Ethical Agility in Dan

Rethinking Technique in British Contemporary Dance

Edited by Noyale Colin, Catherine Seago, and Kathryn Stamp

Routledge
Taylor & Francis Group
LONDON AND NEW YORK

Designed cover image: Common Dance, 2009, *Choreographer Rosemary Lee*, Dance Umbrella, Greenwich London. Photo Simon Weir.

First published 2024
by Routledge
4 Park Square, Milton Park, Abingdon, Oxon OX14 4RN

and by Routledge
605 Third Avenue, New York, NY 10158

Routledge is an imprint of the Taylor & Francis Group, an informa business

Funded by the University of Winchester.

British Library Cataloguing-in-Publication Data
A catalogue record for this book is available from the British Library

Library of Congress Cataloging-in-Publication Data
Names: Colin, Noyale, editor. | Seago, Catherine, editor. | Stamp, Kathryn, editor.
Title: Ethical agility in dance : rethinking technique in British contemporary dance / Noyale Colin, Catherine Seago, Kathryn Stamp.
Description: First edition. | New York : Routledge, 2023. |
Series: Routledge advances in theatre & performance studies | Includes bibliographical references and index. | Contents: Part 1. Concepts — Part 2. Practices — Part 3. Conversations — Part 4. Manifestos. Identifiers:
LCCN 2023025251 (print) | LCCN 2023025252 (ebook) |
ISBN 9780367628673 (hbk) | ISBN 9780367628635 (pbk) |
ISBN 9781003111146 (ebk)
Subjects: LCSH: Dance—Moral and ethical aspects—Great Britain.
Classification: LCC GV1645 .E84 2023 (print) |
LCC GV1645 (ebook) | DDC 792.80941—dc23/eng/20230711
LC record available at https://lccn.loc.gov/2023025251
LC ebook record available at https://lccn.loc.gov/2023025252

ISBN: 9780367628673 (hbk)
ISBN: 9780367628635 (pbk)
ISBN: 9781003111146 (ebk)

DOI: 10.4324/9781003111146

Typeset in Sabon
by codeMantra

Contents

Figures

Tables

About the Editors

Noyale Colin (MA/PhD) is a Senior Lecturer in Dance at the University of Winchester. Her academic writing and practical works relate to her research around issues of embodied practices, health, the notion of the collaborative self in performance. She leads the Research Unit of Assessment 33 and the University's Centre for Performance Practice and Research. She is one of the executive board members (Secretary) of Dance HE.

Cathy Seago (MFA/PhD) is a Senior Lecturer in Dance at the University of Winchester and is the programme leader for its BA(Hons) Dance degree. Cathy's practical and written work is focused by an interest in notions of flow and flux. Her research in this vein explores aspects of dance technique training and of working as a performer-creator and as a collaborator. Cathy has, as Director of Evolving Motion, developed a series of somatically focused interdisciplinary performance projects which have been presented in Europe and SE Asia.

Kathryn Stamp (PGCE/MA/PhD) is a dance researcher and educator, specialising in inclusive dance, the value of dance and dance in education. Kathryn works as an Assistant Professor in Dance Studies at the Centre for Dance Research (C-DaRE) at Coventry University. She is Co-Chair of the Society for Dance Research, an executive board member for Dance HE and Editorial Manager for the *Journal of Dance and Somatic Practices*. Kathryn is an Ambassador for AWA DANCE charity and an advisory board member for We Are Epic.

Contributors

Adesola Akinleye, PhD, is an artist-scholar and Assistant Professor at Texas Woman's University. They have been an Affiliate Researcher and Visiting Artist, MIT and a Theatrum Mundi Fellow. They began their career with Dance Theatre of Harlem Workshop Ensemble (USA) later working in UK Companies such as Green Candle and Carol Straker Dance Company. Adesola creates dance works ranging from live performance to films, installations and texts (include monographs and edited anthologies).

Tamara Ashley is a Senior Lecturer in Dance at the University of Bedfordshire, where she leads PG taught and research programmes in dance. She has recently been part of the AHRC Somatic Practice and Chronic Pain Network and created a video offering practice for chronic pain relief. In the pandemic, she organised ECITE online in the UK and recently co-led the organisation of Contact Improvisation's 50th Anniversary in London. Recent publications include *Developing a Sense Place: The Role of the Arts in Regenerating Community* and *Mapping Lineage: Lineage Maps by Dance Improvisation Artists*.

Fiona Bannon is an Associate Professor in the School of Performance and Cultural Industries, University of Leeds. Research interests include aesthetic education, ethics and practice, site performance and social choreography. Career experiences include Head of Department, Scarborough School of Arts; Co-Convenor of Centre for Practice Research (Leeds); and Education Officer for Ausdance, NSW. Having recently completed her term as Chair of Dance HE in the UK, Fiona is currently working as Chair of World Dance Alliance-Europe. As an experienced academic, Fiona promotes an ethos of practice in dance that seeks to ensure equality, diversity and inclusion.

Jane Carr initially trained and worked as a ballet dancer before studying at Laban and later completing study for PhD (University of Surrey at Roehampton). She has lectured at Central School of Ballet, Trinity Laban, the University of Lincoln and at the University of Bedfordshire where she was the Head of the School of Media and Performance and now serves as a Research Fellow. Jane is continuing to develop her interdisciplinary approach to exploring the significance of performance with recent publications, including in Farinas, R. and Van Camp, J. (eds.) (2021) *The Bloomsbury Handbook of Dance and Philosophy* and Midgelow, V. (ed.) (2019) *The Oxford Handbook of Improvisation in Dance.*

Rosemary (Rosa) E. Cisneros is an artist researcher at C-DaRE (Coventry University) with a background in dance, sociology and films. She works closely with several charities and NGOs in the UK and Europe, and leads several small- and large-scale projects. Her work aims to make dance and education accessible to vulnerable groups and ethnic minorities, and she also works closely with freelance artists developing ethical and equitable standards.

Marie-Louise Crawley is a choreographer, artist researcher and Assistant Professor in Dance and Cultural Engagement at the Centre for Dance Research (C-DaRE), Coventry University. Her research interests include dance, museums and cultural heritage, and areas of intersection between Classics and Dance Studies such as ancient dance and the performance of epic.

Jamieson Dryburgh is the Director of Higher Education at Central School of Ballet. He previously taught contemporary dance technique in conservatoire settings for over 25 years. This led to his dance pedagogy PhD which explored critical feminist and queer perspectives of learning from within the dance studio. He is a Principal Fellow of the Higher Education Academy (PFHEA), Director of the Participatory Arts Qualifications (PAQ), Board member of Dance HE and External Examiner at Leeds Beckett University.

Betina Panagiotara is a dance theorist and dramaturg. Her latest research focuses on cultural policies for dance and disability in Europe, while her PhD explores collaborative artistic practices in Greece. She teaches dance history in professional dance schools collaborates with performing arts artists in dramaturgy and research, and curates educational workshops. Her research focuses on dance history and dramaturgy, politics, archiving practices and inclusive dance. She is a member of the Dance Studies Association, Springback Academy and the European Arts & Disability Cluster.

Jo Read, PhD, is a dancer, maker and trainee Integrative Counsellor and Psychotherapist. She works as a Senior Lecturer in Dance at the University of East London, and also as a trainee therapist at Cherry Tree Therapy Centre. As a performer, Jo was previously a company member of Boy Blue, and Etta Ermini Dance Theatre. Her current practice-led research project 'Dancing with Endo' focuses on relationships between dance, health and wellbeing, collaborating with artists who also have Endometriosis.

Rachel Rimmer-Piekarczyk is a contemporary dance practitioner, performer and scholar who is a Senior Lecturer in Performance at The Manchester School of Theatre and an artist with the contemporary performance group, Reckless Sleepers. She completed her PhD at Manchester Metropolitan University in 2021, which was a practice-led ethnographic-action research study that utilised the work of Pierre Bourdieu to examine undergraduate dance students' experiences of engaging with reflection in dance technique training.

Carla Trim-Vamben is the Arts and Creative Industries Director of Education and Experience, and the programme leader for the BA (Hons) Dance: Urban Practice degree at the University of East London. As a practice-led researcher, her interests centre around club culture and has authored, *From Club to Stage: The Integration of House Dance within Performance Practice* (2013). She is currently evaluating an ACE Transforming Leadership Project called We Move: Transforming Leadership in Hip Hop.

Karen Wood is a dance artist, researcher, educator, maker and producer. She works as an Assistant Professor at the Centre for Dance Research, Coventry University, and as Co-Director for Birmingham Dance Network. Her practice and research focuses on dance as a cultural practice and what it offers society. Her latest research investigates the working conditions of freelance dance artists.

Introduction

Ethical agility in British contemporary dance technique

Noyale Colin

This book relies on the idea that dance fosters both singularity and collectivity in artistic education and thereby offers invaluable techniques to operate within the immediate, interconnected and volatile contemporary professional environment. It is concerned with the potential of dance education for developing socially engaged individuals capable of forging ethical human relations for an ever-changing world; and in this sense, to frame dance as a fundamental part of human experience. It poses the question of how the concept of 'technique' and associated systems of training in dance can be redefined to enable the collaboration of skills and application of ideas required to face the ethical challenges of twenty-first century dancing bodies. In so doing, the volume seeks to widen our understanding of contemporary dance technique and training in view of an expanded field of dance which would include a broad range of areas, including health, community arts, performance, choreography and education.

Julia Buckroyd (2003) argued that the dance profession was, at the turn of the century, 'at a point in its history' where its cultural significance required the creation of code of ethics and practice. Buckroyd finds the origins of the development of such a code in the UK by highlighting the influential British dance educator Peter Brinson's work (1991) towards improving practice in the dance world. She also highlights the Dance UK Healthier Dance Conference in 1990 and the creation of the Dancers' Charter as notable moments for opening up debates around ethical issues in the profession.[1] A code of ethics articulates values and principles and informs the understanding of the moral qualities necessary to work in the profession. While this book is not concerned with the codification of a set of principles, the ideas formulated through the different contributors in this collection of essays, conversations and manifestos can be seen to function as a way to explore, debate and grasp the current values of contemporary dance. Examining these values in the applied field of dance reveals a complex and contrasting range of ideas, encompassing broad themes including the relationships between individuality and collectivity, rigour and creativity, and virtuosity and inclusivity. This volume points to ethical techniques as providing a way of navigating these contrasting values in dance.

DOI: 10.4324/9781003111146-1

Whereas exploring the underlying ideology around the production of the contemporary dancing body is crucial for the continuing development of alternative discourses on dance education and training, the broader aims of this investigation also include the reframing of the practice of dance technique in relation to broader political and social contexts. In the UK, a growing awareness of the need for solidarity, and development of a politics of belonging based on altruism, empathy and connectivity has been widely argued within social commentary in the aftermath of the 2016 Brexit referendum (Klein, 2017; Delgado, 2018) and further intensified by the global COVID pandemic. A global call for the decolonisation of both dance education and dance discourse has challenged the status quo with regard to racism, white supremacy and injustice in the field (Banerji and Mitra, 2020).

Local and international developments with regard to environment, technology and migration have informed a politics of togetherness, whereby collective and individual socially engaged actions have become vital to reassess the ways we breathe, communicate and move. Dance can play a significant role in this reassessment. Yet its ethical value in society including in education – needs to be more widely discussed and acknowledged. American dance scholar, Susan Leigh Foster (2019), recently argued for the revaluing of dance as a social exchange which can be experienced as a commodity or as a gift. As a 'resource' dance can bring people together, energise and adapt to diverse range of social situations (2019: 18). To examine the potential value of dance, its 'resource-fullness' is to assume that value is relational and constantly in flux (2019: 19). The call for greater focus upon ethical concerns in dance technique invites readers, including dance teachers and students, to think critically about the social value of dance in society. A number of our contributors have been motivated by the paradigmatic political and decolonial discourse in dance studies. Together, their voices offer a response to the need to theorise how we learn new techniques and what is being reproduced in space of transmission (Kraut, 2020: 47). The techniques, practices and ideas shared across the different sections of the book offer lenses to approach the current position of contemporary dance training in Britain, and how it has shaped and is still shaping British dance.

Techniques for the contemporaneity of dance

The use of the term contemporary here and in the title for the volume calls for some clarification. Contemporary dance styles in formal dance education in the UK have largely drawn upon codified techniques of American modern dance, European Physical Theatres and more fluid forms of postmodern dance and somatic approaches which are broadly understood by teachers as Release Technique. However, this lineage of contemporary dance needs to be re-evaluated in light of shifting postcolonial perspectives on education. In academia, there has been a tendency to privilege Western techniques of dance as foundational principles, undermining the idea that other genres are also contemporary (Kwan, 2017). While this might be reflecting a lack of diversity in contemporary dance more globally, the intention in using the term 'contemporary' is to invite contributors to problematise, reflect and resist a fixed meaning, and specifically confront its understanding with our overarching ethical concern.

As SanSan Kwan observes (2017) in her article entitled *When Is Contemporary Dance*, the meaning of the words 'contemporary dance' depends on the various contexts within which it is used. In the United States, Kwan distinguishes between concert, commercial and world dance (2017: 38). For some dancers, the term evokes the more process-based approach of the avant-garde aesthetics of modern and postmodern dance. For others, it represents the more lyrical and physical commercial form – as is commonly seen on television whether in advertising or popular entertainment. As Kwan concludes, in a multicultural dance context '"contemporary dance" can encompass a range of practices: Western contemporary dance performed by non-Western dancers, ethnic dance fused with Western contemporary vocabulary and/or compositional techniques, or innovations on a traditional non-Western form' (2017: 48). Kwan reminds us that the signification of 'contemporary' as being 'together with time' points to the ontological nature of dance as ephemeral, performative and therefore in some contexts making it a time-based art (2017: 39). This points to the idea that all dance is contemporary while also designating the dance happening in the current time. However, she warns us that 'opening up the field to all current practices' might dilute its identity and not allow the mean to grasp the 'social, cultural and political significance of a moment in history' (2017: 48). In addition, she demonstrates that defining scholarly concepts of contemporary dance – based in specific aesthetics – could point to exclusive set of artists.[2] This, she argues, undermines 'so many other forms and communities to being "not contemporary"' (2017: 48). This problematising of the term contemporary in dance is important to reframe technique in training through an ethical lens which widens the perspective on what techniques can be seen as key skills for contemporary dance training.

In the UK, formal dance education has been focusing on contemporary dance. Most dance courses at higher education (HE) level are simply called dance, dance performance or dance studies, yet their physical training focuses on traditional contemporary techniques which are seen as foundational training. Additional styles such as ballet for contemporary dancers, commercial dance (urban/street/hip-hop) – and more rarely multicultural techniques, such as African/South Asia/Capoeira – are often seen as a marketing tool to nominally distinguish courses from each other. A recent publication by Melanie Clark (2020) entitled *The Essential Guide to Contemporary Dance Technique* evidences this dominant approach by focusing on only three forms: Martha Graham, Merce Cunningham and Released-based techniques. In this volume, we have intended to draw attention to other forms of contemporary dance which are bringing in different values to examine the link between the practice of technique in dance and its contemporaneity. Rather than defining how contemporary dance looks, we argue that an ethical imperative in dance today might define its contemporaneity.

The etymological root of technique, *techne*, refers to the craft of doing things well. To explore the ethical aspect of techniques in dance is to ask if dancing well can be considered an action in the service of the good or, in other words, what are the techniques that develop the training of dance as an ethical action? In this introduction, I foreground agility as one of the main characteristics of the ethics that we seek to develop in dance. While this may seem familiar in terms of what could be expected in a creative environment, it is something that is not always made explicit or overtly addressed in dance education. Like other physical techniques, dance movements embody social and personal expressions (Mauss, 1973). Training can develop the embodied agency of the dancer who becomes agile in moving in between internal and external emotions. On the one hand, the term agility is used in contrast to the association of technique with virtuosity, and on the other hand, it signals a reassessment of the notion of virtuosity which draws on recent debates in dance studies (Brandstetter, 2007; Foster, 2011; Osterweiss, 2013; Burt, 2017).

The contested term 'technique' is itself intended as a generative provocation enabling contributors to engage with the questions we invited them to consider in relation to the future of dance in Britain, including what ethics means within dance practices, what techniques are emerging out of ethical practices in dance and are these techniques what is being taught within British dance education. A number of key themes emerged from these questions including virtuosity and inclusivity, reflective and critical practice, creativity and imagination, technology and communication, and culture and representation.

In attempting to construct a theory of ethics through which contemporary dance technique might be analysed, I propose the concept of ethical agility as an overarching idea framing many contributions in this volume. In what follows, I develop this concept in relation to the historical development of training in contemporary dance in Britain. I begin by offering a contextualisation of dance education, in which I argue for the need to re-examine the value of dance in society. I reflect on the ways that our contributors have explored the nature and role of technique in dance and its relation to contemporaneity. I then review the ways in which dance has been seen as an ethical practice. I finally discuss how the concept of ethical agility might support the development of a more humane culture in dance.

Shifting contexts

Dance as an art form and as a form of entertainment has had a rise in popularity in recent decades. This is represented by the popularisation of a larger range of styles of dance, ranging from ballroom to ballet, hip-hop, contemporary, folk or South Asian. Dance is performed in theatre venues, has a more prominent position on national television and is found on digital social platforms on the internet. In addition, the benefit of dance for society has been evidenced more widely through community and health-related projects, including its positive affect on individuals' physical and psychological wellbeing and its potential for enhancing social cohesion. What are the implications of these developments on dance education, and especially in the context of British Contemporary Dance?

At the beginning of the 2000s, at the time that Buckroyd (2003) called for further debate around ethics in dance, the sector was starting to be considered a significant cultural asset. The contribution of dance education to prepare young people to enter one of the fastest economic growth industries is even more significant at the time of writing. Pre-pandemic, the creative industries accounted for almost 6% of the UK economy with an increase between 2010 and 2019 of 44%; meaning the economy of the creative industries was growing much faster than the UK economy as a whole (Waitzman, 2021).

However, the COVID health crisis has significantly impacted the creative sector. If the value of dance to promote positive social relations, physical and mental health during the pandemic was recognised (One Dance UK, 2021), post-COVID, the level of support and resources being afforded for dance education – particularly in England – has been curtailed. This shift in the status of dance education had started well before the pandemic. For over a decade, dance in education has been under threat. A series of governmental measures have had a deleterious effect on the quality of the training for young people. These have included both funding cuts and the introduction of the English Baccalaureate which further prioritised STEM subjects (or Science, Technology, Engineering and Maths). These changes have been accompanied by the use of language from the government and media which have sought to weaken the field by identifying dance and other creative subjects as 'low-value' and 'non-priority' subjects. Such rhetoric has a negative impact on the way that young people and their careers perceive dance as a subject of study. The sector's support organisation One Dance UK has identified that the number of those seeking a dance subject-based qualification at secondary school has plummeted with a more than 50% reduction in entries for the dance General Certificate of Secondary Education (GCSE) in less than ten years and down to only 1100 A Level entries in England in 2020 (One Dance UK, 2020). This decline has been exacerbated by the COVID pandemic due to a reduction in provision. In 2021, One Dance UK reported that 'Post pandemic, there are less dance educators and less hours allocated to dance teaching in schools' (One Dance UK, 2021: 11). Nevertheless, this does not mean that students are not interested in dance. Survey data from the Department for Digital, Culture, Media and Sport and the Arts Council of England (ACE) continues to evidence that there is a large demand for dance for young people at both recreational and exam levels (ACE, 2017; DCMS, 2021).

Numerous research projects have demonstrated the benefit of dance activities for the development of children and young people's lives. In particular, recent studies have highlighted the ways in which dance can increase happiness, confidence and self-esteem in people (Yorkshire Dance, 2018). The recent report of the Sport and Recreation Alliance on the social value of movement and dance in the UK underscores the positive effects of dance to create a healthier and happier society (Sport and Recreation Alliance, 2021). A key problem identified by One Dance UK has been the undervaluing of the potential for dance in education by government and media, as reflected in descriptions of the field as 'low value', 'non-priority' and 'dead-end' (One Dance UK, 2021: 6). Teachers have also observed the 'increasing lack of awareness of what dance can be, who it is for and how it can be used, beyond transferable skills, as a tool for social engagement, confidence, mental health and the learning of subject matter' (One Dance UK, 2021: 16).

This undermining of the value of dance is also found in HE where a series of governmental funding cuts have been specifically targeting the performing and creative arts, and media studies. Funding for these subjects was reduced by fifty percent for the academic year 2021–2022, and a further reduction is anticipated in the future (Office for Students, 2021). Although, most contributors to this volume are writing from a higher educational context, it is important to highlight that these issues of the valuing of dance arise at earlier levels in the educational structure. In other words, deeper shifts in cultural attitudes might be required to bring about systemic change that would improve the outlook for dance. This is unlikely to take place without a significant wider revaluation of the role of dance education as a serious academic subject which can positively impact the physical and mental health of young people and their future careers. Foregrounding the ethical value of dance for society in training might form part of such a reassessment. Examining the techniques to learn dance through an ethical lens contributes to the necessary debate about access to high-quality dance education 'as a birth right of every child' (Andrew Hurst in One Dance UK, 2021: 3). Access to the arts is specifically listed as a basic right in Article 27 of the United Nations of the Declaration of Human Rights; and the collection of concepts, practices, conversations and manifestos that is offered in this volume is informed by a call for the recognition of the importance for British people of all ages to enjoy access to contemporary dance as one of the arts contributing to the national culture.

The ongoing nature of technique training in contemporary dance

The end of stable funding for the arts in many Western countries towards the end of the twentieth century influenced a shift in the structure of a typical dance company. In recent years, companies are less often led by a single choreographer; and dancers are required to work alternately or simultaneously for several companies. Accordingly, dancers are more responsible for their own training, and this training must support the versatility required as a result of such instability. As Bales and Nettl-Fiol explain (2008), 'choreographers are no longer training dancers, at least not in the traditional sense of giving technique classes that train the dancers in their personal movement style separate from the rehearsal process. The rehearsal replaces training for many' (x). In other words, the traditional idea of technique based in systematic physical training and codified steps has been replaced by a more individualised exploratory approach to movement, whereby modern techniques, postmodern techniques, urban dance forms, ballet and somatic approaches are being mixed freely.

In this context, contemporary dance students are expected to learn an increasingly diversified range of techniques related to a wide range of performance styles and approaches in dance. Often driven by its own economy, this hybridisation of training in dance reflects an entanglement of creative and learning practices with the market of education in which a faster production of ready-to-use skills is prevailing. In 1986, the American dance scholar, Susan Foster, observed the production of what she coined 'the hired body' of the dancer as a flexible and resilient body trained to create dance quickly and economically. More recently, other scholars have defined the trained dancers' body as 'eclectic' (Bales and Nettl-Fiol, 2008). These characteristics promote a more surface approach to dancing which adopt a traditional mode of learning movement by replication and can prevent the development of creative, responsive and therefore socially aware dancers. If this book is a response to this situation, the argument for a more ethical approach to training in dance is not happening in a vacuum.

Many scholars have identified the problematic tension facing contemporary dancers between the nature of contemporary dance teaching and the eclecticism of the dancer's training demanded by dance markets (Enghauser, 2007; Bales and Nettl-Fiol, 2008; Coogan, 2016; Roche, 2016). On the one hand, the combination of techniques can create a homogenisation effect as 'a rubbery flexibility coated with impervious glossiness' (Foster in Bales and Nettl-Fiol, 2008: 63), and on the other hand, it can create a collage of styles from which a coherent aesthetics is not easy to achieve (Bales in Bales and Nettl-Fiol, 2008: 63). In choreography, this contributed to a 'bricolage' aesthetics, whereby 'something old, something new and something borrowed' would be combined to create the eclecticism which characterised American postmodern dance (Monten in Bales and Nettl-Fiol, 2008: 52). This approach is discussed in detail in a number of contributions in this volume. In particular, the extent of its potential to contribute to more inclusive and ethical relations between students and teachers is explored through action research and personal reflections from contributors who have had lifelong careers in dance.

If we turn to a wider European approach to training, we find further calls for a more meaningful approach to technique in contemporary dance. French choreographer Boris Charmatz points to the physical and academic skills necessary 'to not merely suffer contemporary techniques but instead construct meaning' (Charmatz in Charmatz and Launay. 2011: 96). He argues against training a 'battalion of dancers' and instead advocates preparing 'artists capable of creating their own employment: not all-rounders necessarily, [instead] people with some ideas of what they really want to do both on and off stage' (Charmatz in Charmatz and Launay. 2011: 96). Training based on movement analysis of kinaesthetic principles has been at the heart of this approach in Europe. The expansion of the so-called somatic techniques encouraged dancers to be more attentive to their bodies through the practice of shared principles, such as connectivity, kinaesthetic listening, breath support and process (Brodie and Lobel, 2012). This more internal approach to training has been influenced by somatic scholars in dance education who have advocated for a paradigm shift in learning and teaching by foregrounding processes of creative exploration, reflection and awareness (Shrewsbury, 1993; Shapiro, 1998; Ross, 2000). While these values are often considered essential characteristics of a democratic transformative education in dance, they are not always associated to the practice of dance in the wider current context of education (Rouhiainen, 2008). Considering that knowledge is shaped by sociocultural experiences, the development of somatic awareness in dance training supports the exploration of how the body of the dancer intertwines with the world (Barr, 2020).

In her research on embedding a somatic approach to technique classes, Sherrie Barr (2020) argues that somatic practices can facilitate the training of more active learners. Referring to the work of somatic dance theorists, including Jenny Coogan and Jenny Roche, Barr points to the need to develop what, in my terms, represents a form of ethical agility in dance training. She states that when training, dancers need to balance their sensitivity with a social consciousness and the awareness of an 'everchanging professional field' (Barr, 2020: 456). The use of somatic techniques in dance training signals a shift in the teaching of dance towards challenging students to work with more internal processes of movements. Technique teachers are thereby able to balance the development of an elevated level of physical skill with the encouragement of creativity (Roche, 2016). Such an approach reveals the need to address the hierarchical structure of a traditional dance education.

From a historical perspective, one might argue that inclusive and democratic values were already introduced to dance training by postmodern choreographers. In particular, in a British context, the work of Mary Fulkerson at Dartington College of Arts rejected the competitiveness and ideals of perfection associated with modern dance and its repetitive teaching methods (Colin, 2018a,b). Ideas of accessibility and attention to personal inward qualities in training have influenced the development of the British New Dance and a whole generation of choreographers and dance educators. Yet as Charmatz and Launay recognise, movement work needs to be contextualised: '[t]eaching theory while neglecting to take experience and other fields of knowledge into account is no longer a viable approach' (2011: 98). While in the UK university dance training is usually supported by lectures through the use of core theoretical material where students' reflective skills can be developed, this part of the curriculum is not always valued equally by dance students. The limitations to engagement can be explained partly by a limited diversity in curriculum which creates a gap between theories, practices and students' representations. As Lynn Quinn states in her book *Re-imagining Curriculum*, '[i]t is not sufficient for lecturers to simply transmit the knowledge enshrined in the canons of their disciplines to students – with little thoughts to who their students are, where they come from and what their legitimate learning needs are' (2019: 8).

In dance education studies, warnings concerning the limits of a superficial multiculturalism have been expressed for more than a decade. Susan Stinson and Doug Risner (2010) argue for the need of a nuanced conception of multiculturalism and diversity to activate genuine empathetic perspectives across a range of students' cultural and social backgrounds. They advocate for pedagogical approaches which veer away from learning 'about' the other to adopt inclusive techniques which instead prioritises learning 'from and with those unlike us or those whose dancing is different from ours' (2010: 6).

Karen Schupp, in a recent special edition of the *Dance Education Journal* on dance education and citizenship, investigates how dance education can develop kind and thoughtful citizens. Schupp and the authors of the volume discuss the capacity of dance to develop self and group responsibility, to build communities through learning, to react to shifting cultural, social and political norms and to cultivate reflective action (2018: 93). At the heart of this conception of citizenship through dance lies the practice of differences. Llana Morgan shares her experience as a teacher and researcher:

> I have watched students of all ages see a person, a situation, or a problem with a new perspective after engaging with inquiry-based artistic creation and expression that involves working with people or communities different from themselves. Being able to work with and being able to understand others' perspectives is at the core of thoughtful citizenship.
>
> (Morgan, 2018: 100)

Similarly, in our HE dance courses in the UK, it is not difficult to witness a sense of 'awakening' that students develop after being exposed to differences not only across the cultural and social realms but also involving bodily and neurological differences. The possibility of intertwining critical concerns and embodied learning is crucial to the development of ethical agility in dance training. Beyond self-reflection, approaches to learning dance technique explored in the book include processes which carry 'a character of 'jointedness' providing access to personal and social insights (Bannon, 2018: 2). Several educators and artists' contributions advocate inclusivity and decolonisation as central to a necessary shift in technique training.

In this appraisal of technique in contemporary dance, internal processes of learning are discussed in relation to the need for inclusive historical and contextual underpinnings in dance education which better reflect the wide range of cultural backgrounds of all those that engage in learning dance. Throughout the volume, technique is approached as a way of learning from difference to be physically engaged with 'others' to support dancers to develop their physical, creative and civic capabilities. Contributors in this book refer to techniques of somatic attention to build an embodied knowledge grounded in an ethical awareness in dance.

The development of dance techniques as relational techniques

While embodied knowledge has always struggled to compete with the Cartesian division between mind and body, phenomenological approaches to uncovering knowledge have found currency in research and teaching. Interest in practice in fields, such as sociology, anthropology and ethnography, contributed to a shift in understanding how knowledge might be constructed and transmitted. Two specific moments in academic discourse have signified a foregrounding of embodied knowledge that underlined many of our contributors' thinking on the role of technique in dance. Following in the tradition of Pierre Bourdieu in the 1970s, the 'practice turn' emerged in the mid-1990s as an interdisciplinary concern with 'practice'. Knowledge is no longer understood as a 'possession of minds' but instead it is 'mediated both by interactions between people and by arrangements in the world' (Schatzki et al., 2001: 12). It is therefore understood as a collective process whereby techniques or practical ways of doing (including their contexts) not only represent forms of knowledge but rather knowledge 'depends' on these forms of knowing. If embodied practice is informed by and generative of knowledge, its transmission occurs in the form of technique through processes that take place at the individual and social levels. Accordingly, investigating the embodied knowledge of dance techniques not only reveals ways of doing dance, but it also locates dancing as a way of knowing the world through human relations. Hence, themes, such as collaborative learning and dialogical pedagogies, are central to the discussions developed in this book.

The second theoretical shift that overarched the rethinking of contemporary dance technique is what has been recognised as the 'affective turn' in the humanities and social sciences (La Caze and Martyn Lloyd, 2011). The term can be seen as signifying a shift away from the post-structuralist 'linguistic turn', which tends to underline the medium rather than its impact on others (i.e. relationality). From a sociological perspective, the affective turn 'expresses a new configuration of bodies, technology, and matter instigating a shift in thought in critical theory' (Clough, 2007: 2). From a philosophical perspective, the term might be better understood 'in terms of renewed and widespread scholarly interest in corporeality, in emotions and in the importance of aesthetics' (La Caze and Martyn, 2011: 2). Within this discourse, the philosopher Brian Massumi's theory of affect is useful for understanding the significance of the knowledge emerging from dance technique and its relation with ethical concerns. For Massumi, affect – understood as the capacity of the body to affect and to be affected by others – allows a veering away from self-interested knowledge towards what he calls an ethics of engagement which he defines as:

> [a] knowledge-practice that takes an inclusive, non-judgmental approach to tending belonging-together in an intense, affectively engaged way is an ethics [...] Ethics is a tending of coming-together, a caring for be-longing as such.
>
> (Massumi, 2002: 255)

This ethical perspective allows us to locate technique in dance as a collective doing, whereby different techniques can be considered diverse ways of coming-together to take account for our mutual capacity to affect and be affected. As such, we can understand dance practices as relational techniques. Yet what is central to the reassessment of the notion of technique in the volume is the prioritising of creative and transformative processes in training. Contributors explore the values to be found through the way that dancers may come together in training studios and utilise dance as a dialogical tool to forge discovery, transformation and creative cooperation.

Technique as a self-organisation of the body through time

Considering embodied knowledge as relational is critical to examining the specificity of the kind of learning developed in dance and the agility that is required of the dancer to sustain a more ethical practice. Indeed, the body's knowledge is not fixed or stable. It evolves and develops with the dancer. It follows its own history. Over time, the training of a dancer reflects the tension between the past of the body and the demands of the future. To forge this temporal agility in dancing, it is necessary to conceive of techniques as an open field of knowledge rather than sets of instructions and repeated steps. As Ingo Diehl (2018, np) argues, 'there is no set technique but a relation to it'. Diehl posits that each dancer develops their own body memory and archive of experiences as unique biographies of training (2018, np).[3] This temporal aspect of training is reflected in many of the conversations in this book where contributors share their own training history and their relation to it. The body of the dancer is considered a living flesh with its own genealogy (Van Imschoot, 2005), capable of creating meaning through a repetitive process of training. This approach foregrounds creativity in technique classes. For movement analyst Hubert Godard, in dance training, '[i]t is not the repetition of movement but the experience of gesture and as such the '"creation of sensory meaning" (fabrique du sens) that gives a sense, a direction, to the senses' (Godard, 1994: 30). Memory here is not understood merely as a tool to reproduce existing gestures but rather as a perceptive faculty of the body to create a continuity of sensory meaning. Godard defines the perceptive organisation of the dancer's body as an active projection which he calls a 'project about the world' (1994). This leads us away from an idea of technique in dance which is contingent upon an instrumentalist conception of the body as a mechanical process of learning skills. The dancer's body is understood as an organising structure of respiratory, postural and perceptive movements (Godard, 1994); and thus, the dancer's body is capable of creating meaning through the constant organising of its changeable organic structure. Techniques in dance can then be defined as a way to cultivate through time this self-organisation of the body.

This need for a sense of continuity in training is seen as an ethical concern throughout the book due to the challenges that dancers are facing in navigating fragmented and heterogenous knowledge in late capitalist society. Indeed, somatic and dance educators have been demonstrating the critical potential of bodily knowledge in the face of neo-liberalism (Ginot, 2010; Fortin, 2017). Neoliberal logics challenge the production of culture in society as its policies aim at privatising public services into commercial ventures, including in the fields of education, health and social care, and the arts. Moreover, in the context of post-Fordism, working practices emerged during the shift from the production of goods to the production of information and services. In this new economy, artists have become the role model for contemporary workers as they are described as multiskilled, flexible and resilient (Kunst, 2015). However, the political economy of the dancing body, subsumed into the global forces of the market, can also be seen as being exploited by capitalism. For Kowal et al., dancers 'are disciplined, self-controlled' and become 'expert in self-promotion to avoid the risk of precarity that is the downside of the loosening of social bonds in times when global markets replace nation-states and their systems of social security' (2017: 12). The tension between the blurring of artistic strategies into contemporary life and labour and a resistance to neoliberal agendas informs the discourses that traverse the field and practices of dance – including its education and training.

Whereas the conditions of dance production and education are increasingly formatted by market forces (as seen in increases of short-term project-based creative processes, freelance remuneration for creative workers, network pressures and consumerist universities), one of the consequences of this regime for dancers is an increase of precarious and uncertain working conditions, and an intensification of the eclectic 'supermarket' approach to body-training. How can the 'nomad' dancer going from project to project or class to class resist a fast, fragmented, interrupted sense of time while responding to the imperative of contemporary adaptability? Bojana Bauer questions in her discussion on dance training, '[w]hat set of tools is needed for the work on and with a body trained in versatility' (2009: 77). For Bauer, the 'hopping' from technique to technique does not allow for the transformative processes needed to connect the body-mind of the dancer with the world. It undermines the creative process of learning dance and the role of perception in dancing which is crucial for forging active and critical dancers. Perception, Bauer argues, 'is a matter of creation and of decision, taking responsibility for the world the subject lives in and not the contrary'. She calls for a training practice that explores the critical actions of the dancers, whereby 'learning [is] inseparable from creation' (2009: 78). The concept of ethical agility in dance is proposed as a possible framework to explore such an approach to technique training.

Ethics in dance

The argument that dance entwines embodied knowledge with ethics is timely. It is consonant with the broadly posthumanist feminist discourse (Barad, 2007; Braidotti, 2013) which challenges the dominant role of cognition and language over lived experience in ethics theory. Posthumanist ethics draws on Emmanuel Levinas' understanding of responsibility. It is based partly on the idea that as responsibility is a relation of bodily engagement, we cannot be indifferent to the other who is different from us (Levinas cited in Barad, 2007: 392). Embodied ethical engagement is more compatible with the intra-actions within which the natural and social world are mutually embedded (Barad, 2007).

Following these theoretical developments, ethics in dance has been the subject of recent scholarly concern with the development of a more humane culture in dance (Bannon, 2018; Aili, Katan-Schmid and Houston, 2020; Jackson, 2022). A focus on ethics in dance highlights the rich potential inherent in the way that dancers learn to actively engage with each other (Bannon, 2018). Drawing on Barad and Braidotti, Bannon locates dance as a valuable ethical activity to challenge division in society by exploring what it is to be human in constant relation with each other and the earth (2018: 9). Attention to ethical relations in dance training allows us to explore ways to cultivate a sense of mutuality and maintain the interrelationships among each other. For Bannon, this process is about learning to be *self-in-relation*. She posits that 'Such an ethical approach concerns the manner of engagement, the manner of individual and group behaviours and the chosen values that are put to active use in the complex process of teaching and learning contemporary dance' (2018: 5). These manners can be defined as embodied techniques in dance which are characterised by specific processes of ethical engagement.

If the arts are not simply about the mastery of technical skills, the technical skills that we might be striving for in contemporary dance training can point to non-linguistic modes of thinking (Bannon, 2018: 84). Such thinking, I argue, embodies ethical techniques. For example, through moving, dancers are involved in 'a thinking of decision-making' (Aili, Katan-Schmid and Houston, 2020). Each step or movement – whether produced from a known shape or not – involves a technical knowhow which is coupled with a tacit decision of perception. Regardless of the style of dance, this approach to technique requires the acquisition and the development of skills of attentiveness and attunement to the immediacy of the moment. Using techniques in dance which foreground this heightened sense of agency in training is an ethical activity wherein the dancer is engaged in a balanced and attentive process of ethical decision-making. In the context of community dance, working with attentiveness involves caring for the ways that the participants are feeling, in order to establish a safe and inclusive environment (Aili et al., 2020). Participative dance techniques require dance facilitators to develop the skill of 'moulding' their practice around people rather than the traditional approach to teaching dance as a fixed structure in order 'to mould bodies to the technical demands of the form' (Houston in Aili et al., 2020: 384).

As relational techniques, dance practices can have a profound ethical impact on the expansion of the 'social good' (Bresnahan, 2014). If we consider that art activities (including dance) can foster cooperation, the relations emerging in the techniques we use to teach and learn dance can develop ethical and social exchanges. Levinas' ethics is built around the responsibility of the other (Levinas, 1985). This understanding points to the ethical potential of the collaborative exchange between people moving together in creative practice (Bannon, 2018) and opens the field of possibility for dialogical techniques of working together in educational and professional dance contexts. Furthermore, ethical responsibility can also be thought about in relation to the exchange between dancers and spectators. For Levinas, the central meaning of ethics lies in the inevitability of the exchange with the other. When the Other calls us, we have no options but to respond. Performance theorist Helen Grehan (2009) argues that the inevitability of the Other's call is parallel to the reactive nature of the exchange with audience members in performance. Confronted with the Other, spectators can leave the theatre unsettled with the responsibility to reflect on their position in society (2009: 6). This mutual ethical responsibility needs to be acknowledged and practiced in contemporary dance training. If the presence of the audience is at least frequently central to performance, dance education needs to pay attention to the potential of this ethical exchange. Whereas contemporary society is oversaturated with mediatised performance, the ethical value of live performance is endangered if educators fail to address the challenges and processes involved in spectatorship in arts education curricula (Prendergast, 2004: 36).

This volume gathers theoretical and practical perspectives on embodied ethics in dance which I thematise below in relation to the concept of ethical agility. While this is not an exhaustive list, taken together these ideas characterise a framework from which to explore the training of dance as an ethical embodied practice.

Decision-making

Ethical agility is understood as a movement of internal and external forces in dancing. It relates to the attentive process of decision-making in so far as it involves a movement in between knowing and feeling. When a dancer is engaged in the experience of a movement, they cannot control 'all the instances of movement in advance' (Katan-Schmidt in Aili et al., 2020).

A multitude of micro-moments of embodied decision-making are involved in processes where attentiveness to external and internal forces is required. The agility of the dancer is measured by the degree of connection between her personal capacities (knowing-how) and the environmental conditions (feeling/attuning). In moving, dancers adjust between knowing and feeling in order to organise, project and communicate a perspective 'about the world' (Godard, 1994).

Collaboration

Ethical agility is also the process from which dancers attune to others whether it is other dancers to move within the space or audience members. Such an approach to training requires us to develop 'behaviours towards being-in-community with other, and towards our selves' (Bannon, 2018: 9). The collaborative learning emerging from that process is bound to the responsive attention of the dancer oriented to doing, thinking and feeling with others. In educational setting, this leads to a more dialogical approach to teaching dance techniques. Whereas in socially engaged practice, this process can refer to the ability to be ready to accommodate the others; this 'readiness' is the underlining principles of an ethics of care (Houston in Aili, Katan-Schmid and Houston, 2020).

Virtuosity

Applying the logics of ethics in dance technique invites questions around what virtuosity means in dance. On the one hand, the association of the notion of virtue with the idea of technical prowess led to a mechanical vision of virtuosity. On the other hand, virtuosity can also be framed from a more dynamic perspective. Active participation to social and political life developed virtuosity as a 'performative contribution to the public sphere' (Burt, 2017: 62). While the versatility of styles required by the industry can be seen by some as a mark of virtuosity (Foster, 2011; Osterweiss, 2013), for others, it is in its degree of emancipation from dominating techniques of production in dance that virtuosity can be reframed (Burt, 2017). However, cultural differences need to be considered when defining the value of virtuosity in dance. Osterweiss' work on the concept of virtuoso in African American choreography is helpful for highlighting the importance of decolonising perspectives on virtuosity. Drawing on Africanist aesthetics ideas, she describes what I understand as the ethical agility of the dancer, as a body/mind that mediates between flesh and spirit and connects with the earth through the performance (2013: 65). This perspective can shape a more inclusive rethinking of virtuosity in dance technique away from a mechanic 'soulless' practice and towards an embodied relation with the earth. While this collection of essays, conversations and manifestos offers a wide range of perspectives on virtuosity in contemporary dance technique – including its relationship with spirituality – overall there is something of a shared consensus for recognising what Ramsay Burt observed as 'the potential value of virtue as a quality arising from dance practice' (Burt, 2017: 62–63). Contributors, in this volume, offer a plurality of perspectives on the ways in which in a British context the practising of ethical agility in training is also concerned with cultivating a quality of connectedness with the public sphere.

Enjoyment

An ethics of engagement can be understood as a responsibility which entails a persisting movement between public concerns (other) and enjoyment (self). Joy can link private emotions with public concerns. Through dancing, joy offers an ethical direction to the dancer's individual desire. Grasping the 'in and out' movement is part of the agility developed by the dancer through the practice of relational techniques. By valuing dance as joyful relational techniques, the 'in-between' spaces of ambivalence, flux and flow can be explored as a form of ethical agility.

Conclusion

Redefining contemporary dance through an ethical examination of its techniques is also engaging in a gesture of emancipation for British dance. The collection of contributions in this volume frames the identity of British dance beyond the dominant influence of American and West-European techniques. It engages with a wider range of diverse and inclusive approaches that have characterised the development of dance training in Britain in the past few decades.

Structured into its four parts of concepts, practices, conversations and manifestos, the volume reveals insights from established practitioners and educators. This highlights the possibilities for leading dance practice towards a rebalance of the overpowering hierarchy in Western dance techniques in schools, universities and conservatoires. Our contributors rethink the values of contemporary dance training by offering specific pedagogical approaches which describe alternative ways of teaching dance techniques.

Multiple voices are present across the book, including expressions of African and Asian principles as well as methods emerging from different bodies in training. Together they express ideas about dance training as an ethical embodied practice. I have theorised these ideas through this introduction in relation to issues of representation and inclusivity in dance, collaboration and decision-making processes, virtuosity and enjoyment. This framework is not intended to depict a definitive essence of what contemporary dance training in Britain is. Instead, it suggests a set of concepts, based in the established practices discussed in the book, which, in turn, illuminates important questions about dance and its contemporaneity.

Notes

1 An updated version of the Dancers' Charter can be found on the Dance One UK website at https://www.onedanceuk.org/programme/healthier-dancer-programme/industry-standards.
2 Kwan articulates three characteristics of current dance practice: the 'intrinsic contemporaneity of dance', an aesthetics based in presence and contingency and a desire to reflect of past practices.
3 For more insights into key techniques in contemporary dance in Germany and Europe see Ingo Diehl and Friederike Lampert's publication Dance Techniques 2010 Tanzplan Germany.

References

Aili, B., Katan-Schmid, E. and Houston, S. (2020) 'Dance as Embodied Ethics', in Cull Ó Maoilearca, L. and Lagaay, L. (eds) *The Routledge Companion to Performance Philosophy*. London and New York: Routledge, pp. 379–386.

Arts Council of England (2017) Youth Consultation. Available at https://webarchive.nationalarchives.gov.uk/ukgwa/20210201183852mp_/https://www.artscouncil.org.uk/sites/default/files/download-file/Sound%20Connections_Youth%20Consultation_0.pdf

Bales, M. and Nettl-Fiol, R. (2008) *The Body Eclectic: Evolving Practices in Dance Training*. Chicago: University of Illinois Press.

Banerji, A. and Mitra, R. (eds) (2020) *Conversation across the Field of Dance Studies*. Volume XL. Dance Studies Association.

Bannon, F. (2018) *Considering Ethics in Dance, Theatre and Performance*. London: Palgrave Macmillan.

Barad, K. (2007) *Meeting the Universe Halfway*. Durham, NC: Duke University.

Barr, S. (2020) 'Embodying One's Teaching Identity – Making the Tacit Explicit', *Theatre, Dance and Performance Training*, 11(4), pp. 454–467. https://doi.org/10.1080/19443927.2019.1673473

Bauer, B. (2009) 'When Train(ing) Derails', *Performance Research Journal*, 12(2), pp. 74–79. https://doi.org/10.1080/13528160903319570

Braidotti, R. (2013) *The Posthuman*. Oxford: Polity Press.

Brandstetter, G. (2007) 'The Virtuoso's Stage: A Theatrical Topos', *Theatre Research International*, 32(2), pp. 178–195. https://doi.org/10.1017/S0307883307002829

Bresnahan, A., 'Improvisational Artistry in Live Dance Performance as Embodied and Extended Agency', *Dance Research Journal*, 46(1), pp. 84–94.

Brinson, P. (1991) *Dance as Education: Towards a National Dance Culture*. London: Routledge.

Brodie, J. and Lobel, E. (2012) *Dance and Somatics – Mind-Body Principles of Teaching and Performance*. Jefferson: McFarland & Company.

Buckroyd, J. (2003) 'Ethics in Dance: A Debate Yet to Be Held', in Van der Linden, M. (ed.) *Not Just Any Body & Soul*. The Hague: International Theatre and Film Books, pp. 73–77.

Burt, R. (2017) *Ungoverning Dance*. New York: Oxford University Press

Charmatz, B. and Launay, I. (2011) *Undertraining on a Contemporary Dance*. Dijon: Les Presses du reel.

Clark, M. (2020) *The Essential Guide to Contemporary Dance Technique*. Ramsbury: Crowood Press.

Clough, P. (ed.) (2007) *The Affective Turn: Theorising the Social.* Durham, NC: Duke University Press.

Colin, N. (2018a) 'The Potentiality of Collaboration at Dartington College of Arts and the Future of Performance Training', *Theatre, Dance and Performance Training*, 9(3), pp. 445–456. https://doi.org/10.1080/19443927.2018.1500938

Colin, N. (2018b) 'The Critical Potential of Somatic Collectivity under Post-Fordism', *Journal of Dance and Somatic Practices*, 10(2), 235–249. https://doi.org/10.1386/jdsp.10.2.235_1

Coogan, J. (2016) *Practising Dance: a Somatic Orientation.* Berlin: Logos Verlag.

Delgado, M. (2018) 'Civility, Empathy, Democracy and Memory', *Performance Research Journal*, 23(4–6), pp. 328–336. https://doi.org/10.1080/13528165.2018.1525216

Department for Digital, Culture, Media & Sport (2021) 'Taking Part Survey'. Available at https://www.gov.uk/guidance/taking-part-survey

Diehl, I. (2018) *Bridging Dance Training Contexts Symposium.* Available at https://www.youtube.com/watch?v=BUbkPgkIeVg

Diehl, I. and Friederike Lampert (eds) (2010) *Dance Techniques 2010 Tanzplan Germany.* Berlin: Henschel-verlag.

Enghauser, R. (2007) 'The Quest for an Ecosomatic Approach to Dance Pedagogy', *Journal of Dance Education*, 7(3), pp. 80–90. https://doi.org/10.1080/15290824.2007.10387342

Fortin, S. (2017) 'Looking for Blind Spots in Somatics' Evolving Pathways', *Journal of Dance & Somatic Practices*, 9(2), pp. 145–157. https://doi.org/10.1386/jdsp.9.2.145_1

Foster, S. (2011) 'Interview with Susan Foster (on the Implicit Politics of Dance Training and Choreography)', *Maska*, XXVI, pp. 141–142.

Foster, S. (2019) *Valuing Dance: Commodities and Gifts in Motion.* New York: Oxford University Press.

Ginot, I. (2010) 'From Shusterman's Somaesthetics to a Radical Epistemology of Somatics', *Dance Research Journal*, 42(1), pp. 12–29. https://doi.org/10.1017/S0149767700000802

Godard, H. (1994) 'Le souffle, le lien', *Marsays*, 32, pp. 27–31.

Grehan, H. (2009) *Performance, Ethics and Spectatorship in a Global Age.* New York: Palgrave Macmillan.

Jackson, N. (2022) *Dance and Ethics: Moving towards a More Human Dance Culture.* Bristol: Intellect.

Klein, N. (2017) *No Is Not Enough: Defeating the New Shock Politics.* London: Penguin.

Kowal, R., Siegmund, G. and Martin, R. (eds) (2017) *The Oxford Handbook of Dance and Politics.* New York: Oxford University Press.

Kraut, A. (2020) 'Marie Bryant's Demonstrative Body and the Reproductive Labor of Transmitting Technique', in Banerji, A. and Mitra, R. (eds) *Conversations across the Field of Dance Studies*, Volume XL. Dance Studies Association, pp. 46–49.

Kunst, B. (2015) *Artist at Work, Proximity of Art and Capitalism.* Hants: Zero Books.

Kwan, S. (2017) 'When Is Contemporary Dance?', *Dance Studies Association*, 49(3), pp. 38–52. https://doi.org/10.1017/S0149767717000341

La Caze, M. and Martyn Lloyd, H. (2011) 'Philosophy and the Affective Turn', *Parrhesia*, 13, pp. 1–13.

Levinas, E. (1985) *Ethics and Infinity*, Pittsburgh: Duquesne University Press.

Massumi, B. (2002) *Parables for the Virtual: Movement, Affect, Sensation.* Durham, NC: Duke University Press.

Mauss, M. (1973) 'Techniques of the Body', *Economy and Society*, 2(1), pp. 70–88.

Morgan, L. (2018) 'Arts Education and Citizenship', *Journal of Dance Education*, 18(3), pp. 95–102. https://doi.org/10.1080/15290824.2018.1481964

Office for Students (2021) *Recurrent Funding for 2021-22 Outcomes of Consultation*. Available at https://www.officeforstudents.org.uk/media/c7329f54-2668-431e-ba14-616892a26586/recurrent_funding_2021_22_outcomes_of_consultation_final_for_web.pdf

One Dance UK (2020) *GSCE Dance Statistics*. Available at https://www.onedanceuk.org/gcse-dance-statistics/

One Dance UK (2021) *Everything We Loved About Dance Was Taken*. Available at https://www.onedanceuk.org/wp-content/uploads/2018/10/Everything-We-Loved-About-Dance-Was-Taken-2.pdf

Osterweiss, A. (2013) 'The Muse of Virtuosity', *Dance Research Journal*, 45(3), pp. 53–74. https://doi.org/10.1017/S0149767713000259

Prendergast, M. (2004) '"Playing Attention": Contemporary Aesthetics and Performing Arts Audience Education', *The Journal of Aesthetic Education*, 38(3), pp. 36–51. https://doi.org/10.1353/jae.2004.0030

Quinn, L. (2019) *Re-Imagining Curriculum: Spaces for Disruption*. Cape Town: African Sun Media.

Risner, D. and Stinson, S. (2010) 'Moving Social Justice: Challenges, Fears and Possibilities in Dance Education', *International Journal of Education & The Arts*, 11(6), pp. 1–26.

Roche, J. (2016) 'Moving Between First-Person and Third-Person Bodies in Dance Teaching', in Coogan, J. (ed.) *Practicing Dance: A Somatic Orientation*. Berlin: Logos Verlag, pp. 123–126. https://doi.org/10.1386/jdsp_00065_1

Ross, J. (2000) *Moving Lessons – Margaret H'Doubler and the Beginning of Dance in American Education*. Madison: The University of Wisconsin Press.

Rouhiainen, L. (2008) 'Somatic Dance as a Means of Cultivating Ethically Embodied Subjects', *Research in Dance Education*, 9(3), pp. 241–256. https://doi.org/10.1080/14647890802386916

Schatzki, T., Cetina, K. and von Savigny, E. (eds) (2001) *The Practice Turn in Contemporary Theory*. London; New York: Routledge.

Schupp, K. (2018) 'Dance Education and Responsible Citizenship', *Journal of Dance Education*, 18(3). https://doi.org/10.4324/9780429284809

Shapiro, S. (1998) 'Toward Transformative Teachers: Critical and Feminist Perspectives in Dance Education', in Shapiro, S. (ed.) *Dance, Power, and Difference*. Champaign: Human Kinetics, pp. 7–22.

Shrewsbury, C. (1993) 'What Is Feminist Pedagogy?', *Women's Studies Quarterly*, 21(3–4), pp. 8–16.

Sport and Recreation Alliance (2021) *The Social Value of Movement and Dance to the UK*. Available at: http://sramedia.s3.amazonaws.com/media/documents/b2d16422-1aa7-4c30-a99b-bc205b7e2ba5.pdf

Van Imschoot, M. (2005) 'Rest in Pieces. Partitions, Rating and Trace in Dance', *Multitudes*, 21(2), pp. 107–116.

Waitzman, E. (2021) 'Impact of Government Policy on the Creative Sector', *House of Lords Library*. Available at: https://lordslibrary.parliament.uk/impact-of-government-policy-on-the-creative-sector/#:~:text=The%20department%20noted%20that%20the,faster%20than%20the%20UK%20economy

Yorkshire Dance (2018) *Dance for Health, Well-Being and Empowerment of Young People*, Leeds. Available at https://yorkshiredance.com/wp-content/uploads/2018/06/Yorkshire_Dance_Youth_Research_Report_Full.pdf

Part I

Concepts

Introduction

Part I of the volume focuses on introducing a range of conceptual frameworks to underpin the notion of technique in contemporary dance practice in a variety of contexts, including postcolonial Britain. The chapters in this part extend the book's introduction by setting up a contextualisation of the notion of ethics and value in contemporary dance while considering wider social, historical, political perspectives on British dance. Critically examining ethical issues of techniques in dance, this group of writings investigates alternative approaches to teaching and learning dance. The contributions consist of critical enquiries, self-reflection and case studies drawn from professional dance teaching practice which use a range of registers, including philosophical, historical and personal. Taken together these chapters thematise theoretical ideas which informed the investigation of how technique in contemporary dance can be grounded in values that are more collaborative, inclusive and accessible. These ideas are further discussed in other modes of writing across the subsequent three parts of the book. Each chapter can be read in relation to other specific contributions, including practice chapters, conversations and manifestos.

In the opening chapter entitled 'New Imaginaries: Dance Training, Ethics and Practice', Fiona Bannon offers an exploration of the sensibilities and socially transforming effects of moving, either alone or with others, through dancing and creating dance. Bannon considers the qualitative benefit of dance as a relational technique to forge mutual ethical practices of being together. Drawing on a wide range of theoretical frameworks on arts and education, she argues that the future of civilised dance practice can be strengthened by seeking ethical accountability. Bannon defines ethics in dance as a collaborative process whereby dancers can learn to negotiate the 'inbetweeness' of being an individual while practising a mutuality of purpose and creative attentiveness. This chapter overarches most of the ideas expressed in the book. It is particularly relevant to read in conjunction with the conversation between Heni Hale and Ivan Michael Blackstock, the conversation between Rosemary Lee and Scilla Dyke and, the conversation between Jonathan Burrows and Alesandra

DOI: 10.4324/9781003111146-2

Seutin, Part II Practice chapters from Catherine Seago and, from Rosemary Cisneros, Marie-Louise Crawley and Karen Wood and, the manifesto 'A chorus of dancing voices' curated by Katye Coe.

In an engaging combination of personal experiences and historical perspectives, Jane Carr considers the changing position of contemporary dance within British culture. Writing in tandem with past memories and their historical contexts, Carr focuses on examples of practices that have revealed shifts in technical training while being foundational to contemporary dance in the UK. Her autoethnographic dialogue outlines different phases in the establishment of certain trends with regard to training by highlighting the pull and give between traditional and experimental ethos in contemporary dance. Acknowledging the broader scope and complexity of the interweaving of artistic and social realities, she offers a situated contextualisation of how contemporary dance practices might be understood within the context of postcolonial Britain. Her account on the South East London dance scene at the beginning of the 2000s provides insights on how contemporary dance practices was caught up in the complexities of changing cultural values. Overall, Carr's charting shift 'in techniques' points towards areas for further consideration for British dance institutions aiming to train dancers as artists with the capacity to respond to their twenty-first century contexts. This chapter is particularly relevant to read in conjunction with Part II Practice chapter by Tamara Ashley, the conversation between Shobana Jeyasingh and Alexander Whitley; the manifesto entitled 'The value of 'South Asian' dance technique to 'contemporary' dance training' by Magdalen Gorringe with Shivaangee Agrawal and Jane Chan as well as 'Funmi Adewole's manifesto 'Towards Decoloniality and Artistic Citizenship'.

In the next chapter, Betina Panagiotara asks: what makes a great dancer? Setting this question as a provocative starting point, her chapter, 'Democratising Dance: Inclusion at the Core of Dance Education and its Impact', examines the potential of inclusive practices to generate ethics and value that can be adopted and applied in mainstream dance education. Drawing on the politics of togetherness and an ethos of communing, Panagiotara offers a counterproposal to normative notions of physical ability and virtuosity often found in traditional dance educational methodologies. With references to key practitioners and professional companies of inclusive dance in the UK, she investigates the function of the notions of adaptability, openness, experimentation, imagination, empathy in specific alternatives approaches to teaching dance, including improvisation and collaboration. A number of these artists and educators are expressing their ideas about inclusive dance elsewhere in this book. This chapter is particularly relevant to read in conjunction with the conversations among Alison Ferrao, Laura Graham (Magpie Dance) and Caroline Hotchkiss (Blue Apple Dance Theatre); the conversation between Imogen Aujla and Laura Jones (Stopgap Dance Company); the conversation between Olu Taiwo and Adam Benjamin and Kate Marsh's Manifesto for Inclusion.

Delving into the nature of assessment in dance education, Adesola Akinleye's chapter discussed the importance of finding a place to evaluate the lifelong skills of students studying dance at Higher Education level. Akinleye situates their writing in the specific context of Covid to suggest that drawing on dance somatic and embodied knowledge could be a valuable way to the re-thinking of assessment tools in dance and in other fields of Higher Education. Weaving personal and critical registers, including thoughts-provoking experiences and theoretical thinking on embodied learning, they specifically examines the role of responsiveness, possibility and emergence as the primary tools for the development of a dancer's bodily thinking. Akinleye argues that (re)evaluating how assessment can support a lasting learning process in dance could in turn allow dance department in Higher Education to resist an institutional normative value system and to pave the way for a long-awaited paradigm change in tertiary education examination. This chapter is particularly relevant to read in conjunction with Carla Trim-Vamben and Jo Read's practice chapter in Part II and Lise Uytterhoeven and Baptiste Bourgougnon's Manifesto.

In the last chapter of Part I, Rachel Rimmer-Piekarczyk concludes the conceptual exploration of contemporary dance technique training in Britain by investigating the role that critical reflection plays in cultivating a critical agency for teachers and students of dance. Acknowledging the recent challenges of the Higher Education dance sector in the UK, Rimmer-Piekarczyk argues for the reconsideration of how higher level performing arts education can enable learners to survive within the current socio-cultural and political climate. She suggests that individual agency would allow dancers to effectively navigate and disrupt the different, sometimes contradictory value systems and ethical complexities that are evident both within the dance profession and within a broader social context. Drawing on notion of 'critical consciousness' as understood by educator Paulo Freire, Rimmer-Piekarczyk investigates what agency looks like for the contemporary dancer and how the development of a critical consciousness might facilitate the creation of new choreographic languages. This chapter is particularly relevant to read in conjunction with Part II Practices Chapters from Jamieson Dryburgh and Erica Stanton, the conversation between Theo Clinkard and Seke B. Chimutengwende and Jorge Crecis' manifesto, 'The world needs more Dancers'.

1.1 New imaginaries

Dance training, ethics, and practice

Fiona Bannon

Introduction

In the creation of dance works and any subsequent performances, the journey undertaken by those involved can emerge as a complex and often challenging interchange between artistic experimentation, the forming of relationships, and the shaping of social determinations. Experiences that shape discreet aspects of such processes depend upon the gradual interweaving of cooperative relationships, amidst the people and ambitions that shape ways of working and of emergent, mutual intent. The ideas explored here concern the sensibilities and socially transforming effects of our such moving relations, formed alone and/or with the others with whom we dance. Experiences forged amidst what can be vibrant associations have intercorporeal implications for the ways we learn to interrelate and, in turn, benefit from working in common. The framework of this debate considers ways we might access qualitative benefit, through the relational practices we forge amidst experiences of dance creation.

Dances come into existence through a series of correspondences, requiring those involved to evaluate their attitudes towards material ideas, sociality, and emerging practice. Benefit can be gained through working in contexts where we each attend to mutual responsibilities. Arguably, when working in such generative contexts, we forge a synchrony through the gradual recognition of our shared ambitions. These experiential behaviours, realised through our ongoing associations, have intercorporeal implications with respect to the ways those involved interrelate, *in* and *through* their relations. Considered in this context, the quest to recognise the complexity of experiences found dancing and the forging of mutual ethical practice deserve our attentions. Our ways of being-with-others, the resonance of our evolving sentient intelligence, and our abilities to work in close association deserve greater scrutiny. Together the features of our *being-in-common* can come to underpin the socio-kinaesthetic sensibilities that shape our relations.

Our manner of *being-in-common* is sourced in lived experiences where our awareness of being in associations aligns with our critical, artistic, communicative, and aesthetic selves. Through the synchrony of learning in motion and realisation of ideas through negotiation, there are benefits in recognising

DOI: 10.4324/9781003111146-3

attitudes to practice as a means of facilitating the realisation of shared ideas. Working through such dialogic structures, we can explore ways to engage, and come to appreciate how we can build frameworks for creative endeavours.

In the arenas of exchange in studio practices, a host of ethical conundrums can emerge and ultimately impact upon our creative endeavours. As we experiment with feasible ideas and investigate ways to align our determinations, we can progress towards a gradual realisation of productive outcomes. The trajectory of any such process comes to be shaped through the continued exploration of the emergent values first recognised at the beginning of a process. In experiences forged through what is an attentive interchange, opportunity to foster a socially engaged practice of ethics can emerge. In asking ourselves how we might scope the potential to establish such a practice on common ground, we might consider:

What we need to do to establish feasible ways of working together?
What shared curiosities can we recognise that might inform our practice?
Through what processes will we make decisions and foster debate?

Amidst the responses to these questions, opportunities can arise as we continue to examine *practice* as a generative *common ground*. Through our experiences of improvising and choreography, we experiment with ways to both question and reveal our understandings. Meg Stuart (2018: 9) echoes these ideas when reflecting on her manner of engagement with improvisation, arguing that 'the body has its own intelligence. We only use a very small section of our mind and dancing is a channel for this lost awareness. I try to cultivate synchronicity and force unusual connections'.

In such circumstances, shared company practice is dependent upon cooperative interchange, sensitivity, and allowance of agency through attentions given to power imbalances in attitudes to working. The exploratory ambitions of choreographic challenges can, however, secure a sense of shared endeavour in contexts where ideas emerge gradually, as a group seeks to establish agreed identity and purpose. For Randy Martin, the idea of *meeting at the work* has positive value, for as he suggests, it is, 'in and through the work, that the dancer is moved to act not as an individual but as a social body' (Martin, 1985: 21). Considered from this perspective, we can recognise the experience of creating a dance work as a socially integrating system. The situation is one where those involved may come to recognise shared practice as an interweaving of social ambition, embracing movement awareness, choreographic challenges, social integration, and ethical acumen. Here, it may be feasible to recognise resilience in the forging of ongoing correspondences, for,

- *It is here*, that the qualitative rigour of shared engagement with artistic challenges and choreographic endeavour can emerge.
- *It is here*, that the creation of a dance work can be recognised as a socially integrating project. It is a place where we can explore the ambiguities and feasible possibilities of discovery.

- *It is here*, that we each seek to forge distinct respect for those we work alongside, sustaining regard for our mutuality through the cultivation of shared ethical practice.
- *It is here*, that ultimately, an emergent conceptual and physical work can be identified as a company practice.

To work through 'correspondence' requires those involved to evaluate their attitude towards artistic sensibilities. The journey can be challenging, reliant as it is on abilities to sustain shared intent. The working environment is necessarily one of ongoing negotiation, something we might frame as an *emergent social encounter*. Arguably, what can become apparent through such processes is a shared resilience, a sensation often grounded in the intercorporeal nature of social projects. Any such process relies on there being sufficient time for those involved to attune to the varied energies and creative identities that come to constitute the group. The journey towards such cooperative awareness takes time to evolve, often benefitting from a gradual immersion with ideas and a range of experimental and experiential practices through which choreographic ideas may emerge. Such a working context can present those involved with an array of challenging, social, and ethical conundrums to address as they seek to forge communality of purpose.

Immersed within what can become an interweaving practice, a company can explore feasible ways to embrace differences of perspective, through seeking to facilitate openness, explorative improvisation, and cooperative endeavour. What is notable here is the manner through which intentional explorations forged amidst social interactions can facilitate both a sense of due diligence and a socially aware respect for others.

- *It is here*, we can recognise each of us as 'selves', realised through being amidst others.
- *It is here*, that dancing can be revealed as a social project that benefits from the intertwining of shared, energising sensibilities.
- *It is here*, that we can learn through movement, alone and with the others with whom we generate opportunities to explore physical ideas.
- *It is here*, that we can forge a gradual realisation of productive coherence.

Between ambitions, drives, and aspirations, an interlacing of artistry, sociality, and accountability can emerge. Arguably, it is through energising these explorative sensibilities that any future artistic outcome emerges. When considered from these perspectives, the practice of dance making and indeed, of dancing, can be seen as riven with dialogic challenges; they exist amongst the socially interacting, creative processes that we design. Karen Barad's thoughts on identity can usefully reinforce these ideas when arguing that for each of us, 'Existence is not an individual affair. Individuals do not pre-exist their interactions; rather, individuals emerge through and as part of their entangled intra-relating' (Barad, 2007: ix). In this way, the social network of a choreographed performance emerges during and continues beyond any initial ambition with respect to the tentative intentions established as the project emerged.

In following these trajectories, we can recognise the ways we mobilise our artful, ethic, and aesthetic intentions in the creation and use of performance. In what for many have become unsettling shifts in perspective during pandemic times, there have been valuable opportunities to hear a broader cross-section of the population speak of the sensation of their situated body in relation to spatial tension, proximity, physical contact, and dynamic changes. It is a context that resonates with the work of Gregory Bateson (1982 [2000]) when exploring the consequences of interactional connections between our ideas and our manners of action. In writing with the aim to consider benefits that can be recognised through forms of social practice, his ambitions reveal the ways generative ideas can resonate with respect to our being-with-others, as we each learn to recognise and seek to understand difference.

What we can appreciate from the themes of this work is that ethical practice concerns more than a societal alignment with behavioural rules, and more than a revelation of philosophic debate. In relation to these thoughts, it is feasible to consider how the wealth of dance learning and experience resides in the micro-political practice of cooperative endeavours. Working in a polydisciplinary frame, we gather and generate experiences; embody and transmit ideas; and utilise creative practices of cooperation, transformation, identity making, and the sustaining of community. In these ways, the practice of making dances contributes to our ways of living. As we work and relate, we experiment, we think through visible ideas, we forge associations through making thoughts visible, and we examine ways to resolve complexities and to generate new ways of resolving our communicative intentions through choreographic problem solving.

We can argue that dancing is about sense finding and sense making. It is a place where we each learn and are changed through the process. Although this may not be expected of experiences in dance, it is through advancing bodily knowledge that we each have opportunities to learn from our relatedness to the other with whom we dance. Our human relations are key for our futures, evidently crucial in dance learning and shaped by responsibilities, participation, and contributions made through sustained resilience. Arguably, approaching dance practice via these routes underscores the feasibility of framing dance as a dialogical tool for a civilising society. In mobilising experiences found dancing, we can enhance our associations through being attentive to shifting tides of social integration and cooperation.

When writing the *Ethics* (1677 [2008]), Spinoza examined our means of being-in-common, by considering the feasibility of our interactive ways of living and how we might learn to recognise shifts in our attitudes when engaged in negotiated encounters. Through experiences gained when navigating complex interrelating processes, we can learn to examine variable, social, and personal challenges, and forge commitments to the realisation of new ways of working. For Spinoza, there are clear benefits in working through such associations. Here, experience can be realised as a meeting of our ethics, our aspirations, our sensibilities, and particularities of behaviour. Significant features of Spinoza's ideas revolve around the need to recognise our ways of living through variability. He emphasises that in our striving to persevere there are advantages for each of us in exploring potential synchronies that can come into existence between forging varied associations. If we think of experiences found dancing in these terms, we can shed light on dance as a communicative bodily technology, a place where we each learn through action and through shifting fields of relatedness.

To seek to consolidate ethically informed studio practices draws our focus towards the ways we each engage through adaptability, agility, and care. Though such attitudes to our learning might be considered aspirational, with respect to future practice they are fundamentally foundational, core features of practice. As part of an interactive system, these behaviours underscore how studio practice gains benefit from active engagement with relational responsibilities and shared accountability. Here, it is worth noting considerations made by Oliver (2015: 274) when arguing that if 'subjectivity is fundamentally inter-subjective because it is formed through mutual recognition, then many of the assumptions of liberalism, based as they are on the notion of individual autonomy, are unfounded'.

There are benefits in broadening debates concerning the position of arts learning in our cultural lives, in order that we might secure access to varied practices that share respect for communality, alongside individuality of voice. The current political determination to underfund the arts and to reduce their core role in education seeks to undermine and restrict the cultural voice of future generations, reducing access for the many, whilst retaining it for the few within private institutions. The impact of such actions threatens the provision of opportunity for society at large, impacting on our facility to communicate through varied forms of media and in sharing debate in/through art. The consequences, as can already be seen, are an undermining of our cultural, critical acumen and our shared, social awareness – features that in time will need attentive repair.

Questions re-emerge concerning ways we can seek to work towards synergy, strengthening the effectiveness of arguments that promote the educative value of learning in and through arts. Though this may feel to be a repeating task, it is a necessary one if we are to acknowledge and readdress decline in the provision of learning in and through arts for the sake of future social and societal wellbeing. As I write, there are emerging issues sourced from a host of political actions intent on the privatisation of arts learning, the removal of arts in schools, and cuts in funding for arts disciplines in universities. Whilst this may be familiar territory for those working in the dance field, there is renewed need to address our ambitions through secured access to learning through movement and amidst an education provision that facilitates creativity, artistry, communication, social cohesion, and physical sensibility. Through experiences gained immersed within these differing arenas of exchange, opportunities can arise through recognising correspondences across a range of motivations and sustained amidst social learning systems. We need to remember that meaningful learning experiences emerge in contexts where we each participate in processes that bring us into dynamic relations. In recognising and championing what can be learned through our ways of being in motion, it is valuable to note that such socially integrative learning underpins our societal structures.

What do we learn through practices that seek to share respect for communality, caught up as we are in a *world* where social patterns of art making are becoming increasingly unsettled? Questions continue to circulate concerning ways we might work towards synergy, securing the value of learning in and through the arts as integral to, and formative of, the broader society. Our arts institutions appear to slide towards tentative positions, less sure of the veracity in seeking to promote the development of knowledge amidst arts practices whilst becoming more beholden to a political system that seeks to prioritise elite training for specific systems of industrial production. However, through the arenas of exchange still evident in studio practices, we can acknowledge the correspondences that inform experimentation and that are sustained in/through social learning systems.

Meaningful learning experiences emerge in contexts where we participate with processes that bring us into dynamic relation. Through investigation, interruption, disagreement, and seeding of evolving alignments, a resonance can emerge that makes the immediacy of our proximity effective. With emphasis given to our relatedness, there is chance to recognise our fluid individuality, and our social affordances, as part of a social world. For Gins and Arakawa, authors of the *Architectural Body*, there is a key ethical concern regarding ways we might each succeed in a quest to live well. To address their concern, they asked, how we might '... put all that one is as a body to best use' (2002: xx). Their question resonates with our need to explore how we might each learn to articulate our expanding and deepening knowledge as moving thinking beings, living moving lives, and how we might put the knowledge gained as movers to best use.

Here, we can recognise and promote values found through movement-based learning, where dance works come into existence through a series of encounters that require those involved to actively evaluate their attitude towards what is an, ongoing, negotiated, social arena. The complexity at the core of such activities can reveal an interweaving synchrony of our social psychologies, a practice that binds ideas and motivations. In this way, the inter/intra-social features of a performed event emerge during and exist beyond any agreed intentions that may have been established as the project began. Together, the complex braiding of the known and unknown facets of a company's practice enters close relation through the associative connections found and felt in moving. Through the potential of these integrating connections, we can recognise a synchronising practice of ethics.

In asking, what can moving together facilitate in terms of our social projects of learning, it is worth considering how we learn to coexist, and to recognise the benefit of delving into our ethical encounters as an inevitable part of the practices involved in creating performance. As makers of art, we are familiar with the notion of the 'responsible practitioner' that the relevance of our work addresses more than the creation of a performance. Encounters navigated amidst a creative process offer ways to explore dialogic relations, through social systems of power and through facilitating aesthetic attunement. It is, here, betwixt our patterning behaviours that we can realise synchrony, forging links between our social bonding and cooperative action. In these ways, experiences of dancing often provide an immediacy of the social, underpinning the challenges and ambitions of the individual through an intermingling with *the other*, with whom they work. We dance not only to enhance our own bodily sensation but also to intertwine our sensory, motor, cognitive, social, rhythmic, and creative sensibilities. Experiences found dancing offer ways we can learn to integrate our perceptions from multiple perspectives and to synthesise our responses through creative expression.

In exploring what can be recognised through experiences of collaborative dance making and echoing Spinozian ideas, Phillipa Rothfield (2015) reminds us that 'the ethical is already implicated within the domain of dance simply because we dance. It is found in the tactile flow of information, from one body to another'. Arguably, ethics is implicit in any such co-creative social act in the transmission of ideas. It is a process that binds, and it happens amongst those involved. Here, it is our self-aware practice of ethics that can act as a contributory feature in the generation of interactive engagements and ideas. It is a place where we act as beings-in-common. Isabelle Stengers voice is valuable in offering ambitions we can echo in seeking to consolidate future modes of a civilising dance practice. When addressing our futures through art, Stengers (2015: 73) reminds us that 'we need researchers able to participate in the creation of responses on which the possibility of a future that is not barbaric depends'.

Achieving such ambitions through a practice of shared recognition, ethical accountability in education, training and professional practice whilst seeking to integrate dance artistry as a civilising practice chimes as a worthy ambition. In turn, Stengers' ideas resonate with those of John Dewey when he notes, '...moving and multiple associations are the only means by which the possibilities of individuality can be realised...' (Dewey and (ed) Boydston, 2008: 122–123). For Dewey (1934), the challenge in building sustainable communities of practice is dependent upon each of us starting from 'home', the place where we need to learn to recognise the complex interweaving of our individuality. Interestingly, he argues, that to gain an integrated individuality, each of us needs to commit to working with others through seeking to cultivate collaborative, respectful, imaginative, committed, and adaptable processes. Arguably, it is here, through what might be recognised as an imaginative synchronicity, that we have opportunities to forge benefits found through a responsive, attentive ethics.

In *Meeting the Universe Halfway* (2007), Karen Barad speaks of an approach to ethics not dissimilar to Gatens (1995), Braidotti (2006), or Lloyd (2013) when asking, 'what might we need in order to facilitate advancement with respect to our understanding more of what it is to be human, to live in relation with each other and with the planet?' (Barad, 2007: ix).

When considering how we might prosper through our ways of being in association, Barad acknowledges the significance of the task when noting:

> To be entangled is not simply to be intertwined with another, as in the joining of separate entities, but to lack an independent, self-contained existence. Existence is not an individual affair. Individuals do not pre-exist their interactions; rather, individuals emerge through and as part of their entangled intra-relating.
>
> (Barad, 2007: ix)

Evident here is the sense that we gain experience through the individual and multiple associations that we forge with one another. In such variable circumstances, we can evolve integrative communities of practice, learning to appreciate the nuance and distinct potential of the individualities involved. Braidotti (2006) and Genevieve Lloyd (2013) both signal modes of sustainability as key determinants of our ethics in the encounters formed, in, and through our lived experiences. In their framing of ethics, they perceive it to be a form of philosophic inquiry that offers guiding principles towards what can be utilised as part of a civilising society.

With such encounters as a key feature of the interpersonal work experienced in performance, we can recognise the ways our intermingling presence impacts on the potential to be found when we investigate ideas together. As Hans-Georg Gadamer (1975) notes, it is ultimately through the manner of our appreciation and respect for each other, and the different experiences we each bring to collaborative practice that responsive, creative challenges and practices emerge.

With evident benefits to be found through our ways of being in association, it is worth exploring what can be learned through the cooperative collaboration that underpins art making as a vital arena for the exploration and the communication of ideas. Rothfield's (2015) echo of Spinoza highlights the social adventures to be found through our means of moving together, a practice we can recognise as riven with the immediacy of ethical relatedness. For Rothfield, there are ethical implications in the movement and flow of information that comes into existence between bodies. However, with the inherent values found in learning through such bodily motion and respect to our potential synchronicity, identity, and relationality, it is apt to note Schenck's observation that it is through our bodily, emplaced self that we '...

literally are, selves expressed' (1986: 46). Implicit here are values to be found through the ways we might come into association, in the sense that we each learn through giving focussed attention to the opportunities we jointly foster through dialogic relations.

In the complexities of experiences found dancing, there are opportunities to learn to perceive and manage aspects of ourselves through giving cooperative attention and seeking chance to recognise more about the other/s with whom we dance. Through exploring processes that include interactive engagements, we can examine our ways of being-in-common and thereby learn to cultivate our aesthetic awareness and ethical attunement. Through such active processes, opportunities arise where we can capture and put to good use our means of relating to, and with, one another.

In 'Dancing Through the Crisis' (2010) Randy Martin, writing amidst the financial crash, asks us to consider the idea of risk, pondering what we might be willing to risk in the hope of gaining 'something altogether different'. His challenge seems ever more appropriate as I write in Spring 2021, amidst a worldwide pandemic. Martin argues for experiences of dancing to be mobilised, shaping a vibrant body of possibilities, and underscoring the relevance of dance practice as a '...profound sentient intelligence'. Starting from the familiar premise that dance in Western cultures is often dismissed as '... a minor art form, academically and aesthetically marginal' (2010), he reminds us of the need to recognise knowledge as both grounded in and emerging through movement, and that such knowledge has the potential to contribute to our ways of securing social integration.

With evidence across the globe of the social role of our mutuality through movement, the Western resistance to acknowledging the bodily contribution in realms of shaping knowledge, and our social integration, stubbornly persists. For Martin, it is clear that we need to recognise that through engagements in dancing we experience an immediacy of our social immersion. In experiences, found, felt, and shared when dancing we '... take up the question of what we can make together' (Martin, 2010).

As we delve into experiments with movement, we examine forms of social interaction, embracing varied means of communication, co-creation, and negotiation. It is evident that through such practice we learn to recognise forms of composition in the generation of artistic responses to our experiments. Here, we have opportunities to re-evaluate and repurpose our behaviours in ways that might better reflect our sensibilities and articulate our creative intent. In a return to where we started the discussion, it is the sensibilities and socially transforming effects of our moving, alone or with the others with whom we dance, that inform our identity making and remain evident in our interwoven experiences of life.

Ultimately, the creation of a *choreographic work* emerges through experimentation amidst a social interchange. It is through negotiation, interaction, and dynamic social integration that choreographic ideas are forged and come to be articulated. The challenges of choreographic working afford opportunities to explore ideas through innovative critical engagement whilst fostering a unity of purpose.

For Spinoza, it is through such continuing examination of our interactive manners that we learn to facilitate and negotiate our lived experiences. In the *Ethics* (1677), Spinoza explores the ways we function as *beings-in-common*, examining the potential for each of us to use interactive ways of living in/through our various contexts of encounter. He argues that we learn to navigate social challenges, recognise, and rehearse the practise of variable, complex, and cooperative actions. Arguably, in these experiences, we learn to incorporate various shifts and differences in our behaviours. We learn to interweave combinations of accommodations in the ways we assimilate and share information and how we address sometimes confrontational behaviours. Through continuing and complex exposure to variable, integrative situations, a versatility emerges in the ways we might each manage our engagement with experiences. For Spinoza, it is through an emerging, sustained recognition of our individual identities and the ways through which we learn to integrate facets of experience with the others we work amongst, that we establish our ethics and recognise our identities.

In the breadth of experiences found learning through dance, we gain an ease of access to unspoken codes, we learn to read the 'other' with whom we create and with whom we dance through complex and varied facets of our social interactions. Through exchanges of ideas, we shape interpretations, and we forge varied meanings. Through complex ways of being in association, opportunities emerge, where we recognise value in forging synchronies. Here, it is through honing ourselves as socially integrating sensibilities that our ideas come to be revealed. In dance learning, dance creation and performance, we work immersed within modes of transcontextual and interdependent practices. It is through such complexity that we generate practice, and in the process, a unity can emerge as we strive to integrate our self, our shared identity, and our interdependence with those we work alongside. To deepen our understandings of the shifting discourses that shape shared studio and performance practices, we can benefit from recognising the values to be found in meeting difference. Be it stylistic, choreographic, artistic, political, or ethical, our task is to forge a unity of understanding through the differences in practice of those we work alongside.

Through the shared experiences of our coordinating interactions, there are evident values to be found, something Elizabeth Waterhouse (2010) recognises as our human facility to make meaning in action. For Waterhouse, it is through our ways of working that we can come to realise dependence on our spatial integration, it is a facet of dance practices often forged through communal endeavour. These coordinating interactions are part of each of our everyday living contexts. They are something we experience as shifting arenas of exchange and gradually learn to facilitate through an interweaving of our ethics, aesthetics, arts practice, and the forging of interactive relationships that evolve in performative, social projects.

Closing

There is a continuing need to remain open to experiences both in recognising and being challenged by difference. Here, we have chance to learn through sustained inquisitiveness, delving into emergent possibilities by allowing ourselves to consider ideas from varied perspectives. Losing the ability to sustain an inquisitive nature diminishes the advantages that can be found through experimentation in relation to our mobility, our ingenuity, and the forging of imaginative, social kinaesthetic associations with others.

> The encounter of people working together is characterised by interruption, rifts and disagreements, forming a certain discontinuous community that needs time and proximity before it can begin to articulate and employ its differences, and it is very likely not to happen in expected or preferable ways.
>
> (Georgelou et al., 2013: 88)

As we come to appreciate the interpersonal fields in which we work as dance makers, where the subtleties of dynamic bodily interactions impact upon the translation of ideas, we can appreciate benefits in the facilitating abilities, which shape processes of working and the communication of ideas. There are benefits in sustaining an openness to experience, where there are opportunities to be challenged through adaptive changes to your own practice, and where new possibilities can emerge when recognising the feasibility of exploring emerging arenas of exchange.

In learning through ethically engaged, socially alert arts practices, opportunities emerge for us to process distinct experiences in the gaining of knowledge. Here, we can establish key guiding principles including the need

- ... *to give* and *take* in the *absence of fixed rules* and in the forging of tentative, agreed ways of working,
- ... to learn to value time given to being uncertain, to being with chaos and unevenness,
- ... to recognise responses to situations, to the ideas of others, to the energy and attention needed in shaping a response,
- ... to learn that each time you start a project, you are entering a process of change.

Through the social project of ethical engagement, we can realise the distinct practices that inform our ways of working; of observing, of communicating, and of corresponding with one another. It is through experimentation amidst such emergent modes of dialogic thinking that we can come to shape future practice. When working amidst modes of engagement where we forge shared sensibilities and generate resilience, opportunities to cultivate a mutuality of practice can emerge. In such environments, and existing between order and disorder, new knowledge can emerge that exhibits characteristics of inclusivity, of mutuality, and collaborative respect. It is perhaps this intermingling of ideas in generating material that comes to reinforce a socially situated, practice of ethics, and can often reveal a mutuality of physical sensibility amongst the company.

For Deleuze, it is through engagement with such ethical and social endeavours that we can identify negotiated territories of both our interrelationships and practices. Through our '…effort to organize our encounters based on perceived agreements and disagreement' (1990: 280) we each continue to explore ways of learning through which we might shape as a self-regulatory system. In the impetus for self-preservation, and the attentions we give to our striving to survive, there is need to learn of the benefits gained through interactions with the others with whom we work. As we learn to give more determined attention, opportunities can arise for integrative, social intertwining through creative practice. In the ways we each relate, live, learn, and work together, a sense of identity making can emerge through varied extending, engagements in practice. This we can recognise as more than an individual honing of talent, as it usefully reveals a form of social interaction where – in *being with 'another'* – we further enhance the possibilities for opportunities as they emerge.

What is of interest for us here in shaping the identity of experimental work in performance is a deepening awareness of related practice through learning of our situated 'inbetweeness'. It is a place where an acknowledged respect of being an individual blends with a mutuality through social relations. Through what is effectively a web of relationality, we gain experience through ethics as a collaborative process. Here, it is appreciation for sustainable practice that guides the principles of working through relations.

References

Barad, K. (2007) *Meeting the Universe Halfway*. Durham, NC: Duke University Press.

Bateson, G. (1982 [2000]) *Steps to an Ecology of Mind*. 2nd ed. Chicago, IL: The University of Chicago Press.

Braidotti, R. (2006) *Transpositions: On Nomadic Ethics*. Cambridge: Polity Press.

Deleuze, G. (1990) *The Logic of Sense*. New York: Columbia University Press.

Dewey, J. (1934) *Art as Experience*. New York: Minton, Balch & Company.

Dewey, J. and (ed.) J. A. Boydston (2008) *The Later Works of John Dewey: 1929–1930, Essays, the Course of a Science of Education, Individualism, Old and New, and Construction of a Criticism*. 1st edition. Carbondale: Southern Illinois University Press, 122–123.

Gadamer, H. (1975) *Truth and Method*. New York: Bloomsbury Press.

Gatens, M. (1995) *Imaginary Bodies: Ethics, Power and Corporeality*. New York: Taylor & Francis.

Georgelou, K., Gallier, E. and Silva, J. (2013) *Inventing Futures: Doing and Thinking Artistic Research with(in) the Master of Choreography Programme of ArtEZ Institute of the Arts, the Netherlands*. Amsterdam: ArtEZ Press.

Gins, M. and Arakawa (2002) *Architectural Body*. Tuscallosa: The University of Alabama Press.

Lloyd, G. (2013) *Enlightenment Shadows*. Oxford: Oxford University Press.

Martin, R. (1985) 'Dance as a Social Movement'. In *Social Text*. No 12. Duke University, 54–70. https://doi.org/10.2307/466604

Martin, R. (2010) 'Dancing Through the Crisis'. *Affinities: A Journal of Radical Theory, Culture, and Action*, 4(2), Fall 2010, pp. 55–60. Available at: https://ojs.library.queensu.ca/index.php/affinities/article/view/6137

Oliver, K. (2015) 'Witnessing, Recognition, and Response Ethics'. *Philosophy and Rhetoric*, 48(4), pp. 473–493.

Rothfield, P. (2015) *Dancing in the Dark, Spinoza's Ethics of the Body*. [online] DANCEHOUSE DIARY. Available at: http://www.dancehousediary.com.au/?cat=708

Schenck, D. (1986) 'The Texture of Embodiment: Foundation for Medical Ethics'. *Human Studies*, 9, pp. 43–54.

Spinoza, B. (1677 [2018]) *Ethics. Ethica Ordine Geometrico Demonstrata*. CreateSpace Independent Publishing Platform. Available at: https://www.createspace.com/

Spinoza, B. (2008) *The Ethics* (pt 11). New York: Biblio Life.

Stengers, I. (2015) *In Catastrophic Times Resisting the Coming Barbarism*. La Decouverte: Open Humanities Press.

Stuart, M. (2018) Mono. Kultur No. 41 Meg Stuart. MonoKultur.

Waterhouse, E. (2010) 'Dancing amidst the Forsythe Company Space, Enactment in Living Repertory'. In G. Brandstetter and B. Weins (eds), *Theater without Vanishing Points: The Legacy of Adolphe Appia: Scenography and Choreography in Contemporary Theatre*. Berlin: Alexander Verlag, 153–181.

1.2 Contemporary dance in postcolonial Britain

Charting shifts in 'techniques'

Jane Carr

Introduction

I have organised an annual dance concert in South-East London, and my goal to ensure equality in the presentation of a variety of dancing chimes with the 'New Labour' politics of the era. In spite of my efforts, more people want to perform ballet, jazz and tap than contemporary dance,[1] African-Caribbean or South Asian dance: the responses to performances within 'classical' traditions of ballet and kathak are polite in contrast to tap and jazz dancing which at every concert always raise some whoops and cheers; while contemporary dances often seem to perplex even the performers' friends and families. At this concert we also have a guest performance by the newly formed Irven Lewis Dance Theatre. I am happy to see the audience respond very positively to their virtuosic performance, but I am surprised that, as someone active in the dance field, I have not been aware of their style of jazz dancing previously.

The above recollection of a concert in 2001 provides a snapshot of those experiences which led me to consider the impact of the wider social and political context upon how dance is valued, understood and appreciated (Carr, 2008). That the UK jazz dancing performed by Irven Lewis Dance Theatre operated in such a different field to the theatre dance and community education I had experienced speaks volumes about the cultural and social divides in postcolonial Britain. To understand how contemporary dance is situated within British culture, it is necessary to grasp something of the complexities of its histories. As a first step, in what ideally would be a much larger undertaking, I draw upon autoethnographic reflections of my experiences of contemporary dance, in tandem with reference to their historical contexts, to reflect back upon its development. This informs consideration of how elements of technical training, related to creative practices and choreographic styles, have come to constitute contemporary dance in the UK as a field that may be understood in relation to wider cultural and social values. It is important however to emphasise that values perceived as embodied in contemporary

DOI: 10.4324/9781003111146-4

dance should not be considered to be located solely in the dance but rather understood by virtue of techniques and practices being enmeshed within a complex of interrelating cultural, social and political fields (Carr, 2008).

Inevitably my perspective of such a vast field of activity spread over half a century is limited and my memory is fickle. Memory as those who study it tell us:

> ...is at once situated in social frameworks (e.g., family and nation), enabled by changing media technologies (e.g., the internet and digital recording), confronted with cultural institutions (e.g., memorials and museums), and shaped by political circumstances.
>
> (Olick, Vinitsky-Seroussi and Levy, 2011: 37)

The dialogue I construct between my past memories and what now seems their relevant context is a product of a play between my past and present, and research shaped by the social, cultural and political landscape of contemporary Britain. Attempting such a broad sweep through history, I cannot do justice to the complex interweaving of different artistic and social perspectives. Building on an earlier survey of dance in the UK which recognises the 'many contradictions' within the dance field (Rowell, 2000: 188), I acknowledge how at times I gloss over details that would benefit from further interrogation. Moreover, due to my particular geographic location, I focus more on some of the issues facing black British dancers than British Asians.[2] Rather than a comprehensive history, my aim is to point towards areas for further consideration for British dance institutions aiming to train dancers as artists with the capacity to respond to their twenty-first-century contexts.

1970s

> I am studying at ballet school. We are nearly all girls and overwhelmingly white. Some students are supported by local authority grants but, by virtue of the private sector dance lessons needed to pass an entry audition, most come from fairly affluent backgrounds. Ballet technique seems to be the pinnacle of a dance hierarchy that replicates a very British sense of 'class': we study for Royal Academy and Imperial Society examinations and learn repertoire from 'classics' such as The Sleeping Beauty and The Nutcracker.
>
> In a time before the internet, occasional news of a changing dance field reaches us through visiting teachers and students. Yet reports of Pina Bausch, Alwin Ailey and the developing London Contemporary Dance Theatre and School seem as if from another world. For us the alternative to ballet is what is called modern stage dance which develops the skills required for 'West End' shows. None of us have a sense of the African diasporic heritage of jazz that informs the choreography. Coming from a small town, I am surprised by the lifestyles of a few of

the richer students, particularly by one girl who reveals that at home in Zambia a 'house boy' does her ironing. However, questioning such things is not part of ballet school, or indeed any school, syllabus.

While the relationship between the social and cultural fields should not be assumed as simple and direct, in general terms, the contemporary dance field at its inception in Britain may be understood broadly as a challenge to an established order that was bound up with a sense of tradition. By the mid-1960s, recognition of persistent social and economic inequalities fuelled political opposition to the Conservative Government of Harold Macmillan and also informed the development of alternative modes of theatre production. These prioritised the interests of disadvantaged communities viewing theatre as a means of cultural intervention linked to opposition to the status quo (Kershaw, 1992). The contemporary dance that became established in Britain was aligned with this turn away from the values of a 'class' based unequal society shaped by the traditions of its imperial past and a shift towards the values of social democracy.

By the 1970s, there were however a number of different strands of contemporary dance that would influence what is now a complex field. One key influence was that of American modern dance training that was transplanted to Britain largely through the establishment of London Contemporary Dance School (LCDS) in 1966 and followed by London Contemporary Dance Theatre (LCDT) a year later. It chimed with a more general turn against outdated convention to follow the example of the American modern dance 'pioneers' of the 1930s. They had dispensed with the many different ranks of dancers that in ballet reflected the rigidly hierarchical class systems of the European societies in which ballet first developed. American modern dance artists had also challenged the aesthetics of a dance form that prioritised visual splendour and the illusion of effortless grace. Instead, their dancing acknowledged the physical effort required to combat gravity and embraced movement that could represent the harsh realities of life, particularly in the context of a depression-hit America. The establishment of contemporary dance in Britain similarly challenged the conventions of 'old-world' traditions and the hierarchies perceived as embodied in the nineteenth-century 'classics'. Ballets that were created initially for bourgeois French or aristocratic Russian audiences had been revived in mid-twentieth-century Britain with an emphasis on a lineage to the courts of France and Russia in a conscious attempt to 'divorce British ballet from what was perceived as its less than respectable music hall past' (Rowell, 2000: 193). By the second half of the twentieth century, ballet in Britain was situated at the pinnacle of both dance and social hierarchies, a position formalised by the establishment of the Royal Ballet in 1946.

LCDS was not the first alternative to ballet in Britain (Nicholas, 2004). Margaret Morris Movement preceded the establishment of ballet in the UK as did the work of Margaret Barr and later Kurt Jooss and Sigurd Leeder, initially at Dartington Hall.[3] During the Second World War, they were joined at Dartington by the dance theorist and choreographer Rudolf Laban. Laban's work was initially an influence on dance in education but it would later become influential on dance theatre practitioners graduating from Laban (later Trinity Laban).[4] Dartington Hall, as Dartington College of the Arts, would continue to foster new developments in dance based in its founding ethos that emphasised the social values of the arts. However, it was LCDS and LCDT which spearheaded the wider acceptance of contemporary dance. At the time, they became established in London in the 1960s, by virtue of being set in opposition to ballet, contemporary dance enjoyed the status of being avant-garde. Yet, arguably, LCDS and its related company were already positioned to become part of the British arts establishment. The aesthetic of the later Martha Graham Dance Company had smoothed out the radically abrupt actions and grounded quality of Graham's early work to incorporate more fluidity and balletic technique (Bannerman, 1999). With support from the American heiress Batsheva de Rothschild and drawn into the USA Government's use of cultural diplomacy to combat the perceived communist threat (Barnhisel, 2015; Prevots, 1999), by the mid-twentieth century, the Martha Graham Dance Company was part of the American modernist establishment co-opted into a bourgeois arts sector (Barnhisel, 2015). The dominant mid-twentieth-century modernist aesthetic adopted a formalism that set the arts apart from everyday life within an autonomous field of the arts conditional upon a set of socioeconomic circumstances particular to modernity and in which only a few artists would develop the cultural capital necessary to gain wider status and recognition (Bourdieu, 1993). With ballet and historical dancing also included in the LCDS curriculum (Kane, 1989: 17), contemporary dance was ready to assert its place in the progressive development of high-cultural British theatre dance, albeit in a form more seemingly relevant to contemporary society. This trajectory was emphasised by a parallel development: in the same year as LCDS was founded Ballet Rambert changed in structure and focus to become a smaller company no longer requiring (or supporting) a corps de ballet and incorporating the choreographic and technical influence of the Martha Graham Dance Company (Mackrell, 1992: 160).[5]

By the 1970s, a new generation of young British contemporary dance artists emerged who were attracted to more recent developments in American dance. In particular, LCDS graduate, Richard Alston studied and then taught Cunningham technique. Cunningham's turn away from seemingly outdated modern dance styles, his use of chance to disrupt movement habits and his experiments with decentralised space and non-hierarchic structures secured his position, and hence Richard Alston's, within an avant-garde milieu. Yet, Cunningham's adaptation of elements of ballet technique and insistence on rigorous spatial and temporal clarity in the execution of his dances also attracted acclaim from traditional dance enthusiasts who admired the classically formalist qualities of his work (Copeland, 2004: 93).

Even as the development of the British contemporary dance scene became established around Alston and fellow LCDS graduates such as Siobhan Davies, an alternative scene emerged that drew on countercultural values that emphasised the relationship between art and politics. Dancers Jacky Lansley, Fergus Early, Emilyn Claid, Mary Prestidge and Maddée Duprèes initiated the X6 Collective in 1976 in a London warehouse (Butlers Wharf, Block X floor 6). Their 'New Dance' was aligned with alternative political movements of the period. In particular, addressing inequalities in terms of gender and sexualities and challenging the gendered assumptions underpinning traditional ballet were key concerns that were informed by feminist theories of the time (Thomas, 2003). Developing ways to organise danced actions in time and space through non-hierarchic structures was a means to address the structural inequalities the dancers criticised both in arts and society (Jordan, 1989). The influence of American postmodern dance can be seen in this group's embracing of contact improvisation as an approach that emphasised co-operation, informal structures and inclusive non-gendered opportunities for partner work. Their approach to dance cohered with the socially situated artistic ethos that continued at Dartington College of the Arts, and in particular, in the work of the American dance artist, Mary Fulkerson, who was based there (Lansley and Early, 2018). Through Fulkerson, the dancers of X6 were introduced to an approach to release technique that 'prioritised the value of accessibility and personal inward qualities' in dancing taught through alternative methods 'based on mutual relations between teachers and students' (Colin, 2018: 446).

By softening Cunningham technique with principles of release, that he too studied with Mary Fulkerson, and with an awareness of his dancers as individuals who could make his choreography 'their own' (Kane, 1989: 18), Alston could be understood as seeking to align his approach to technique with the alternative values of New Dance. However, the tension between the expectations on dancers to train to meet the extrinsic demands of specific aesthetics as codified in formal techniques and a political awareness of dancers as individuals who might challenge the norms embodied in those techniques would become an ongoing dialectic.

In spite of their inclusive agenda, the collectivist spirit within New Dance did not always engage all British citizens as equally as was their aim. The overt racism prevalent in many post war British communities shaped the experiences of living in Britain for people of African and South Asian ethnicities (Gilroy, 2013). As Steve Paxton, the founder of Contact Improvisation, recently acknowledged in relation to his experience of Contact Improvisation in America '… it might well be that rubbing skins with your oppressors is not an appealing prospect within contact' (cited in Mitra, 2018: 13). In the British context, the founder member of X6, Emilyn Claid, reflects on her discussion with a former student of LCDS, Greta Mendez, who was part of the short-lived MAAS movers, which in 1977 became the first 'Black' dance company in Britain since Ballet Nègres (1946–1952):

In the 1970s and '80s, many white post-modern performers were letting go of established dance structures and styles in order to re figure subjectivity in performer spectator relations. But this was not necessarily the same for black dancers. In the 1970s there was no established presence in the UK of which to let go.

(Claid, 2006: 106)

In contrast to the struggle for black dancers to be integrated into ballet companies (Bourne, 2018), black dancers were accepted into contemporary dance companies. However, finding ways to represent diasporic heritage within a contemporary genre was not always easy. In part this was down to the lack of recognition of diasporic influences upon American modern dance (Dixon-Gottschild, 1998). Even tap and jazz dancing only later acknowledged its African American influence (Stearns and Stearns, 1979). Claid reports that according to Mendez some of the MAAS Movers dancers trained in Graham technique were wary of dance moves seen as stereotypically 'black' including 'wriggling hips' and 'undulating shoulders' (Mendez cited in Claid, 2006: 106). Actions of the hips and shoulders found in a number of dances of the African diaspora had not only become stereotypes but also, detached from their cultural context, had been fashioned by predominantly white Broadway choreographers into the glitzy, sexualised style exemplified in Fosse's choreography for shows such as Sweet Charity (1966). Much dancing that draws on a diasporic heritage is situated within cultures with very different value systems in relation to sexuality (Hanna, 2010). By being placed within a western commercial theatre context, elements of diasporic traditions had been co-opted into dance styles sold on their sexual content. Without recourse to a nuanced 'intersectional' feminism that might counter the colonial gaze to which all black bodies risked being subjected, dance moves rooted in diasporic traditions were not easily presented as 'art'. In contrast, within diasporic communities in which dancing played an important social role, jazz dancing was one outlet for people faced with the racist attitudes to many immigrant communities to find ways of articulating new forms of British identities. However, in the 1970s, there was little crossover between this dancing and more formal field of dance performance (Carr, 2018).

1980s

The conservative leader, Margaret Thatcher has just become Prime Minister but this causes little concern amongst ballet students. We are taken to see Rambert and, unaware of his Royal Ballet School training, I watch a young Michael Clark dancing in Richard Alston's Rainbow Ripples (1980) with a sense of awe tinged with sadness due to my feeling that contemporary dance is beyond me. Yet on joining a small ballet company I find myself dancing in works by contemporary choreographers.

A few years later I study at Laban. There are classes in Graham based, Cunningham, Horton and Limon techniques which I adapt my ballet trained body to with varying degrees of success. Visits to see new work reveal how many professional contemporary dancers are demonstrating the technical skills associated with ballet. This is especially noticeable in the works of Richard Alston and Michael Clark. High leg 'extensions' with pointed feet, sustained balances, turns, big jumps and fast footwork all seem now to have a currency in contemporary dance - albeit performed in a more every day, and in Clark's case nonchalant, manner without the conventional regal carriage of the upper body and geometric arm gestures.

Nevertheless, there are still artists who continue to eschew these more balletic elements in favour of release and contact improvisation. Something different again, is presented by Lea Anderson whose graduation piece, 'The Cholmondeley Sisters', is based around carefully structured sequences of hand gestures, looks and small travelling steps to create a highly visual aesthetic that both delights her tutors (who see the impact of an innovative, small-scale application of Laban's spatial theories) and will go on to attract a fashionable arts audience. Another shift in style comes from Matthew Bourne, who while at Laban makes a pastiche of the Hollywood dance extravaganzas of Busby Berkley. His humour highlights the anti-commercial predispositions of Laban as a high-cultural, contemporary dance institution while perhaps heralding how contemporary dance would need to adapt to the advancing neoliberal economy.

In part due to a developing youth dance sector, contemporary dance students draw from a wider range of backgrounds than at ballet school. While initially the majority seem to have little interest in the world beyond dance, the politics of gender and sexuality gain our attention, especially when 'Clause 28' prohibits the promotion of homosexuality in education. Then, as the 1980s progress there is growing anger with the 'Tory' government that we all seem caught up in. Even so the politics of representation are rarely mentioned in our practical classes although such concerns informed some of the artists who shared their work with students.

During the 1980s, the contemporary dance sector secured its place in British culture with different strands of activity continuing to develop in ways that shaped training regimes. While Robert Cohan remained at LCDT (although his role reduced from 1983), his previous student, Richard Alston, became Ballet Rembert's resident choreographer in 1980 and six years later artistic director of what would soon become Rambert Dance Company. Alston's Cunningham influenced work was presented in established theatres by dancers whose balletic skills outstripped those seen in Alston's early productions. This fuelled an eclecticism which informed many British institutional approaches to training that incorporated Cunningham and ballet techniques

Other LCDS graduates explored related but different paths: Siobhan Davies, who joined Alston at Rambert as an Associate Choreographer (1986–1989) had danced for Robert Cohan but like Alston, was also influenced by Cunningham. Davies also mined a more somatic exploration of movement. Her own company, Siobhan Davies Dance (founded 1988), focused on the practices that were aligned with release technique and thus challenged dance techniques that subordinated the body to geometric ideals.

In addition to the developing prevalence of release-based dance techniques, the continuing legacy of Dartington was also evident in the work of alumni, including Rosemary Butcher who, inspired by American postmodern experimentation, emphasised conceptual explorations of movement. The shared influence of X6 and Dartington on the development of accessible, collaborative practices allied to an anti-elitist political agenda also supported work within community dance companies such as Fergus Early's Green Candle Dance Company (established in 1987). In tandem with initiatives spearheaded by the National Association of Dance and Mime Animateurs (established 1986), community dance artists aimed to increase participation in dancing, challenging dominant notions within British society of dance as an art form being solely the preserve of highly trained professionals selected against very narrow aesthetic criteria.

With the economic development of London's riverside, the X6 collective had to move from Butler's Wharf but found space in Bow that, as Chisenhale Dance Space, continued to provide a place for experiment while the original members went on to play roles in a continuing alternative dance scene.[6] However, the approaches to dance they had instigated to challenge traditional norms became increasingly vulnerable within a changing political climate. The collectivist and socialist ideals that had informed radical experimentation in the previous decade were now the target of the neoliberal politics that were the cornerstone of the Conservative Government during the 1980s. Even where an attempt was made to align innovation in dance with 'a culture of individualism and neo-liberal consumer empowerment', dance experiments that strayed too far from established expectations of dance struggled in a market economy (Claid, 2016: 259). Nevertheless, as opposition to Thatcher's conservative politics grew, some artists successfully managed to attract audiences to engage with alternative approaches to dance. In particular, the challenge to norms of gender and sexuality in dance was given a boost by Michael Clark's mix of flamboyant and fashionable queer performance and balletic grace. Moreover, a new company on the British landscape, DV8, whose early dance theatre works such as *My Sex: Our Dance* (1986), that featured a same sex couple, flew in the face of the 'Tory' led heteronormative policies.[7] Newly emerging Laban alumni, Lea Anderson and Matthew Bourne, offered alternatives to the now established forms of contemporary dance by making work that, while often critiquing social norms, did so with a very marketable sense of style and humour.

In spite of an increasing opposition in many artistic circles to the alliance of neoliberalism and nationalism in Thatcher's Britain, for the most part contemporary dancers were still predominantly white. Outside the recognised field of contemporary dance, artists trained and performed in techniques and styles from Africa, Asia and the Caribbean. The Academy of Indian Dance, established in 1979, developed training in Indian classical dance styles, while Adzido, established in 1984, soon became the leading 'Pan African' dance company. Support for 'traditional' dance forms was provided by multicultural policies in the arts and local politics, but it was still difficult for dance artists wanting to draw on their diasporic heritage within the field of contemporary dance. Indeed, youths drawing upon their diasporic heritage to innovate new styles of dancing in clubs might find their activities of interest to the police (Cotgrove, 2009: 137). In this context, Harehills Youth Dance was notable for developing young black contemporary dancers. The leader of this youth dance group, Nadine Senior, worked to establish Northern School of Contemporary Dance (1985). Previously she had taught David Hamilton, Donald Edwards and Vilmore James who started Phoenix Dance Company (1981). Initially the dancers drew on their African-Caribbean heritage to combine elements of jazz and reggae with contemporary dance and ballet in a style that provided for *contemporary* black British culture to shape dance that could be recognised as art. However, the identity of a company that considered itself as 'contemporary' in which the dancers were all black British and drew on dance traditions beyond Europe and North America proved to be a source of tensions in its relationship with the British arts establishment (Adair, 2000). At this time, contemporary dance was firmly rooted in the modern dance traditions of Europe and America. The aesthetic values located within modernist western artistic traditions emphasised qualities perceived in terms of clearly identifiable spatial and dynamic forms. This, as Deborah Baddoo remembers, resulted in continuing difficulties for black British contemporary dance artists: 'I remember feeling like a square peg in a round hole as I tried to fit my approach to dancing into work that could be accepted within the dance field of that time' (Carr and Baddoo, 2020: 70).

1990s

My creative work, like that of many others, has become interdisciplinary and collaborative and eschews the contemporary dance techniques I learned at Laban. I sometimes take Gaby Agis' Skinner releasing classes, enjoying the 'undoing' of years of movement habits. I also take some classes in Feldenkrais and try out a contact improvisation class at Chisenhale, although my training so far has not prepared me for the upper body strength needed. I am happier in Gill Clark's classes taking place at the Holborn Centre that draw on some actions reminiscent of a Cunningham or Limon class but with more attention to somatic awareness of the relationship between pelvis and head.

I notice that Matthew Bourne, who had worked previously with Laban graduates, now often employs dancers with more advanced ballet skills. At a performance for emerging artists at the ICA (1994), a solo dance by Wayne McGregor demands balletic virtuosity combined with a greater upper body rang of actions than found in ballet, while ex Royal Ballet dancer Russell Maliphant, also on the same triple bill, has been learning Tai Chi and capoeira to develop a graceful, fluid but strong dance style.

1997 seems momentous as at last the 'Tory' Government ends. Under New Labour, funding for dance in community settings becomes more available and this supports a new generation of dance artists to work within youth and community contexts. While some of this work draws on what is now an established eclectic mix of contemporary dance techniques and choreographic approaches, in the South-East London boroughs in which I am working, street dance classes become a means to engage young people in areas such as Brixton and Peckham.

While Alston and Davies were now established names, Christopher Bruce took over as Director of Rambert Dance Company in 1992. His work offered a flowing, balletic form of contemporary dance with a sense of narrative content that was popular with wider audiences. Alston returned to the Place as Director in 1994 – LCDT had been disbanded and his was now the resident company marking the final step in the transition from the dominance of a Graham-based technique to Alston's somatic informed Cunningham technical basis.

The work of Michael Clark and Lea Anderson retained loyal audiences while the contemporary dance sector, that now included graduates from a growing number of dance degree courses, grew faster than government sourced funding could sustain. Yet with the fall of the Berlin Wall in 1989 and the ousting of Margaret Thatcher by her own cabinet in 1990, dance artists, while often short of funds, were optimistic, creating work that reflected their visions for the future. For example, Candoco was established in 1991 to integrate disabled dancers within a professional company. One of Siobhan Davies' dancers, Gill Clark, spearheaded what was now termed the 'Independent Dance' sector, leading release-based classes that sustained a number of younger artists and influenced a growing interest in somatic practices. Many newer choreographic practices drew on the contribution of dancers through improvisational tasks. There was also an upsurge of work in non-conventional sites and/or drawing on a range of media as a new generation built upon the artistic legacies of New Dance alternative practices and postmodernism. While the work of Independent Artists was performed to niche audiences at venues such as Chisenhale, they were often supported by Higher Education institutions and those arts organisations that valued the continuation of the tradition of alternative practices allied to the challenge to those the neoliberal values which continued in spite of the change in government in 1997.

Ballet in Britain still remained very popular with audiences and by the end of the 1990s, within established companies, the boundaries between ballet and contemporary had continued to weaken. As the numbers of new contemporary dance companies grew and competed for scarce Arts Council funding, it was Matthew Bourne's synthesis of ballet and contemporary dance to remake the 'classics', such as his Swan Lake (1995) that attracted support. Towards the end of the 1990s, new dance theatre companies Protein and Jasmin Vardimon Dance Company (both formed in 1998) developed brands of visually compelling dance theatre that, as with Bourne's choreography, was attractive to a new generation of young people and transferred well to video and, from the mid-1990s, to DVD.[8]

In this diversifying and growing sector, crossovers between the different sub-fields of the contemporary dance field were also becoming more common so that, for example, contact improvisation might be used more widely to develop partner work in dance theatre (see, for example, *Enter Achilles*, Van Gool and Newson, 1995). For contemporary dancers, and those training them, the skills that might be demanded of them embraced a wide range of techniques from ballet to release and contact improvisation. Working within a growing sector largely reliant on project funding, contemporary dancers needed to be versatile in order to respond to contrasting different choreographer's visions as they moved from one short contract to another. Moreover, as Susan Foster (1997) noted in relation to North America, newer choreographers were starting to require dancers who could draw on a combination of skills related to what previously had been distinct disciplines.

While the boundaries between the techniques of ballet, modern dance and the alternative practices of release and contact improvisation diminished, the distinction between dance as art and commercial dance still seemed clear: ballet and contemporary were placed on one side of a divide and tap, modern jazz, and street on another. However, while New Labour's 'Third Way' meant a continuation of much of the neoliberal economics that had transformed Britain in the 1980s, what was different under New Labour was that the arts were co-opted through Policy Action Team 10 into an agenda to combat social exclusion. This led to support for work that could, 'engage people in poor neighbourhoods, particularly those who may feel most excluded, such as disaffected young people and people from ethnic minorities' (DCMS, 1999: 5). Community dance practices that were focused on equality and committed to developing participation in dance could find new sources of funding. Alongside the continued adaptation of the principles of New Dance, as British institutions grappled with the concept of 'institutional racism',[9] an emphasis on engaging marginalised groups raised the profile of styles originating in African or Asian diasporic dance traditions. Especially where engaging young people was important, Street Dance forms based on African

American styles of Breakin', Poppin' and House dancing became widespread in the youth sector. Nevertheless, within the field of contemporary dance, while artists might draw upon a wide range of dance vocabularies, within a contemporary dance idiom, there was still an expectation that such work was presented within the structural and conceptual framework of twentieth-century western theatre dance. Although Akram Khan's *Loose in Flight*, filmed at the end of the 1990s, heralded a more intercultural aesthetics that would gain in importance in the years to come (Mitra, 2015).

After the Millennium

It's a few years now after the performance in South-East London and I am teaching in a conservatoire for contemporary dance. While the ballet classes have changed little from my time as a student, contemporary dance training now incorporates release-based techniques and somatic practices, while contact improvisation has become a well-known source of virtuosic partnering techniques. Graham, Cunningham, the New York Judson era and British New Dance are now topics for history classes, although students still have some Graham-based and Cunningham technique classes. Together we reflect on Cunningham's distinction between 'license' and 'freedom' which for me has political connotations (Carr, 2010). In seminars the students have quite heated debates in relation to issues of representation and identities. With the students I start to explore how an early (Judson) postmodern dance that, in its transfer to the UK, continued a modernist interrogation of the medium of dance, has given way to a newer form of postmodernism in dance which is breaking down boundaries between disciplines and between 'high art' and consumer culture. While some of them still see working for Siobhan Davies, Richard Alston or other established choreographers as the ultimate career goal, some recognise there are a broadening range of opportunities.

With boundaries between genres weakening, British contemporary dance in the years following the turn of the millennium shifted towards an 'analogical 'postmodernism (Connor, 1997: xii) bringing it into a global, multidisciplinary cultural field. Neoliberal economics, hardened by the global financial crisis of 2008–2010, increased the pressure on the arts to prove their value in economic terms. In this context, the homogenisation of techniques Foster (1997) acknowledged in America in the twentieth century became more prevalent in the UK which was increasingly aligned to global trends. For the twenty-first century, Foster now posited as three key 'hired' bodies:

The balletic body cultivates a geometry of shape and the standard notions of virtuosity associated with high extensions of the legs, weightless jumps, and multiple turns. The industrial body emphasises its labor and its sexiness while selling itself. And the released body promotes a neutrality and efficiency of execution that disencumbers the dancer from being committed to what it is dancing about.

(Foster cited in Čičigoj, 2011: 141)

Foster also proposed counterparts to these hegemonic forms that 'undermine the workings of global uniformity and spectacle'. Against the globalised balletic body, she posited one 'highly trained in a tradition and with strong connections to a community'. She proposed the processual body, 'that doesn't produce a product through its dancing' to counteract the 'industrial body' while 'the released body' is disrupted by 'the volunteer body' which she suggested is 'unconcerned with efficiency but instead gambling on making a difference in its community' (cited in Čičigoj, 2011: 141).

Within a changing global cultural economy, much British contemporary dance built upon a continuing interplay with the ballet establishment in which the boundaries between ballet and contemporary dance continued to blur. For example, Russel Maliphant's works, such as *Push* (2005) featuring Sylvie Guillem, were very popular, while Wayne McGregor became resident choreographer at the Royal Ballet in 2006. More generally, the balletic body, now able to move with increasing fluidity through a wide vocabulary of movement, was increasingly found in much contemporary dance.

Also in this changing context, the neutral body associated with release techniques became less the outcome of a resistance to the technical norms of the past but a recognised product of training that emphasises biomechanical efficiency. As such its practices, which emphasise access to the space and time to escape the strains of daily life risked, in the context of British society, becoming associated with the privileges of both 'class' and 'whiteness'. However, with intercultural practices becoming more prevalent and previous 'multicultural' policies giving way to those that supported 'community cohesion' (Zetter et al., 2006), there seemed to be more encouragement for dance artists to draw on their diasporic heritage to create contemporary work that explored the complexities of Black British and Asian British identities.

Many choreographers increasingly made work collaboratively with their dancers by setting the dancers tasks and crafting the results rather than teaching their material to dancers. This approach also worked well within the arena of work which integrated disabled dancers and community dance practices which continued the inclusive legacy of New Dance to celebrate the more everyday (or 'volunteer' body) of the participants.

Perhaps the most noticeable change in the years after the millennium was the breaking down of artistic and commercial boundaries: Rambert dance artist Rafael Bonachela, for instance, made work for Kylie Minogue's 'Fever' tour in 2002 before becoming the artistic director of Sydney Dance Company. This early instance may say more about how the music industry repositioned itself culturally as much as contemporary dance embracing dancing bodies that reveal their labour and sexuality. However, more recently dance theatre programming has revealed a growing body of work that challenges the divide between commercial and contemporary dance, particularly where choreographers, such as Kenrick Sandy and Tony Adigun, draw upon Hip Hop dance traditions that themselves have a complex relationship with the (commercial) record industry. This change also provided for contemporary diasporic traditions to influence contemporary dance opening opportunities for intercultural explorations within contemporary dance even as those dance companies, such as Agido, whose work was more consistent with a multicultural celebration of diasporic heritage, lost support.

> As I try to make sense of the past, I acknowledge all those moments which didn't quite fit the historical narratives I have proposed. I am writing at a time of great uncertainty both for what it means to be British and for the future of the arts and especially dance. It may be in the future I will look back to reflect upon different issues that will take on more relevance. For example, I have hardly mentioned the impact of video that is the subject of a previous paper (Carr, 2012). Yet the role of dance in the era of digital communications emerging out of the pandemic will be interesting to watch. What makes any one narrative difficult to sustain is that dance training is far more complex than learning how to execute movements and the fostering of a particular physical aesthetic. It is through the play between self, others, the environment and the normative demands of any technique or style through which the dancer finds a way to come to terms with the context s/he/they finds her/him/themself. As a dancer, teacher and audience member what I have cherished is a sense, if only momentarily, of surpassing contextual constraints, on a journey that can take unexpected turns that do not always fit preconceptions or historical narratives.

In the above, I have tried to make sense of the past by constructing one among many possible narratives. I have suggested how historically contemporary dance in Britain may be considered as aligned initially with those seeking alternatives to the norms of established British culture and society. Yet contemporary dance would quickly become established within the high culture of a western and privileged social position. British contemporary dance can be seen to be aligned with the growing cultural dominance of America after the Second World War. While a North American sensibility might be thought to undo an older British colonial and class ridden mentality, both societies were marked by a historic racism that would have an impact on the value placed on dancing that drew on African American, black British and wider diasporic influences. An alternative dance scene provided a counterbalance to the formalist artistic values of much contemporary dance to emphasise the social values embodied in dance practices, and in particular to apply feminism to challenge gender stereotypes perceived as embodied in ballet. While these alternative dance practices were threatened by the rise of the neoliberal policies of the 1980s onwards, their influence continued. Artists of diasporic heritage also challenged the norms of established theatre dance but initially found it difficult to engage with the artistic values of much twentieth-century contemporary dance. It has only been comparatively recently, with the later 'analogical' postmodernist embrace of broader cultural influences that British contemporary dance could engage on a more equal basis with movement traditions emerging from beyond the narrow confines of North American and European 'high' culture. Yet the terms under which such engagement takes place still risk being framed within wider inequalities, not only in terms of 'race' but also class, gender, ability, age and sexualities.[10]

Contemporary dancers are now confronted by a global economy in which alternative approaches, be they inclusive of dancers with disabilities or embracing diasporic dance traditions or providing comment on social issues, often become absorbed by the mainstream they once challenged, losing some of the distinctiveness of their initial innovation. Within an economy of bodily techniques, many choreographers often seek dancers who can adapt quickly to their vision and dancers require a palette of dance expertise to compete for work. It is thus becoming increasingly difficult for contemporary dancers to undertake in depth exploration of alternatives to hegemonic dance forms and practices and sustain themselves financially (Farrer and Aujla, 2016). Yet the histories of British contemporary dance have always included more radical contingents that have served to counteract established norms, destabilising them through examples of alternative practices that have then often shaped wider changes. If British contemporary dance is not to lose the legacy of its radical innovators, just as important as contemporary dance institutions offering students the opportunity to learn how to dance in different styles is to offer them, as future artists, the conceptual tools and the time to explore how values may be understood as embodied in the dancing they study.

Notes

1 'Contemporary' dance is in many ways a contested term as explored by Grau (1998) but is used here as delineating a field constituted through practices in the UK.
2 Data from The Office for National Statistics reveals that in Southwark and Lambeth (the boroughs where I worked in Adult and Community Education) and also in Lewisham (where I trained and later taught) the largest BAME/Global Majority populations identify as 'black'. (Office for National Statistics, n.d.).
3 Margaret Morris opened her school in 1910. Margaret Barr taught at Dartington Hall from 1930. Kurt Jooss and Sigurd Leeder fled Nazi Germany in 1934 and commenced teaching at Dartington Hall which later as Dartington College of the Arts.
4 A diploma course commenced at Laban in 1974 and a BA (Hons) in 1979.
5 Rambert company member, choreographer and from 1966 Associate Director, Norman Morrice studied in New York and was initially strongly influenced by the work of Martha Graham.

6 In addition to Fergus Early's Green Candle Dance Company, Emilyn Claid led the alternative dance company Extemporary, Mary Prestidge supported the development of a course at Liverpool Institute for Performing Arts (LIPA), and Landsley and Duprèe worked as independent artists.
7 In particular, Clause 28 added to the Local Government Act in 1988 made it illegal to promote homosexuality in schools.
8 The influence of video on dance is something I explore in Carr (2012).
9 Institutional racism was highlighted by the McPherson report (1999) into the police handling of the murder of Steven Lawrence.
10 There is a whole discourse on intercultural performance, and similarly the fields of disability studies and intersectional cultural analyses have implications for equality in dance.

References

Adair, C. (2000) *Dancing the Black Question: The Phoenix Dance Company Phenomenon*. London: Dance Books.

Barnhisel, G. (2015) *Cold War Modernists: Art, Literature, and American Cultural Diplomacy*. New York: Columbia University Press.

Bannerman, H. (1999) 'An Overview of the Development of Martha Graham's Movement System (1926-1991)', *Dance Research*, 17 (2), pp. 9–46. https://doi.org/10.2307/1290837

Bourdieu, P. (1993) *The Field of Cultural Production*, in Johnson, R. (ed.). *Essays on Arts and Literature*. Cambridge: Polity Press.

Bourne, S. (2018) 'Tracing the Evolution of Black Representation in Ballet and the Impact on Black British Dancers Today', in Akinleye, A. (ed.) *Narratives in Black British Dance: Embodied Practices*. London: Palgrave Macmillan, pp. 51–64.

Carr, J. (2008) 'Embodiment, Appreciation and Dance: Issues in Relation to an Exploration of the Experiences of London Based, "Non-Aligned" Artists,' unpublished PhD thesis. London: University of Roehampton. Available at: http:// roehampton.openrepository.com/roehampton/bitstream/10142/47593/13/openning.pdf

Carr, J. (2010) 'Issues of Control and Agency in Contemplating Cunningham's Legacy' Dance *History Symposium 2010*. Roehampton University, UK, 13 March. Available at: http://societyfordanceresearch.org/wp/conference-proceedings/

Carr, J. (2012) 'Record, Pause, Replay, Repeat: Video and the (Re) Production of Dance Knowledge,' *The Theory, Practice & Art of Movement Capture and Preservation*, AHRC funded symposium, The Knowledge Lab, London, 19th–20th January.

Carr, J. (2018) 'Battling Under Britannia's Shadow: UK Jazz Dancing in the 1970s and '80s', in Akinleye, Adesola (ed.) *Narratives in Black British Dance: Embodied Practices*. London: Palgrave Macmillan, pp. 217–233.

Carr, J. and Baddoo, D. (2020) 'Dance, Diaspora and the Role of the Archives a Dialogic Reflection upon the Black Dance Archives Project (UK)', *Dance Research: The Journal of the Society for Dance Research*, 38 (1), pp. 65–81. https://doi.org/10.3366/drs.2020.0291

Čičigoj, K. (2011) Interview with Susan Foster, *Maska*, XXVI, Autumn, pp. 141–142.

Claid, E. (2006) *Yes? No! Maybe…: Seductive Ambiguity in Dance*. London: Routledge.

Claid, E. (2016) 'Messy Bits', in Colin, N. and Sachsenmaier, S. (eds.) *Collaboration in Performance Practice: Premises, Workings and Failures*. London: Palgrave Macmillan, pp. 259–279.

Colin, N. (2018) 'The Potentiality of Collaboration at Dartington College of Arts and the Future of Performance Training', *Theatre, Dance and Performance Training*, 9 (3), pp. 445–456. https://doi.org/10.1080/19443927.2018.1500938

Connor, S. (1997) *Postmodernist Culture: An Introduction to Theories of the Contemporary*. 2nd edn. Oxford: Blackwell.

Copeland, R. (2004) *Merce Cunningham: The Modernizing of Modern Dance*. New York and London: Routledge.

Cotgrove, M. (2009) *From Jazz Funk and Fusion to Acid Jazz*. London: Chaser Publications.

DCMS (1999) *Policy Action Team 10: Arts and Sport a Report to the Social Exclusion Unit*. London: HSO.

Dixon-Gottschild, B. (1998) *Digging the Africanist Presence in American Performance Dance and Other Contexts (Contributions in Afro-American & African Studies)*. Santa Barbara, CA: Praeger Publishers.

Farrer, R. and Aujla, I. (2016) 'Understanding the Independent Dancer: Roles, Development and Success', *Dance Research: The Journal of the Society for Dance Research*, 34 (2), pp. 202–219. https://doi.org/10.3366/drs.2016.0159

Foster, S. (1997) 'Dancing Bodies,' in Desmond, J. (ed.) *Meaning and Motion: New Cultural Studies of Dance*. Durham, NC: Duke University Press, pp. 235–257 (Originally published in *Incorporations* (Zone 6), Crary, J. and Kwinter, S. (eds.) Cambridge, MA: Zone/MIT Press, 1992. 480–495.)

Gilroy, P. (2013) *There Ain't No Black in the Union Jack*. London: Routledge (Originally published 1987).

Hanna, J. (2010) 'Dance and Sexuality: Many Moves', *Journal of Sex Research*, 47 (2–3), pp. 212–241. https://doi.org/10.1080/00224491003599744

Jordan, S. (1989) 'British Modern Dance: Early Radicalism', *Dance Research: The Journal of the Society for Dance Research*, 7 (2), pp. 3–15. https://doi.org/10.2307/1290769

Kane, A. (1989) 'Richard Alston: Twenty One Years of Choreography', *Dance Research*, 7 (2), pp. 16–54. https://doi.org/10.2307/1290770

Kershaw, B. (1992) *The Politics of Performance: Radical Theatre as Cultural Intervention*. London and New York: Routledge.

Lansley, J. and Early, F. (2018) 'Radical Connections: The Dartington Dance Festival and/X6 Dance Space Axis', *Theatre, Dance and Performance Training*, 9 (3), pp. 380–388. https://doi.org/10.1080/19443927.2018.1482230

Mackrell, J. (1992) 'Step by Step: The Cautious Revolution in Dance', in Moore-Gilbert, B. and Seed, J. (eds.) *Cultural Revolution? The Challenge of the Arts in the 1960s*. London: Routledge, pp. 156–170.

Mitra, R. (2018) 'Talking Politics of Contact Improvisation with Steve Paxton', *Dance Research Journal*, 50 (3), pp. 5–18. https://doi.org/10.1017/S0149767718000335

Mitra, R. (2015) *Akram Khan: Dancing New Interculturalism*. Basingstoke: Palgrave.

Nicholas, L. (2004) 'Dancing in the Margins? British Modern Dance in the 1940s and 1950s', inCarter, A. (ed.) , G. (eds.) *Rethinking Dance History*. London and New York: Routledge, pp. 119–131.

Office for National Statistic (n.d) *Ethnic Groups by Borough*. Available at Ethnic Groups by Borough - London Datastore.

Olick, J., Vinitsky-Seroussi, V. and Levy, D. (eds.) (2011) *The Collective Memory Reader*. Oxford: Oxford University Press.

Prevots, N. (1999) *Dance for Export: Cultural Diplomacy and the Cold War (Studies in Dance History)*. Middletown, CT: Wesleyan University Press.

Rowell, B. (2000) 'United Kingdom: An Expanding Map', in Grau, A. and Jordan, S. (eds.) *Europe Dancing: Perspectives on Theatre Dance and Cultural Identity*. London: Routledge, pp. 188–212.

Stearns, M. and Stearns, J. (1979) *Jazz Dance: The Story of American Vernacular Dance*. New York: Schirmer Books.

Thomas, H. (2003) *The Body, Dance and Cultural Theory*. New York: Palgrave Macmillan.

Van Gool, C. and Newson, L. (1995) *Enter Achilles*, DV8 Films and BBC in association with RM Associates and Arthaus Musik.

Zetter, R., Griffiths, D., Sigona, N., Flynn, D., Tauhid, P. and Beyno, R. (2006) *Immigration, Social Cohesion and Social Capital What Are the Links?* York: Joseph Rowntree Foundation.

1.3 Democratising dance

Inclusion at the core of dance education and its impact

Betina Panagiotara

How do we want to live together?

Since the start of the millennium, the world has witnessed a series of crises – environmental, financial, refugee, educational, health – that are still ongoing and accelerating, creating precarious living conditions that seem inescapable. In this impasse, with no foreseeable alternative to neoliberalism and its agendas, the question raised is how do we want to live together and how is art relevant?

The aim of this chapter is to examine the alternative approaches to teaching, grounded in a philosophy of working with one another, while also embracing rigour and excellence as professional standards in the field, that inclusive dance and its educational methodologies propose. In doing so, inclusive dance practices forge a specific ethos of commoning and politics of togetherness that challenge prevailing conditions of individualisation and also act as a counterproposal to normative educational methodologies that often focus on notions of physical ability and virtuosity. My basic argument is that the underlying philosophy of inclusive dance educational methodologies generates ethics and values that can be adopted and applied in the wider spectrum of dance teaching, cultivating active dancers and citizens.

The starting point of my examination of inclusive dance practices was research I conducted in 2018, in the framework of the European project iDance (Panagiotara, 2019). This project examined the cultural policies and educational infrastructures of inclusive dance in four European countries. It argued that while it is important to take into account the specificities of each sociocultural context when discussing issues of policy, it is also crucial to highlight similarities such as the need for visibility of inclusive dance practices, so that they can be ingrained into the mainstream dance field as a best practice approach, making contemporary dance accessible to all. The research indicated that the UK is a pioneer in the field but even in its case the overall educational structures are not inclusive. It also highlighted how inclusive dance methodologies are based on notions of collaboration and collectivity that in turn lead to the creation of micro-communities. Practices of togetherness become the central topic of this article that focuses on inclusive

DOI: 10.4324/9781003111146-5

practices, the ethics they cultivate in the dance community, and the impact they have on socio-political terms. My basic argument is that this underlying philosophy of inclusive dance educational methodologies generates ethics and values that can be adopted and applied to the wider spectrum of dance teaching, regardless of the technique used.

Thus, this study is rooted in the previous research that highlighted the need for more inclusive dance practices, both on stage and in educational frameworks. Its aim is to explore the ways in which inclusive dance methodologies and techniques are essential to the further diversification and accessibility of the dance field, also as a cultural practice reshaping the social sphere. To that end, this article in its beginning draws from the work of arts sociologist Rudi Laermans (2012) to examine how dance practices that invest in collectivity are in some cases experiments in reshaping democratic societies. Then, it focuses specifically on educational settings and techniques, drawing amongst others from arts theorist Florian Schneider (2010) who highlights the importance of education in reshaping society, cultural sociologist, Toby Siebers (2010), arguing against a dominant ideology of ability, and disability scholar Dan Goodley (2014) discussing notions of ableism in education and the potential of inclusive practices. In order to unpack the argument that inclusive dance practices are best practices for all, this chapter starts with a provocative question.

What makes a great dancer?

'What makes a great dancer?', the question the Stopgap Dance Company posed to the participants of a workshop on inclusive dance education, makes a good starting point for the examination on the one hand of the stereotypes and values attached to contemporary dance and, on the other hand, of opening up space for alternative responses. Participants of the workshop wrote their answers on a sheet of paper, where a body was drawn. The answers included comments such as to 'keep on learning', 'to be determined', and 'explore your abilities', as well as descriptions of skills, such as having 'awareness of own body, others, space and time'. What was missing from that paper were technical efficiency, virtuosity, experience, and discipline, to name only a few from the numerous answers that could be given to this question. My point being that each of the answers given suggests diverse visions of what contemporary dance is or could be, shaping at the same time what a dancer is or could be, and so suggests different educational methodologies. The aim and core philosophy of inclusive dance is to be a best practice for all, catering and always readjusting to different needs on the spot, and to that end, it is an experimentation with and articulation of new vocabularies, possibilities, and methodologies for thinking about dance education anew. However, inclusive dance is not examined here as a specific technique like, for example, release or Graham, but as a methodology of teaching dance on an amateur and professional level, embracing a worldview of diversity and participation for all, through a collaborative practice that is co-shaped by participants and teachers alike.

Returning to the question of what makes a great dancer, one answer could be that a teaching approach that acknowledges and addresses difference as a vital component of designing a class can make a great dancer. As Lucy Bennett from the Stopgap Dance Company stresses 'difference is our means and our method' (2014). How is that difference achieved and what does it mean to work-with one another in this context? Starting from this collaborative aspect, inclusive dance practices nurture a state of mind where every class is a different class, depending on the participants. Core elements of their approach is enabling **communication** through the careful and targeted use of language, continuously **adapting** the practice and technical level through responsive teaching to address the needs of both the individual and the group, and nurturing an **ethos** of participation and collaboration where difference works for the benefit of everyone in the room. In what follows, I will examine the notion of working-with theoretically and practically, provide specific teaching methods used in inclusive settings and their underlying values, discuss the need for more visibility and accessibility in the field, and argue for a change of mindset in relation to how we teach dance.

What makes a great dancer: an ethos of working-with

'Collaborating is like two people banging their heads against each other, and the collaboration is the bruises that are left behind', comments performance theorist Joe Kelleher emphasising the difficulty and the effect of collaborating as an artistic practice (Burrows, 2010: 59). Since the 1990s, there have been many theoretical debates in the performing arts field in relation to collaborative and collective working modes, examined as an antidote to neoliberalism as well as conditions of extreme individualisation. Nonetheless, such notions have also been appropriated by neoliberal agendas in so far that collaboration is equated to networking for personal purposes rather than for a common good. Even so, this reality does not necessarily diminish the potential of such working modes for creating communities of people. In fact, I suggest that inclusive dance practices are essential for the forging of an ethos that fosters heterogeneity and encourages criticality and adaptability, as it will be further examined through specific examples, such as the practice of translation, the use of improvisation, and responsive teaching. According to arts sociologist Rudi Laermans, collaborative practices in dance are significant as they cultivate an 'ethics of doing with others' that brings forth diversity and difference as essential driving forces of artistic creativity (2012: 97). What is at stake in this discussion about collaboration and inclusive dance is the democratisation of the field aiming to make it accessible, diverse, and inclusive for all, for, as Laermans suggests, 'each artistic collaboration is in essence a micro-political experiment in democratizing society' (2015: 37). In other words, dance is a vehicle for initiating change and therefore its values and ethics are of major significance.

Hence, this ethos, which is quintessential to collaborative practices examined here, is rooted in values, such as harnessing heterogeneity, respecting otherness, enabling diversity, and creating common grounds. To start a new class by inviting everyone to voice their needs and/or anxieties in relation to the class, and to name the rules of their engagement (e.g., not being late, not talking over one another) – as most inclusive dance practices do – already creates a common ground amongst participants, allowing them to have a voice in the process, as well as the right to differ, and inviting them to co-shape the class as a group, questioning the figure of an authoritative and distant teacher, while also compelling everyone to take responsibility for one another in a collective. Within the prevailing neoliberal system that supports productivity and individuality, while encouraging a culture of ability set against a precarious reality, inclusive dance is an alternative proposal that is driven by equality, equity, commonality, and openness.

Furthermore, theorist Florian Schneider argues that in this neoliberal context that praises the individual, her abilities along with her productivity, it is imperative that educational structures and methods enable heterogeneity and difference. He supports that we need a notion of 'learning [that] is decoupled from the possession of knowledge' and in that sense an educational approach that is imaginative and grounded in working-with one another (2010: 1). Inclusive dance cultivates horizontal relations – in and outside the classroom – empowering participants to have a voice, to communicate their needs, and to be aware of others, enabling trust amongst participants and a sharing of knowledge that transcends established positions of power, giving them agency in the teaching and learning process.

Pointing again at this need for commoning, Schneider posits a timely question in relation to learning: 'How can we envision, design, develop, and enjoy environments in which one learns with someone else instead of from or about others...?' (2010: 2). In practical terms, inclusive dance practices use a wide range of teaching methodologies to ensure this working-with ethos, varying from codified techniques to the translation method and from facilitation to improvisation and reflective processes. All these methodologies are structured on notions of adaptation and communication that make it possible for teachers and students to work together.

What makes a great dancer: adaptability, openness, experimentation

One of the vital tools in inclusive dance practices is the use of **translation** as a way of making movement material accessible to everyone in the class. In particular, translation 'is a way of re-inventing existing terminology but also practical tasks in imaginative ways that reproduce the aim, the purpose and quality of the movement so that it can be tried by different bodies'

(Panagiotara, 2018: 73). So, with translation, dance teachers inventively communicate the mechanics and intention of movement using metaphors, imagery, and other descriptions, subsequently making movement and dance education accessible to all. Translation dissects the movements into their parts preserving them 'in terms of transfer of weight, dynamics, relational proximity, or spatial and directional orientation', causing a rethinking of the relationship between language and movement, and initiating a critical understanding and reading of codified techniques (Urmston & Aujla, 2018: 15). For example, the generic skills associated with executing a double pirouette are those of balancing and turning, maintaining control over the movement and the body. The aim is not to copy the movement in aesthetic terms, in a homogeneous and uniformly manner, but to translate it into its dynamics and mode of operation so that it becomes accessible to a diversity of bodies, while at the same time, setting the criteria with which to evaluate the competence of the dancer in a professional or amateur context. For example, pirouette can be translated into a vortex, or a battement tendu can be thought of as a rocket. This creative method of teaching necessitates solid educational experience, openness to difference, imagination, and criticality as it involves reinventing a set of techniques so as to formulate a flexible, adaptable, and diverse mode of teaching with set educational aims, 'working towards greater equity of opportunity and access to dance participation' (Urmston & Aujla, 2018: 14).

However, such a method is often very challenging for both teachers and students as it requires a questioning of specific ideals that are ingrained into the dance profession after years of practising. A participant in one of Stopgap Dance Company's workshops described the notion of translation as a 'process of unlearning', followed by an anxiety about devaluing a universal dance language, even if the latter often results in the exclusion of different bodies. Translation is a challenging teaching method because it questions and reformulates a dominant dance discourse along with its seemingly universal values and stereotypes, bringing forth what cultural theorist, Toby Siebers (2010), names the ideology of ability, which will be examined further below. However, without questioning established notions and codes, as the translation tool does, learning is diminished into 'adding information rather than rethinking a structure' like inclusive methodologies such as translation do (Rogoff, 2006: 99). Theorist and curator Irit Rogoff maintains that critical thinking is associated with risk, arguing that the former originates from letting go of learnt patterns of thought, set techniques, and analytical tools so as to be open to exploring, experimenting with, and articulating new ones, as inclusive dance does.

Moreover, translation is only part of a wider philosophy cultivated in inclusive dance that has to do with the careful and attentive use of language while teaching. Instructions such as 'stand tall' can be reformulated into 'be upright' and 'reach tall', or 'travel with accelerated pace in space' can be used instead of 'stand and run', or the phrase 'return to your neutral position' in place of 'stand with parallel feet'. These are everyday examples derived from dance classes that make evident the significance of the language used in order to acknowledge and at the same time smooth out the differences between students, inviting everyone to participate, and thus creating an inclusive framework. This language use awareness that inclusive methodologies promote uncovers learnt patterns of speaking and subsequently frames of thinking that are useful in repositioning ourselves to be more inclusive not only within our dance communities but also in our social lives, highlighting the politics of language and how these relate to issues of gender, ability, age, and race. In other words, the way we choose to work together in difference, is, as Laermans proposes, a partial democratisation of our societies through our practices.

Moreover, any and every discussion on inclusion should be framed in relation to dominant social and cultural contexts for its political significance to emerge. Inclusion is a much wider social demand relating not only to disability and dance but also to race, gender, ethnicity, sexual orientation, and age, as causes for social discrimination. According to cultural theorist Toby Siebers (2010), western societies have long been dominated by an ideology of ability that is characterised by notions of perfection, independence, and productivity forming the basis for social and political exclusion of people with disabilities, and other minorities. By the same token, disability studies scholar Daniel Goodley (2014) discusses the term ableism – a set of practices and processes that favours certain abilities in the expense of everyone not fitting said abilities – as crucial in generating a culture of marginalisation and discrimination, which is also dominant in educational environments.

Dance as a field has been historically shaped by social constructions of the body, its physicality and aesthetic readings of it. Dance scholar and practitioner Ann Cooper Albright (1997) in her pivotal text *Moving Across Difference* examines how, early on, theatrical dance has fabricated an ideal body of the dancer that is flexible, thin, strong, white, and abled, which is still central to the contemporary dance field even if it is nowadays challenged by many professionals. This construction makes evident the socio-historical background of bodily stereotypes that still prevail today causing exclusion in the field, while it also stresses the importance of challenging and reassessing them both through theory and practice. Dance might be a practice based on physical abilities, but it is not defined or limited by them (Panagiotara, 2019). Nowadays, the body of the dancer has become a prototype of neoliberalism in its need to emphasise productivity, efficacy, virtuosity, discipline, youth and strength. On the contrary, inclusive dance practices detach specific notions of physicality from the dancing body, challenging stereotypical depictions of the body and the dancer, questioning a 'corporeal hierarchy' and its effects, and making evident the associations between the artistic field and dominant socio-political norms (Whatley, 2010: 12). Inclusive dance is significant in challenging such notions, reconsidering the body and its abilities, and proposing alternative educational methods that will lead to the renewal of the field and the creation of a more inclusive and diverse artistic discipline.

Overall, this ideology of ability that is dominant in society but also in dance as a prerequisite to enter the field – there are numerous stories about how people with disabilities have been asked to leave a class or have been prevented from attending (see Nadarajah, 2017) – is firmly associated with the prevailing neoliberal agenda that promotes a culture of endless productivity, individualisation, and virtuosity along with a devaluing of social and communal structures (Lazzarato, 1996; Virno, 2004). In this setting, disability, according to Siebers (2010), challenges this faith in ability and independency, proposing alternatives that take into account human vulnerability, fragility and, in essence, the notion of a community of people rather than a notion of individuals. Disability studies, and, in this case, disability and dance is a fertile ground to bring forth difference as an agent of change, to stress that vulnerability and precarity are cornerstones of the human condition and, thus, of modern societies, and to generate alternative working models that address important needs and make sure to create open communities of people.

What makes a great dancer: imagination, empathy, experimentation

Another vital technique used by inclusive dance that builds on responsive teaching and collaboration is **improvisation** as a means of teaching, learning, and choreographing. Improvisation – a technique common in the contemporary dance field since postmodern dance in the 1960s – is a working mode that calls for problem-solving qualities within a group of people, ignites imagination, and allows for individuality within a collaborative working group bound by a set of rules. Improvisation encourages creativity, spontaneity, and agility, enables decision-making processes here and now, while also forming groups of people who work horizontally on a common code contributing even more to a shared ethos within the group. According to Susan Foster:

> As dancers practice this relationality with one another, they learn more about each other. They respond creatively to mistakes; they help each other out of ruts; they move beyond their limits. They disagree; they make mistakes and reject decisions; they stumble into something new; they concentrate. Most important, they take collective responsibility for the time they spend together.
>
> (Foster, 2002: 240)

During the 1960s and the 1970s, the use of improvisation was also a means for the democratisation of the dance field as part of a wider socio-political change taking place as a result of a variety of social movements, especially in the USA. Nowadays that, according to sociologist Richard Sennett, contemporary societies have 'weakened cooperation in distinctive ways', it is crucial to form alternative frameworks that enable and encourage the exercise of collaboration (Sennett, 2013: 29). Working with one another is a social and dialogical skill that 'emerges from practical activity', and, as such, the use of improvisation in inclusive dance is part of its wider working philosophy aiming at educating dancers in different practical but also social skills (Sennett, 2013: 6).

However, it is also the case that associating improvisation with notions of freedom and democracy has also led to the over-idealisation of a technique that is now used widely in the contemporary dance field without always aiming at or encouraging collaboration or even differentiation. Improvisation is not per se inclusive, but it can be depending on the way it is used and its educational aims, which is why it is widely used in inclusive settings. For example, a popular exercise in mainstream dance classes is Mirroring where a pair of dancers faces one another, mirroring each other's movement, changing the lead from one to the other, and initiating a process common in dance, that of demonstrating and copying. How does this exercise work with different bodies and abilities? Participants in an inclusive dance context are invited to translate the other's movement into their own bodies, instead of copycatting in exact physical terms, while also having the liberty of letting go of phrases that don't work for them and suggesting new movement material in a mutual exchange with their partner. They are in essence practising working-with one another in a collaboration where, 'one co-stimulates the other's otherness' permitting and generating difference and multiplicity (Laermans, 2012: 97). Dance teacher Jürg Koch (2010) maintains that shifting this copying mechanism inherent in dance techniques into translating and improvising allows for more experimentation but, primarily, for participation and inclusion. In her own experience, such an approach to teaching, and specifically in relation to the Mirroring exercise, highlights 'exploration and play', produces 'more and different movement material', while also giving agency to the participants to find their own solutions in this partnering (2010: 13).

In another example from Stopgap Dance Company's workshops on developing an individual movement vocabulary, improvisation is used throughout the process from warming up to cooling down the group, focusing each time on different tasks, accumulating knowledge towards creating an individual movement vocabulary through a collaborative and improvised process. For example, the dancers are invited to work individually by exploring specific words such as rotate, press, and lengthen, and to repeat the sequences the dancers develop that they feel are important to them. Finally, they need to share these sequences with other dancers, exchanging and commoning, while the teachers give a set structure within which the dancers need to work on these vocabularies creating set sequences that can be repeated. These and other sets of exercises that are based on improvisation as a learning and teaching technique are made available through various online sources, mainly by professionals in the field of inclusive dance that share their working experience and expertise.[1] Thus, in this framework, improvisation is useful as a methodology which allows for differently abled bodies to come together, to work both independently but also as part of a group, to find ways to work on and translate terms and techniques in each body, nurturing difference within a collective process provoking 'a reconsideration of ableist education' and its entrenched values (Goodley, 2014: 104).

All these teaching tools and approaches, such as improvisation, the use of inclusive language and of translation, offer an alternative approach to mainstream learning methods based often on imitating/copying paradigms where the crucial difference is between do as *I do* and do *with* me; essentially a difference between knowledge as reproduction and knowledge 'developed in heterogeneity' (Schneider, 2010: 1). What is more, is that they counteract to some dance educational settings that only value technical efficacy, discipline, virtuosity, and competency as if being a dancer or a teacher is not a multi-faceted professional identity formed also by collectiveness, empathy, social awareness, solidarity, curiosity, and difference. A similar dispute in relation to the aims and breadth of education occurred in 2015 in the UK, when three prominent UK-based choreographers published a joint press release asking for a dance education that will be aimed primarily at technically competent dancers, receiving several responses as to the needs for education to lead to life-long careers that are not always and not only dependent on technical efficacy (BBC News, 2015). This debate further explicates how education was and remains a significant field of negotiation amongst different visions of what contemporary dance is or could be.

What makes a great dancer: working in common

Revisiting the opening of this article, inclusive dance practices use a set of techniques that nurture a philosophy of working with one another that is crucial for cultivating ethics of collectivity and togetherness for the twenty-first century. According to scholars Urmston and Aujla (2018), inclusive practices nurture important qualities such as patience in a time-driven productive society, generosity, humility, honesty, empathy, and confidence to teachers and students alike. These attributes are significant as they bring forth the affective impact of inclusive practices, grounded in working in common and respecting difference. As Urmston and Aujla suggest, '[t]hese qualities determine and describe how the artist acts, what they do and how they relate to bring out the best in the people with whom they work as well as themselves' and in so doing, they are urged to 'reflect on their persona, their values and the attributes that drive their practice' (2018: 15). Essentially, inclusive dance is effective dance education for all; encouraging working modes that are built on notions of togetherness that, in turn, as sociologist and dance theorist Gabriele Klein claims, 'test new forms of community, friendship, and complicity', experimenting also with 'alternative social practices' (Klein, 2013: 139).

However, as disabled artist Claire Cunnigham has pointed out during the Danceable conference in Holland in 2019, the danger inherent in canonising inclusive dance methodologies is that they become detached from their political backdrop arguing for equity, equality, openness, and experimentation for all. To that end, she recounted how she is self-educated, working at first with people outside the field of dance so as to create her own movement vocabulary. Her work '4 legs good' portrays this process, emphasising how her crutches are part of her body and of her relation to the world, as well as the diverse ways with which an artist can form her own language without necessarily being part of specific educational frameworks. That is to say, inclusive dance is not a purpose in itself, but rather a fertile, moving ground and methodology with which we can keep on learning and creating, posing questions as to the aims and values of education, remaining open as a platform of investigation in or outside of institutions, and in or outside of our dancing communities. By the same token, inclusive dance pioneer and practitioner, Adam Benjamin, argues that inclusive dance, or his preferred term integrated dance, is not 'a dance form, organisation or style' but that '[i]t may, unless we are very careful, end up as one' (2002: 16).

Conclusion

According to Ann Daly, dance is 'a place where diverse groups of people can and do meet to share a common experience' (2002: 9). However, it is important to investigate what kind of common experiences are shaped each time through different educational and professional structures, so as to critically reflect on them. When examining dance and disability, and in particular, inclusive dance educational methodologies, what is at stake is a restitution of the dance scene leading to a more diverse and inclusive field. The latter corresponds to and engages with shifting social and political realities, investing in communities built on mutual trust and difference, nurturing socially engaged dancers. Inclusive dance practices, and their techniques, such as translation, improvisation, facilitation, and processes of reflection, aim primarily to establish a working ethos that is founded on collaboration, and that in turn leads to the creation of smaller communities, which are part of the expanded field of dance, and, in essence, part of wider society. As dramaturg and critic Marianne Van Kerkhoven (1994) argues, when discussing the arts nowadays, we need to take into account not only the minor dramaturgy, which has to do with the artwork production at hand, but also the major dramaturgy, which relates to the world. In her own words:

> We could define the minor dramaturgy as that zone, that structural circle, which lies in and around a production. But a production comes alive through its interaction, through its audience, and through what is going on outside its own orbit. And around the production lies the

theatre and around the theatre lies the city and around the city, as far as we can see, lies the whole world and even the sky and all its stars.

(Marianne Van Kerkhoven, 1994)

Inclusive dance techniques and practices are, in fact, inclusive of this major dramaturgy making sure that a dancer is positioned within this changing world, having the skills necessary for the twenty-first century.

What are these skills? Returning to the question of what makes a good dancer in today's context, the answers deriving from this article are multiple. A good dancer should be a self-reflective one, with the necessary technical proficiency, social awareness, dialogical skills, and an ethos of working-*with* that takes into account the minor and major dramaturgies of the art world, or, in other words, what Laermans identifies as the 'thinking dancer' (2015: 366). Someone who in relation to her cultural and socio-political context is engaging with, committing and contributing to creating common grounds, producing a 'social commonality', experimenting, failing, and retrying (Laermans, 2015: 371).

Inclusive dance pedagogies and especially the techniques they use are a platform for innovation, creativity, and renewal of the dance scene, as they question the ideology of ability that dominates society and, by extension, the field of dance, and propose a philosophy of teaching and performing accessible to all, cultivating alternative values in society. At the same time, inclusive dance techniques – as discussed in this article – produce a working ethos founded on respecting difference, learning from the other, and working-with, as part of a communal project that then penetrates society through socially aware dancers, leading to an 'experimentation with new forms of subjective organisation, with new forms of subjectivity, clearly in a sort of dialectical connection to a new concept of community, of the common' (Manchev, 2016: 49).

In conclusion, inclusive dance is a move towards the democratisation of the contemporary dance field and as such 'a contingent experiment in *democratizing democracy*' (Laermans, 2015: 391). It is a way to keep on dreaming of and experimenting with alternative worlds in an epoch where everything seems dead-end and dystopic. It is a fertile ground for new social imaginaries that are grounded on being, working, and living with one another. It is a practice of responsibility through which to develop 'the inclusive society we stand for', to fight for the future we wish for as artists and citizens (Saša Asentić in Marsh & Burrows, 2017: 24).

Notes

1 For more information and available resources, please visit online Stopgap Dance Company https://www.stopgapdance.com/learn-and-practice/dance-teachers-and-artists/inclusive-dance-and-iris-teacher-training/ and idance Euroepan Programme http://www.idancenetwork.eu/lessons/

References

Albright, A. C. (1997) *Choreographing Difference: The Body and Identity in Contemporary Dance*, Middletown, CT: Wesleyan University Press. Hanover, NH: University Press of New England.

BBC News (2015) *Akram Khan Criticises Quality of UK Dance Training*. Available at: https://www.bbc.com/news/entertainment-arts-32236406

Benjamin, A. (2002) *Making and Entrance; Theory and Practice for Disabled and Non-Disabled Dancers*. London: Routledge.

Bennett, L. (2014) 'Arts Head: Lucy Bennett, Artistic Director, Stopgap Dance Company: Interview by Matthew Caines', *The Guardian*. 8 April. Available at: https://www.theguardian.com/culture-professionals-network/2014/apr/08/Stopgap-dance-company-disabled-artists

Burrows, J. (2010) *A Choreographer's Handbook*. London and New York: Routledge.

Daly, A. (2002) 'Dancing democracy', *Dance Research Journal*, 34(2), pp. 8–11.

Foster, Leigh S. (2002) *Dances that Describe Them*selves. Middletown, CT: Wesleyan University Press.

Goodley, D. (2014) *Dis/ability Studies: Theorising Disablism and Ableism*. London: Routledge.

Klein, G. (2013) Dance Theory as a Practice of Critique. In: Brandstetter, G. & Klein, G. (eds), *Dance [and] Theory*. Bielefeld: Verlag [transcript], pp. 137–149.

Koch, J. (2010) *Find Your Own Pace and Move Together: The Application of Universal Design of Instruction in Dance Degrees in Higher Education*. Unpublished Manuscript. Available at: https://static1.squarespace.com/static/537f912ce4b0f33d47e8549a/t/5880a049be6594efd28522d0/1484824650400/Koch+UD+in+Dance+web+17.pdf

Laermans, R. (2012) 'Being in Common': Theorizing Artistic Collaboration', *Performance Research, A Journal of The Performing Arts*, 17(6), pp. 94–102. https://doi.org/10.1080/13528165.2013.775771

Laermans, R. (2015) *Moving Together: Theorizing and Making Contemporary Dance*. Amsterdam: Valiz.

Lazzarato, M. (1996) Immaterial Labor. In: Virno, P., & Hardt, M. (eds), *Radical Thought in Italy: A Potential Politics*. Minneapolis: University of Minnesota Press, pp.133–147.

Manchev, B. (2016) 'Nothing in Common: Collaborations, Relations, Processes, and the Actuality of Artistic Labour', *TkH Journal for Performing Arts Theory*, 23, pp. 49–52. Available at: http://www.tkh-generator.net/portfolio/tkh-23-commons-undercommons/

Nadarajah, N. (2017) '...sight, smell, touch' in Marsh, K. & Burrows, J (eds), *Permission to Stare. Fresh Perspectives on Arts and Disability*. Brussels: IETM, p. 17. Available at: https://www.ietm.org/en/publications

Marsh, K. & Burrows, J. (eds.) (2017) *Permission to Stare. Fresh Perspectives on Arts and Disability*. Brussels: IETM. Available at: https://www.ietm.org/en/resources/fresh-perspectives/fresh-perspectives-7-permission-to-stare-arts-and-disability

Panagiotara, B. (2019) 'Dance & Disability: A Research on Inclusive Dance Education & Training', iDance European Programme, Available at: http://www.idancenetwork.eu/activities/dance-disability/

Rogoff, I. (2006) *What is a Theorist?* Available at: http://kein.org/node/62 (Accessed: 12/11/2020)

Schneider, F. (2010) '(Extended) Footnotes on Education', *E-flux*, 14 (1). Available at: https://www.e-flux.com/journal/14/61318/extended-footnotes-on-education/

Sennett, R. (2013) *Together. The Rituals, Pleasures and Politics of Cooperation.* London: Penguin Books.

Siebers, T. (2010) *Disability Aesthetics.* Michigan: University of Michigan Press.

Urmston, E. & Aujla, I. (2018) *Developing Potential Amongst Disabled Young People: Exploring Dance Artists' Qualities as Educators in the Context of Inclusive Dance Talent Development.* Available at: http://www.idancenetwork.eu/wp-content/uploads/2018/09/Developing-Potential-Amongst-Young-Disabled-Dancers-Report.pdf

Van Kerkhoven, M. (1994, October 01). *Sarma.* Available at: http://sarma.be/docs/3229

Virno, P. (2004) *A Grammar of the Multitude.* Los Angeles: Semiotext(e).

Whatley, S. (2010) 'Strategies for Inclusion in Dance; Disability, Performativity and Transition Into and Out of Higher Education', in 2010 International VSA Education Conference Proceedings. The Kennedy Center. Available at: https://www.kennedy-center.org/globalassets/education/networks-conferences--research/research--resources/vsa-resources/2010-conference/whatley_sarah_strategies_for_inclusion_in_dance.pdf

1.4 Finding a place for responsiveness, possibility, and emergence in dance education assessment systems

Adesola Akinleye

In this chapter, I reflect on assessment tools for dance in higher education/ tertiary education environments, specifically university dance departments and dance conservatoires accredited by higher education institutions. My focus is on Western settings and as such I draw on my own experience as lecturer and as external examiner in universities and conservatoires in the UK, Canada, and the USA over the last 25 years. In understanding the culture of dance in this context, it is important to note the histories of how a dance department might have come to be in the position of accrediting learning. Often university dance departments are the younger siblings in longer established academic areas. This has meant most university dance departments have been expected to take on generalised aspects of pre-existing assessment systems that extend across a range of other subjects within the further/ higher education setting. Similarly, dance conservatoires accredited by further or higher education organisations find themselves in the already existing systems of appraisal used by the institutions they have partnered with. In this way, dance education curriculums inherit modes of evaluation that are often adjusted from existing assessment tools originally associated with non-physical theoretical study. Examples of this are the use of tests (assessments through observation of a single technique class) and summative grading that originally derive from static theoretical based inquiry rather than the heuristic and experiential learning of the arts.

Dance departments can find themselves straddling the nuanced nurturing of a student's lifelong art practice on the one hand while on the other assessing that student on the fleeting event of a single test-class or performance. Subsequently, key continuities in dance-arts learning (such as the responsiveness of creativity and divergent possibility of imagination) risk being devalued due to a lack of appropriate assessment tools for their appraisal. Of course, many dance departments have accomplished hard fought repositioning of assessment criteria and been able to significantly adapt wording on grading grids. However, I feel there are further ontological shifts that dance can offer the wider education system as we find ways to resolve issues of assessment within our movement practices. Where better than in the corporeal knowledges of a dance department would we find the expertise of

DOI: 10.4324/9781003111146-6

learning underpinned by the embodied nature of the human experience. The somatic nature of dance practices fosters alertness to the process of experiencing the moving body that reveals the flux of the human experience. The dance department is thus an apt environment for the development of assessment tools fit to recognise responsiveness (context), possibility (creativity), and emergence (process) as fundamental to the humanity of the learning experience (Deloria Jr. & Wildcat, 2001).

Now more than ever: the now-ness of context more than the ever-ness of perfection

I began to write this reflection on how we evaluate and assess in dance education during the years of 2020/2021 when Covid-19 affected the where and when of all I had anticipated I was entering while I sang Happy New Year on the first of January. The sudden shift in routine, connection, and habit that the pandemic created drove home the importance of being able to respond and work creatively. The numerous changes and modifications of my life through Covid were marked by the companionship of my iPad and the films, performances, Zoom dance classes, and songs it brought me to keep me company. For myself and millions of people moving through quarantines, lockdowns, and their isolation, the arts brought the humanity of responsiveness, possibility, and imagination into rooms where we would sit otherwise alone. Post-Covid's arrival, the arts now more than ever, help hold the population in hope and yet the dance students I teach are ongoingly confronted with their industry being devalued. For example, in the initial 2020 response to devastating unemployment and furlough caused by worldwide lockdowns, rather than recognise how vital the arts were to people in isolation, the UK Government assume a hierarchy for career training that placed arts, specifically dance, at a lowest most point. This is illustrated by the recalled UK Tory Government campaign that saw posters of a female dancer sitting with ballet shoes on her feet next to the caption '*Fatima's next job could be in cyber. (she just doesn't know it yet)*' signed off with the Government slogan '*Rethink. Reskill. Reboot*' (Bakare, 2020). A response to this from across the UK dance world could be summed up by adapting the sentiment attributed to Emma Goldman (Shulman, 1991): *If I can't dance, I don't want to be part of your revolution* or your rethink or your reboot!

It is important to point out that education is not the same as training for a job. Nevertheless, historically in the West, there has been a divide between schooling as learning a trade through practical doing and education as classical theoretical inquiry (academic study). Sir Ken Robinson discusses this divide when he lectures on Western education in the well-known Ted Talks *Do schools kill creativity* and *Changing Educational Paradigms* (made into RSA animation).[1] In these talks and through his other published works (such as Robinson, 2001; Robinson & Aronica, 2013), Robinson criticises structures within formal education as stifling individuals' potential for creativity.

Robinson points out that practical education – including dance – has long been on the periphery of the academic paradigm. He suggests that the emphases on some kinds of ability, such as the memorising and reproducing of test material, is so celebrated in formal education that it starts to appear to be the only indication of intelligent learning that can be strived for. This could be why dance is expected to take on the assessment systems of its theoretical study siblings in academic organisations.

However, dance education is stifled by the larger university or further education institution's expectation that dance departments will willingly assess their dance students through tests and summative grades. Within these formal test systems, that universities impose and Robinson critiques, a student would be seen as successful when they silently reproduce the aesthetic of a dance form at the prescribed time of a test-class or performance to receive a grade for the whole period of the term/semester. In this Western academic paradigm, the practicality of *doing* is seen as means to an end, a means to arrive at a point of perfection. Thus, within the larger educational institution, the dance department inherits an assumption that knowledges in dance resides in the mind's ability to reproduce shapes in the body at a given time. The moving body as a site of knowledge is then compromised because the act of learning is expected to be demonstrated in the reproduction of movement rather than the movement itself being the activity of knowledge making. Thus, the somatic nature of learning done in the dance department could be seen as misunderstood or even out of place in the traditional higher and further educational setting. However, alternatively to feeling dislocated from the wider university, the dance department can spearhead methods that extend the learning experience beyond the static consumption and reproduction of information that test-driven teaching is limited to.

In the economic climate of the Post-Covid period, the arts are even more charged to defend their worth. Yet, rather than engaging in a challenge to justify dance through conforming to pre-existing assessment systems, dance's presence in tertiary education could be seen as the opportunity to share wisdom in alternative modes of learning. Conceiving the dancing body as a site of knowledge (and not just evidence of a mind that can control and contort it) requires us to consider how we recognise qualities of dance knowledge that are elusive in the type of testing systems that require students to manufacture a perfectly reproduced/memorised outcome. Dancers, dance scholars, choreographers, and dance teachers are familiar with thinking through the response of doing (Henley & Conrad, 2021). In *Thought in the Act*, Erin Manning and Brian Massumi argue that doing is in itself a mode of thought, and dance particularly is 'thinking in movement' (Manning & Massumi, 2014: vii). Dance is in the unique position that by enriching our practices for assessment and progression, we can offer alternatives to wider pedagogical approaches beyond the field.

Ken Robinson also points out that Western traditional systems of assessment have routinely suppressed the self-worth of people who do not excel in test settings (Robinson, 2001; Robinson & Aronica , 2013). This is because test settings conflate students' depth of knowledge with their ease of performance during the time of the test. Robinson's critique calls for change in the general educational paradigm. Following Robinson's (2001) long-standing calls for formal education to critique itself, dance education has the potential to be at the forefront of new ways to understand how knowledge can be assessed and valued in university settings in the twenty-first century. The embodied nature of dance education offers students the challenges to engage with their own humanity, fragility, empathy, and relationship as they dance together and in the wider world. Standing behind these values requires dance departments to have the courage to engage with ongoing self-reflection and to look at how movement education values can contribute to equity and humanity across the rest of the university. Elsewhere (Akinleye, 2018), I have discussed this to be no mean task, as the Western dance forms that are ubiq-uitously taught in higher education are thus required to look at their own value systems which include colonial misogynistic, ableist, racist, and classist authoritarian histories. As what is assessed tacitly reveals what is valued, subtleties of assessment ricochet across the faculty and student members of tertiary education into society (touching students' families, employers, and future members of the university and society in primary and secondary edu-cation). What is assessed and how it is done is crucial to the learning culture of a department and thus part of any shift away from cultures of misogyny, ableism, and racism. Addressing how we appraise the work of dance stu-dents, how we encourage them to value their lifelong emergent relationship with the art form is a vital component towards this larger humanitarian shift.

Dance, learning to be human

There used to be a homeless man, a homeless artist, who I would see when I rode the One Train in New York from my apartment on 86th street to class and rehearsals at Dance Theatre of Harlem (DTH) on 152nd street. And later, when I moved around the corner from DTH, I would see him on the A Train on evenings when I went downtown to performances at Lincoln Centre. I remember a number of his subway *concerts* even though this was 30 years ago: the colour of the subway seats, his smile, movements he made with his body as he was playing are all clearly recalled, and the recollection keenly takes me to myself sitting on the train speeding through New York to and from dance rehearsals and classes. He would move from train carriage to train carriage performing with a saxophone. He would say he was an alien and as if to prove this he wore a headband with googly silver balls attached to it by metal springs like antenna. He played 'alien' music; he played music that was not harmonious. He would say if we (the train passengers) gave him money he would stop playing! A short stocky brown skinned man with a beard from behind which he would cheekily smile. On one journey, he got on my train with a bruised eye and cuts on his cheeks; his saxophone was dented in a couple of places. He said that he could still play it and proceeded to perform. It was not the funny-give-him-money-to-stop-odd melody, it was a horrible sound, and it was his artistic response to his situation. It made the passengers acknowledge the violence it had taken to dent the instrument which was so precious to him and his livelihood. This was not the last time I saw him perform. The memory of his concerts on the train carefully opens my feelings, thoughts, sensation of my dancing life from years ago. This is what art does, art reaches across memory confounding time by making a moment part of a timeless continuity (Dewey, 2005; Jackson, 1998; Mahina, 2004).

Likewise, art confounding time, I have seen, with elderly relatives when there are moments when we both wonder, fear, they will forget their own story, and in them doing so, I will also lose their story of my history. But the felt sensation in the notes of a tune, in the companionship of the musical harmony of a song, in getting up to move through steps of a dance together brings them vividly back to the moment of us. Dancing together to radio, a gift the musician, gives me and my relative purposefully yet unknowingly through their artwork.

In his Ted Talk *We are larger than our definitions*, choreographer Alonzo King (2016) speaks of the journey in dance to find out who and what we are. The talk includes a performance by his company LINES Ballet. In a breath-taking performance, the dancers embody the music, the space, and the journey of self-discovery King speaks of. As I watch the dance on the computer screen, I feel it in my physical response as if my heartbeat took up the pace of what I am watching. Time disappears as the ballet becomes part of me, part of my inner recall at instants when I feel broken or overwhelmed by an everyday task.

These are encounters that shape my personal dance history, they flesh dance with context and meaning for me. All three descriptions are instances when artists (artist-on-train, singer-my-relative-always-dances-along-to, King-and-the-artists-he-works-with) enter my life, effect how I allow myself to be deeply touched and thus shape my definition of self. They are three instances that awakened my understanding of responsiveness, possibility, and emergence. Knowledge made available to me through the artist's ability to be genuinely a part of the moment and extend the offer of being time-lessly present, through their artwork, to me. The instant of my encounters with them all involves dance and has shaped what dance means to me when I am moving. Each encounter (on train, caught in a tune, captivated by the computer screen) unexpectedly ignited my own knowledge of past experiences, an openness to being aware of the moment of now-ness and the possibility of what future engagement could bring forth. What a responsibility art has – it connects us to ourselves across time-space. John Dewey captures this when he writes, '*Art celebrates with peculiar intensity the moments in which the past reenforces the present and in which the future is a quickening of what now is*' (Dewey, 2005: 17). Thus, dance-art suggests we are multi-dimensional: the past is present in the habitual of our daily movements and shaped by the anticipation of the future given what has been. When we meet and assess the students who have arrived at our classes to learn to dance (stand at the front of a studio or turn on our video feed on a computer) we meet the people who hope to respond to the possibility of time-space to create a sense of art. As teachers, we are entering our student's history for a few years, minutes, lifetimes depending on how well we nurture or hinder them. The dance teacher is tasked to exemplify how we hold the fragile of possibility and emergence without weakening it while also giving meaning to the unverbalised timelessness of dance-art. Aware of this, the dance teacher is in the dichotomy of assessing while not unwittingly condoning the standardisation of educational policies that stifle the dance-artist in their students (Risner & Schupp, 2019). The student artist requires an educational environment that values and prepares them for engaging with the folds and rough edges of their lives; timelessly engaging with the unexplored and unexpected encounters of human lives.

The importance of responsiveness

Education is about meaning making, that is the 'educated' moving body has much more ability than just being able to ever reproduce a perfected shape to a given prescription. As I dance, I am responding to music, gravity, other dancers, histories of technique and aesthetics of shape, and the physicality of my own organs and muscles second by second. This is the somatic development of being aware of the moment and responding to it. The dance student who has developed knowledges in responsiveness is able to read, interpret, and contribute to the present situation informed by past experience and anticipation of possible futures. In this responsiveness is a fundamental aptitude for lifelong learning in general.

Responsiveness that requires understanding of context, togetherness, and agency is a key element for dancing. Explicit examples are in African and Indigenous diaspora dance forms for which dance is an overt exploration and expression of philosophical/worldview and world around (Welsh-Asante, 1990). In these dance forms, understanding of music, space, community connection, and community values are learnt through the responsive embodied participation of dancing (Mabingo, 2022). Western forms of contemporary improvisation and contact improvisation also draw on the togetherness and agency of responsiveness as threads woven into the aesthetic of the movement. Unfortunately, African, Indigenous, and Improvisational dance forms are often treated as secondary or elective classes on the dance academy curriculum. In conversations with colleagues in Western educational settings, those teaching dance forms that involve improvisation and contact improvisation highlight the insufficiency of test-class/performance assessment events for evaluating a dance student's knowledge and skills. Colleagues have also noted that problems with assessment can be used as an excuse for not making those dance forms required classes. Highly codified European dance forms, such as ballet, can be shoehorned into test situations more easily. This is not just a problem for the particular movement genres that use improvisation. Rather, it is a problem across all dance education as it highlights how academic assessment tools from outside the field are in danger of driving the value systems within the field.

A racist past in Western dance effects how the skill of improvisation can be mistakenly dismissed as randomly uninformed rather than considered, spontaneous, and open interaction (Lewis & Piekut, 2016). In the nineteenth- and early twentieth-century, when Western observers encountered non-Western dances they concealed their own lack of knowledge of movement by the suggestion that these dances were the result of mindless compulsion (for example, reading Sachs [1937]). Thus, the nuanced interaction and exchange of improvisation within non-Western dances was originally missed by those contributing to early Western dance scholarship. Burdened with not having fully shaken off its prejudiced history, the Western dance academy can miss the importance of articulating responsiveness as a set of applied knowledges. The first step is to reposition (improvisation and) responsiveness as clear examples of applied knowledge in action (De La Roche, 1992; Heil, 2019). Numerous African dance forms can be used to exemplify this (once they are on the curriculum). This repositioning underlines the stance that any action (including ones through the responsiveness of improvisation) is part of a larger continuum of experience and meaning making. Then the question becomes how we trace the development of this applied meaning making which by its nature is not about a single incident exemplifying knowledge (such as a test-class). Rather assessment calls for the student to demonstrate their continuing processes for finding meaning, with responsiveness being an important tool for this process. As Western dance institutes untangle legacies of colonialism and liberate themselves from their misogynistic and racist past, they advance their own ability to flourish as a site of knowledge in the twenty-first century (Silva, 2017).

There are devices, such as reflective journals, which can capture student learning through revealing the students reflexive understanding of their own application of responsiveness. Reflective journaling has a long history as a tool in settings where diligence to ongoing responses to new advancements is a vital part of professional responsibility, such as in nursing and health care (Moon & Dawson, 2006). It is not new for dance departments to use journaling and diaries as useful sustained reflection (Risner, 2017; Zeller, 2017). The issue is how we continue to raise the profile and credibility of these ongoing modes of capturing process beyond specialised settings and into more general educational policy. That is, at the general university board, the dance department representative is not expected to justify journals once again, but rather is in conversation about how more formal academic subjects could benefit from how dance engages reflexive learning through their use.

The easy access of internet use in Western educational cultures adds a further imperative for seeing learning how to respond as an integral skill for dance students. The web 2.0 culture of daily updates on one's emotional and physical environment has a noted impact on dance students (Harrington, 2020). For many dance students, navigating the pressure of evaluation of their ability through a social media post is exacerbated by a culture of evaluating dance through observation of a 'test' performance (Hoff & Mitchell, 2009). Developing and using skills in self-assessment through self-reflection, particularly in terms of alternatives to aesthetic-based summative evaluation tests, are key to the dance students' emotional stamina in the online culture of the twenty-first century. Reflective journals as self-assessment models that can be overseen by the dance teacher appear to provide significantly important skills for the students to evaluate processes of feedback from their educational setting to their personal lives.

Reflective journaling and self-assessment become tools for the meaningful tracing of the self-awareness needed by the dance student to develop their skills in responsiveness physically and emotionally. Journals and the robust documentation of self-reflection are modes that require regular formative feedback. This means a letting go of the inherent power dynamic between student and teacher created by the *grade reveal* at the end of a semester adorned by an after-the-fact summative feedback paragraph (Akinleye & Payne, 2016). Assessment using regular journaling requires the kind of ongoing transactional feedback that echoes the somatic experience of dance where feedback and response are continually derived from multiple entities (feedback when dancing such as *music, gravity, other dancers, histories of technique and aesthetics of shape, and the physicality of my own organs and muscles second by second*). In recognising responsiveness as a valuable component of dance education, modes of evaluation that use formative feedback and reflexive practices are vitalised.

Possibility and teaching technique

Influenced by the University system's need to commodify attainment, a dance department can be pressured to use test-classes (assessments through observation of technique class). But within this system, nuances of a technique can be usurped by the student's quest for a general aesthetic that will get them through the one-off event of the test. This is done to the detriment of knowledge gaining for the dance student. The dance student becomes adept in mirroring what they are told to do without seeing the *possibility* of the movements they are engaging with. Their potential for movement is thus reliant on the teacher telling them what to do. The power dynamics created by this becomes an accepted structure for the student to avoid thinking for themselves. Catherine Seago points out the importance of dance students engaging with different types of attention and sense making (beyond the single skill of being able to reproduce moves as directed). She suggests '*students can benefit from an increased knowledge of different types of attention and by exploring this they can experience a greater sense of agency*' (Seago, 2020: 245). Without this developed sense of agency, when the dance teacher is removed, for instance after the student's graduation, the student can only cling to a sense of perfecting their bodies into the different exercises which they had been directed to undertake in order to pass their exams. Then, student is locked in the limited possibility of movement produced for a test. Their sense of being an artist is lost to the very thing (technique) that is there to service their art. I am not suggesting less rigour in the teaching of technique. However, I am suggesting that technique is for the purpose of dancing and thus should be in service to the dancer not the end goal itself. As such dance technique is about the aesthetic of the student's steps but importantly also about the student's engagement with the possibilities of their dancing.

I have suggested above that art steps out of time, confounds time (such as the artist-on-train, singer-my-relative-always-dances-along-to, King-and-the-artists-he-works-with). Therefore, above I use the phrase '*possibility of their dancing*' suggesting possibility can be a verbal placeholder for the idea that knowledge of what has gone before and anticipation of what can be, starts to describe the multiple engagement with time-space that is dance-art. I propose that the person who has a dance education has spent time reflecting on, and practising their individual sense of physicality in time-space. The educated dancer is the person who can recognise the potential for dance to happen in themselves and in others and has the wherewithal to engage with the opportunity for dance to happen.

One of the main tools that allows the educated dancer exploration of movement possibility is knowledge of a movement technique. This allows the dancer to seize the offer for dance to happen while keeping the mechanics of their individual body safe. Dance techniques allow the individual to continue to engage with dance over extended periods of time, for their lifelong learning. Thus, dance technique can be seen as a personal tool which grows with the dancer instead of pre-determined knowledge that is acquired at a certain point in training. Education in a dance technique opens knowledge of oneself that allows the individual to pursue dancing. Knowledges in one particular movement technique can then reveal the possibility of movement in another dance form (even if the aesthetic of that form falls outside of the dancer's range of experience). A dancer adept in the possibility of movement using the technique of one particular dance form knows their moving body fluently enough to glimpse the somatic knowledges present in an unfamiliar dance technique. Thus, a dance technique provides at least two kinds of knowledge simultaneously. First, knowledge of the possibility of movement in time-space which encompasses the worldview and history of the dance form the technique is associated with. Second, knowledge that allows the dancer to notice the differences, nuances, worldviews of another dance form through understanding the possibility of movement that technique allows for. This is about the dance student understanding *where they can go* in the movement, possibilities which are overshadowed if their primary focus is on what a movement looks like during a test. In simplifying the attainment of dance to being a momentary execution of aesthetic body movement, assessment systems can again tacitly adhere to the notion that dancing is the result of thinking rather than the thinking itself (Manning & Massumi, 2014).

In measuring dance through summative evaluation, the Western dance academy is vulnerable to students missing the idea that dance engages with philosophical worldviews, speaks to ontology, and is in dialogue with the world beyond the dance studio mirrors. Dance students can omit to notice the links between the history, sociology, activism, and philosophy of dance, seeing them as passing additions to attaining the best-looking moves for the best grades in technique class. Dance assessment becomes treated as the acquisition of a set of movement vocabulary, the meaning of which can be emoted by the student but not understood.

Emergence: responsiveness and possibility create emergent and relational learning experiences

The dancing body is transactional, historied, and emergent, given context by the world around. Dance learning is rarely done in isolation; it is relational and emerges from the embodied context. Dance education supports and develops techniques and knowledges that allow the dancer to recognise within themselves the potential, possibility, and incompleteness of responsive interact with world around through movement. This is dance education as creating the ability to spontaneously respond in movement to the possibility of the moment of dance with others. Dance educators are aware of the myriad of qualities that we would like our student dancers to grasp: the behaviours of empathy, the subtlety of presence and absence, and the poetics of breath in movement are clearly a part of the dance studio. The embodied nature of learning dance offers students, '*the concept of the learning self as the sensation of coming into relation with outside world and to the other selves who inhabit and create that world with us*' (Ellsworth, 2005: 117). The nature of the world is intra-actional in the making, in other words, an emerging relational experience. Massumi (2002) suggests that fields of emergence, becoming, possibility, responsiveness are tools for thinking about agency and social change. The dance class can be a micro space for exploring the relationality and transaction between self and others. Just as the dance class also resonates with the macro emergence of agency, identity, society building, social change, and resilience that dance has historically been a part of, particularly Africanist and Indigenous dances (Graff, 1997; Shea Murphy, 2007; Thompson, 2014).

No doubt emergence into the moment of now is exemplified in the practicality of learning dance. This is learning dance as the skills of to-be-in-interaction, to develop a sense of transaction, to build together. The question for dance is, how possible is it to assess emergence as the accomplishment of an individual student? It seems tools for group assessment, peer assessment, and self-assessment offer apparatus to recognise learning is not achieved in isolation; it is relational and emerges from context.

I realise, that in this chapter, I have only given a few practical alternatives to test-driven and summative testing models. This is partly because I feel the system that produces a need for these kinds of assessments is what is in need of change. As Ken Robinson encourages us, the point is to change the paradigm.[2] In order to do this, we can look to other dance systems (which have a distinctly non-Western influence). For instance, standing (in the different system) the club, on the street, in the rented gym hall at the end of a gathering or a hip hop, or Capoeira, or Ghanaian Adowa class, it is familiar to stand in a circle. An individual or two enter the circle/cypher and move. The group of the circle anticipate beats, moving together in a reflective responsive rhythm to the dancers in the centre, all building the movement. At another point the circle/cypher creates shared sound as we all breathe out or in response to a movement. Sometimes when someone in the centre notices another has not stepped into the circle yet. They approach with outstretched open gestures. Play replaces test.

The movers in the circle still have to demonstrate understanding of the movement, they have to use techniques to be able to be a part of the movement conversation, they also have to be responsive to and see the possibility of movement. Assessment is shifted from the linear observational experience to a circular shared self, peer, and elder/teacher experience. These circles at the end of class are joyful moments of celebration of the attainment of knowledges. The formal Western dance educational setting is challenged to transform the silent, judgemental test space into the multiple registers of the creative space of exchange, possibility, and transactional for instance of the circle.

Across the period of writing this chapter, I have felt a growing urgency to highlight the arts' fight for existence as a vital part of humanising Western society's mental and physical resilience. Clearly within the context of this book, this importantly requires the 'us' of those in dance education to constantly adapt how we prepare dance students for a lifelong interest in exploring their artistic practice. Along with how we deliver dance training that encourages a sense of humanity in students (towards themselves and others). I wonder how we encourage students to be resilient and eager to grow. This seems to directly relate to the value system we place on students through assessment of their dance attainment and progression. Specifically, how assessment tools deal with giving value to students' responsiveness, possibility, and emergence.

In this chapter, I have suggested that dance's moving somatic knowledges inculcates dance education with (re)evaluating how assessment can support a lasting learning process. I have questioned how we use appropriate tests and summative feedback for the assessment of key attributes of dance-arts. Specifically, I feel responsiveness, possibility, and emergence are primary tools in dancer's bodily thinking that are often overlooked because many formal assessment systems do not have the capacity for acknowledgement of them. The recent unexpected history of Covid demonstrates the importance of the artistic skills of being able to imaginatively respond and recognise possibility. Rather than be swallowed up in the system, across the wider field of higher education, the dance department can contribute to unravelling how we address assessment as part of a long-awaited paradigm change.

Notes

1 https://www.ted.com/talks/sir_ken_robinson_do_schools_kill_creativity? language=en (accessed Nov 10 2022); https://www.ted.com/talks/sir_ken_ robinson_changing_education_paradigms (assessed Nov 10 2022)
2 If we keep using to the system of X, we will keep finding ourselves the system of X.

References

Akinleye, A. (ed.) (2018) *Narratives in Black British Dance: Embodied Practices.* London: Palgrave Macmillian.

Akinleye, A. & Payne, R. (2016) 'Transactional space: Feedback, critical thinking and learning dance technique'. *Journal of Dance Education*, 16(4), pp. 144–148. doi: 10.1080/15290824.2016.1165821

Bakare, L. (2020) 'Government scraps ballet dancer reskilling and criticised as 'crass''. *The Guardian*, 12th October 2020 17:40 BST. Available at: https:// www.theguardian.com/politics/2020/oct/2012/ballet-dancer-could-reskill-with-job-in-cyber-security-suggests-uk-government-ad

De La Roche, E. (1992) 'Critical thinking and improvisation'. *Inquiry: Critical Thinking across the Disciplines*, 10(1), pp. 16–17. doi:10.5840/inquiryctnews199210141

Deloria Jr., V. & Wildcat, D. R. (2001) *Power and Place: Indian Education in America.* Denver, CO: Fulcrum Publishing.

Dewey, J. (2005) *Art as Experience.* Paperback edition. New York: Penguin.

Ellsworth, E. A. (2005) *Places of Learning: Media, Architecture, Pedagogy.* Oxon: Routledge.

Graff, E. (1997) *Stepping Left: Dance and Politics in New York City, 1928–1942.* Durham, NC and London: Duke University Press.

Harrington, H. (2020) 'Consumer dance identity: The intersection between competition dance, televised dance shows and social media'. *Research in Dance Education*, 21(2), pp. 169–187. doi:10.1080/14647893.2020.1798394

Heil, J. (2019) 'Dancing contact improvisation with Luce Irigaray; intra-action and elemental passions'. *Hypatia*, 34(3), pp. 485–506. doi:10.1111/hypa.12479

Henley, M. & Conrad, R. (2021) '"I'm not thinking about it to understand it, I'm thinking about iot to do it": Student's sensemaking experiences from the modern dance classroom'. *Journal of Dance Education*, pp. 1–10. doi:10.1080/15290824 .2021.18848870

Hoff, D. L. & Mitchell, S. N. (2009) 'Cyberbullying: Causes, effects, and remedies'. *Journal of Educational Administration*, 47(5), pp. 652–665. doi:10.1108/09578 230910981107

Jackson, P. W. (1998) *John Dewey and the Lessons of Art*. New Haven, CT and London: Yale University Press.

King, A. (2016) *We Are Larger Than Our Definitions*. Ted Talk, filmed at TEDWomen 2016. Available at: https://www.youtube.com/watch?v=YpMUCwOO-yk)

Lewis, G. E. & Piekut, B. E. (2016) *The Oxford Handbook of Critical Improvisation Studies*. Vol. 2. New York: Oxford University Press.

Mabingo, A. (2022) 'Decolonizing assessment in dance education: Ubuntu as an evaluative framework in indigenous African dance education practices'. *Journal of Dance Education*, pp. 1–12. doi:10.1080/15290824.2021.2004313

Mahina, 'O. (2004) 'Art as ta-va 'Time-Space' transformation'. In *Researching the Pacfic and Indigenous Peoples: Issues and Perspectives*, edited by T. Baba, N. Williams & U. Nabobo-Baba. Auckland: Center for Pacific Studies, University of Auckland, pp. 168–202.

Manning, E. & Massumi, B. (2014) *Thought in the Act: Passages in the Ecology of Experience*. Minneapolis and London: University of Minnesota Press.

Massumi, B. (2002) *Parables for the Virtual: Movement, Affect, Sensation*. Durham, NC: Duke University Press.

Moon, J. A. & Dawson, B. (2006) *Learning Journals: A Handbook for Reflective Practice and Professional Development* (2nd ed.). London: Routledge.

Risner, D. (2017) 'New reflective practices research in dance education'. *Journal of Dance Education*, 17(3), pp. 8990. doi:10.1080/15290824.2017.1355183

Risner, D. & Schupp, K. (eds.) (2019) *Ethical Dilemmas in Dance Education: Case Studies on Humanizing Dance Pedagogy*. Jefferson, NC: McFarland.

Robinson, K. (2001) *Out of Our Minds: Learning to be Creative*. Oxford: Capstone.

Robinson, K. & Aronica, L. (2013) *Finding Your Element How to Discover Your Talents and Passions and Transform Your Life*. London: Allen Lane.

Sachs, C. (1937) *World History of the Dance*. New York: Norton.

Seago, C. (2020) 'A study of the perception and use of attention in undergraduate dance training classes'. *Research in Dance Education*, 21(3), pp. 245–261. doi: 10.1080/14647893.2020.1757636

Shea Murphy, J. (2007) *The People Have Never Stopped Dancing: Native American Modern Dance Histories*. Minneapolis: University of Minnesota Press; Bristol: University Presses Marketing [distributor].

Shulman, A. K. (1991) 'Women of the PEN: Dance with feminists'. *The Women's Review of Books*, 9(3), p. 13. doi:10.2307/4021093

Silva, J. C. D. (2017) *Reflections on Improvisation, Choreography and Risk-Taking in Advanced Capitalism*. Helsinki: University of the Arts Helsinki, Theatre Academy.

Thompson, K. D. (2014) *Ring Shout, Wheel About: The Racial Politics of Music and Dance in North American Slavery*. Urbana: University of Illinois Press.

Welsh-Asante, K. (1990) 'Philosophy and dance in Africa: The views of Cabral and Fanon'. *Journal of Black Studies*, 21(2), pp. 224–232. Available at: http://www.jstor.org/stable/2784475

Zeller, J. (2017) 'Reflective practice in the ballet class: Bringing progressive pedagogy to the classical tradition'. *Journal of Dance Education*, 17(3), pp. 99–105. doi: 10.1080/15290824.2017.1326052

1.5 Facilitating individual agency in British contemporary dance technique training

A praxical pedagogical approach

Rachel Rimmer-Piekarczyk

Introduction: agency in turbulent times

In recent years, the higher education dance sector in Britain has faced a series of unprecedented challenges including the marginalisation of arts subjects in lower-level education, increased university tuition fees and a shortage of jobs in the performing arts profession. This has led to a significant number of undergraduate dance programme closures in UK universities. Exacerbating an already challenging landscape for the higher education dance sector is the global Covid-19 pandemic, which resulted in the temporary closure of performing arts venues across the UK and the cancellation of numerous arts-based festivals and events. Although much has been done to improve the conditions of the performing arts industry since the pandemic, this series of events has created a discourse around higher-level performing arts education,[1] which has called its value into question. Consequently, as dance educators, we need to reconsider how the skills acquired within a higher-level performing arts education can enable learners to survive within the current socio-cultural and political climate. A key aspect of this survival is the need for individual agency in order to allow dancers to effectively navigate and disrupt the different, sometimes contradictory value systems and ethical complexities that are evident both within the dance profession and within a broader social context.

In response to these ideas, in this chapter, I examine the relationship between higher-level contemporary dance technique training and the notion of agency. I explore how the teaching and learning practices of dance technique, which originate from the traditions of the choreographic practices of western theatre dance,[2] have constructed a dominant pedagogical discourse that limits opportunities for teachers and learners of dance to exercise agency. According to Michel Foucault (1977, 1981), 'discourse' refers to the different ways of structuring areas of knowledge and social practice. The dominant choreographic discourse of western theatre dance has traditionally foregrounded notions of authority, discipline and physical rigour (Stinson, 1993; Smith, 1998; Roche, 2011; Stanton, 2011). This discourse has been reinforced by an overt lack of reflection and critical thinking, meaning that dancers

DOI: 10.4324/9781003111146-7

have tended to be viewed as unthinking objects of the choreographer's vision. This dynamic establishes a power-based relationship between choreographer and dancer where, as dance scholar Susan Leigh Foster writes, the dancer's body is structured by the 'discourses or practices that *instruct* it' (1997: 235). Consequently, the training practices of western dance techniques have been significantly influenced by the dominant choreographic discourse of the west, which conveys rules of engagement that determine how dance teachers and students should participate in the dance class; the rules at play within a given social arena are what Pierre Bourdieu (1977) describes as the 'doxa'. Without opportunities for reflection and critical thinking, teachers and students may remain unaware of the doxa, which subsequently allows dominant training structures to remain intact. In view of these ideas, the first part of this chapter examines how the external forces of discourse and doxa have, over time, structured the body-minds of teachers and learners of contemporary dance technique in a way that is not conducive with agency.

In the second part of the chapter, I use the work of Brazilian educator Paulo Freire (1972) as a lens to examine the findings of my own ethnographic-action research, which was conducted in a British university in collaboration with undergraduate contemporary dance technique students. I explore the role that critical reflection plays in cultivating agency for teachers and students of contemporary dance technique. I propose the notion of a praxical pedagogy for dance technique training; that is, a pedagogical approach that employs reflection in the process of embodying dance techniques. This is by no means to suggest that dancing is a thoughtless act; in fact, contemporary choreographers such as Wayne McGregor have discussed how dancing itself can be viewed as a thinking process. For example, in his 2012 TED talk, McGregor uses the term 'physical thinking' to explain how choreography can function as a tool for breaking movement habits and stimulating innovation. This is an interesting idea to consider in relation to the agency of the contemporary dancer. In proposing the notion of a praxical pedagogy, the intention is to draw a distinction between the kind of 'pre-reflective' (Maitland, 1995; Zarrilli, 2009) thinking that occurs in the body-mind as the dancer is moving, and the subsequent reflections that arise from the physical practice, once the dancer pauses and steps back to make sense of what has been experienced within the body-mind. This is a key idea within arts practice-as-research methodology, as articulated by Robin Nelson (2013) who proposes that there are different 'modes of knowing' (2013: 38); as such, for the dancer, cognitive knowledge acquired through reflection can be viewed as one mode of knowing that exists on a non-hierarchical spectrum alongside other modes, including embodied knowing. Discussing the findings from my own research, I propose that reflection can allow teachers and learners of dance technique to become aware of the doxa at play within the learning environment and to exercise agency in navigating and disrupting it. A practical illustration of this conception of agency is explored in the final section of the chapter when I discuss the work of contemporary choreographers

Igor and Moreno and explore how these artists display agency through their choreographic practice.

The 'discursive practices' of British contemporary dance technique training

In Foucault's view, discourses, or 'systems of domination' (Foucault, 1981: 52–53) are generated by what he refers to as 'discursive practices'; these are particular ways of thinking, speaking and acting that are determined by the broader discourse. According to Bacchi and Bonham (2014: 174), discursive practices are concerned with understanding:

> how knowledge is formed in the interaction of plural and contingent practices within different sites...The term "discursive practice/s" describes those practices of knowledge formation by focusing on how specific knowledges ("discourses") operate and the work they do.

As such, discursive practices can be considered as the 'practices *of* discourses' (ibid.), such as the specific behaviours, rules and regularities that determine how a social setting, or 'field' to use Bourdieu's (1977) term, operates. It is important to remember that the term 'discursive' does not necessarily relate to verbal modes of communication – in the field of dance technique training, much of the communication that occurs between teachers and students happens through the body and words are not always required to convey a particular meaning. Through regular participation in the field of dance technique training, discursive practices become inscribed within the body-minds of dance teachers and students. For example, this could include the movements and gestures of specific dance techniques, as well as the broader behavioural practices that are used to communicate the rules and values of the field, such as standing at the barre in a ballet class or lying down on the floor in a release-based technique class. Returning to Bourdieu, the embodiment of these practices would be considered as the construction of one's 'habitus' (1977, 1993), which he proposes is comprised of two entities:

- The cognitive perceptions of the field that allow the individual to make sense of her own actions and the actions of others in relation to the rules of engagement. For example, it could be said that dance students gain an understanding of how to participate in the field of the technique class by interpreting the verbal and visual instructions provided by the teacher and observing how other students behave.
- The 'hexis', which refers to the physical dispositions/habits that are acquired by participating in a given field. Since different technique classes (ballet, release, breakdance) operate in accordance to different rules of engagement, the hexis acquired will be different – an example of this would be the physical disposition of turnout in ballet, which is different to

how the legs are organised in a release-based class where dancers usually move from a parallel position.

According to Bourdieu, the habitus determines the extent to which an individual feels at ease within a given field and attuned to the 'rules of the game' (Maton, 2012: 53). For example, a classically trained ballet dancer is likely to feel like a fish out of water in a breakdance class since the habitus a dancer acquires through participation in ballet is significantly different to that of a breakdancer. This is not just because the dance moves have a different aesthetic but because, as dance forms, ballet and breakdance are grounded within different social and cultural discourses; the discursive practices of these discourses determine how each dance class operates and how participants should engage.

Within the dominant teaching and learning practices for contemporary dance techniques, training tends to be structured around the idea of embodying principles from codified vocabularies of movement such as Cunningham, Hawkins, Limón or release-based techniques in order to develop specific skills for performance. This process is directed by the teacher who is viewed as the key source of knowledge and therefore, as the most powerful individual in the room (Stinson, 2015). This sense of power is facilitated by a range of discursive practices; for example, the teacher positioning herself in front of her students who stand behind and attempt to replicate the movements of her body through continuous repetition, thus, establishing a social hierarchy through the spatial organisation and orientation of bodies. Furthermore, students receive verbal or physical 'corrections' from the teacher, presenting the idea that the teacher's body is the ideal example to conform to. Interaction between students is also not customary practice and in fact, 'The teacher's voice is expected to be the only one heard, except in the case of a well-focused question' (Stinson, 2015: 34). Over time, the prevalence of codified techniques has also resulted in an aesthetic where dancers embody the same movements as each other and then perform these movements in unison, the aim being to construct multiple versions of the same dancer who is primed and ready to embark on a career as a professional performer.[3] As such, the notion of being a thinking, feeling individual is not something that has traditionally been foregrounded in contemporary dance technique training.[4] This overtly physical approach to training has also constructed a discourse whereby the reflective capacity of the mind is viewed as having less value than the physical aptitude of the body.

In facilitating a praxical approach to contemporary dance technique training that involves integrating reflective activities, it could be said that the field of the technique class is significantly disrupted. Reflection breaks the traditional rules of engagement by inviting teachers and students to participate differently, therefore producing new behaviour or discursive practices. However, this process of disruption is often not straightforward as before they arrive into higher education, students acquire a habitus that is structured through participation in other dance education fields. This is not to suggest, however, that the habitus is a fixed entity that is unable to shift and change in response to the conditions of new social fields, as discussed later on. Since the dominant discourse for contemporary dance technique training has influenced other educational contexts for dance, the notions of authority, discipline and physical rigour have become normalised. As such, many undergraduate dance students begin their higher-level education with specific expectations around how they will be educated and preconceived ideas about what it means to be a dance student. Thus, if the dance technique class does not operate in accordance to such expectations and ideas, this may create what Bourdieu (1977) refers to as a habitus and field clash.

In the following sections, I explore how the learning environments that dance students participate in before they enter higher education have contributed towards the construction of the dominant discourse for contemporary dance technique training. I examine the discursive practices at play, exploring where reflection and critical thinking are absent and the subsequent impact of this on a student's ability to exercise agency. Although this chapter focuses on employing reflection as a way to empower dance students, it is necessary to acknowledge that there is a dialogical relationship between teachers and students; teachers too are subjects of the dominant discourses and like their students, many will not have been provided with opportunities to become aware of this phenomenon through reflection and critical thinking. Indeed, it could be said that a deliberate lack of reflection and critical thinking is how the British dance profession maintains power and control over its participants. By maintaining specific expectations around how dance teachers should train their students, the dominant discourses are perpetuated, meaning that often, teachers teach in ways that they believe their students expect them to, which establishes a cyclical process that can be difficult to intervene with. I have struggled with this in my own teaching-research where the choice to use reflection as part of my training approach for dance technique has led me to question the extent to which I am providing students with what they perceive as a 'good' learning experience, as discussed later.

The influence of earlier learning: the British BTEC and AS/A Level Dance curriculum and the private dance school syllabus

Before entering the higher education system, whether this be in a university or conservatoire setting, many dance students will have received training in another educational setting such as a private dance school, youth group, sixth form or college. Providing guidance on the various pathways that are available for individuals wishing to embark on a career in teaching dance, One Dance UK (2017: 2) suggests that dance can be taught in a range of educational settings including higher education, further education, secondary school or sixth form (KS3–KS5/S1–S6), primary school (EYFS–KS2/

Primary 1.7), syllabus teaching in a private dance school and community dance settings such as through sport, fitness, health and wellbeing initiatives. This information gives a useful indication of the various routes that students may take towards studying dance in higher education. Based on my experience of teaching dance in a British university from Level Four to Level Seven, the most dominant routes into higher-level dance study tend to be further education, secondary education and private dance schools.[5] As such, students tend to apply to higher education having either attained, or while working towards, one or more of the following level 3 qualifications: AS or A Level Dance, BTEC Level 3 National Extended Certificate in Performing Arts (Dance), as well as graded exam qualifications awarded by national organisations that, in some cases, can be converted into UCAS points.[6] In view of this, it is necessary to explore the role that these educational pathways play in constructing the dominant pedagogical discourse for contemporary dance technique training and, thus, in constructing the habitus of those students who embark on higher-level dance study.

Process driven vs. output driven

In Britain, many undergraduate dance degree programmes assess students through coursework and continuous assessment, particularly where practice is concerned, placing equal emphasis on the process of the learning journey as well as the outcome of the learning, which may take the form of a performance or equivalent performative output. This approach to programme design emphasises the idea that knowledge acquisition in dance is a generative process and there is in fact no conclusive 'end point' to the learning; this idea is particularly relevant to the area of dance technique training as it requires regular daily or weekly practice to enable the embodiment of specific movement skills and the refinement of these skills over time. Speaking about arts practice-as-research where the idea of 'praxis' is key, Nelson (2013: 20) draws a distinction between 'knowledge' and 'knowing', suggesting that knowledge pertains to something more finite and tangible, whereas 'knowing', in the present tense, 'acknowledges a subject engaged in a processual relationship spatially more proximal to the object to be understood'. By using reflection to uncover further layers of knowledge that may be implicit within her embodied practice, the dancer can be viewed as being engaged in a praxical, processual pedagogy that allows her body-mind to exist as an unfixed entity, evolving through space and time.

This conception of dance technique training seems to directly contradict the approach to learning and assessment that is foregrounded within the British AS and A Level programme design for dance. The 2021 version of the AQA specification for AS and A Level Dance proposes that it gives students 'the skills and experience to better prepare them for the demands of higher education or the workplace' (2019: 5) by placing equal emphasis on the practical and theoretical aspects of dance. However, the assessments for both the practical and theoretical areas take the form of examinations, with no coursework element built into the assessment framework. The idea of acknowledging process seems absent in this programme design and, thus, reinforces the notion of output-driven learning that allows dancers' bodies to be externally objectified by an examiner who may have little sense of the physical and cognitive journey undertaken, unless the written assignments incorporate a reflective dimension.

This approach to learning is reinforced by representations of dance seen within popular culture. For example, reality television shows such as *So You Think You Can Dance, The Greatest Dancer* and *Strictly Come Dancing* show individuals (who are in some cases celebrities) competing against each other to perform dances with the greatest level of technical virtuosity and spectacle. Contestants' bodies are externally objectified by a public audience and a celebrity judging panel who at times, appear to 'empower' them by applauding their performance and at other times are highly critical or even derogatory. In this environment, contestants are the subjects of the judges' vision and the underlying power imbalance in this relationship mirrors that of dance technique teacher/examiner and student. Although some television shows do try to present participants as having a sense of agency by inviting them to reflect on their individual journeys during conversational video pieces, the extent to which individual agency can be exercised in a controlled environment that views dance, and its participants, as commodities for the purpose of entertainment is debatable.

In contrast, the BTEC Extended Certificate foregrounds the practical aspects of learning dance with a view to preparing learners for direct progression into the workplace or 'via study at a higher-level' (Pearson, 2021: 5). Thus, BTECs have been traditionally viewed as a vocationally-orientated qualification and this is reflected in the nature of the assessments, which are both internally and externally assessed (depending on the unit being studied) and must evidence knowledge through the 'practical demonstration of skills' (Pearson, 2021: 45). Forms of evidence can include projects, recordings of performances, oral or written presentations and logbooks (ibid.). Interestingly, reflective journals are also cited as a form of evidence. While on the one hand, this is reassuring, the degree to which BTEC students will be prepared for keeping reflective journals is not easily determinable in the specification itself. Experience has shown me that often, it is assumed that students will automatically know how to reflect on their practice, yet this is largely dependent upon a teacher's enthusiasm towards nurturing a reflective disposition in students. Based on what has been learned about the lack of reflection and critical thinking in dance training more generally, it cannot be presumed that all dance teachers in further education will understand how to enable BTEC students to reflect on their practice; and this reinforces the need for a praxical pedagogy to more effectively support dance teachers and students in reflecting on their practice, much earlier in their educational journeys.

Linear learning

Posing a further challenge, the AQA AS and A Level specification describes the qualification as being 'linear' in nature, meaning that 'students will sit all their exams and submit all their non-exam assessment at the end of the course' (AQA, 2019: 9). This approach to assessing students appears to view the learning of dance as a chronological process, with the examination symbolising that the learning is now 'complete'. As established earlier, the embodiment of dance movements is a skill that is acquired over time, and often, the learning is rarely linear but engages the dancer in a continuous process of physical discovery, supported through ongoing reflection on her practice. This idea can be viewed in relation to psychophysical approaches to actor training. Scholars Jane Turner and Patrick Campbell (2021: 150–151) state that: 'Psychophysical practices are not necessarily assimilated in a sequential order; they are deeply embodied processes wherein learning actively occurs in and through the body over time.'

Psychophysical training also incorporates a reflective dimension, which allows the actors to exercise agency by taking up the position of 'autodidact' (Turner and Campbell, 2021: 155) in relation to their performance practice and engaging in a continuous process of exploration and questioning. In contrast, the extent to which learners undertaking an AS, A Level or BTEC qualification in dance are able to be inquisitive and reflective is unclear and this poses a question regarding the value that is placed upon reflection within these different pathways.[7] Given that the BTEC and AS/A Level are the two of the most dominant routes into higher education, perhaps this is one of the reasons why scholars have questioned the extent to which further education prepares individuals for studying dance at undergraduate level (Stevens, 2006). This topic was explored at the 2006 Palatine seminar where HE lecturers were invited to discuss their experiences of delivering dance in UK universities.[8] The findings from this seminar demonstrate that often, there is a 'mismatch' (Stevens, 2006) between students' expectations of how dance will be taught within UK higher education and the reality of how provision is actually delivered.[9] This is of particular interest where dance technique is concerned since students generally expect a fast-paced mode of delivery that pushes their physical limits; the quieter and slower practices of reflection or somatic-based explorations often come as a surprise to students, as I discovered in my own research, discussed later.

Embodied capital

Another common training route through which students access higher education in Britain is the private dance school sector. In this setting, training typically focuses on learning a syllabus of sequences of a perceived level[10] and dance 'style' such as ballet, tap, jazz, freestyle and so on. Students are then assessed on their ability to embody the specific style being learned and practical examinations are the only method of assessment (www.onedanceuk. org). Similar to the AS and A Level syllabus, the emphasis on examinations seems to reinforce the idea of output-orientated learning, since this method of assessment does not appear to place any value on the starting point of the learner and the physical and cognitive learning journey that has taken place. In this way, examiners are encouraged to perceive students merely as objects rather than thinking, feeling individuals who have been through a process. Alongside exam preparation, students may also participate in annual showcases hosted by the school in which they perform dances for the public or in some cases, national competitions in which they compete against other schools or groups from the UK.

The approach seen in the private dance school sector seems to position dance as a purely practical pursuit that constitutes a form of entertainment. Furthermore, the emphasis on competition that is evident in some private dance school settings appears to privilege the notion of physical virtuosity, or what Bourdieu (1977) would refer to as embodied capital, a form of power that allows the individual to move further up the hierarchy within the field. From this perspective, it could be said that dance students are encouraged to view embodied capital as being of more value than cognitive capital, as opposed to placing an equal value on both. This training seems to offer a rather narrow experience of dance that emphasises physical virtuosity, entertainment and hierarchy. With that said, speaking as a woman who grew up in a working-class city in Britain and initially trained in a private dance school setting myself, I am aware of how many students access higher education through this route. Although I have mainly discussed the challenges surrounding the training practices in this sector, it could be argued that there are many positives to taking this route into dance, especially in relation to class and widening participation. For example, private studios can offer an accessible and generally inclusive introduction to dance that subsequently provides a route into higher education.[11] Indeed, the majority of the students who participated in my study discussed their experiences as students in private dance schools and many of these students were also first-generation university students. Although the private dance studio shapes a student's habitus in a very particular way, a praxical pedagogy can allow the individual to explore how she has been structured by the training practices in this field and how her body-mind can be used as a positive force for change.

A pathway to individual agency in British dance technique training

In view of the ideas discussed, it is necessary to examine what agency means for the dancer who has entered higher education through one of the routes discussed and to explore the role that reflection plays in cultivating agency. 'Agency' is the idea that individuals have control over their ability to act autonomously, to exercise choice and free will (Barnes, 2000). However, as established earlier, in the case of dance technique training, teachers and students assume a 'subject position' (Davies, 1991: 53) in relation to a doxa that determines how the dance technique class operates and how its participants behave. In reality, this means that any agency is always going to be exercised within the constraints of the doxa. Therefore, it is necessary to rethink the idea of doxa by departing from the notion that the rules of engagement are fixed and unchangeable, and instead viewing the doxa as a flexible structure through which agency emerges.[12] Many dance scholars have attempted to do this by teaching from critical, emancipatory and somatic perspectives; and this is evident in the work of many of the dance scholars who have contributed to this volume. While this work is essential for the field, research by dance scholar Dragon (2015) demonstrates that progressive pedagogies fall short when there is a lack of reflection and dialogue between teachers and students and as such, the underlying value and belief systems of these teaching approaches remain silently embedded. This means that a pedagogy which is meant to empower dance teachers and students inadvertently becomes another form of control. Speaking from the perspective of critical pedagogy, which has historically emphasised the idea of empowering communities whose voices have been suppressed, Freire (2005: 125–126) writes, 'Human activity is theory and practice; it is reflection and action...revolution is achieved with neither verbalism nor activism, but rather with praxis, that is, with *reflection* and *action* directed at the structures to be transformed.' This quote reinforces the importance of a praxical relationship between reflection and action in order to expose teachers and learners of dance to the underlying doxa that controls their behaviour. By employing reflection as a learning tool in contemporary dance technique training, teachers and learners of dance can develop an understanding of the discourses they are shaped by, which are often operating simultaneously and, at times, with contradictory value systems (Fortin et al., 2009).

Embedding reflection and action in dance technique training: a praxical pedagogy

As discussed earlier, nurturing a reflective disposition in undergraduate dance students is not straightforward. I know this from the first-hand experience of conducting my own ethnographic-action research in which I have examined the use of what I refer to as a 'reflexive-dialogical' approach to teaching dance technique in an undergraduate university dance class.[13] Contact hours between students and teachers are extremely precious in the HE environment,[14] opportunities to go 'flat out' with dancing may be sparse and so, understandably, students do not want to spend this time talking or writing, but being immersed in the flow of dancing. As such, it could be said that the physical and mental states of dancing and reflecting do not easily align with each other.

In my own teacher-led research, I have explored methods for enabling dancers to move fluidly between these body-mind states, allowing what could be considered as a 'feedback loop' (Ehrenberg, 2010: 175) to occur between the dancing and reflective practices.[15] Peer feedback activities involving observation to facilitate reflective discussions around the technical components of a dance sequence, as well as the performative aspects, are one approach I have explored. By allowing students to observe and feedback to each other about their dancing, not only does it empower learners by shifting the onus away from the teacher, but a dialogue emerges between dancer and observer that arises out of a kinaesthetic empathy. For example, within the context of my research, students often commented on the experience of watching someone else dancing and having a sense of empathy because they understood how a particular movement felt on a bodily level; and not only did this allow them to reflect on their own execution of that movement, but they could offer more informed feedback to their partner by drawing on their own embodied experience of it. With that said, the use of a more democratic learning approach such as peer feedback does not come without challenges, especially in a learning environment that is built upon the idea that the teacher is the fountain of knowledge. For example, enabling students to articulate feedback effectively or to value each other's comments in the same way that they value feedback from the teacher can be problematic, but this does not mean that it is not worth exploring as part of a praxical pedagogy.

In addition, within my teaching, I have researched the idea of developing a culture of scepticism by enabling learners to question dominant ideas or truths that are communicated through the teaching of dance techniques. For example, on occasions when students have questioned technical or performative details of the movement being taught, I have made conscious efforts not to provide straightforward, concrete answers, but to open questions out for dialogue. Although some students have expressed frustration with this approach as it interrupts the physical practice, my argument is that it disrupts the dominant narrative that dance techniques are fixed entities for which teachers hold all the answers. With that said, it should be acknowledged that in adopting a critical stance, it is the responsibility of teachers to communicate with students about their reasons for doing so – this allows students to ask questions and to contribute towards the development of critical pedagogical approaches, ensuring that this a dialogical process.

During the course of my research, the students frequently questioned my use of a reflexive-dialogical approach to teaching dance technique. This was initially difficult for me, but I have now come to accept such questioning as an essential part of instigating change. Many students have discussed the challenge around finding reflection to be a disruptive activity that jars with the body-mind state occupied when dancing. This is something that I have often found myself grappling with, and still do in my current teaching practice. While there are no easy answers to this dilemma, my research findings demonstrate that overall, the students viewed reflection as having value within the broader educational and professional dance landscape, and they were able to recognise how it contributed to their development as contemporary dance practitioners and their ability to exercise agency.

Concluding thoughts: the value of a praxical pedagogy in relation to the contemporary dancer and the creation of new choreographic languages

The intention of a praxical pedagogy is by no means to undermine the embodied knowing of the dancer or to somehow privilege the cognitive capacity of the mind over the body, but rather to view reflection as an additional skill that empowers the dancer to develop what Freire (1972) calls a 'critical consciousness'. For the dancer, a critical consciousness encompasses a cognitive awareness of the dominant discourses at play, and the ability to use the body-mind as a force to intervene with such discourses. This process of intervention can allow the dancer to consciously construct her own moving identity (Roche, 2011, 2015) by embodying ideas from a range of pedagogical and aesthetic discourses, as opposed to passively allowing techniques to be layered onto her body-mind. Through this praxical approach to dance technique training, the dancer not only exercises agency to navigate and disrupt the discourses available to her, but she constructs new and alternative discourses in the process.

A practical illustration of this conception of agency can be seen in the work of contemporary dance duo, Igor and Moreno who describe themselves as contemporary dancers, makers and thinkers. To create their choreography, the artists draw upon their eclectic backgrounds in Sardinian Basque folk dance and singing, Latin American, Ballroom, modern and contemporary dance techniques. In their 2015 choreography, *Idiot-Syncrasy*, the pair present a physical language of continuous jumps, twists and turns that is grounded in the principles of Basque folk dance, yet appears inflected with aesthetics from modern and postmodern dance. For example, the spiralling torso from Cunningham technique and the loose-limbed execution of release-based techniques – presumably a result of their training undertaken at the London Contemporary Dance School – is meshed with the continuous jumping from Basque folk dance, creating a distinctive aesthetic that demonstrates the duo's ability to navigate and embody ideas from several different movement discourses. This ability to incorporate a 'multiplicity' (Roche, 2011, 2015) of ideas into the body-mind could be viewed as a physical conception of agency that arises out of critical engagement with the underlying values of each movement system and the deliberate disruption of such values through choreographic innovation. A praxical pedagogy incorporating reflection is one way to facilitate agency of this nature, allowing the dancer to survive within a constantly evolving dance profession, situated within a complex socio-cultural and political context.

Notes

1 By 'higher-level', I am referring to British universities and conservatoires that offer undergraduate and postgraduate provision in the performing arts.
2 When using the term 'western', I am referring to the choreographic practices of North American and British dance that have significantly influenced the pedagogical practices and content of the dance curriculum in British higher dance education. However, I also recognise the problematic nature of this definition and although this chapter does not deal directly with the decolonisation of the curriculum, it should be acknowledged that engagement with dominant 'western' dance practices constructs a body-mind in which particular perceptions and dispositions are incorporated.
3 I acknowledge that more recently, the area of dance studies has questioned this view of the dancer and this approach to training in response to the shifting landscape of professional dance performance and the individuality of dancers (see Roche, 2011, 2015).
4 The area of somatic practices has greatly assisted the field of contemporary dance training by offering methods for enabling dancers to acquire greater levels of authority over their body-minds. See Fortin (1994, 1998), Fortin et al. (2002), Green (1998, 1999, 2001, 2002), Enghauser (2007), Fortin et al. (2009), Dyer (2009, 2010), Weber (2009), Burnidge (2012) and Reed (2016).
5 I know this from my experience as the Programme Leader for the BA Hons Dance Programme at Manchester Metropolitan University (2014–2019) where I worked closely with the recruitment and admissions team to assess applications for entry onto the course.
6 For example, higher-level qualifications such as those awarded by The Royal Academy of Dance, International Dance Teachers' Association or the British Ballet Organisation.
7 This lack of value around reflection is also evident in the OCR AS and A Level Drama and Theatre syllabus, which features the work of the physical theatre company *Frantic Assembly*. In a recent critical text by Evans and Smith (2021) exploring the training and devising processes of *Frantic*, the body is clearly foregrounded and viewed as a highly energetic tool for creating performance. Yet the quieter process of reflection is not discussed or acknowledged as a method for informing the creative process or the embodiment of the movements being learned.
8 Palatine was the former Higher Education Academy subject centre for the performing arts.
9 This was a finding from the 2006 seminar report by Palatine for which lecturers were invited to discuss their experiences of teaching contemporary dance techniques in British universities.
10 For example, Grade One, Two and so on.
11 I say generally because there can be many invisible costs associated with a private dance school training such as lesson payments, uniforms, costumes and exam fees, which can make it an expensive pursuit and therefore, more exclusive than inclusive.
12 In previous research, I have referred to this flexible structure as a 'doxic agreement', suggesting that through the discursive practices at play in the dance class, teachers and students enter into an unconscious agreement with each other

that determines how they will behave; and furthermore, different dance classes operate in accordance to different doxic agreements. See Rimmer (2017).
13 The findings from this research, which was conducted between 2014 and 2021, can be viewed in my PhD thesis, 'Doxic agreements and the mobilisation of agency: examining students' engagement with cognitive reflection in relation to the dominant pedagogical discourses of western dance technique education' (2021), which can be accessed online at: https://e-space.mmu.ac.uk/629427/
14 Here, I am predominantly referring to university programmes, which, unlike conservatoires which may have more autonomy, come under pressure to conform to the timetabling structures determined by the institution.
15 In my own teaching and research, I have employed Phillip Zarrilli's (2009, 2020) psychophysical approach to actor training as a lens to explore how the dancer slips between a nexus of body-mind states in which body and/or mind come to the fore at different moments. Again, my analysis of this idea can be viewed in my PhD thesis.

References

AQA (2019) *A Level Dance Specification*. Available at: https://filestore.aqa.org.uk/resources/dance/specifications/AQA-7237-SP-2016.PDF

Bacchi, C. and Bonham, J. (2014) 'Reclaiming discursive practices as an analytic focus: Political implications', *Foucault Studies*, 17, pp. 173–192. https://doi.org/10.22439/fs.v0i17.4298

Barnes, B. (2000) *Understanding Agency: Social Theory and Responsible Action*. London: SAGE.

Bourdieu, P. (1977) *Outline of a Theory of Practice*. Cambridge: Cambridge University Press.

Bourdieu, P. (1993) *Sociology in Question*. London: SAGE.

Burnidge, A. (2012) 'Somatics in the dance studio: Embodying feminist/democratic pedagogy', *Journal of Dance Education*, 12(2), pp. 37–47. https://doi.org/10.1080/15290824.2012.634283

Davies, B. (1991) 'The concept of agency. A feminist poststructuralist analysis', *Social Analysis*, 0(30), pp. 42–53. http://www.jstor.org/stable/23164525

Dragon, D. (2015) 'Creating cultures of teaching and learning: Conveying dance and somatic education pedagogy', *Journal of Dance Education*, 15(1), pp. 25–32. https://doi.org/10.1080/15290824.2014.995015

Dyer, B. (2009) 'Merging traditional technique vocabularies with democratic teaching perspectives in dance education: A consideration of aesthetic values and their socio-political contexts', *Journal of Aesthetic Education*, 43(4), pp. 108–123. https://www.jstor.org/stable/25656251

Dyer, B. (2010) 'The perils, privileges and pleasures of seeking right from wrong: Reflecting upon students perspectives of social processes, value systems, agency and the becoming of identity in the dance technique classroom', *Research in Dance Education*, 11(2), pp. 109–129. https://doi.org/10.1080/14647893.2010.482978

Ehrenberg, S. (2010) 'Reflections on reflections: Mirror use in a university training environment', *Theatre, Dance and Performance Training*, 1(2), pp. 172–184. https://doi.org/10.1080/19443927.2010.505001

Enghauser, R. (2007) 'Developing listening bodies in the dance technique class: When you dance, what is your body telling you?', *The Journal of Physical Education*,

Recreation and Dance, 78(6), pp. 33–54. https://doi.org/10.1080/07303084.2007. 10598039

Evans, M. and Smith, M. (2021) *Frantic Assembly*. Abingdon: Routledge.

Fortin, S. (1994) 'When dance science and somatics enter the dance technique class', *Kinesiology and Medicine for Dance*, 12(2), pp. 88–107.

Fortin, S. (1998) 'Somatics: A tool for empowering modern dance teachers', in Shapiro, S. (ed.) *Dance, Power, and Difference: Critical and Feminist Perspectives on Dance Education*. Champaign, IL: Human Kinetics, pp. 49–71.

Fortin, S., Long, W. and Lord, M. (2002) 'Three voices: Researching how somatic education informs contemporary dance technique classes', *Research in Dance Education*, 3(2), pp. 15–179. https://doi.org/10.1080/1464789022000034712

Fortin, S., Vieira, A. and Tremblay, M. (2009), 'The experience of discourses in dance and somatics', *Journal of Dance and Somatic Practices*, 1(1), pp. 47–64. https://doi.org/10.1386/jdsp.1.1.47_1

Foster, S. (1997) 'Dancing bodies', in Desmond, J.C. (ed.) *Meaning in Motion: New Cultural Studies of Dance*. London: Duke University Press, pp. 235–257.

Foucault, M. (1977) *Discipline and Punish: The Birth of the Prison*. New York: Pantheon Books.

Foucault, M. (1981) 'The order of discourse', in Young, R. (ed.) *Untying the Text: A Post-Structuralist Reader*. London: Routledge, pp. 48–78.

Freire, P. (1972) *Cultural Action for Freedom*. Harmondsworth: Penguin.

Freire, P. (2005) *Pedagogy of the Oppressed*. London: The Continuum International Publishing Group.

Green, J. (1998) 'Engendering bodies: Somatic stories in dance education'. Paper presented in the *Annual Meeting of the American Educational Research Association* conference proceedings, April 13–17.

Green, J. (1999) 'Somatic authority and the myth of the ideal body in dance education', *Dance Research Journal*, 31(2), pp. 80–100.

Green, J. (2001) 'Socially constructed bodies in American dance classrooms', *Research in Dance Education*, 2(2), pp. 155–173. https://doi.org/10.1080/14647890120100782

Green, J. (2002) 'Somatic knowledge: The body as content and methodology in dance education', *Journal of Dance Education*, 2(4), pp. 114–118. https://doi.org/10.1080/15290824.2002.10387219

Maitland, J. (1995) *Spacious Body: Explorations in Somatic Ontology*. Berkley: North Atlantic Books.

Maton, K. (2012) 'Habitus', in Grenfell, M. (ed.) *Pierre Bourdieu: Key Concepts* (2nd ed.) Abingdon: Routledge, pp. 48–64.

McGregor, W. (2012) *A Choreographer's Creative Process in Real Time*. TED Talk. 14 Sept. Available at: https://www.youtube.com/watch?v=KPPxXeoIzRY

Nelson, R. (2013) *Practice as Research in the Arts: Principles, Protocols, Pedagogies and Resistances*. London: Palgrave Macmillan.

One Dance UK (2017) *Dance Teaching Pathways: Guidance on Routes into Teaching and Qualifications*. Available at: https://www.onedanceuk.org/wp-content/uploads/2018/10/Dance-Teaching-Pathways.pdf

Pearson (2021) *BTEC Level Three National Extended Certificate in Performing Arts Specification*. Available at: https://qualifications.pearson.com/content/dam/pdf/BTEC-Nationals/Performing-Arts/2016/specification-and-sample-assessments/9781446938362_BTEC_Nat_ExtCert_PA_Spec_Iss2C.pdf

Reed, S. (2016) 'Dance somatics as radical pedagogy: Reflections on somatic practice within UK higher education and training in dance', in Coogan, J. (ed.) *Practicing Dance: A Somatic Orientation*. Berlin: Logos Verlag, pp. 176–180.

Rimmer, R. (2017) 'Negotiating the rules of engagement: Exploring perceptions of dance technique learning through Bourdieu's concept of 'Doxa'', *Research in Dance Education*, 18(3), pp. 221–236. https://doi.org/10.1080/14647893.2017.1354836

Roche, J. (2011) 'Embodying multiplicity: The independent contemporary dancer's moving identity', *Research in Dance Education*, 12(2), pp. 105–118. https://doi.org/10.1080/14647893.2011.575222

Roche, J. (2015) *Multiplicity, Embodiment and the Contemporary Dancer: Moving Identities*. Basingstoke: Palgrave Macmillan.

Smith, C. (1998) 'On authoritarianism in the dance classroom', in Shapiro, S. (ed.) *Dance, Power and Difference: Critical and Feminist Perspectives on Dance Education*. Champaign, IL: Human Kinetics, pp. 123–146.

Stanton, E. (2011) 'Doing, re-doing and undoing: Practice, repetition and critical evaluation as mechanisms for learning in a dance technique class 'laboratory'', *Theatre, Dance and Performance Training*, 2(1), pp. 86–98. https://doi.org/10.1080/19443927.2011.545253

Stevens, J. (2006) 'Re-thinking dance technique in higher education', *Higher Education Academy: Palatine Report*. Available at: http://78.158.56.101/archive/palatine/events/viewreport/309/

Stinson, S. (1993) 'Journey towards a feminist pedagogy for dance', *Women & Performance: A Journal of Feminist Theory*, 6(1), pp. 131–146. https://doi.org/10.1080/07407709308571170

Stinson, S. (2015) *Embodied Curriculum Theory and Research in Arts Education: A Dance Scholar's Search for Meaning*. London: Springer International Publishing.

Turner, J. and Campbell, P. (2021) *A Poetics of Third Theatre: Performer Training, Dramaturgy, Cultural Action*. London: Routledge.

Weber, R. (2009) 'Integrating semi-structured somatic practices and contemporary dance technique training', *Journal of Dance and Somatic Practices*, 1(2), pp. 237–254. https://doi.org/10.1386/jdsp.1.2.237_1

Zarrilli, P. (2009) *Psychophysical Acting: An Intercultural Approach After Stanislavski*. Abingdon: Routledge.

Zarrilli, P. (2020) *(Toward) A Phenomenology of Acting*. Abingdon: Routledge.

Part II

Practices

Introduction

This second part of the volume features perspectives from current studio practice. At the Dance Technique and Performance Training roundtable, which took place at University of Winchester in 2018 as a precurser to this edited collection, dance teachers from various contexts shared concerns regarding the challenges of evolving more inclusive, mindful and socially engaged ways for practicing dance together. Appetite for a reassessment of what we are each doing with the principles and passions upon which we build our pedagogies appeared to be widespread. This part of the collection thus features a series of chapters examining the values embedded in dance technique training and offers proposals for embedding an ethical dance practice. The chapters each explore ways in which practitioners are developing and using dance technique classes to build up skills and awareness that are necessary to prepare students for the ethical challenges of twenty-first century dance work. In her Introduction, Colin asks if 'dancing well can be considered an action in the service of good?' Taken together the chapters in this section point to values for social engagement foregrounding the diverse, distinctive, inclusive and mindful approaches through which we share practice. Techniques that enable training in dance to be considered as an ethical action ring out and echo across these six chapters. They include skills for building ethical relationships through attention, care, empathy, moral judgement, somatics, collectivity, togetherness and kinship as part of training to dance 'well'.

The first chapter in part two is rooted in the premise that learning in dance is exploratory and relational. From this premise, Jamieson Dryburgh examines how classes can generate practices that help learners to navigate social values of human agency, connectivity, collective effort and interrelatedness. Dryburgh examines dance technique pedagogy from his perspective of teaching contemporary dance practice at a Higher Education conservatoire, proposing that through precision, particularity and plurality dance techniques can be a means to discover how to move purposefully through the world in ethical relationship with others. Dryburgh draws on examples from his own class work as he unpacks the value of opportunities for learners to

DOI: 10.4324/9781003111146-8

develop curiosity and an alert responsiveness, recognise difference and build up individual distinctiveness, and to be attentive to changing circumstance for revealing possibilities. In this chapter, Dryburgh examples how inclusive dance practice can build capacities for social engagement.

In the following chapter, Carla Trim-Vamben and Jo Read also reflect on opportunities offered by curricula design foregrounding distinctive and shared practices. Their concern is with effectively navigating the intersections of popular dance culture and Higher Education level study, as part of a commitment to challenging the Eurocentric canon which dominates Higher Education dance training. Their chapter draws on their experience of running the BA Dance: Urban Practice course to discuss the ethics and values inherent within rich diverse cultures and the challenges and opportunities these contribute to dance technique training. They discuss the value of embodied knowing and the ethical considerations of contextual historical referencing and new technologies. In critically examining the influences of terminology, expectation and relationships on the learner and the wider community, they probe the socio-cultural connections which are embedded in urban dance which has roots in popular, social, Afro-diasporic and Asian-diasporic dance practices.

Catherine Seago's chapter reflects on connectedness within contemporary dance training, proposing that an agile and empathetic use of attention in dance technique practice can foster a sense of connectedness with others, as well as amongst ideas and practices. Seago draws on her Higher Education teaching practice and recent action research to explore how attention is commonly viewed and valued in dance training and how a bricolage-style approach to classes can help to enable an agile use of attention and build up empathetic skills when practicing with others. Seago proposes that attentional awareness should be foregrounded as part of dance training arguing that greater awareness of how we attend to practicing physical agility together can help dancers to develop an ethical agility through awareness, sensitivity and empathy. In this chapter, Seago reflects on the usefulness of attentional awareness for building up skills and values of connectedness for working within and beyond dance.

In the next chapter, Tamara Ashley similarly foregrounds the importance of being ethically agile. She begins from the premise that racism permeates every aspect of social, cultural and political life and her concern is with developing teaching and learning processes and dialogues that can respond to and serve the student through care in changing times. In her chapter, she outlines her steps towards an ethical anti-racist teaching practice. In seeking to further decolonise her teaching of Contact Improvisation (CI), she expands on the three steps she is using. She draws on wider CI practices, locating them within a current socio-political context, to demonstrate her critical, activist and reflective processes in approaching class work. She explores the entanglements evident in embodied histories and considers the ethics of acknowledging bias and uncovering embedded references and the values and challenges of inclusivity and feeling safe.

Foregrounding ethics, Rosemary (Rosa) Cisneros, Marie-Louise Crawley and Karen Wood's chapter asks how the values of care, empathy, moral judgement and inclusivity can be central to dance training experiences which negotiate entanglements between the physical and the digital. Their chapter uses two European-funded dance projects, WhoLoDancE and CultureMoves, to discuss how digital toolkits can promote collaboration, reflection and analysis to reveal hidden aspects of embodied knowledge and co-creation processes, expanding learners' understanding of dance material can be created, transmitted, stored and archived. They introduce ethical considerations using theories of Ethics of Care and Embodied Ethics to discuss data collection and ownership when dancing bodies become bodies of data, identity formation and social engagement.

In the final chapter, Erica Stanton's looks closely at her own experience of dance practice and daily life. She asks how each of us is informed by our training and questions what is preserved and possible, as well as what we should do with lofty visions and past relics to enable our classes to stay alive through the exciting instability that we find. Her chapter draws from the 'Simply for the doing' project (see also the manifesto) which brings together peers and has been motivated by personal illness and medical diagnosis. The 'tools for survival, resistance and kinship', she says, 'are all present in the dance technique class'. Stanton's writing moves fluidly between the present and the past; voices, ghosts and possibilities. She sees class as a gathering of dance, people and daily life. She proposes 'togethering' and explores the rich possibilities coming from triangulating the teacher, learner and the work which allows we, us, conversation and kinship.

2.1 Material matters

Jamieson Dryburgh

Entering in

Learning through dance technique can be a practice of bodily discovery through which embodied knowledges are honed. It can simultaneously enable understandings of oneself as part of a collective learning/living among others (Bannon 2018). Therefore, instead of the dance technique class being a place of coercion and conformity, it can be a location from which learning is explorative and relational. Entering into such thinking about dance technique counters the conventional limitations of learning in the studio as the development of body skills alone (Stinson 2004). Through this chapter, I argue that dance technique affords opportunities for the learner to develop curiosity and positively recognise difference as it is embodied in the studio. As such, learning dance technique offers pathways towards increasing bodily sophistication and social engagement. I am speaking from my experience as a contemporary dance technique teacher in conservatoire settings in the UK for over 25 years. Consequently, this chapter opens up the concepts of dance technique pedagogy from my perspective as a practitioner, and with reference to the strategies, I employ in the studio.

As is commonplace, my teaching of dance technique utilises set movement materials. Movement materials, as I use the term here, refer to dance content generated by me, the teacher, and taught to the students as 'set' exercises, tasks, phrases or sequences. These materials provide the means by which the dancers practice the stylistically defined technique concepts (release-based contemporary dance in my case) and train their bodily capabilities. In a process of training, the materials may be repeated and returned to multiple times during a session or subsequent sessions. However, when the materials are approached exploratively, the dance technique class can open up many opportunities for the learner to enhance movement sophistication while developing their unique sense of the moving self among others. To contextualise this, I will later use social anthropologist Tim Ingold's (2018) consideration of precision as the focus of skilful practice.

When the materials of a dance class are considered matter with which to inquire, thinking about active learning in the dance technique studio

DOI: 10.4324/9781003111146-9

shifts beyond being right in a fixed or singularly defined way. Learning flows from that which is revealed uniquely through/in/of the body. As such, dance technique is a practice that enables distinctiveness through the honing of details and ownership of movement concepts that are intrinsic to the materials. Thus, I employ the terms particularity and plurality to signal the personal and relational experiences of learning in the dance technique class. In a dance class with peers, the possibilities for learning with/through movement materials are expanded by drawing from each other, navigating dissonance and being accountable to those among whom one is learning (Dryburgh 2020). Consequently, the dance class can generate practices that navigate social values of human agency, connectivity, collective effort and interrelatedness. For dance education, this is essential if a technique is to be more than the acquisition of an exclusively specific skill set that is only relevant in a narrowly defined context for the chosen few. Techniques of the body can rather teach us about how to navigate the world, build our capacities to engage in socially complex contexts and find our ways to share space in common projects. Therefore, dance technique can be a means to discover how to move purposefully through the world in ethical relationship with others.

I believe that the dance technique class can be a location within which all students are enabled to contribute to the shared learning experience. Towards this, dance pedagogy can work progressively for inclusion such that normative and hierarchical attitudes of ability are challenged and more socially just values might be enacted. I believe this is important in our experiences of learning in the studio because it models ways of being that are democratic, working towards greater social equity and resistant to current educational/industry pressures of competition, self-promotion and individualisation. It is argued that the value of dance training is evidenced not only in the quality of achievements by the individual student but also their quality of life and roles as artistic citizens (Bannon 2018, Schupp 2018, Tregear et al. 2016). I concur, and through the ensuing discussion, I advocate for learning dance technique as a relational practice that both emanate from the personal while also being collectively experienced. Later, I shall describe an activity from my teaching practice called 'Gatherings' that is designed to enable such an approach to shared learning. To put this teaching strategy in context, I expand the thinking that underpins my pedagogical approach.

Technique as practice

Dance technique is not a fixed entity defined by a singular set of criteria. Technique styles are various, and each has specific priorities that are culturally, aesthetically and historically influenced. Even within a particular dance style, movement principles can be codified in diverse ways and with different emphases. My particular interest, as a dance technique teacher, is to enable an involvement with movement possibilities. Honing dance technique can be approached as an increasingly sophisticated engagement with stylistically defined movement concepts. A useful way of thinking about how dance technique might be thus approached is encapsulated in the term 'Technique-ing'. This term originated in the explication of dance technique training by eminent contemporary dance practitioner and visionary, Gill Clarke, as something that one is engaged with rather than a thing to be achieved (Clarke, Cramer and Muller 2011). As such, dance technique is not about the acquisition and attainment of body skills but rather a movement intelligence that opens up choices about how to move (Parviainen 2002, Reed 2018). Such embodied knowing arises through the practice of moving and sensing wherein mind and body are 'holistically intertwined' (Spatz 2015: 11). Flowing from this, learning dance technique can be engaged with as a practice through which knowledge arises by tuning-into the body.

Precision

Tuning-into the body enables the dance technique learner to hone the skilfulness of their practice. According to Ingold (2018), skilful practice concerns precision. He makes a clear distinction between skill and habit stating that the ability to perform a motor operation without thought indicates the loss of skill rather than the acquisition of it. Thus, the possibility to perform an action automatically, while accurate and efficient, serves to render the action as mechanistic. Conversely, Ingold suggests, skill lies in the sensitivity with which movements can be adjusted. This is because precision flows from 'a close perceptual monitoring of the task as it unfolds' (Ingold 2011: 161). Consequently, skill concerns doing/moving responsively such that the practitioner adjusts the operation while in the midst of performing it. Translation of this idea to the dance technique class lies in the dancer's attentiveness to the changing circumstances of movement through the body, in space, among others.

As such dance technique can be redefined more holistically as skilful practice through which the dancer pays attention or 'stretches toward' (Ingold 2018) that with which they are kinetically engaged. This concerns an attentiveness to how one is physically located, sensorially attuned and emotionally connected within one's evolving context. Thus, in training environments, we might cultivate practices that enable learners to discover more about who they are and how they might move into and through the world. Dance academic and practitioner, Ann Cooper Alright, describes such learning experiences as 'training students for a life of thinking with, though, and about their embodied perspective' (2017: 63).

In order to enable this alert responsiveness in my teaching, I locate the movement materials as propositions. They are the content through which the learners can explore, practice and hone technique concepts. Functioning as dance problems, or puzzles, the movement materials invite inquiry rather than a replicable form. In class, I might set up inquiry by initiating a specific focus, for example the relationship of the Sitz bones and heels, weight of the arms or sequential actions across the centreline. Alternatively, I might raise questions about the learners' movement experiences to expand and simultaneously direct exploration. For example, 'What's going on through the vertical reach of the body?', 'In what ways can you change the dynamic as you transition into the next action?' and 'What are you noticing feels important right now?'. These prompts are intended to reorient the dancer from 'getting it right' to tuning-in to the live possibilities of their dancing through the materials. These, and other, strategies work to progressively shift the learning approach from unthinking replication dependent on teacher instruction, to unrelenting discovery and precision.

Particularity and plurality

Malleability of the movement materials enables particularity and plurality in the dance technique class (Dryburgh 2018). What I mean by this is that as teacher, I encourage leaners to make individual choices about how they dance the materials. This can lead to the materials being danced distinctively as each learner attends diversely to their specific features. For example, one learner may choose to emphasise suspension of a particular movement and in this way take longer in its execution, while another learner might focus on the initiation of each action to infuse the materials with dynamic impulses. They may choose to attend to one of the foci I had offered and/or focus on an area of interest of their own. Consequently, this renders the materials open to the wilful curiosities of the learners. It invites them to become aware of their involvement in the unique realisation of the materials through each dancing moment. Importantly, this is not to negate the rigour with which the specific technical details of the materials are being activated but to acknowledge each dancer's individuality and the potential for variation and thus, deepen embodied understanding.

The invitation to inquire of the materials in this way can shift perceptions of what we are engaged in together in the dance technique class. The implication is that rather than aiming for something beyond ourselves, dance technique can be realised through that which comes from ourselves. It is an approach that ascribes value to who we are and can become rather than what we are not. Thus, difference can be foregrounded in the dance technique class because the manifestations of the movement materials are not exclusively defined. Neither are the experiences or interests of learners assumed to be homogenous or static. Rather, the materials are positioned in ways that go beyond the prescribed such that plurality can be purposefully realised. Plurality of dance technique can be enabled through teaching strategies that encourage learners to expand upon that to which they are paying attention in themselves and the similarly inquiring bodies of peers around them.

Learners might observe/sense/feel the deliberate choices made by peers in the dancing moment that provide new perspectives of the concepts being explored. By paying attention to the nuance of how others dance the materials, learners can be inspired and/or provoked. It is akin to hearing a persuasive argument. The dancing of the materials by peers can be compelling, motivating and propelling. For example, the ways in which one dancer 'plays with' the articulation of a movement might stimulate a peer to do the same, not as replication, but as a way of thinking-through-bodily that which has been declared. In this way, observing/sensing/feeling each other in the dance technique class need not objectify other learners but rather serve as embodied acts of recognition (Dryburgh 2020). Therefore, opportunities to watch each other dancing through the materials can be prioritised in dance training contexts as reciprocal means of accumulative learning. This is a process of embodied dialogue (Anttila 2004), whereby each learner is connected in common projects.

In what has been described, it can be understood how a dancer might express themselves as an individual while simultaneously making connections with others. Thus, as a way of practicing being in relation with others, the dance technique class affords a three-fold engagement. First, with precision as alert responsiveness; second, with particularity as capacity to be distinctive; and lastly, with plurality as availability to possibilities beyond the prescribed. In what follows, I describe an activity that I use in the studio to enable these ways of engaging with learning dance technique. The 'Gatherings' is part of a process that is structured to enhance embodied knowing. The process is designed to prioritise choice making by the learners with respect to what they do while encouraging inclusivity and collectiveness. Through what follows, I ground the ideas discussed so far in the 'sweaty realities' of the dance technique studio.

Gathering – an example from practice

To ground our thinking of material matters, I outline here a process I undertake with learners, called Gathering. This process is one way that the materials might be put to work so that we can foster precision, particularity and plurality. I will describe this example from my teaching practice in terms of the various structural components of the process and the pedagogical considerations that underpin them. In offering this example, I do not intend to present it as a formula or model of best practice. Rather what I hope to do is to bring our thinking about learning through materials in the dance technique class to a concrete example. By describing the Gathering process in its various components, I appreciate that it may seem overly complicated. However, while the exercise is admittedly complex with respect to the options available to the learners, it is important to bear in mind that it develops out of an explorative way of working with the materials that would have been established as part of our shared learning experience.

- The living circle – never out

To begin with, the learners form a circle around the perimeter of the studio to create an enlivened dancing space (Chatterjea 2011). This space can be entered into by any learner to dance through the materials. The learners choose when and how they enter the dancing space. However, everyone is included as participant observers simply by being part of the living circle. This is an active attending wherein we all 'hold' the space for each other.

The living circle is responsive such that when a dancer steps in to dance the materials, the learners that were on either side of that person move around thereby closing the gap. This can involve the observing learners in moving around and along the circle numerous times even when they have not chosen to go into the dancing space themselves. It reduces the stasis of having a fixed place in the circle and helps to manifest a sense of implication when a peer enters in. For example, it is less possible to be passive as an observer, and even if one chooses not to dance inside the circle, the learner is attentive to the unfolding experience. Most importantly, the living circle is an inclusive manifestation of the collective ideal. We are all part of that which is unfolding regardless of what roles we assume.

For the learner that has entered the dancing space, their place is not held vacant for them, and in this way, their dancing does not need to be determined by a returning to that place. While this might at first seem to suggest that their place is gone, the receptivity of the living circle to absorb them back-in means that a space will always be provided for them. In this way, the dancing of the materials has no fixed end point/location but may extend outwards.

- Familiar and fresh materials

In setting up this Gathering process, I have found that it can be useful to have a substantial amount of material to 'chew through' (inquire of). I usually ensure we have three 'chunks' of movement materials that are available to us to explore. For example, this would include a recent sequence we had been exploring that travels through the space, a floor sequence with a different dynamic and a previous sequence that can be remembered. These different materials offer various means for exploring technique foci.

The recent sequence affords a continuity of exploration such that the dancers can redo (Stanton 2011) movement features that are relatively well known to them. These materials are potentially the most available to the dancers with respect of knowing them well and having confidence to dance them while being observed by their peers. This can be particularly important for learners who are less confident and provides direct links to the experiences of our most recent dance classes. The inclusion of a floor sequence can offer the opportunity to connect ways of moving that are dynamic and aerobic to the fluid and sensuous at low level. Ultimately, the aim would be for the dancers to be able to choose to employ a variety of dynamics at each level of travel. However, the juxtaposition of different 'types' of material can present fresh challenges and new inquiries.

The utilisation of an older sequence can afford ways of expanding the materials pallet and generate a reflective practice that revisits technical concepts previously explored. To return to materials that were previously well known and readily available in the body can be an interesting proposition as it allows the dancer to build on and re-evaluate understandings. That which was previously easily achievable might be reimagined alongside other materials with different foci/concerns/questions. Additionally, this revisiting can help to reconsider the seeming disposability of the materials and encourage a deeper engagement with them. The various ingredients of Gathering, the different materials, as I have described them are not formulaic but rather an example of the range of 'matter' with which the dancers are invited to explore. Importantly, the range of materials is not intended to overwhelm but rather excite. The dancers are invited to dance through any or all the materials and as I will go on to explain, the possibility for the student to make their own choices is vital.

• Both sides, all or some

In order that the quantity of the materials to be explored does not overwhelm the learners, it is essential that there is choice to do as much or as little as each person would like/feel able. It is my experience that less confident learners can feel inhibited to move into the dancing space and therefore the accessibility of stepping in (literally) can be prioritised. One way, I try to achieve this is to state explicitly to the dancers that they can do any amount of the materials. As I set up the process, I make it clear that they need not do the materials completely. They may choose to do a section and then return to the living circle. At the other end of the readiness continuum, some learners will feel enticed by the vastness of the task and energised by the possibilities to perform the different materials in this way. The range of challenge of the Gathering can accommodate this ambition. However, it is important for me, the teacher, to remember that this excited response will not be the case for all. The primary focus of the process is not concerned with the quantity of materials that each dancer 'performs' but rather their engagement with inquiry and personal discovery.

The materials enable bodily attunement with the multidimensional possibilities of movement as they unfold (Dryburgh 2018, Farnell and Wood 2011). They provide the frame through which processes of exploration, discovery and honing deepen embodied knowing (McWilliams 2009, Rouhiainen 2008). For those students who would like the extra challenge, I extend the possibility to do the various materials as a repeatable and linked sequence of movement available 'on both sides'. This generates a potential longer looped dancing experience. With this extended range of possibilities, I hope to enable learners to galvanise their daring as part of an ongoing invitation. I believe that legitimating the learners' choices in this way will encourage them to take risks, to put themselves out there and delve deeper.

Thus, explicitly stating that the learners may take part within this range of possibilities can reduce the sense of pressure to have to do the same as everyone else.

- Plus impro

An additional feature of this already complex process that I might introduce is to improvise 'in relation to' the materials. My instinct with this layering of the experience is to not be too prescriptive. I trust that the dancing body will bring an increased awareness to sensed knowing. By introducing the possibility to improvise my intention is not to obfuscate but rather to open up the ways in which the features of the materials, the technique concepts, might become known/felt/sensed. For example, if one of the technical concepts we had been exploring is the use of suspension, then this idea may surface through the experience of improvising alongside the materials.

The use of improvisation may also occur following on from the end of a sequence, alongside a peer doing the materials or as an interweaving between parts of the materials. It is a relational response to the materials. In my experience, the integration of improvisation serves as a way of bringing counterpoint to the enlivened space that stimulates further alertness rather than distraction. Consequently, improvisation adds new perspectives with which to see, do and feel through the materials in the lived environment. Dance scholars Dyer and Löytönen state that 'bodily or embodied encounters ultimately shape modes of thinking, interacting and processes of inquiry within a community' (2012: 139). Consequently, learners may understand not only the ways in which they learn from their peers but also the unique and particular ways in which their own dancing contributes to the collective experience. Thus, students can affect 'a snowballing' of understanding that has the potential to galvanise shifts in their technical capabilities by expanding awareness, provoking attention, cultivating precision and inspiring alternative propositions.

- Invite in, join with

A facet of Gathering that I feel enables a collectively conducive experience is the possibility for learners to invite each other to dance with them or join others as they dance. The pedagogical intention of inviting a peer to dance can be useful to encourage learners who appear reluctant to find their way to the dancing centre. My experience is that peers are well placed to know how to encourage each other in this way. This can serve to prevent the teacher from being the sole encourager of engagement and thus provide bridges into the fullness of the learning process.

The other possibility, to join with, is useful as an explicit instruction as it opens up the possibility for peers to come alongside a dancer who has proposed a certain starting place. What is exciting from my point of view about this is that the 'joining with' can stimulate a group of learners to come together to dance in accord. This is a deliberate coming to be with each other in an experience of dancing. From where I stand this appears to generate solidarity and pleasure in moving as a connected body.

Gathering as a shared learning experience enables listening, seeing and sensing others. This fosters a reflective dwelling upon the engagement of peers with the materials. Thus, learning dance technique is furthered as a shared experience that can inspire personal change. Learning through materials in this way concerns a mutual accountability of shared space; reflecting upon that which is bodily perceived. This goes hand in hand with the use of materials as a personally meaningful process of discovery (Rouhiainen 2008). Students can better understand themselves and their relatedness to others through opportunities for individual and group reflection alongside and in concert with movement activities. By drawing from the dancing of others, one's perspectives of technique potentialities can expand. This is important because it means that the experience of learning dance technique can foster exchange, shifting perceptions and mutuality. As such dancing is aligned with socially engaged ways of learning and living well with others, a joining with. As stated by Ingold, 'every being finds its singular voice in the sharing of experience with others' (2018: 26). Therefore, the learner can develop their own emanating technique as part of an enmeshed symbiotic process with peers.

• Wash and remain

Lastly, a function that I may sometimes use to refresh the experience as it unfolds is to 'wash and remain'. This instruction calls for the group to 'wash across the space' wherein all participants move from one side to the living circle to the other. While doing this, the invitation will be extended for some learners to 'remain' in the space to dance the materials. This wash and remain strategy functions to enable a further breaking down of the perceived barrier between those who are in and those who are out of the dancing space. It is my experience that this simple device can be the stimulus that offers some dancers their way to dancing inside the living circle. Simply by passing through the space in this way, some learners are emboldened to try.

The Gathering process has the potential to extend for a considerable period of time. As teacher, the focus is about cultivating an environment of inquiry that enables learners to assume responsibility to discover for themselves how their technique may be honed. It is a space that privileges curiosity with the aim that technique will become increasingly relevant for individuals. Gathering is designed to engage learners with inquiry of the materials without the expectation that they must do so in a singularly defined way. It prioritises choice making and connectivity. This is important because the learner should feel able to respond to the invitation to inquire on their own terms. At the same time, the learner can come to recognise that their choices influence the collective experience. Thus, dancing together in processes such as the one described above can model social engagement in a world where one might act/move in declarative, collective and ethically responsive ways among others.

Returning from

The materials of the dance technique class matter in as much as they can afford opportunities to hone precision, develop particularity and recognise plurality as part of an accumulative process in common projects. Learning as part of a collective in the dance technique class has an exponential function in that peers can shape and reshape their moving/thinking/being together. Thus, it is argued, the dance technique class holds potential for developing relational capabilities of social engagement. By paying attention to oneself and each other, we can galvanise our shared accountability for learning/ living. This is a relational practice that recognises the contribution of others and ourselves. Consequently, we affect change, progression and growth for/with each other.

This expansive pedagogy appeals to me because it asks us to engage in ways that are not self-indulgent, narcissistic or negatively competitive. Beyond selfish ambition, the honing of dance technique can foster an ethical relating in the studio that enhances learning for all while simultaneously being a means of practicing citizenship. As an educator, I want to cultivate experiences of learning, like Gathering, that are stimulatingly expansive. In so doing, the materials of the dance technique class enable embodied discoveries that resist deficit thinking and promote plurality. Thus, the embodied and relational capabilities arising from the dance technique class can galvanise collective ways of being/moving in the world that are responsively alert, distinctively declarative and constantly available to possibilities beyond the prescribed.

References

Anttila, E. (2004) 'Dance learning as practice of freedom', in Rouhiainen, L. et al. (eds.) *The same difference? Ethical and political perspectives on dance.* Helsinki: Theatre Academy, pp. 19–62.

Bannon, F. (2018) *Considering ethics in dance, theatre and performance.* Cham: Palgrave Macmillan.

Chatterjea, A. (2011) 'Body knowledges: dancing/articulating complexity', *Brolga: An Australian Journal about Dance*, 35, pp. 9–16.

Clarke, G., Cramer, F. A. and Muller, G. (2011) 'Minding motion', in Diehl, I. and Lampert F. (eds.) *Dance techniques 2010: tanzplan Germany.* Leipzig: Henschell, pp. 196–229.

Cooper Albright, A. (2017) 'The perverse satisfaction of gravity', in Nakajima, N. and Brandstetter, G. (eds.) *The aging body in dance: a cross-cultural perspective.* Oxon: Routledge, pp. 63–72.

Dryburgh, J. (2018) 'Unsettling materials: lively tensions in learning through "set materials" in the dance technique class', *Journal of Dance & Somatic Practices*, 10(1), pp. 35–50. https://doi.org/10.1386/jdsp.10.1.35_1

Dryburgh, J. (2020) 'Vital entanglements: an exploration of collective effort in the dance technique class', *International Journal of Education & the Arts*, 21(34). http://doi.org/10.26209/ijea21n34

Dyer, B. and Löytönen, T. (2012) 'Engaging dialogue: co-creating communities of collaborative inquiry', *Research in Dance Education*, 13(1), pp. 121–147. https://doi.org/10.1080/14647893.2012.640143

Farnell, B. and Wood, R. N. (2011) 'Performing precision and the limits of observation', in Ingold, T. (ed.) *Redrawing anthropology: materials, movements, lines*. London: Routledge, pp. 91–113.

Ingold, T. (ed.) (2011) *Redrawing anthropology: materials, movements, lines*. London: Routledge.

Ingold, T. (2018) 'Five questions of skill', *Cultural Geographies*, 25(1), pp. 159–163.

McWilliams, E. (2009) 'Teaching for creativity: from sage to guide to meddler', *Asia Pacific Journal of Education*, 29(3), pp. 281–293. https://doi. org/10.1080/02188790903092787

Parviainen, J. (2002) 'Bodily knowledge: epistemological reflections on dance', *Dance Research Journal*, 34(1), pp. 11–26. https://doi.org/10.2307/1478130

Reed, S. (2018) 'A conversation with Gill Clarke', *Journal of Dance & Somatic Practices*, 10(1), pp. 9–22. https://doi.org/10.1386/jdsp.10.1.9_1

Rouhiainen, L. (2008) 'Somatic dance as a means of cultivating ethically embodied subjects', *Research in Dance Education*, 9(3), pp. 241–256. https://doi. org/10.1080/14647890802386916

Schupp, K. (2018) 'A call to action: dance education and responsible citizenship', *Journal of Dance Education*, 18(3), pp. 93–94. https://doi.org/10.1080/1529082 4.2018.1486074

Spatz, B. (2015) *What a body can do: technique as knowledge, practice as research*. Oxon: Routledge.

Stanton, E. (2011) 'Doing, re-doing and undoing: practice, repetition and critical evaluation as mechanisms for learning in a dance technique class 'laboratory", *Theatre, Dance and Performance Training*, 2(1), pp. 86–98. https://doi.org/10. 1080/19443927.2011.545253

Stinson, S. W. (2004) 'My body/myself: lessons from dance education', in Bresler, L. (ed.) *Knowing bodies, moving minds: towards embodied teaching and learning*. Dordrecht: Kluwer Academic Publishers, pp. 153–168.

Tregear, P., Johansen, G., Jørgensen, H., Sloboda, J., Tulve, H. and Wistreich, R. (2016) 'Conservatoires in society: institutional challenges and possibilities for change', *Arts and Humanities in Higher Education*, 15(3–4), pp. 276–292. https://doi.org/10.1177/1474022216647379

2.2 Questioning values in the delivery of dance practices at the University of East London

Carla Trim-Vamben and Jo Read

What do you have in you? Why do you connect to that style? And I also feel like, when you do different things, even though you're not used to it… I think it shows you a lot about yourself, […] you notice how you learn, how you learn things, […] you're like okay, how do I be me in this style?

(Focus Group, 2021: 20)

Popping, contemporary, locking, house, bharatanatyam, kalaripayattu, modern Afro, capoeira, breaking, dancehall, hip-hop… These are the current dance and movement practices studied by students during their three-year journey on the University of East London (UEL) BA (Hons) Dance: Urban Practice course. This offering is part of an ongoing commitment to challenge the Eurocentric canon which dominates Higher Education (HE) dance training and contributes to some of our success and reputation with our students and the wider dance community over the past 15 years. Despite progress, we encounter many challenges as the course continues to develop, in our role as co-lecturers who have worked collaboratively on the course since 2014. This leads us to important critical discussions about the ethical considerations and questions of value that other popular and social dance scholars (Amin, 2016; Dodds, 2011; Malnig, 2009; McCarthy-Brown, 2014) consider in their work. Consequently, these considerations are at the forefront of our delivery, which we are reflecting on in this chapter.

This research focuses on the teaching of diverse dance practices on the course, and how we prepare our students to enter into the creative industries by inviting them to confront a range of challenges and contradictions. Through a combination of textual analysis, discussion with students, studio-based class observations and experiences through programme leadership and teaching, we consider the value of the course, and how it translates to critical thinking and embodied skills for our students. Despite notable contributions to the field of Afro-diasporic dance forms and the discourse on Black British dance (Adewole, 2016a,b; Akinleye, 2018; Castelyn, 2018), there are limited sources that focus on a diverse dance curriculum delivered in the context of UK HE. Consequently, we turn to valuable contributions by scholars, such

DOI: 10.4324/9781003111146-10

as Hyun Jung Chang and Azaria Hogans (2021), Takiyah Nur Amin (2016) and Nyama McCarthy-Brown (2009, 2014), whose research focuses on delivering Afro-diasporic dance forms in undergraduate dance degrees in the United States. We acknowledge that there are many differences between the structure of US and UK degrees, such as the credit weighting of foundational and elective courses (Monroe, 2011: 38). We also recognise that when discussing Afro-diasporic dance practices, 'Black British dance deserves explication on its own terms' (DeFrantz, 2018: ix), which is made difficult when drawing from scholars who work outside of the UK. Therefore, we felt it was important to also draw from detailed studio examples and discussions with our current students, in order to capture aspects of their experience as a crucial part of this research.

As co-authors of this chapter, we share a wealth of experiences having worked together across several modules over the last eight years.[1] Despite areas of similarity and overlap through our shared interests and practice in the area of popular and social dance, our specific dance experiences and cultural backgrounds differ. Carla Trim-Vamben identifies as a British Mauritian, cis-gendered woman, whose current dance practices include house and waacking. Jo Read identifies as a white, British, queer, cis-gendered woman who currently trains in litefeet, along with a dance movement practice informed by past training in popping, hip-hop and contemporary dance. Blind spots and individual privileges impact on this research, often at the forefront of our conversations together, both professionally and personally within our friendship. To attempt to address this, we are committed to individual continuous reflection and critical conversations (Brookfield, 2017) on our practice. This involves evaluating and debating our biases which is supported by ongoing institutional and personal Equity, Diversity and Inclusivity activity and training, and listening to and centring the student voice wherever possible. We also understand that there are ethical issues connected to the delivery of popular, social, Afro-diasporic and Asian-diasporic dance practices within the context of UK HE, which are far removed from their original roots, which we revisit later in this chapter. All of this also comes with an understanding and awareness that limitations, misjudgements and areas of misunderstanding are inevitable within our work and practice, which we acknowledge as part of this research.

We begin this chapter by situating the programme within its geographic and historical context, highlighting key areas of practice that contribute to the overall ethos of the course. Following on from this, we focus on a critical discussion of aspects of the delivery of dance practices which feature on the curriculum. In addition to scholarly debate, our work is informed by a small focus group discussion, which took place in November 2021 with student representatives from first, second and third year on the course. Furthermore, due to the broad range of dance practices included on the course, the chapter focuses on one specific pairing of popping and contemporary dance, offered in tandem on the course. We chose to place more emphasis on this because it is the entry point for our students at the beginning of their first year, and the initial dance practices that they learn in the first term. This part of the chapter is arranged in a series of key themes which encapsulate our thinking: Contradictory Principles and Points of Intersection, Inadequate Terminologies, Embodied Histories and Knowledge, and New Micro-Hierarchies. Through this work, we intend to begin an important discussion about the unique value of offering a broad range of dance practices on a UK degree course, and share some of our considerations as part of our ongoing quest to create equitable and ethical embodied dance experiences for our students.

Contextualising the dance course at UEL

In 2007, UEL validated the BA (Hons) Dance: Urban Practice degree course in partnership with a consortium of East London based leaders, lecturers, dancers, producers and community advocates across dance, theatre and New Vic college. The vision was to offer an undergraduate degree that reflected the diverse range of dance practices that were being offered in East London at the time. Furthermore, the programme aimed to challenge the Eurocentric dance canon of Ballet and Western contemporary dance techniques, which permeated HE dance training. Before the course's inception, the borough of Newham in East London historically funded many community dance activities, particularly through the work of East London Dance (East London Dance, 2022). Dance companies, such as Boy Blue (Boy Blue, n.d.), also delivered community hip-hop and 'street dance' classes and activities in the area.[2] As East London also had a high demographic of South Asian communities, South Asian dance classes were also taking place led by Akademi (previously known as the Academy of Indian Dance), in London (Akademi, 2019; SADAA, n.d.).[3] Ballet and Western contemporary dance were not the predominant dance forms delivered in East London, and so the programme at UEL was designed to reflect this reality.

The historical and social context of East London has led to ongoing connections with local communities, as an important and ongoing part of the design and development of the course. Furthermore, UEL as an institution names 'civic engagement' as part of its core aims and is historically known as 'the people's university' (University of East London, 2022). Over the years, we have worked closely on various exchange and collaborative projects with East London Dance and Boy Blue, amongst other organisations, dance companies, local schools, colleges and communities to maintain this ethos as a core part of the course. Stratford, East London, where the course is mostly based, has also seen a huge amount of local change as a result of gentrification and regeneration since the London 2012 Olympics. The impact of these shifts is felt by the local population, leading to 'displacement and the loss of a sense of place for local young residents' (Kennelly and Watt, 2012: 151). In response to this issue, the course centres the geographical and socio-political landscape of East London and the position of UEL within this.[4]

During 14 years of delivery and two compulsory university-wide revalidation processes, the vision to raise the value of popular, social, Afro-Diasporic and Asian-Diasporic dance forms in HE has always been withheld. The modular framework of the course is designed around four central pillars, which are embedded into three years of core study; dance practice and training, skills and employability, practice-led research and choreography and dance making. The course focuses on dance in various contexts, such as stage, screen, studios, clubs and other community and social spaces. The modules and projects are designed sequentially through the years and aim to cross subject content laterally. The course structure offers dedicated spaces for students to identify the cultural similarities and differences which underpin their learning, and time to consider what this means in their developing practice as emerging artists. Specific examples are discussed later in this chapter.

The course was designed to include core training and study of a more equitable balance of dance forms, and a broader range of movement practices. All dance practices offered on the course are compulsory and are also weighted equally in terms of assessment credit. This aspect is crucial, to avoid 'making personal favorites the center of our programs, [and] perpetuating Eurocentric dance hierarchies' (McCarthy-Brown, 2014: 128). Over the last 14 years, the dance technique offering in UK HE has slowly expanded, with multiple institutions now including a wider range of dance practices as a core part of study and training. Other courses which remain focused on contemporary dance practices have also become more inclusive, designing additional programmes and introducing new dance forms into the curriculum.[5] These ongoing shifts are underpinned by current threats to the position of dance within Higher and Further Education (Weale, 2021), as a result of governmental guidance to reprioritise Office for Students HE funding towards provision of high-cost 'STEM' subjects, which are Science, Technology, Engineering and Mathematics (Williamson, 2021). This has led to several UK dance course closures,[6] so there is a strong motivation for courses to stay current and relevant, with 'good' graduate outcomes.[7]

Where appropriate, the course rejects the idea of theory and practice as binary oppositions, and alternatively, students are encouraged to consider how their developing embodied knowledge informs their critical thinking skills, and vice versa. This is reinforced by the structure of learning in the studio, which usually features a combination of moving, doing, thinking, reading, writing, watching and discussion across all modules. This is echoed through wide ranging modes of assessment and innovative approaches to feedback, depending on the module or project. One assessment is a 2vs2 competitive battle event in house dance and popping, recently led by artists Clara Bajado and Vicky 'Skytilz' Mantey. A team of visiting specialists deliver specific dance and movement forms on the programme each year, such as Baris Yazar teaching capoeira, Shelaine Prince teaching dancehall and Kamala Devam teaching bharatanatyam and kalaripayattu. These modules use audio feedback in order to utilise a conversational approach, and practitioner-led terminology. These approaches, amongst others, underpin an antiracist pedagogic practice that we are constantly striving for, to decolonise approaches to the curriculum since the inception of the course in 2007.

Contradictory principles and points of intersection

Our detailed studio examples are from a series of technique classes that we observed in the Autumn term of 2021, including popping classes taught by Senior Lecturer Fred 'Realness' Folkes, and contemporary dance classes with influences from Graham, Cunningham and Release. The contemporary dance classes were taught by Senior Lecturer Robert Nicholson, and Visiting Lecturer Delene Gordon.[8] The classes are the technique starting point for our students during their first term on the course. It is important to note the typical entry points for students on the programme, as they often arrive with a varied knowledge base of popular, social, Afro-diasporic and Asian-diasporic forms of dance. Our students have a diverse range of cultural and socio-economic backgrounds, with many being the first in their family to attend university. Out of the 123 students for the academic year 2021–2022, 45% identified either as Black, Asian or Minority Ethnic backgrounds and 55% identified as white or from white European backgrounds. If students have had formal dance training at school or college, contemporary dance forms are inevitably part of this. Many of our students, however, have had no formal dance training and have learnt popular dance styles informally through online platforms, community dance settings or in recreational dance studios.[9]

Hyun Jung Chang and Azaria Hogans note that when their students study West African dance and hip-hop dance, they struggle to adjust to key principles of the forms, such as maintaining the 'bounce' or to 'ground and rebound continually to the beat' (2021: 9). This implies that their students do not usually have previous experience of these dance cultures. For our students, the challenge is often the opposite, and we observed that many students struggled to adjust to key principles of Western contemporary dance, such as 'the erect body dictated by the straight, centred spine' (Gottschild, 1998: 14). One student admitted that they found learning key principles of Western contemporary dance more 'restrictive' and 'fixed' (Focus Group, 2021: 28). Another student noted that popping gave them more opportunity to implement their own personal style (Focus Group, 2021: 14).

Students are encouraged to value and appreciate all forms of dance, whilst also acknowledging that the 'Africanist aesthetic is often in direct opposition to Western Philosophical principles' (Osumare, 2016: 26), with Western contemporary dance and ballet historically being privileged above other dance practices. One way to invite students to reflect on that opposition is through identifying intriguing points of similarity and difference between the movement principles and value systems of the techniques. For example, a central theme in both the popping and contemporary dance classes at UEL is contraction and release. Despite being the same overall principle, this is explored very differently in each dance form. One student describes this contrasting experience as follows, 'in contemporary, it's a big contraction, then that extends to the rest of the body. And in popping it's loads of [small] contractions that make a big movement' (Focus Group, 2021: 7). Simultaneously, students become aware of their need to shift, when moving from one dance practice or space of learning to another. One student commented, 'if I have a hip-hop freestyle, then I need to change everything about myself, I need to change my clothes, I need to change my environment, I need to change the music...' (Focus Group, 2021: 5). Consequently, students begin to develop skills when analysing different movement practices, discovering parallels, compatible aspects and aesthetic clashes that they may not have initially observed.

Understanding points of intersection and stark contradictions between dance cultures becomes crucial for students, when considering that many of the industry professional choreographers, choreographic platforms and projects are based on a combination of aesthetics from Afro-diasporic and contemporary dance forms. UK choreographers, such as Botis Seva, Dickson Mbi and Julia Cheng, all work with a combination of Afro-diasporic and contemporary dance practices, amongst other artistic influences. Frequent mentorship projects, such as *Back to the Lab* and *Open Art Surgery* at Breakin' Convention, also draw from different artistic practices, where emerging hip-hop dance theatre artists are paired with mentors from hip-hop dance theatre, contemporary dance and theatre directing.[10] At the end of the intensive project, the work-in-progress is presented at the Lilian Baylis Theatre (Breakin' Convention, n.d.) with opportunities for audience response and feedback. Making theatre-based choreographic works is a popular career path for our graduates, and it is notable that even when development opportunities are designed for hip-hop dance artists, they still draw influence from contemporary dance. Frequently, it often appears that the only way to be accepted or funded as a theatre choreographer working with dance practices outside of this canon, is to utilise and draw from Western theatre dance compositional and structuring devices as part of 'tactical ways of working' (Adewole cited in DeFrantz, 2016a,b: 68). This is further emphasised through the many core textbooks that are published on choreographic practice, which are typically rooted in white Western theatre dance principles. It is important for us to prepare students for the reality of the industry, whilst also exploring ways to challenge traditions and inform creative and choreographic decision making.[11]

Whilst training in popping and contemporary dance, first-year students simultaneously undertake a choreography and dance making project. This is an example where contradictions emerge through major differences in where value is placed in the music-dance relationships for each dance practice, a theme explored in Jo Read's (2018, 2020) doctoral research and subsequent article focused on musicality. Popping has Afro-Diasporic roots and is characterised by a close, detailed music-dance relationship where 'significant beats of the music' are emphasised (Miyakawa and Schloss, 2015: 340). The aim is to create an illusion that the dancer is causing the sound through their movements, and different sounds in the music (e.g. snare drum, hi-hat) often correspond to specific qualities and textures in the movement. Contemporary dance forms, however, are often associated with a rejection of musicality (Banes, 2011: xxii), and the 'non-relationship' became a conventional feature of modern dance, propelled by the famous collaborations between John Cage and Merce Cunningham (Jordan, 2007: 12). Notably, it has since been established that the primary aim was not necessarily to disconnect music and dance (McMains and Thomas, 2013: 199) in this example. A 'righteous aesthetic high ground' (White, 2006: 68), however, can sometimes prevail when working with popular dance forms in choreographic settings.

One example of this is in response to hip-hop dance company Boy Blue's work, *Blak Whyte Gray* (2017), with whom the dance course has regularly worked in collaboration. When opting for an abstract, episodic structure for this particular work, the work was praised as more 'artful' (Roy, 2017) as a result of its contemporary influences. There are also many contemporary dance choreographers who are also well known for working with close and intricate relationships with music, such as Mark Morris, Matthew Bourne and Akram Khan. Nevertheless, considering the musical traditions and clashes in values of different dance practices creates space for dynamic debate and 'creative problem solving' (Amin, 2016: 22) for students. Students are invited to undertake their own creative tasks that often flex the boundaries of these musical traditions. A simple introductory task might involve playing with popping movement vocabulary, but working closely with a piece of classical or experimental music, or experimenting with abstract movement to hip-hop or other forms of popular music and evaluating how meaning is changed. Consequently, an 'unusual synthesis of aesthetic influences' and values (Read, 2018: 41) are explored in a creative context as a result of the dance practices being studied by the students. Through engaging with critical discussion about musicality and musical choices, they are encouraged to think reflexively when making their own creative choices, as emerging choreographers and dance makers.

Inadequate terminologies

If you go to a battle, no one says, "that was a great improvisation".
(Focus Group, 2021: 3)

When we talk about improvisation in class, people are less shook than when we say freestyle.
(Bajado and Johnson, 2019)

Dance techniques, training, styles, forms and practices, are a few of the many terms in circulation on our course, used by staff and students to describe a serious and sustained commitment to their craft. As the programme spans the study of many dance cultures in a wide range of commercial, community, underground and educational contexts, we acknowledge that there are many different spaces that staff and students occupy to experience different dance cultures. Resultantly, and as the quote above alludes to, there are many instances when ideas of a shared common language and assumptions of the meaning of specific dance terminology is challenged in practice.

Frequent discussions about the course name itself and the problems with the term 'urban' are constantly raised as part of our reflection on uses of terminology on the course. This was made all the more urgent in the aftermath of the tragic murder of George Floyd in 2020, which became a turning point for anti-racism and 'the largest anti-racist demonstrations in Britain in the 21st or 20th Century' (Mohdin, Swann and Bannock, 2020). Hyun Jung Chang and Azaria Hogans discuss the problems with this term along with others, such as 'global' and 'world' dance (2021: 7). We acknowledge the issues with the use of the term 'urban', and the negative impact it has on black cultures. Although it is likely that the course name will be changed, we have been hesitant about doing this in a performative or reactive capacity, in order to first engage in full consultation with our current students, which is currently in process. Until this has been completed, the existing course name presents an opportunity to engage in critical debate with students, staff and our collaborators in the dance community.

As part of this discussion, we also invite critical reflection of other terms used on the course, such as 'technique', as it often implicitly indicates ballet and contemporary dance forms. Acknowledging Racquel Monroe's (2011) work on the meaning of the term 'technique', we notice a similar hierarchical pattern in our audition process for new applicants for the course. When engaging in small group discussion, we frequently overhear applicants state that they train in 'technical styles' but also do 'urban' or 'hip-hop styles'. When we ask about this, the 'technical styles' are usually contemporary and/or ballet forms, and applicants therefore insinuate that the other dance practices are not part of what they consider to be their dance technique. Monroe's work has been a successful access point to introduce technique as a 'loaded term' (2011: 52), and to bring about an expanded awareness of its meaning. Technique is a term that is still frequently used on the course, with a shared understanding that every dance practice on the course contributes to this equally.

Amongst UK practitioners, similar debates have taken place in relation to issues with the terms 'Hip-Hop' and 'Street Dance', along with discussion about which dance practices can be considered to be included under those terms (Moser-Kindler, 2018). This has been further complicated by (mis) representations of various dance practices in commercial contexts, such as reality television competitions (DanceMadnessTV, 2012) or social media viral trends. In these instances, although they make a positive contribution by dance becoming more widely accessible, the movement and vocabulary used by the practitioners for whom these dance practices are an integral part of their daily embodied and lived experience is often misconstrued or absent entirely. We connect students with these debates early on in their journey on the course, through introducing practitioner-led sources, such as *The Capsule*, which is a UK Street Dance Media Platform.[12]

Other terminology that is often used interchangeably can also present opportunities for critical debate in class. Carla Trim-Vamben's research on Freestyle Practice in UK House Dance (2019) highlights problems with the difference in students' responses to the terms 'improvisation' and 'freestyle' in practical house dance classes. This research, along with the Focus Group discussions (2021), focuses on the limitations and issues when using these terms to indicate the same meaning. Students describe a fear of the term freestyle, which is predominately used in dance cultures with Afro-diasporic origins, and tend to feel more at ease when the term improvisation is used in technique classes. This phenomenon is not synonymous to house dance, as we observe students grappling with this conflict on the course more generally, as most of the popular and social forms that are learnt have freestyle as a core element, such as popping, locking, breaking and hip-hop. Consequently, learning to freestyle and getting more comfortable with freestyling is fundamental to many of the dance practices that are delivered as part of the technique strand of the course.

> So, for me, when I think about improv, I always take it to the contemporary side. Very western very European.
>
> (Focus Group, 2021: 2)

Danielle Goldman (2010) and Brenda Dixon Gottschild (1998) discuss how European American improvisational practices have shaped the meaning of the term 'improvisation', which has roots in Afro-diasporic and Asian-diasporic cultural practices. This meaning is where improvisation is seen as having, 'no outside set of rules to remember' (Blom and Chaplin, 1988: 6) and where, 'a spontaneous mode of creation...takes place without the aid of a manuscript or score' (Goldman, 2010: 5). These general definitions have continued to shape the idea of improvisation in dance training spaces in various educational settings such as HE. Freestyle is not fully represented or visible in these definitions, as it is based on learning and mastering foundational codified movement and creating personal unique variations. The aim is to share and exchange with other dancers to inspire new pathways whilst dancing in synchronicity with the music (Trim-Vamben, 2019: 30).

The difference in the meanings of these terms presents an ethical issue when enabling the use of them interchangeably, and the transmission of freestyle dance practice involves a clunky transmission into a white institutional space that is steeped in European aesthetics. Scholars such as Jacqui Malone (1996) and Jonathan Jackson (2001) offer definitions and frameworks to analyse improvisation in African American vernacular dances that supports the analysis of the British experience of popular and social dances in HE. The lack of acknowledgement of definitions through Afro-diasporic and Asian-diasporic lenses also contributes to the misconceptions and cultural misunderstandings of freestyle dance practice (Trim-Vamben, 2019: 28). Students sometimes misunderstood the importance of the use of music in freestyle, often dancing offbeat or at times not acknowledging the music at all. Students frequently did not understand and, at times, did not value the importance of mastering and demonstrating the codified movement in sync with the music. In an approach to help students feel more at ease, the use of inadequate terminologies had created another layer of complex problems, which in turn created more fear and anxiety.

Delivering dance forms outside of the dominant canon in HE settings inadvertently creates a hybrid conflict of meanings and values that needs more thought and attention. As a result of these findings, we have created supportive approaches to students' development in their technique classes. We guide students to raise their awareness of the differences, similarities and the possibilities of new frameworks when studying a broad range of dance practices. The Eurocentric interpretation of terminology holds value in dance practice, and we ask students to acknowledge that whilst questioning and giving space to frameworks from Afro-diasporic and Asian-diasporic dancing cultures. Engaging with the nuanced complexity of how HE institutions impact meaning in dance training reminds us that students should not be viewed from a deficit model when their environment and prior learning have had an impact on their understanding of terminology.

Embodied histories and knowledge

The time allocated to contextualise the historical and socio-cultural contexts of the movements being taught varies according to different dance practices on the course. In the contemporary dance classes, there was a clear acknowledgement that vast documentation of theories, core principles, pioneers and histories were readily available in the library and through online archives for students to access. In popping classes, however, the oral transmission of history through class discussion featured much more, partly due to the scarcity of historical and published documentation. Furthermore, there is also a history of distrust towards academics in university settings who have published material about hip-hop and other closely associated popular dance and music cultures. Craig and Kynard note that when this occurs, 'these so-called experts are far removed from the everyday cultural production of hip-hop' (2017: 146–147). Additionally, de Paor-Evans acknowledges the 'marked difference between hip-hop artists and practitioners visiting academic institutions and academics developing hip-hop research from within academic institutions' (2018). This highlights the importance of practitioners who have lived experiences in these styles and those who have learnt first-hand from leading pioneers to tell 'their stories'. Early representatives from the course identified this issue when it was first designed, and as a result, the university sustains its commitment to employ practitioners who have a rich embodied knowledge to share with students.[13]

As popping teacher, Fred 'Realness' Folkes, has been taught directly by members of the Electric Boogaloos, students value learning from him enormously. The focus on the cultural context in technique classes on the programme enables students to connect with the movements in a deeper way. One first-year student describes how Folkes offers context on why movements were created, and how and why they were used. They reflect that their prior knowledge of popping was more focused on copying the outline of the moves, rather than understanding their meaning (Focus Group, 2021: 13). Folkes' focus on the socio-historical context of the dance practice clearly resonates with the students, as they describe Folkes' intricate explanations of different movements in class. He teaches specific social dances from decades earlier such as the 'Twist', which he then references by showing the students how traces are embodied and still visible within popping movement vocabularies. This emphasis on oral histories is also prevalent in the delivery of other dance and movement practices on the course, such as capoeira, locking and breaking.

The consequence of this approach is that students begin to develop an in-depth understanding of and appreciation for the different influences that inform their own dance practice and personal movement style. One student below reflects on their process of identifying the emerging influences in their own personal practice.

> I do use a lot of influence from popping in my Hip-Hop. And, I do use a lot of Hip-Hop in my house. But because of this course, I kind of learned how to transform it or adapt it so people can see, oh there's the influence, for example, in my hip hop freestyle, but you don't say that that's popping, because it's deconstructed in a way that I take what I've learned in popping but I put it on myself.
>
> (Focus Group, 2021: 12).

This statement evidences the ways that students are able to grasp the crucial importance of referencing a range of movements' influence, in order to protect and share knowledge about dance practices that are historically excluded from the canon. In addition to this approach which is adopted in the technique aspect of the course, students are also encouraged to consider the ethics of their practice in other modules and projects. The careful handling of the embodied knowledge learnt, when applied in other contexts, becomes a central focus in all course content. This ethos is sustained when working with students on making, teaching, leading, producing, managing and researching dance. One example is, during a project called 'Border Crossings' led by

Dr Sarahleigh Castelyn, where students engage in practice-led research to explore how dance forms and practices 'rarely have pure roots or routes' (Castelyn, 2022). As part of this choreographic project, students learn how the dance practices 'adapt to shifts in economies, the migration of bodies across geographies, and the exchange of values, politics and labour' (Castelyn, 2022). Students therefore 'increase their capacity to learn cultural sensibility and responsibility' (Chang and Hogans, 2021: 10), whether they eventually work as teachers, performers, dance makers, producers or choose to transfer their skills to another area of work entirely.

New micro-hierarchies

Once the programme was established, we quickly came to realise that challenging the canon through a dance degree course in UK HE had potential to create new problematic views, often in the form of an implicit 'anti-ballet' and/or an 'anti-postmodern dance' sentiment. This is fuelled by understandable student frustrations about the dismissal of their dance interests as serious topics of study in their previous schools, colleges or dance spaces, and consequent realisations about issues of erasure and appropriation. When reflecting on learning capoeira and bharatanatyam, one student commented 'I didn't really realise until now how much release and contemporary has pinched and pinched from these styles' (Focus Group, 2021: 9). Students are welcomed to share their previous experience and voice their frustrations in a discussion context, as this may be the first time that they are in a space where their dance practices and experiences are deemed valuable and worthy of serious study. Simultaneously, students also begin to identify the new local value systems and micro-hierarchies that emerge when this resentment becomes collective, and shared amongst the student cohorts, and UEL dance community.

Encouraging students to reconnect with and appreciate ballet and contemporary dance practices helps to gently challenge this binary way of thinking. A particular focus on investigating professional companies who challenge stereotypes of race, gender and sexuality within their forms, such as Ballet Black (balletblack, 2020) and Ballez (Ballez, n.d.), helps to add complexity and depth to the debates. For many, this increases relatability and provides an access point to connect with the appreciation of dance practices which students may have felt historically excluded from. As many of the dance practices that our students learn are often associated with freedom of expression and assumed as being more inclusive in terms of representation, this is also an opportunity to complicate the debate. Students are introduced to dance companies, such as Ill Abilities (Ill Abilities, 2022), who challenge the ableist structures within Breaking. In an article published for *Ink Cypher*, Emily Tisshaw asks the question, *Where Is Disability in Hip Hop Dance?* (2021), as ableism is a hugely neglected area of research in relation to hip-hop dance and other popular and social dance practices. Students then have the opportunity to identify areas of ignorance, and re-examine their personal prejudices, assumptions and value systems (Brookfield, 2017), whilst developing their skills and learning on the programme.

In our quest to challenge the canon and develop the course, predictable debates surface about which dance practices to include and omit from the curriculum. In these discussions, inevitable tensions emerge about how these choices construct 'systems of classification and criterion of worth' (Dodds, 2011: 99). Studying multiple dance forms also sometimes inadvertently leads to new micro-hierarchies within the programme, where specific dance practices (e.g. West African social dances to Afrobeats music)[14] become suddenly more favourable amongst some students due to the sudden rising popularity within popular culture transmitted through social media channels. There is of course space for personal preference, and self-discovery in relation to the dance practices that feel more or less comfortable for students is a crucial part of the journey through the programme. When one particular dance culture seems to be positioned as suddenly more valuable by a majority or a collective cohort, however, it presents another opportunity to open up a debate. For the aforementioned example, we introduced our first-year students to a recent documentary in the *Netflix Explained* series, called 'Dance Crazes' (2021). This short episode draws attention to examples of Tik Tok's viral dance challenges, a phenomenon that allows for fast spreading of dance 'trends'. Crucially, it also highlights issues of appropriation by corporations and explains how specific dances often made by black creators become sensationalised by white creators. After watching and relating this to other sources and reading material, students 'face ambiguity' and 'wrestle with diversity' (Amin, 2016: 23), whilst having the opportunity to think critically about the impact of the widespread popularity of some of the dances they enjoy most.

Conclusion

Students graduate from the BA (Hons) Dance: Urban Practice course with a broad range of embodied movement experiences, and a rich knowledge and awareness of dance cultures and practices. Many of our graduates go on to have exciting and varied careers in the industry, including but not limited to performing, making, directing, producing, teaching and managing dance. Often, graduate pathways reflect the ethos of the programme, as they continue to challenge stereotypes in dance through their entrepreneurship and artistry.[15] What happens in the technique strand of the course becomes increasingly meaningful when this knowledge is applied in other contexts and is given the necessary space for exploration and reflection during other projects on the course. Similarly, critical thinking skills that develop from other projects such as choreography and dance making, are applied in the technique classroom to inform and make a valuable contribution to embodied learning.

In this chapter, we have outlined some of the challenges that we confront when considering values and ethics in our delivery of a wide range of dance practices on the course. Encouraging students to consider contradictions and similarities in their learning often allows for innovative exchanges and the creation of original dance work. Grappling with tricky terminologies presents many opportunities to question uses of language, and how meanings are impacted by wider socio-political issues, causing frequent shifts and ethical adjustments. Students learn the value and importance of documentation and oral histories, through the realisation that the learning materials for many of the dance practices are limited when compared to that of ballet and contemporary dance forms. Many of them go on to engage in research projects dedicated to this discovery in their final year, focusing on aspects of dance cultures that they find to be absent from scholarship. Finally, we revealed that challenging hierarchies that exist in dance practice and study can inadvertently create new ones, and there is a subsequent shared acceptance that this work will never be complete. Consequently, students have opportunities to develop a sustained commitment to critique and awareness of their own biases and value judgements, whilst still working as part of a collective effort to challenge the canon.

It is important that students develop the ability to consistently question and critically reflect on their practice. This ethos remains at the crux of our work on the course. It is only possible through openness and a willingness to challenge, both staff members and students. Often this involves honesty and frankness from staff members about the problems we encounter, and a clear acknowledgement that we do not have or hold all of the knowledge and the answers. This encourages a reflexive approach at the heart of all collaborative work, allowing for questions such as why am I doing what I'm doing? What kind of mover do I want to be? And what does this mean for me and for others? This is made possible because questions of value are embedded at the core of learning across all modules.

We are excited by the increasing numbers of dance degree courses in the UK which are continuing to expand and diversify the dance forms that they offer for practice and study, and widening the offering of dance technique classes led by expert practitioners' acts as a useful starting point to consider the value of embodied history and knowledge in action. We believe strongly, however, that if a wider range of dance practices are offered on a programme in terms of technique, the work does not end here. All areas of a dance programme need to shift because if modules or projects aiming to develop skills in areas, such as choreography, improvisation and critical thinking, are still firmly rooted only in Western theatre dance principles, the same problems around hierarchies of value are perpetuated. Thus, we have an ethical responsibility to not only continually review the institutional frameworks of HE but also to consider shifts in values which are created through changes in the curriculum by looking at the course as a whole.

Despite the inclusive approach that we strive for, we will continue to face challenges when working within UK HE with a broad range of dance cultures and practices, and this is not always an ideal fit. The BA (Hons) Dance: Urban Practice course, however, consistently presents a critical and crucial space to identify and challenge our personal and collective hierarchies of value, which continue to be inherently influenced by the Western dance principles that dominate Higher Educational practices in the UK. As the course continues to develop, we remain committed to ensure that the rich and diverse dance cultures that are practised in East London are celebrated as legitimate and serious contributions to dance technique and training.

Notes

1 Carla Trim-Vamben has also been the Programme Leader of the course since 2015, and Jo Read joined her briefly as Co-Programme Leader for an interim period during the academic year of 2021–2022.
2 In the UK, although now used less frequently, 'street dance' was often used as an umbrella term to describe dance practices including but not limited to: popping, locking, house, hip-hop, breaking, waacking and krump.
3 The organisation was set up in 1979, aiming to connect South Asian dance with the wider contemporary arts sector.
4 This is explored in a second-year project, "Hip-Hop and Digital Activism", led by Senior Lecturer Dr Claudia Brazzale.
5 Examples include BA (Hons) Diverse Dance Styles at Irie Dance Theatre, BA (Hons) Dance at Kingston University and BA (Hons) Professional and Commercial Dance at Shockout Arts. The Northern School of Contemporary Dance (NSCD) started a Cert HE in Cultural Dance Forms, and London Contemporary Dance School (LCDS) offers a broad range of dance forms on their BA (Hons) Contemporary Dance.
6 Dance degree courses that have closed or suspended recruitment at the time of writing in the UK include the University of South Wales in 2019, University of Surrey in 2019 and University of Wolverhampton in 2022.
7 'Good' graduate outcomes refers to those students who graduate with either first class (70% and above) or a 2:1 (60–69%) for their overall degree classification.
8 Frederick Folkes is a dancer, choreographer and actor, who has been practising Popping since 1982 and has trained with the Electric Boogaloos. Robert Nicholson is a dance artist and researcher who trained at London Studio Centre; he is currently working on his PhD which focuses on the unwritten and oral histories of drag performers on the London scene. Delene Gordon is a dance artist who trained at Northern Contemporary Dance School and also works as a massage therapist and trainee biodynamic psychotherapist.
9 In the past, we have had students enter the programme with their main dance practice as bone-breaking, krump and Salsa Caleña, as examples.
10 E.g. Jonzi D, Jonathan Burrows and Anthony Ekundayo-Lennon.
11 *Czerwone Korale* is an example of a piece choreographed by recent graduate Wiktoria Grzes on the course, inspired by both polish folk dances and hip-hop dance. Wiktoria was selected to be developed for *Open Art Surgery* at Breakin' Convention.
12 This platform can be found on Instagram using the tag @thecapsule.ldn and the weekly Podcast (*The Duke LDN Podcast*) is available on Youtube, Apple Podcasts and other podcast platforms.

13 Popping and locking teacher, Fred 'Realness' Folkes, recently transitioned from a visiting lecturer to a permanent core team member and Senior Lecturer on the course at UEL.

14 This is a dance practice commonly referred to as 'Afro Dance', but there are many ongoing debates within this community about terminology and naming. For the academic year of 2021–2022, our teacher George 'Unkle TC' Dukz settled on 'Modern Afro Dance Styles', for the naming of his class.

15 Examples include Tia Denton (@empowered.movement_ on Instagram), Charlie Blair and her company The Blair Academy (@theblairacademy on Instagram) and Karine Goudout who previously worked as the Coordinator at Breakin' Convention (www.breakinconvention.com) and has now joined the core dance team as a lecturer at UEL.

References

Adewole, F. (2016a) 'The Construction of Black Dance/African Peoples Dance Sector in Britain: Issues Arising for the Conceptualisation of Related Choreographic and Dance Practices', in Adair, C. and Burt, R. (eds.) *British Dance: Black Routes*. London and New York: Routledge, pp. 139–162.

Adewole, F. (2016b) 'Carribean Dance: British Perspectives and the Choreography of Beverley Glean', in DeFrantz, T.F. (ed.) *Choreography and Corporeality. Relay in Motion*. London: Palgrave Macmillan, pp. 67–82.

Akademi (2019) *Akademi*. Available at: https://akademi.co.uk/

Akinleye, A. (2018) *Narratives in Black British Dance: Embodied Practices*. Cham: Palgrave Macmillan.

Amin, T.N. (2016) 'Beyond Hierarchy. Reimagining African Diaspora Dance in Higher Education Curricula', *The Black Scholar. Journal of Black Studies and Research*, 46 (1), pp. 15–26. DOI: 10.1080/00064246.2015.1119634

Bajado, C. and Johnson, F. (2019) Interviewed by Carla Trim-Vamben for *An Investigation of Freestyle Practice in UK House Dance*. Unpublished MA Dissertation, 5 June.

balletblack (2020) *balletblack*. Available at: https://balletblack.co.uk/

Ballez (n.d) *Ballez*. Available at: https://www.ballez.org/

Banes, S. (2011) *Terpsichore in Sneakers: Post-modern Dance*. Connecticut: Wesleyan University Press.

Blom, L.A. and Chaplin, L.T. (1988) *The Moment of Movement: Dance Improvisation*. Pittsburgh: University of Pittsburgh Press.

Boy Blue (n.d.) *Boy Blue*. Available at: https://boy-blue-2.webflow.io/

Breakin' Convention (n.d.) *Breakin' Convention*. Available at: https://www.breakinconvention.com/

Brookfield, S.D. (2017) *Becoming a Critically Reflective Teacher*. New York: John Wiley & Sons.

Castelyn, S. (2018) '"Why I am Not a Fan of the Lion King": Ethically Informed Approaches to the Teaching and Learning of South African Dance Forms in Higher Education in the United Kingdom', in Akinleye, A. (ed.) *Narratives in Black British Dance: Embodied Practices*. Switzerland: Springer International Publishing AG, pp. 115–129.

Castelyn, S. (2022) 'Crossing Borders Project Guide', *21–22 Border Crossings Project*. University of East London. Unpublished.

Chang, H.J. and Hogans, A. (2021) 'Teaching Communal Dance Forms. Expanding Student Perspectives and Assisting Dance Educators in the 21st Century', *Journal of Dance Education*, 21(1), pp. 4–13. Available at: https://www.tandfonline.com/doi/full/10.1080/15290824.2019.1652754

Craig, T. and Kynard, C. (2017) 'Sista Girl Rock: Women of Colour and Hip-Hop Deejaying as Raced/Gendered Knowledge and Language', *Changing English*, 24(2), pp. 143–158. Available at: https://www.tandfonline.com/doi/full/10.1080/1358684X.2017.1311034

'Dance Crazes' (2021) *Netflix Explained*, series 3, episode 1. Netflix. 24 September.

DanceMadnessTV (2012) *What Impact Have TV Talent Shows Had on Street Dance*. 7 October. Available at: https://www.youtube.com/watch?v=t_3aVgKrozE

de Paor-Evans, A. (2018) Why *Hip-Hop Needs to be Taken More Seriously in Academic Circles*. Available at: https://theconversation.com/why-hip-hop-needs-to-be-taken-more-seriously-in-academic-circles-95177

DeFrantz, T. (2018) 'Forewards', in: Akinleye, A. (ed.) *Narratives in Black British Dance: Embodied Practices*. Cham: Palgrave Macmillan, pp. 3–6.

Dodds, S. (2011) *Dancing on the Canon: Embodiments of Value in Popular Dance*. Basingstoke: Palgrave Macmillan.

East London Dance (2022) *East London Dance*. Available at: https://www.eastlondondance.org/

Focus Group (2021) *Interview with First, Second and Third Year Students on the BA (Hons) Dance: Urban Practice course*. 15 November, Stratford: University of East London.

Goldman, D. (2010) *I Want to be Ready: Improvised Dance as a Practice of Freedom*. Michigan: The University of Michigan Press.

Gottschild, B. (1998) *Digging the Africanist Presence in American Performance Dance and Other Contexts*. Connecticut: Praeger.

Ill Abilities (2022) *Ill Abilities. International Dance Crew*. Available at: https://www.illabilities.com/

Jackson, J. (2001) 'Improvisation in African-American Vernacular Dancing', *Dance Research Journal*, 33(2), pp. 40–53.

Jordan, S. (2007) *Stravinsky Dances. Re-Visions across a Century*. Alton, Hants: Dance Books.

Kennelly, J. and Watt, P. (2012) 'Seeing Olympic Effects Through the Eyes of Marginally Housed Youth: Changing Places and the Gentrification of East London', *Visual Studies*, 27(2), pp. 151–160. DOI: 10.1080/1472586X.2012.677496.

Malnig, J. (2009) *Ballroom, Boogie, Shimmy Sham, Shake: A Social and Popular Dance Reader*. Champaign: The University of Illinois.

Malone, J. (1996) *Steppin' on the Blues: The Visible Rhythms of African American Dance*. Urbana: University of Illinois Press.

McCarthy-Brown, N. (2009) 'The Need for Culturally Relevant Dance Education', *Journal of Dance Education*, 9(4), pp. 120–125.

McCarthy-Brown, N. (2014) 'Decolonising Dance Curriculum in Higher Education: One Credit at a Time', *Journal of Dance Education*, 14(4), pp. 125–129. Available at: https://www.tandfonline.com/doi/abs/10.1080/15290824.2014.887204?journalCode=ujod20

McMains, J. and Thomas, B. (2013) 'Translating from Pitch to Plie: Music Theory for Dance Scholars and Close Movement Analysis for Music Scholars', *Dance Chronicle*, 36(2), pp. 196–217. DOI: 10.1080/01472526.2013.792714

Miyakawa, F.M. and Schloss, J.G. (2015) *Hip Hop and Hip Hop Dance. Grove Music Essentials.* Oxford: Oxford University Press.

Mohdin, A., Swann, G. and Bannock, C. (2020) 'How George Floyd's Death Sparked a Wave of Anti-Racism Protests', *The Guardian.* Available at: https://www.theguardian.com/uk-news/2020/jul/29/george-floyd-death-fuelled-anti-racism-protests-britain (1 June 2022).

Monroe, R.L. (2011) '"I don't want to do African… What About My Technique?:" Transforming Dancing Places into Spaces in the Academy', *Journal of Pan African Studies,* 4(6), pp. 38–55.

Moser-Kindler, F. (2018) 'It's Time to Familiarise Yourself with the Coolest Styles of Street Dance', *Red Bull.* Available at: https://www.redbull.com/gb-en/dance-your-style-different-styles-guide

Osumare, H. (2016) *The Africanist Aesthetic in Global Hip-Hop: Power Moves.* New York: Palgrave Macmillan.

Read, J. (2018) *Cadences of Choreomusicality: Investigating the Relationship between Sound and Movement in Staged performances of Popping and Animation in the United Kingdom.* Unpublished PhD Thesis. DeMontfort University.

Read, J. (2020) 'Animating the Real: Illusions, Musicality, and the Live Dancing Body', *International Journal of Screendance,* 11, pp. 59–75. DOI: 10.18061/ijsd.v11i0.7100

Roy, S. (2017) 'Boy Blue Entertainment: Blak Whyte Gray Review – Explosive Hip-Hop Robot Ballet'. Available at: https://www.theguardian.com/stage/2017/jan/15/boy-blue-entertainment-blak-whyte-gray-review-explosive-hip-hop-robot-ballet

SADAA (n.d.) *Akademi.* Available at: https://sadaa.co.uk/archive/dance/akademi

Tisshaw, E. (2021) 'Where Is Disability in Hip Hop Dance', *Ink Cypher. Hip Hop Dance Almanac.* Available at: https://www.hiphopdancealmanac.com/ink-cypher-where-is-disability-in-hip-hop-dance

Trim-Vamben, C. (2019) *An Investigation of Freestyle Practice in UK House Dance.* Unpublished MA Dissertation. Roehampton University.

University of East London (2022) *University of East London.* Available at: https://www.uel.ac.uk/

Weale, S. (2021) 'Funding Cuts to go Ahead for University Arts Courses in England Despite Opposition'. Available at: https://www.theguardian.com/education/2021/jul/20/funding-cuts-to-go-ahead-for-university-arts-courses-in-england-despite-opposition

White, B. (2006) 'As If They Didn't Hear the Music, Or: How I Learned to Stop Worrying and Love Mickey Mouse', *The Opera Quarterly,* 22(1), pp. 65–89.

Williamson, G. (2021) Letter to Sir Michael Barber to give *Guidance to the Office for Students — Allocation of the Higher Education Teaching Grant funding in the 2021-22 Financial Year,* 19 January.

2.3 Fostering attentional awareness for connectedness, with agility and empathy as core values

Catherine Seago

Introduction

This book seeks to reflect upon what dance technique might mean today in response to the myriad changes of the past half century since dance became widespread in arts and physical education. During this time, massive evolutionary change across the dance field has been motivated by a growing diversity of styles and purposes, expanded approaches that are more inclusive and interdisciplinary, and influences rooted in technology and digital media. Shifting perceptions and expectations of what dance 'is' have impacted on dance training practices. Attitudes and methods of dance training and education today are more varied than ever before and young people encounter a wide range of approaches. It is with an interest in this broad context that my dance teaching practice has been driven to understand how young people use their attention in dance classes, and if awareness of making different attentional choices in various scenarios can lead to owning a deeper embodied understanding of dance, through finding interconnections within the lived experience. In my practice and research, I have explored the ways in which developing an agile use of attention as part of dance technique practice can facilitate discoveries of interconnectedness amongst dance's varied principles, styles and ideologies, as well as with others.

This chapter proposes that attentional techniques should be foregrounded as part of dance training. I argue that greater awareness of how we attend in practicing physical agility together can help dancers to develop an ethical agility – by encouraging sensitivity to connections with others and developing empathetic skills. This argument contributes to a concern shared with others in this volume for considering the ways that dance techniques can be used to help young people build life-long habits through the values and ethics embedded in dance's various outcomes and purposes. I propose that developing an ethos of practicing attention together in dance classes can cultivate greater interconnectedness, by fostering an agile and empathetic point of view. The discussion below is rooted in my recent action research project which explored how dance students perceive and use attention in dance classes (Seago 2020). Its outcomes indicated that nurturing an agile

DOI: 10.4324/9781003111146-11

use of attention in dance technique practice fostered a mindful state through letting go of fixed ideas and being present and encouraged a greater facility for empathy through multisensory alertness to all that is happening. Building on these findings, I will discuss the ways in which interconnectedness can be cultivated through an agile use of attention and the implicit value of realising connections within and beyond dance skills development, for well-being, care, health and education.

How is attention currently viewed in the technique class?

Attention, first and foremost, allows us to make sense of the world, actively and effectively processing particular information while at the same time withdrawing from other stimuli in our environment. Commonly, expectations of dance and music training for young people have been about improving the brain's executive attention networks (Posner and Patoine 2009). Cognitive science research has evidenced the usefulness of these in building coordination, concentration and efficiency, often through repetitions. However, as one withdraws from other stimuli to concentrate on recreating one single fixed thing, it can be damaging to the process of learning deeply. Brown, Ryan and Creswell (2007: 213) claim that 'concentration entails a restriction of attention to a single interoceptive or exteroceptive object, leading to a withdrawal of sensory and other inputs'. They explore the distinction between concentration and mindfulness (Engler 1986). In dance classes, repetitions can indeed seem narrowing and in my research project assumptions about the value of fixing, controlling and restraining concentration on a single end goal was initially shown to be common amongst participants. The rather out-of-date interpretation that practices, including attention, should be disciplined to enable the performance of an ideal which is fixed, targeted, automatic and second nature might be unhelpful in our current, pedagogically informed, dance training landscape. Mihaly Csikszentmihalyi (1990) has proposed that a 'flow experience' is helpful for deeper engagement and is often evident in being thoroughly absorbed in an activity. He proposes that flow is achieved, in part, through attentionalities which involve balancing, merging and responding. While many of the participants in my project reported that allowing such fluidity in their attention use was disorienting and distracted them from focusing on task at hand, others found a renewed sense of agency through the flexibility they experienced. Indeed, cognitive scientist and educational psychologist Guy Claxton has illustrated that a gliding attention is an important aspect of a learning process by allowing variation in its intensity, direction and social-ness throughout. He imagines a 'three dimension attentional 'crate' of creativity (2006: 67) which contains a 'glide space' (2006: 66). Through this he offers to help us perceive how different mindsets enable us to work in different and flexible ways as we direct our attention inwards or outwards toward others, operate from solitary or social positions and zoom in and zone out various stimuli. Claxton's diagrammatic crate models the interconnected dimensions of attention throughout a learning process and the mutual impacts on the whole. Claxton's crate for attentional flow shares similarities with Csikszentmihalyi's theory of flow in its focus on articulating the productivity of mindsets that are present to all that is happening and responsive to changing conditions to allow for an individual's creative success or, as Csikszentmihalyi's theory indicates, a way to achieve happiness.

An agile attention, flowing easily amongst internal and external targets via oral, visual, tactile and kinaesthetic modes, can promote a sense of fluid interconnectedness. Robert Sawyer (2006) has investigated Csikszentmihalyi's flow theory, which focuses on a state of consciousness for achieving individual flow, to examine how flow operates in relation with others – specifically in collaborative, emergent creative practices. Sawyer's 'group flow' (2006) shares the conditions which produce easy enjoyment and success in the process of doing something but proposes additionally a state of 'interactional synchrony' (2006: 157) in successful group working. This state sees an entire group feeling strongly connected and 'in sync' as they flow *together*. In group flow, the inter-relational attention can enable anticipation of what fellow performers will do even before they do it (Sawyer 2006: 158) in addition to propelling individuals beyond themselves. Lucznik, May and Redding's research showed a group of improvising dance students experienced a state of 'becoming one with the group' (2021: 199), describing an 'effortless attention' (204) as they practiced together. My study is not concerned with being in sync with others in emergent practices but finds similarities with the expression of a feeling of being one with others in flow – through developing an ethos of practicing agile attention together. Group flow produces a strong sense of connectedness to others who we are 'in sync' with, it is owned by the whole group and happens as a result of their interaction. Sawyer (2006: 158) quotes Jazz bassist Chuck Israels who articulates, 'If it's working, it brings you very close. It's a kind of emotional empathy that you develop very quickly. The relationship is very intimate' (as quoted in Berliner, 1994: 349–350). In listening and sensing others in parallel with our own attentional practice in dancing an intimate and empathetic sense of mutuality can arise, provoking awareness of the impact we have upon each other. As Sawyer says, 'you can't relax your attention or you will fall behind' (2006: 159). Practicing attention *together* in dance class can help to develop alertness to and with others and, in a common flow experience, a sense of being connected with them. It can encourage not only dancing together but being present in our attention together.

As dancers attend with other dancers by observing and translating particular visual forms into a kinaesthetic sense they go further in their connectedness, with the production of a 'felt' response to the movement of others. This is kinaesthetic empathy – widely documented since the discovery of the mirror neuron system (MNS) in the early 1990s. As the MNS fires it recreates what is seen by and in the seer, involving a precise physical change and inviting a particularly intimate sense of being connected by physically experiencing a sense of 'putting myself in your shoes'. This intimate process has been explored in relation to studio practice by Shantel Ehrenberg (2012) who has examined, from a practitioner's perspective, how a dancer tries to imagine ways to feel and do the movement that one sees performed by another. The interconnectedness of our sensory system is apparent as we attend to seeing (in the mirror or on video) and feeling ourselves while moving ourselves as well as imagining our appearance to others and trying to feel the way that another looks in dance class. When dancing amongst others our fundamentally empathetic responses are foregrounded in this process. As attention flows amongst your, my and our experience as we dance together, we anticipate moments and feelings of connectedness.

Feeling connected with others is a familiar and richly rewarding aspect of dancing. It is most often foregrounded by improvisational practices and ensemble composition as well as in dance company working. My interest is in how attentional use in dance technique classes can help to build up values of connectedness through agile and empathetic responsiveness. Discovering emotional and physical connections is helpful in building up a sense of community. Psychological theories (Deci and Ryan 1985, Maslow 1954) have shown the importance of social connection in growth, development and motivation. Making connections is vital for versatility, creativity, criticality and synthesising new ideas. Feeling connected is important for physical and emotional health and well-being. It is widely recognised that a sense of connectedness can lead to people becoming more trusting and cooperative as well as greater self-esteem and empathy rooted in lower levels of anxiety and depression (Seppala 2014). Developing an ethos of practicing attention together in dance classes can help in recognising the value of connectedness for versatility, creativity, growth and cooperation within and beyond dance skills. Recent research has examined how universities could foster a sense of connectedness to better support student mental health (Di Malta et al. 2022). Moreover, social prescribing has been adopted as part of National Health Service (NHS) care in England in recognition of the 'interconnections between activity levels, social connectivity, and mental health' (Husk et al. 2019). Foregrounding attentional use in dance technique practice to develop an agile and empathetic point of view can help students to build life-long habits for valuing connectedness – an ethos which can be carried into a range of contexts.

Exploring attention and connectedness with students

An initial aim of my research and practice has been to explore ways to encourage dancers to be more available to potential connectedness within an often bricolage-style approach to their dance training. Bricolage-style approaches have replaced the singular approaches to training dancers proposed by modern dance and the subsequent notion of training of dancers for more varied roles, or 'for hire' which Susan Foster articulated in 1997. Bales and Nettl Fiol (2008) adopted the term bricolage to characterise the 'self-styled' training approach amongst practitioner teachers which emerged from the dialectics and bricolage of post modernism. A bricolage-based approach to dance training for students can promote a more inclusive curriculum, offer unique juxtapositions and produce new insights into ways of knowing and applying dance. However, discerning, synthesising and making connections amongst often dialectical concepts, approaches, values and languages in each's own dancing body is its own challenge. While having a 'go at everything' (Rafferty in Rafferty and Stanton 2017: 197) provides a rich terrain for individual discovery, Rafferty has suggested that as teachers we might seek to connect our broad yet 'kindered' principles to assist our students in finding and making connections for themselves. With this in mind, a main aim underpinning my research project was to facilitate greater agency for uncovering intra and inter-relational connectedness amongst dance experiences. Attention techniques can enable a greater awareness of habit, choice and potentialities, encouraging agency to identify available connections as dancers move amongst different experiences, demands and ideas.

My research project sought to investigate students' lived experience of the different modes, manners, targets and values of attention through contemporary dance. The research was underpinned by two principles. First, that particular uses of attention are embedded within different approaches and styles of dance training. Second, that it is beneficial to dancers to utilise reflexively a range of modes and values in order to have consistent framework for attentional practice. Rather than comparing the principles of techniques and the attentional values they foreground, I was motivated by Kirsty Alexander's call for a 'consistent framework of values' which, she suggested, might be found in kinaesthetic experiences, to underscore a 'continuum of somatic and traditional practices' (2008 in Reed 2015: 214). My intentions were to raise awareness of perceptual choice, encouraging students to use their reflections to enable connections amongst their lived experiences and to allow their attention to flow between modes and targets as they dance. I hoped to help students to build up a sense of agency in testing and fine-tuning their attention, in order to discover potential connections amongst approaches and embodiments.

The questions driving my action research project were: to what extent are dancers aware of their uses and choices of attention in training classes; what is the impact of expectations about distinct dance practices on attention use; how can free-flowing attention rather than fixed (concentration) benefit dancers and how can a greater sense of agency result from awareness of uses and choices? To explore my questions, I worked with 16 final-year undergraduate dance students in regular physical skills classes. Second-person participatory action research (Reason and Bradbury 2008) enabled me to assess the students' active engagement with concepts of attention and gather data about their practices and understanding through teaching observations, multi-mode journals, anonymous questionnaires and focus group with semi-structured questions. Potential ethical issues linked to scale, the complexity of my joint position as teacher and researcher and perceptions of assessment and conformity were considered and addressed through discussion and consent to data use. The aim was to create an environment in which the distinct demands and experiences of attention in dancing could intermingle so the methodology featured a combination of formal exercises and open-ended movement tasks, peer observation, annotating movement and written, diagrammatic and discursive reflections. Bricolage-styled sessions enabled participants to explore various values and modes of attention. In my sessions, technique exercises focused on embodying fragmentation and micro-rhythmic patterning to enable coordination, drawing on Cunningham-based technique practices. Improvisation tasks encouraged present-ness, spontaneity and external/ensemble relations. Yogic directions reinforced flow in the dimensions and directions of movement, whole-ness and new-ness in repetitions. Choreological concepts such as were used to articulate the nature of changes taking place within movement structures and virtual spatial forms. To encourage reflective strategies and individual feedback loops, the group were introduced to concepts, uses and values of attention, for example sensory modes of attending kinaesthetically, visually and aurally, verbally, musically and spatially; internal and external targets; the qualities, multiples and intensities of attention; and allowing, placing, tracing and fixing it. Examining established attentional values was encouraged, for example the introspective values of inward listening and soft sensational attention are championed by somatic practices and the historically visually dominated attentional use of codified forms. Further, adopting a wider field of attention is often cultivated by associative, generative practices. We used a growing knowledge and experience to build up techniques for noticing, triggering and shifting attention, for example, using mapping techniques to represent when, how, what and why particular attentionalities dominate what is being practiced and to experiment with interchangeable aspects and opportunities.

Interpreting experiences of attention

The research findings showed initially limited, but consequently increased, awareness of attention use in my study group. The two-way engagement of this pedagogic action research, as Gibbs et al. (2017: 10) has summarised, encouraged deeper learning and, for some, resulted in higher achievement. For most, Stanton's lab-style (2011) mixed-mode approach enabled exploration of attention in new and productive ways. As Rachel Rimmer-Piekarczyk argues in this volume, dance training approaches can struggle to shift the 'doxa' – the established unspoken understanding of the way of things. During my project, dependency on the teacher as owner of dance knowledge lessened because a focus on their own attention use encouraged personal reflection and reflexive practice. Noticing, shifting and letting go of attentional targets and modes provoked many to be present to what was happening, less fixed on the outcomes and more available to potential connections that they sensed, noticed and felt within the materials, the environment and with others – without an underlying resistance to being 'distracted' by these things. Some experienced agency in a new way, and others became more aware of the impact of others in the class. Some felt overwhelmed but, for most, a greater confidence to refine and shape the dance experience for themselves became apparent.

Knowing what different attentional strategies are, together with an awareness of how they impact on dance practice evidently benefited students involved in my project. Outcomes indicated that attention training benefited students in the following ways:

1 Engaging with attention use enabled recognition of habitual practices and reflections on the impact of attentional choices on the lived experience;
2 Being open to and present in how they attend enabled potential connections to appear;
3 Exploring strategies for negotiating multiple attention flows in an ever-shifting world encouraged flexibility in response to change and led to agility;
4 Making choices about attention by not focusing on fixed goals led to a deeper sense of agency;
5 Fostering a sense of the feeling of the movement of others encouraged empathy.

The outcomes of the action research highlighted particular attributes being drawn out from the dancer via knowledge and skills of attention. Attributes exhibiting particular values came to the fore such as recognising and owning behaviour, being mindful in approaching new challenges, resilience, agency and empathy. Bill Lucas proposes, in his report questioning '21st century skills' that weaving together such knowledge and skills with attributes and values form the competencies that drive actions (Lucas 2019). In seeking ways to build life-long habits for an attentional awareness through being present for agile and empathetic connections to arise, both within and beyond dance class, attention training evidently has something to offer. However, in defining attention as 'focused noticing', dancer Peter Fraser (2016) captures the tension of balancing a singular deep investigation and a wider and more open awareness, illustrating Claxton's polarities in practice. To develop an agile practice of attention requires building confidence to remain in the inevitable moments of uncertainty within the sudden shifts afforded by noticing, allowing, letting go and catching on to things, while at the same time to be committed to deep investigation of each fleeting awareness. To cultivate a quiet and focused commitment to exploring attentional shifts that can be fluid, sudden, light and surprising has an ethical aspect.

This approach is the antithesis of current UK education frameworks. It can be enormously challenging for the teacher (a) to foster the open heartedness of 'allowing' when our students so often crave definitive direction and (b) to invite an investigation of potential connectedness when students can often perceive their bodies and experiences in isolation, reiterated by digital environments in which they are often operating. Yet this is what an attention training can offer – a transformative pedagogy, facilitating an understanding of how mindful attention use can encourage an open, flexible and present point of view which can foster resilience through persistence in pursuing the ever-changing and unfixable connections within our lived experience.

Agility as a core value of dance technique

Encouraging an agile attention for discovering connections rather than fixing attention on a single goal/approach varied in its impact. First to note is that some participants reported feeling overwhelmed at the notion. Many reported the need for familiar or slower paced materials during what might have been a disorienting experience of recognising attention flow. Csikszentmihalyi's flow theory highlights the need for a balance of established skill and challenge in an activity while both Claxton and Csikszentmihalyi's concepts of flow foreground the importance of demarking clear progression. One student in my group reported that, when working towards an agile attention, potential connections appeared making 'much more to develop' apparent as a growing sense of 'inquiry' emerged, 'rather than just getting it done'. She became deeply absorbed in a process of inquiry, through a flow experience. The importance of agile attention for deepening dance practice has been articulated by Danny Lepkoff (2011). He explains that in Contact Improvisation (CI) '[w]hen my attention stops moving, my interpretation of what is happening becomes fixed and my vision becomes conventionalized, and thus the questioning disappears' (2011). He is talking about being available to external as well as internal stimuli in indeterminate dancing with others and indicating the excitement and inquiry of potential connections. Being absorbed and energised by the process of doing challenging but attainable things is part of Csikszentmihalyi's state of flow. I found that during the familiar repetitive practices of, for example, Cunningham-based phrases, mobilising attention better enabled participants to access a similar experience of freedom from fixed visions and interpretations which Lepkoff identifies in CI. A number of participants became confident with a lively negotiation of attention during activities, phrases and exercises. One participant reported 'it never occurred to me to choose what to focus on – it has completely changed my experience of dancing'.

Participants reflected on how they attended to the tone, dynamic and imagery of instructions; the effects of self-chat, ambition, preconception and deep remembering on their attentional choices; and on how the feeling states, tactility, kinaesthetic awareness as well as motor skills and physiological responses impacted on their attention use. Second to note is that exploring attention helped participants to be more present to what was happening across this spectrum of targets and modes- a vital condition of Csikszentmihalyi's concept of flow. Presence, Seigel (2007) says, is our capacity to be open to what is happening as it happens. It is a fundamental component of mindfulness which encourages letting go of outcomes to be present to what might be happening now. In practicing agile attention, something akin to a mindful state became apparent for participants in my project. Letting go of fixed ideas, goals and interpretations one said, 'I can relax more, being present to what is happening'. Being 'fully present in the moment' and perceiving by the 'whole body, not just my eyes' is, says American dance educator Stinson (2015: 2), a state of consciousness which she says is shared by mindfulness and dance. A holistic engagement is underpinned by present-ness to all our senses. Independent dance artist Gill Clarke encouraged being simply present to sense different possibilities in movement. These, she says, are available through 'tasting sensations' in the body rather than 'forming of movement' which has visual definition (in DeLahunta et al. 2012: 247). She highlights the value of clearing away the 'clutter' of the principles and complexities of codified movement vocabularies to explore different feelings of movement via looking/listening and sensing with a light touch. Clarke valued 'letting go' in order to focus the 'skills of attention' which she saw could help to develop 'discrimination and differentiation of fine nuance in the process of moving' (in DeLahunta et al. 2012: 248).

Jenny Roche (2015) reflects on Clarke's pedagogy for developing dancers as 'investigative artists' who can make things their own. She recognises the vitality of agency for the dancer for whom agile responsiveness is essential. Roche has characterised the current contemporary dance landscape as continually rupturing the 'stability of the familiar'. For choreographer William Forsythe, this rupture is a necessary element in seeking to 'detach ourselves from positions of certainty' (2011 in Roche 2015: 254). For the continual evolution of movement approaches and vocabularies, the field might be best served by a bricolage approach to training. Dancers are required to build an embodied understanding which is both consistent and agile. However, the question of deep or wide approaches to training, refuelled recently by the publicised concerns about the rigour of contemporary dance training in Britain by three international choreographers (Mackrell 2015), persists. A bricolage approach can be useful in building skills for making connections and for experiencing dance as an inclusive practice – a vital aspect of the dance training needed for working across dance today. Building up skills for seeking out new intra- and inter-relational connections amongst peers, styles, approaches and experiences can be a valuable outcome of honing an attentional practice as part of dance training, preparing dancers to bring a range of perspectives to their work. One student in my project specified that agile attention 'allows me to choose to work on particular things, and to deal with how I'm feeling that day'. Struck by her separation of a more personal

'I' within her learning process, I was reminded of Roche's findings. Roche has investigated how a dancer's personal lived experience can shape their own movement and the valuable contribution this makes to new choreographies. Roche terms it a dancer's 'moving identity' (2011). I propose that an agile attentional practice can help ready dancers to identify with their own, vitally shifting 'moving identity' through building versatility and resilience for resisting certainty and finding unique new connections. Project findings indicating that fixed growth mindsets, interpretation and self-evaluation, which can cause a resistance to building agency, were reduced through an agile use of attention were promising – 'since being aware of my attention it has completely changed how I think when I'm dancing' reported a student on the project.

Empathy as a core value of dance technique

My research findings indicated that an intrinsic value of finding intra-relational connectedness in dance experiences might not only build up a sense of inquiry, presence and agency but also a more empathetic point of view. In my project, dancers attended not only to their own embodied experience but also to the attention of others as they practiced together. Many developed a greater awareness of the attention of others in reciprocal and shared ways, developing a sense of the feeling of movement of others while attending to their own attentional practice. New inter-relational connections were often seeded through exploring attention through improvisational and peer-to-peer work. An increased awareness of the intraconnectedness of their multisensory systems of perception and attention promoted greater fluidity in looking, listening and feeling. An exercise highlighted kinaesthetic empathy as dancers used touch as well as observation to trigger and modify movement in peer work. Welton (2010) articulates that touch is a metaphor for attentive listening in Rosemary Lee's Common Dance (2009), explaining that it is a 'mode of perception in which one is reciprocally giving as well as receiving'. Indeed, our intrinsically fluid sensory systems allow 'listening' attentively for movement intention and detail to involve touching, sensing and looking. In highlighting a full multisensory attention, participants reported that feelings of empathy for others emerged more strongly as they anticipated each other's listening through greater bodily awareness. In this volume, Lee, in conversation with Scilla Dyke, expresses her sense that the skill of being finely attentive in listening to others often does not currently appear highly valued, or visible in dance training and performance. Finding connections with others through practicing attention together has, for me, indicated a potential value of attention training as part of dance techniques. Nurturing attentive egalitarian sensibilities for listening to, for and with others most often appears as part of Contact Improvisation in dance training. Here tactility and softening promote sensitive listening in non-hierarchical relations. The mutual connectedness found in the reciprocity of contact work echos the deep listening of group flow. We are reminded by Miranda Tufnell (2017) that in touching we are also touched – simultaneously giving and receiving. However, in training, there is often limited opportunity for the expansion of these vital multisensory, empathetic skills of attention into other areas of practice. Building up empathetic skills as an intrinsic part of refining the dancer's own physical agilities should be a fundamental aspect of dance training in the now expanded field of dance. Developing skills of cross-referencing the senses in different activities, to enable tuning into the feeling of others, could help prepare dance students for work in the caring and social professions as well as performative and collaborative work by fostering ethical human relations.

Practicing attention together in my project revealed characteristics of Sawyer's group flow. Listening, anticipating movement of and synchronicity with others led to strong empathetic relations in duet and group improvisational exercises and in set material. A sense of being one with the group emerged from building up a dance together although such connections happen more commonly in ensemble improvisation or improvisational composition where dancers depend upon the interactions and deep listening, to produce group flow in their practice. Practicing phrases of set 'technique' materials – solitary although synchronous – can produce a sense of shared attention in 'coming in' together or preparing for specific partner work such as the moment of a lift with cooperation and trust. Participants in my project also noted a sense of shared attention in anticipating external stimuli together – for example listening/sensing for indeterminate cues from 'within a dance'. Some found that the experience of being *one* with others was intensely moving as they anticipated together in different ways. These skills and experiences of non-hierarchical, cooperative and shared ways of being in relation are vital in developing socially engaged dancers. It calls for an ethos of practicing attention together to be developed as part of dance classes. As Claxton has invited us to see, fluidity amongst our modes of social and solitary attention, inner-outer resources and detailed and wide lenses can enable us to use our attention flexibly and responsively. An ethical attention might use this agility to dig deeper, wider, softer and find greater open-ness and inclusivity through being present and synchronous with each other as we dance.

Closing

So, what is the usefulness of practicing agile attention together and developing students' empathetic skills to build up a sense of connectedness?

Nurturing an awareness of our attentional habits, the ways in which we pay, give and receive attention and the way that these choices can colour our worlds is a useful practice for personal growth as well as for developing relevant skills for a diversifying British dance industry. A bricolage-style dance training is a fertile ground for seeding attentional awareness through enabling skills for multisensory engagement, letting go and being present to difference and change. Actively seeking out connections within our lived experience builds up capacities for inquiry, creativity, empathy and cooperation, as well as versatility, resilience and agency. Attention training as part of dance education has the potential to promote an ethos of practice which is about awareness of attention with each other, and these attributes underpin the development of ethical human relations. Practicing attentional agility together can help us grow as socially engaged individuals who are more aware of the nature of our relations with others and the experience of others in relation to our own. Connecting with others in these ways can develop vital skills for working in a range of collaborative and developmental settings. Practicing being present, flexible and responsive to environmental demands and to each other can help to foster a greater sense of connectedness. Being connected with others can be said to be a twenty-first-century obsession. The Covid pandemic highlighted the importance of connectedness for many and saw a massive increase in the use of digital devices for social media, messaging applications and video platforms to stay connected. However, it has been shown that 'coronavirus has atrophied the social skills of many individuals in the absence of peers' (Apurvakumar and Pragya 2021). The reason for this is that people interact differently in digital environments. Our use of attentional modes is more limited and our capacity to be present with each other is reduced on screen. Connecting with the subtle nuances of social interaction and etiquette found in non-verbal interactions is not fully possible with virtual online communication. It is evident that for a greater sense of connection we need to practice being more attentive to each other in live, bodied contexts, particularly in an era where excessive digital use leads to increasing attention-deficit symptoms, impaired emotional and social intelligence, social isolation and mental illnesses such as depression [and] anxiety (Apurvakumar and Pragya 2021). Attending to each other's attention in different ways can help us build courage to move amongst others sensitively as we share experience, space and time. As I have probed through a dance technique context, practicing attention together can help to build up an ethical agility in the dancer's ability to be present with others.

Developing an ethos of practicing attention together in dance classes can cultivate values of connectedness by being present, alert and empathetic. An ethics of attention can be a way of being together which is present, alert to wide field of perspectives and possibilities and open to seeking connections. In reflecting on what dance technique might be today I have tried to convey the usefulness of practicing an interconnected physical, ethical and attentional agility, together, in ways that allow new connections to appear as we tune into our whole selves and to others with sensitivity and vitality.

References

Apurvakumar, P., and Pragya, L. (2021) "Social Connectedness, Excessive Screen Time during COVID-19 and Mental Health: A Review of Current Evidence." *Frontiers in Human Dynamics* 3. https://doi.org/10.3389/fhumd.2021.684137

Bales, M., and Nettl Fiol, R. Eds. (2008) *The Body Eclectic: Evolving Practices in Dance Training.* Urbana and Chicago: University of Illinois Press.

Berliner, P. (1994) *Thinking in Jazz: The Infinite Art of Improvisation.* Chicago, IL: University of Chicago Press.

Brown, K., Ryan, R., and Creswell, D. (2007) "Mindfulness: Theoretical Foundations and Evidence for Its Salutary Effects." *Psychological Inquiry* 18 (4): 211–237. https://doi.org/10.1080/10478400701598298

Claxton, G. (2006) "Creative Glide Space." In *Navigating the Unknown: The Creative Process in Contemporary Performing Arts,* edited by C. Bannerman, J. Sofaer, and J. Watt, 58–69. London: Middlesex University Press.

Csikszentmihalyi, M. (1990) *Flow: The Psychology of Optimal Experience.* New York: HarperCollins.

Deci, E.L., and Ryan, R.M. (1985) *Intrinsic Motivation and Self-Determination in Human Behavior.* New York: Plenum.

DeLahunta, S., Clarke, G., and Barnard, P. (2012) "A Conversation about Choreographic Thinking Tools." *Journal of Dance and Somatic Practices* 3 (1+ 2): 243–259. https://doi.org/10.1386/jdsp.3.1-2.243_1

Di Malta, G., Bond, J., Conroy, D., Smith, K., and Moller, N. (2022). "Distance Education Students' Mental Health, Connectedness and Academic Performance during COVID-19: A Mixed-Methods Study." *Distance Education* (Early Access). https://doi.org/10.1080/01587919.2022.2029352

Ehrenberg, S. (2012) "A Contemporary Dancer's Kinaesthetic Experiences with Dancing Self-images." In *Dance Spaces: Practices of Movement,* edited by S. Ravn and L. Rouhiainen, 193–213. Odense: University of Southern Denmark.

Engler, J. (1986) "Therapeutic Aims in Psychotherapy and Meditation." In *Transformations of Consciousness: Conventional and Contemplative Perspectives on Development,* edited by K. Wilber, J. Engler, and D.P. Brown, 17–51. Boston, MA: Shambhala.

Foster, S. (1997) "Dancing Bodies." In *Meaning in Motion: New Cultural Studies of Dance,* edited by J. Desmond, 235–258. Durham, NC: Duke University Press.

Fraser, P. (2016) "Gaps in the Body: Attention and Improvisation." *Brolga* 40: 73–84.

Gibbs, P., Cartney, P. Wilkinson, K., Parkinson, J., Cunningham, S., James-Reynolds, C., Zoubir, T., et al. (2017) "Literature Review on the Use of Action Research in Higher Education." *Educational Action Research* 25 (1): 3–22. https://doi.org/10.1080/09650792.2015.1124046

Husk, K., Elston, J., Gradinger, F., Callaghan, L., and Asthana, S. (2019) "Social Prescribing: Where Is the Evidence?" *British Journal of General Practice* 69 (678): 6–7. https://doi.org/10.3399/bjgp19X700325

Lepkoff, D. (2011) "Contact Improvisation: A Question." *Contact Quarterly* 36 (1): 38–40. Available at: https://contactquarterly.com/cq/article-gallery/view/contact-improvisation-a-question#$

Lucas, B. (2019) "Why We Need to Stop Talking about 21st Century Skills." *Melbourne Center for Strategic Education Seminar Series Paper #283* May 2019. Available at: www.expansiveeducation.net

Lucznik, K., May, J., and Redding, E. (2021) "A Qualitative Investigation of Flow Experience in Group Creativity." *Research in Dance Education* 22 (2): 190–209. https://doi.org/10.1080/14647893.2020.1746259

Mackrell, J. (2015) "Are British Dancers Really Outclassed on the World Stage?" *The Guardian dance blog* 13 April.

Maslow, A.H. (1954) *Motivation and Personality.* New York: Harper & Brothers.

Posner, M., and Patoine, B. (2009) "How Arts Training Improves Attention and Cognition." *Cerebrum*, September 14.

Rafferty, S., and Stanton, E. (2017) "I Am a Teacher and I Will Do What I Can: Some Speculations on the Future of Dance Technique Class and Its Possible Transformation." *Research in Dance Education* 18 (2): 190–204. https://doi.org/10.1080/14647893.2017.1354841

Reason, P., and Bradbury, H. Eds. (2008) *The Sage Handbook of Action Research*. 2nd ed. London: Sage.

Reed, S. (2015) "Attending to Movement." In *Attending to Movement. Somatic Perspectives on Living in This World*, edited by S. Whatley, N.G. Brown, and K. Alexander, 207–218. Axminster: Axminster Triarchy Press.

Roche, J. (2011) "Embodying Multiplicity: The Independent Contemporary Dancer's Moving Identity." *Research in Dance Education* 12 (2): 105–118. https://doi.org/10.1080/14647893.2011.575222

Roche, J. (2015) "Disorganising Principles." In *Attending to Movement. Somatic Perspectives on Living in This World*, edited by S. Whatley, N.G. Brown, and K. Alexander, 253–262. Axminster: Axminster Triarchy Press.

Sawyer, R.K. (2006) "Group Creativity: Musical Performance and Collaboration." *Psychology of Music* 34 (2): 148–165. https://doi.org/10.1177/0305735606061850

Seago, C. (2020) "A Study of the Perception and Use of Attention in Undergraduate Dance Training Classes." *Research in Dance Education* 21 (3): 245–261. https://doi.org/10.1080/14647893.2020.1757636

Seigel, D.J. (2007) *The Mindful Brain: Reflection and Attunement in the Cultivation of Well-Being*. New York and London: W.W Norton.

Seppala, E. (2014) "Connectedness & Health: The Science of Social Connection." *The Center for Compassion and Altruism Research and Education*. Available at: www.ccare.stanford.edu

Stanton, E. (2011) "Doing, Re-Doing and Undoing: Practice, Repetition and Critical Evaluation as Mechanisms for Learning in a Dance Technique Class 'Laboratory'." *Theatre, Dance and Performance Training* 2 (1): 86–98. https://doi.org/10.1080/19443927.2011.545253

Stinson, S. (2015) "Dance Education as the Practice of Living." https://ausdance.org.au/uploads/content/publications/daCi-2015/education/Dance-Education-as-the-Practice-of-Living-Susan-Stinson.pdf

Tufnell, M. (2017) *When I Open My Eyes*. Dance Books Ltd.

Welton, M. (2010) "Listening-As-Touch: Paying Attention to Rosemary Lee's Common Dance." *Performance Research* 15 (3): 47–54. https://doi.org/10.1080/13528165.2010.527203

2.4 Steps towards decolonising contact improvisation in the university

Tamara Ashley

To begin the work of anti-oppression and anti-racism is to start from an acknowledgement of positionality and privilege or oppression. Mine is a privilege of a mobile life lived in many countries as well as the complexity of a multi-lineage family, with traumatic histories of migration and displacement, as well as arrival and settlement. I am of Scottish, English, Portuguese and South Asian descent, and my pronouns are she/her. I am a dancer, teacher, researcher, yoga and somatic practitioner, with degrees from universities in the UK and United States. I have focused my work in somatic practice, contact improvisation (CI), yoga, bodywork and contemporary dance through the lenses of critical pedagogy and ecological justice for over 20 years. I have been interested in how oppressions intersect and how harm is perpetuated across minorities and marginalised populations as well as the planet itself. As a teacher, I also believe that practices such as CI provide contexts in which critical, activist and reflective processes of individual and social transformation can occur through the engagement with the form itself. Decolonising the practice of such a form is a logical extension of a critically engaged pedagogy and becomes essential to an ethical anti-racist teaching practice when it is acknowledged how racism permeates every aspect of social, cultural and political life.

CI is an open-ended practice that is taught through a wide range of methods from the teaching of partnering forms, to the exploration of scores for improvisation, to anatomically based explorations that serve as impetus for moving and relating. A core principle is negotiating weight flow through relating in touch/contact, whether that is with the earth, or other with other bodies, and there are several techniques that aim to refine this skill in practitioners. These techniques are principles for moving rather than specific movements, and they are open to interpretation by each individual practitioner. CI already reorients the ethics of teaching dance technique, in that there is no imposition of form on the body. The details of the movement developed are the responsibility of the practitioner, and work within the practitioner's own experience and capacity, developing agency and ownership of the movement learning and process from the very beginning. Advanced- and beginning-level dancers can explore the same principles, and an advanced dancer might

DOI: 10.4324/9781003111146-12

be recognised for their nuance and sensitivity, over perhaps, form-based virtuosic accomplishment. At the University of Bedfordshire, the assessment criteria for CI technique assessments privilege skill in sensitive response to self and others, skill in navigating one's own capacity in weight flow, trust and touch and creative response within one's expressive and physical range. Because of this open-ended exploration of key principles, and the freedom to create and innovate with the form, I have mostly regarded the form as accessible, inclusive and progressive in that dancers of mixed levels can be in the same class. However, when starting to investigate CI from a decolonial perspective, it can be seen that the practice contains within it both tools to aid processes of decolonisation as well as practices and assumptions that are exclusive and harmful to people of colour.

I was initiated into practicing the form of CI by white teachers from the United States. I have noticed, over the years, a lack of participation in jams, festivals and other such events by black dancers and also of efforts by leading teachers and organisations to reach out to some of these dancers. It has been a concern of one of the form's founders, Steve Paxton, and, in a recent interview with Mitra, he acknowledges that the form has not been very successful at integrating black dancers. Paxton explains:

> As the recent Black Lives Matter movement signals to us, what we once considered was institutionalized racism as practiced by the police is in fact systemic in our society, our culture. So, it might well be that rubbing skins with your oppressors is not an appealing prospect within contact. It seems to be a bit of a canary in a coal mine situation this. It warns us that something might be up, and has been, for the whole time that contact has been around.
>
> (Paxton in Mitra, 2018: 15)

What is interesting about the development of CI is that despite its roots in the inclusive politics of the 1970s American counterculture, the form is acknowledged as predominantly white and yet it draws heavily upon aikido, and in the approaches developed by Nancy Stark Smith, Tibetan Buddhism. CI is simultaneously hybrid, by incorporating diverse cultural and indigenous knowledges, and exclusive, through its implicit and systemic failure to truly engage a diverse range of people in the practice. Nonetheless, I have taught the work extensively in education settings and universities, trying to integrate a critical pedagogical approach that offers a questioning approach to the somatic experiences of the body and mind in the practice. The recent thinking and scholarship outlined above have prompted me to reflect more deeply and consider what it might mean to decolonise CI as a practice for the twenty-first-century curriculum.

In this chapter, I will discuss three steps that I am developing in my own practice to decolonise my teaching in order to develop some ethical agility as a practitioner committed to developing anti-racist progressive relations in teaching and learning. These three steps are rendered from experiential insights, ongoing research in critical pedagogy and current research in dance on racism, anti-racism, decolonisation, whiteness and oppression of the body. The three steps are not definitive and I am open to developing them. However, it is useful to ground teaching practice and action in tangible steps. I have explored the three steps in practical teaching, in the development of my own research and in the context of research supervision. In this chapter, I will offer a discussion on the application and development of each of the steps in detail. In summary, these three steps are:

1 Understand the body as a site of identity development and change and that oppression is embodied (Caldwell and Leighton, 2016).
2 Understand that my teaching begins from an inherently racist standpoint.
3 Critically interrogate white privilege and embed critical questioning from the beginning (bell hooks).

What does it mean to engage in a process of decolonisation? Shifting from a focus on diversity to a focus on decolonisation.

Before going in-depth into each of the three steps, it is useful to discuss a broader meaning of decolonisation of teaching in dance and somatic practices. Decolonisation is a contested and debated term subject to multiple renderings and applications. However, broad definitions can be gleaned from the literature. In the UK, there has been a growing movement to decolonise the curriculum, which further develops the concerns of postcolonial studies, cultural studies and social and environmental justice movements through the works of scholars such as Sarah Ahmed, bell hooks, Paul Gilroy, Stuart Hall and many others. Initiated in 2015, #whyismycurriculumwhite, for example, is led by the National Union of Students Black Students' campaign. The campaign seeks to deconstruct the concept of whiteness in higher education, where whiteness 'exceeds the individual and is a ubiquitous, multifaceted and inconsistent manifestation of power' (Magd, 2016). Further to that, Magd asserts that the normative white curricular bias of the university is no longer acceptable. Such bias is seen not just in curriculum and reading lists but in student admissions, staff representation, and assumptions pertaining to knowledge ownership, fees, rent and the broader economic structures of universities. In fact, the legacies of colonialism are present in campuses in highly visible ways such as in statues of benefactors and in the naming of buildings. Activists have focused on some of these symbols as catalysts to raise awareness around issues of colonisation.

Gebrial's essay *Rhodes Must Fall* (2018) foreshadows events of summer 2020, when in the aftermath of the murder of George Floyd in the United States, and a resurgence in support for the Black Lives Matter movement, the statue of Coulston was thrown into the dock by protestors in Bristol. Earlier in 2015, students at the University of Cape Town in South Africa campaigned for the removal of the Rhodes statue from their campus. The protest movement inspired the Rhodes Must Fall in Oxford campaign in 2016. Gebrial discusses how an impact of the Oxford campaign was a shift in the rhetoric in anti-racism work from one which focused on diversity, to one which focused on decolonisation (2018: 20). What is significant about this is that, in Gebrial's view, decolonisation calls for structural transformation at all levels of the institution and goes far beyond measures developed to encourage campus diversity and inclusion. In the discussion of the Rhodes Must Fall campaign, Gerbrial calls for a 'reorientation in the antiracist framework from diversity to decolonisation, and what this might look like' (2018: 20). The recent shift towards decolonisation as a focus in anti-racist work means that what it might look like is still under refinement, definition and development. In fact, *decolonisation* is defined by its active process-oriented approach to developing anti-racist perspectives for individuals, institutions and society.

Dance scholars have developed critiques concerned with making explicit racist assumptions and exclusivity in the field. Contemporary dance, particularly postmodern dance, has been problematised by anti-racist thinkers, such as Mitra, in the UK, for its use of abstraction in choreography. The film *Racism and Contemporary Dance* by Mitra, Arabella Stanger and Simon Ellis (2020) touches upon the tendency of white patriarchal culture to write the body itself out of discourse, to make it visual, objectified and conceptual. This is a reason why abstract concept-based work in dance can be experienced as racist and exclusive. If the experiential body is silenced, so is the violence acted upon it. This happens in choreography when the virtuosic and visual are given privilege over feeling, energy and aliveness of each individual performer.

Similarly, Chaleff's analysis of postmodern dance in the United States critiques the construction of the ordinary and neutral body in postmodern dance, asserting that 'Any body does not have the potential to be read as neutral, and so not every body has the same access to what is presumed to be ordinary' (2018: 79). While Chaleff focuses on the works of Trisha Brown and Yvonne Rainer, the tacit values of embodying ordinary neutral bodies, pedestrian movement and the natural in the moment state of moving are present in allied practices of somatics and CI. Moreover, to start to consider the decolonisation of these practices, as well as considering who feels they are able to participate, the lineage and knowledge sources should be investigated. These practices often draw heavily on techniques derived from martial arts, Buddhist meditation and yoga. Stark Smith, who was a practicing Buddhist and a co-founder of CI, has been referred to as a dancer bodhisattva. Because postmodern dance, which would include practices of CI and some somatic practices, developed in a context of white privilege, the acknowledgement of these forms as exclusive and white, and potentially culturally appropriative, would seem to be necessary for an inclusive environment to truly develop.

As dance scholar Davis points out, 'inclusivity without explicitly naming Whiteness when it presents is not an inclusive environment at all' (2018: 125). Moreover, *inclusion* might not be a sufficient term in that it assumes inclusion to something established, when perhaps what should be sought is a co-created environment that evolves and changes with those who are present.

Decolonising contact improvisation through the three steps

To engage critically in a process of decolonisation is complex in a postcolonial, globalised world in which migration, knowledge exchange, hybridity and fusion are commonplace. What is it to look openly to other cultures for inspiration and guidance while also holding anti-racist decolonising attitudes? How can CI, for example, be decolonised? How are its foundations in postmodern dance, Buddhism and martial arts made sense of in current contemporary discourses of decolonisation? In the wider practice of the form, CI is not only practiced as art and performance but also shared through international festivals, retreats and events in exotic locations, where rich Westerners, clearly privileged, practice in the vicinity of communities of extreme poverty in a scenario that might be described as *contact tourism*. For the purposes of this chapter, I am focusing on CI practice and teaching within the university teaching setting but investigation into the development of contact tourism, and the decolonisation of the international travelling practitioner are certainly worthy of further discussion in the future.

Discussing the three steps in detail

For the remainder of the chapter, I will discuss the three steps with detailed reference to teaching examples and situations.

1 **Understand the body as a site of identity development and change and recognise that oppression is embodied,** and that it manifests in discomfort, pain and resistance (Caldwell and Leighton, 2016). Co-create a non-judgemental space for free expression of ideas, actions, reactions and processes. Understand how embodiment can generate meaning and worldview, and that movement systems are value systems, inherently exclusive to different modes of embodiment, and thereby meaning, experience and sense of self. Deconstruct the authority of codified systems and approach them as tools and technologies for learning. Offer choice and the chance to follow different paths.

  The film *Racism and Contemporary Dance* (2020) is critical of conceptual and abstract works that do not provide space for experiential narratives of trauma and the oppressed. In contexts of oppression, Caldwell points out that 'oppression in any form does violence to identity development' (2016: 33). Caldwell further explains that where body identity development is suppressed there is no acceptance of the body and the body is made to feel wrong in relation to the dominant culture. Remedying this feeling of being wrong in the body can mean taking on behaviours of the dominant culture – a form of internalised oppression. Caldwell advocates for the development of a practice called *bodyfullness* in which the practitioner pays attention to 'our moving bodies in response to sensory signals' (2016: 34). Given that CI is based upon principles of sensing and somatic awareness, it would seem that it might accommodate a bodyfullness approach.

While the practice of CI is essentially a score that is organised around following the points of contact between bodies in relation to gravity and momentum, the ways in which skills for that score can be developed can include a great deal of experiential exploration that encourages the development of self-exploration and self-knowledge; a form of bodyfullness, perhaps? Such an exploration might begin with the Small Dance/The Stand, a foundational exercise developed by Paxton, where one listens to the inner movements of the body as organised by the breath in its resting state. The exercise offers opportunities for dancers to come into a relationship of self-sensing while being guided by the teacher. In a teaching and learning context sensitive to decolonisation, the position of knowledge between teachers and learners is important to interrogate. Imposition of knowledge, for example, might be experienced as a colonising force on bodies. Offering choices and cues that are invitational, on the other hand, enables students to choose how to interact with the information on offer. Moreover, when practiced regularly, the small dance reveals to the dancer the changing states of mind, body and organisation and starts to release students from perceptions of fixed and stable identities. Each time that they come to practice the small dance, the student can perceive and accept the different sensations of body and mind that arise, and let go of ideas that the practice gives a particular imprint on the practitioner. Rather the practice enables the practitioner to observe themselves, their own habits and reactions and enables them to develop movement knowledge that starts in self-awareness.

In the practical learning of CI, tasks are designed to help dancers become sensitive to their in the moment sensations: their senses of weight, momentum, flow and relationships that include partnering through space, level and touch. These become the ground from which the dance develops. Foundational tasks such as lying on the floor to sense weight, to be in touch-based relating with a non-family member or partner and to support and give weight can all give rise to culturally exclusive environments. Consent and giving overviews of sessions with clear choices for a range of participation options can help students to feel safer, if not completely safe. Students can be given tasks to adapt and invent their own tasks that enable safer participation, and the definitions of safety and safe practice can be discussed and agreed upon with each individual. Even when consent is agreed and there is a committed engagement from students, because the trauma of racial and other oppressions is embodied, it will be present in the dancing and, since also in CI, the practice is about following sensation, the practice may bring up strong feelings that manifest as pain, resistance and discomfort. I have observed that sometimes resistance can manifest both in injury and in emotional pain, which has been the case in my own practice and is also what I have witnessed in the practice of others. Many students are drawn into the performing arts precisely because they have stories to tell, strong emotions and expressions that they can channel and release in performance. It is also important to recognise that the teacher is not a therapist and to offer a supportive yet clearly defined non-judgemental space.

The creation of a non-judgemental space that can enable free expression of processes is skilful, particularly when artistic and educational assessments are part of the learning environment. To be able to look at pain, suffering and trauma in any practice requires courage from the practitioner and a supportive environment in which to do it. It is well documented that CI practitioners often stop attending jams and events when they feel unsafe, which has happened recently in the context of #metoo (see Beaulieux, 2019) as well as in situations of implicit racial exclusivity (see brooks, 2018). It is an ongoing work of dialogue and reflection to hold space in a non-judgemental way that enables dancers to feel accepted with the permission to be themselves.

When teaching CI in an educational setting, such as a university, students are often in a situation where the curriculum requires them to study the form, rather than them being able to make an independent choice to learn. This makes the teaching and learning situation of the institution very different from the open class or jam that might be offered in the community. There are often students in a class who would not have elected to be there, given a choice. Such a situation can compound the dynamics of exclusion that might ordinarily be present and sensitivity to this can be helpful in developing the teaching and learning relationships.

A teacher can initiate students into the form with confidence by designing tasks that meet the students where they are, all of which take listening, good communication with students and responsive task design, and it is not always successful. Teaching is a process of failing and nearly failing, again and again, trying to develop the confidence of students in practices and forms that might be of use to them. In CI, it is important not to assume consent to touch. It is usual that there are students in a group who wish to engage in the practice without touching, and the practice includes many scores for solo, and spatial partnering. No matter how critically aware and reflective the teaching practice, there may also be behaviours and values in the form that are inherently exclusive or alienating for some students that the teacher has not foreseen, leading to potentially harmful engagements in the learning environment in terms of social, psychological and overall well-being. For this reason, it is necessary as an educator to enter into the teaching learning dialogue with an attitude of fallibility and incompleteness, where openness to not knowing gives permission for imperfection and failing. Such an attitude can help generate compassion and greater understanding between teachers and students.

2 **Understand that teaching begins from an inherently racist standpoint** due to the racist viewpoints that we have inherited, the inheritance of dominant knowledge, canonical knowledge that has systematically excluded, and struggled to include people of colour, women and the global majority. At the same time, acknowledge and be fully explicit of your knowledge lineages being unafraid to critique them and being aware of the dynamics of cultural appropriation.

   Attending a recent training on Racial Equity in the Dance Classroom in November 2020, led by the organisation *Race Forward*, I was reminded that teaching begins from a racist standpoint. Due to the inheritance of racist views, dominant narratives of white supremacy and internalised oppression, it is not possible to engage in teaching and learning environments that are free from racial bias and oppression. In UK higher education, there are documented attainment gaps in progression, retention and completion of undergraduate degrees, and there is documented bias in curriculum, reading lists and representation of racial groups (Advance HE, 2021). When it is accepted that racism is inherent in the teaching and learning environment, then the work of anti-racism can take hold in a meaningful way because all are endeavouring to question the biases and assumptions that affect the learning environment. Such biases and assumptions typically include curricula that prominently feature the work of white artists, while failing to include artists of colour, and that contemporary dance is a western form of dance, when in fact it has culturally appropriated movements and ideas from a wide diversity of global traditions, both with and without acknowledgement. By interrogating these biases and assumptions, anti-racism can become a collective endeavour that can build critical and supportive relationships among teachers and learners. This work requires trust and sensitivity because anti-racist work can bring up feelings of anger, shame, guilt and blame, as well as trauma.

   The racist standpoint in teaching is concerned with not only our personal views and histories but with the forms that we teach. CI is a distinct and unique form that developed on from a creative research project undertaken by Paxton at Oberlin College in the United States in 1972. The form was then developed by Paxton and collaborators such as Stark Smith and took hold as a social movement, with jam culture proliferating as dancers shared the work, as well as an artistic practice that continued to develop in the context of postmodern and contemporary dance. CI did not set out with an exclusionary agenda, rather, as can be seen from the work of Rebecca Chaleff, introduced above, it could be understood as implicitly exclusive to people of colour and marginalised groups. But it is interesting that in the context of the 1970s counterculture that there was not a decision to be actively inclusive either, as opposed to the preceding work of Anna Halprin in leading the Dancer's Workshop in San Francisco, which in 1968 created the first racially integrated dance company in the United States. Privilege often plays out in the non-actions and implicit frameworks of a practice. It is also interesting that part of decolonising the practice of CI also means understanding its influences from indigenous sources, such as aikido and Tibetan Buddhism, in order that they not be culturally appropriated, which I will discuss below.

The influence of aikido on CI is profound and many practitioners take up aikido as a complementary study to their dancing. The contact between bodies has evolved from a rough and tumble approach that can be seen in *Magnesium* (1972), to more informed and nuanced uses of touch that have drawn from massage, bodywork and somatic practices. In the Kagyu lineage of Buddhist meditation, as beginners, we are invited to sink down through the layers of the earth, and Stark Smith invites us, in no small amount of detail to bond with the earth, to drop down into nothing, no tone, to see what movement comes, so that we can follow the rituals of body patterns or see what arises. I experience incredible somatic resonance across the traditions where the feeling states of my body are similar if not the same in guided dance improvisations and Buddhist meditations. I have taken refuge as a Buddhist myself in the Kagyu lineage of Tibetan Buddhism, which is the lineage of Chögyam Trumpa Rinpoche, a teacher of Stark Smith. While Stark Smith did not explicitly frame her teaching as Buddhist, I consider Stark Smith a significant teacher in my Buddhist path, in that she opened my mind to the potentials of mindfulness through movement, and following my studies with her, I was intuitively drawn to the Buddhist path. The *shakedown*, as taught by Stark Smith, and a meditation documented in Akong Rinpoche's book *Taming the Tiger* are two such exercises that generate these similar feeling states of relaxation and openness. In the dance, the feeling state opens the practitioner to movement possibility, relationship and co-creation of movement, while, in meditation, the feeling state opens the practitioner to deep relaxation that enables the mind to release tension, generating a sense of spaciousness and awareness.

In the dance, I have adopted and inhabited Buddhist teachings, often starting sessions, as my teachers have done, with simple focus on breath, sitting and awareness of body. These tasks are not introduced as meditation or mindfulness and in the moment of teaching, I do not always attribute them to a tradition. Contextualisation and lineage reflection might occur at the end of the session, which in regard to being rigorous by not culturally appropriating and drawing on forms without due acknowledgement is important. However, the practice seeks to foreground the dancers' experience and support the development of presence. Offering too much information ahead of the activity can occupy the mind and distract from the embodiment process. So where to offer historical, contextual and philosophical information on the practice raises questions about the design of the learning environment, what is privileged in that learning environment, how learning happens and what order of activities and tasks are undertaken. I do think that this is highly individual based on teaching style, student needs and the overall situation of a session within a course and learning programme because in teaching and learning the development of trust between learners is a foundation of the whole enterprise. Teachers and learners negotiate the dynamics of trust daily, and it influences what all members of a learning community feel comfortable and empowered to share. Racism and other oppressions inhibit the development of trust.

The lines between cultural appreciation and cultural appropriation are not always easy to perceive. As the generations move on, the lineage of practices is less acknowledged and less known. Teaching styles that focus on practical in the moment tasks do not often give their reference points or background, partly because the focus of a session is to practice and to tune bodily intelligences that are not in the worlds of language or rational thought. Because of the focus on bodily sensations of self, the dance is mindful and it can resemble a moving meditation. There can be states of motion and feeling that comprise bliss, flow states and expansive inclusive perception that are also experienced in yoga and meditation practices. The practice of CI can also be performed with these spiritual goals in mind but I would assert that the distinctness of the form, its orientation towards artistic knowing, means that practitioners can appreciate the cultural and spiritual influences on the form without appropriating them and so can clearly distinguish that the influences on the form are not the form itself.

As a teacher, I develop tasks that cultivate presence, sensitivity and awareness of the moving body solo and in relation to others. Some tasks come intuitively, although with reflection perhaps lineage influences can be found, but overall I am guided by my knowledge of the form of CI and what I perceive to be valuable to the students with whom I am working. I have developed much of my knowledge through experience and immersion in the form. CI, like the Kagyu lineage Buddhist practice, is primarily an oral tradition, passed in the doing of practice from one practitioner to the next and this generates a context of fragility where knowledge is mostly known in bodies that move, change, grow, age and forget. There are documents to support the practice, such as videos, interviews, scores and symbols, such as those used in the underscore that are only decipherable to the initiated. Initiation is through moving, doing, improvising and learning in workshops the protocols and conventions of the form. It is the teaching that passes the form from one generation to the next and it is in the teaching that the ethics of contemporary practitioners intersect the practice and perhaps change it. Knowing that the lineage of a form is infused with confusion, undocumented and unacknowledged cultural and religious influences, scandals and abuse, the ethics of introducing students to that form are important to consider.

3   **Critically interrogate white privilege and embed critical questioning from the beginning** (bell hooks). Ask students to reflect upon their embodied experiences, training, body histories and body stories and the knowledge that they bring to the classroom. Empower students to develop self-knowledge and self-actualisation as part of the teaching and learning. Reflect on meanings of safety and inclusion and co-create these with students.

   In *Teaching to Transgress* (1994), bell hooks discusses how self-actualisation processes in the classroom must be undertaken by both students and teachers if the classroom is to truly empower students. Both teachers and students need to be vulnerable and take risks. hooks points out that it is often the teacher that should take the first risk, to link personal narrative to curriculum content, and show how 'experience can illuminate and enhance our understanding of academic material' (1994: 21). Of course, experience can also show how the relevance of curriculum content is questionable and subject to change; such is the importance of critical questioning and being open to review in order to develop learning environments that are progressive and do not simply reproduce the status quo. It is healthy to view forms and contents as open to change, with the potentials for transformation that serve the needs of students.

While tasks that develop skills for CI do invite experiential reflection on the sensing self, more explicit invitations for narrative explorations of individual histories and experiences can be a foundation for student empowerment. It might seem paradoxical to engage in practices that seek to develop acceptance of impermanence and change while also encouraging students to come to know their own stories better. However, by using tools from art practice such as journaling, drawing, dancing and devising with text, emerging stories can be appreciated as truthful tellings of life experience which while also being released through imagination and creativity can be encountered with qualities of fluidity and change. Moreover, where body identity development has been suppressed, telling stories and developing narratives offers possibility for reclamation of a fuller identity, a reclamation to feel right in the body. This ability to feel right in the body, to inhabit a sense of ease, well-being and comfort is not to be taken for granted and the embodiment process is inhibited where discomfort, pain and lack of well-being prevail.

To start the teaching and learning endeavour from the assumption that a safe and inclusive space is inhibited from the outset by the presence of white privilege is a step towards decolonisation. It is perhaps in moments of introduction that structural intervention towards decolonisation can be made. Simply stating values of inclusion and equality is not seen as sufficient by many current practitioners. Practitioner, Taja Will reflects that she does not believe in 'spontaneous equality' (2018: 38). Will writes:

> I hear in CI spaces sound something like "all are welcome here; here we are all equals," which perpetuates a guise of radical acceptance. This definition of inclusion **does not** promote the visibility of people of colour (POC) in CI culture.
>
> (Will, 2018: 38)

CI Sessions often begin with an opening circle in which dancers talk about feeling states, injuries and anything else that they would like to share with the group. There is opportunity in such situations to engender trust through listening, mutual respect and empathy. In the beginning, trust cannot be assumed and lack of trust in the teacher, the group and the learning process may be present for all kinds of reasons that go beyond the individual into collective histories of racial oppression, slavery, migration and poverty. While the UK and United States experiences of slavery are different, the histories of slavery and white supremacy continue to permeate our consciousness. For example, mayfield brooks attributes a lack of trust in a student group to that where she writes:

> I noticed this deep distrust. I don't think it was just because they were mostly African American, but I think it is part of it. There is that feeling that you have to watch your back, and the young people named it. I think it's directly related to slavery, this incredibly traumatiz- ing, disruptive history, and we have to figure out how to negotiate that now.
>
> (brooks, 2016: 37)

Similarly, Kent Alexander calls for an active critically engaged approach to the facilitation of CI spaces, where 'when all participants acknowledge the limitations of white normative spaces, the CI community learns to liberate itself from a white normative reality' (2018: 37). If a student starts a session with the feeling of having to watch their back, their potential for allowing their nervous system to relax enough to come into a state of weight sensing is going to be inhibited. In this respect, the very foundational qualities of the dance arise from the privilege of safety, of feeling safe and not having to watch your back. My own experiences as a beginner echo this where weight sensing was so foreign to me that when I finally experienced it, it felt indulgent and luxurious in ways that I had not experienced before in my body and I felt guilty for the sense of joy that I also experienced. I did not know that my body could feel so relaxed, expansive and spacious while at the same time I would feel panic at the vast openness engendered by the practice; both freeing and terrifying at the same time. I also felt shame for coming into positive experiences of my body that I had not witnessed in my upbringing and had not been modelled to me in family or community settings.

I think about how essential it is to the practice of CI for dancers to have a true felt understanding of the weight of their bodies in order to find the momentum and flow in their bodies that enables the dance to happen. In CI, the dance is too fast to be conscious of the muscle support. This can also be challenging for dancers with classical training who have been taught to pull their muscles up and away from the earth to create images and sensations of lightness in the body and have often trained their minds to entrain the muscles with particular movements. Such students are not used to moving without tracking the movement with the mind and the dance in CI has the potential to move faster than the mind can track. Improvisation calls for in the moment intuitive responsive organisations of the musculoskeletal system, and other body systems, which can be challenging for beginners to trust. This is why many beginning-level exercises are repetitions of rolling, falling and catching, so that these gradually become instinctive responses that can be relied upon in the dance. Teaching a workshop to predominantly 18- and 19-year-old students in the university sector, directions to sense the weight can not only be racially exclusive but also be provocative to students who may have struggled with body image and eating disorders, as well as the implications of cultural interpretations of the word weight.

When teaching principles of weight, I often use touch and bodywork to access the sensations of weight without necessarily explaining to students that this is a focus of the exercise to sense the weight. Students support and manipulate the body parts of others, and practice giving up their weight entirely to the support of their partner and the floor. Use of gentle shaking and moving the joints can give experiential sensations of differentiation in the musculoskeletal system, experiencing joints, muscles and bones as separate, and sometimes a sense of more space. Taking these sensations immediately into dancing in the space and together can help to integrate the understanding in motion. Discussion can follow, where students are given space to articulate their experiences and insights. Discussion is one of the most important elements of a critical learning environment that aims towards decolonisation and social justice, giving learners the chance to not only make sense of their experiences but to also continue the dialogue of consent, trust and safer practice with peers and facilitators.

Conclusion

The concept of decolonisation has reinvigorated the ethics of my teaching practice. The explication and application of the concept of decolonisation have helped me to develop tools to teach with an anti-oppressive and anti-racist attitude. Because teaching and learning is a process and a dialogue that is not fixed, the attitudes that are cultivated in the teaching and learning exchange have profound effects on the development of relationships in terms of trust, depth and human development. Being able to develop tools that move my practice from one that promotes diversity and inclusion to one that engages in a process of decolonisation is a significant and meaningful adjustment in attitude that I am still coming to appreciate the full impact of. As an educator with commitment to practicing engaged critical pedagogy, I find resonance in the words of bell hooks who writes that 'To teach in a manner that respects and cares for the souls of our students is essential if we are to provide the necessary conditions where learning can most deeply and intimately begin' (1994: 13). Caring is an aspect of teaching practice that brings the educator into ethical relations with students. By caring for each student and by asking what serves each student, the educator can discern tensions, oppressions and obstacles to the teaching and learning process. When those oppressions and obstacles are institutionally and systemically inherent, as with racism, it is not only ethically agile to develop teaching and learning dialogues that deconstruct such oppressions but ethically necessary.

References

Advance HE. (2021) *Understanding Structural Racism in UK Higher Education: An Introduction*, York: Advance HE.

Alexander, K. (2018) 'On CI Intersections', *Contact Quarterly*, Summer/Fall, 34(2), p. 36.

Beaulieux, M. (2019) 'How the First Rule Brought #Metoo to Contact Improvisation', *Contact Quarterly*, Winter/Spring, 44(1), pp. 46–50.

brooks, m. (2016) 'Improvising While Black', *Contact Quarterly*, Winter/Spring, 41(1), p. 37.

brooks, m. (2018) 'Touching Myself: A Refusal of Contact Improvisation', *Contact Quarterly*, Summer/Fall, 43(2), p. 39.

Caldwell, C. and Leighton, BL. (2016) *Oppression and the Body*, Berkeley, CA: North Atlantic Books.

Chaleff, R. (2018) 'Activating Whiteness: Racializing the Ordinary in US American Postmodern Dance', *Dance Research Journal*, 50(3), pp. 71–84. https://doi.org/10.1017/S0149767718000372

Davis, C. (2018) 'Laying New Ground: Uprooting White Privilege and Planting Seeds of Equity and Inclusivity', *Journal of Dance Education*, 18(3), pp. 120–125. https://doi.org/10.1080/15290824.2018.1481965

Gebrial, D. (2018) 'Rhodes Must Fall: Oxford and Movements for Change', in Bhambra, G., Gebrial, D., and Nişancıoğlu, K. (eds.) *Decolonising the University*, London: Pluto Press.

hooks, b. (1994) *Teaching to Transgress*, London; New York: Routledge.

Magd, N. (2016) *Why Is My Curriculum White? Decolonising the Academy*, Available: https://www.nusconnect.org.uk/articles/why-is-my-curriculum-white-decolonising-the-academy

Mitra, R. (2018) 'Talking Politics of Contact Improvisation with Steve Paxton', *Dance Research Journal*, 50(3), pp. 5–18. https://doi.org/10.1017/S0149767718000335

Mitra, R., Stanger, A. and Ellis, S. (2020) *Contemporary Dance and White-Ness*, Available: http://danceandwhiteness.coventry.ac.uk

Rinpoche, A. (1988) *Taming the Tiger: Tibetan Teachings for Improving Daily Life*, London: Rider.

Will, T. (2018) 'Inclusion or Invisibility for POC in CI', *Contact Quarterly*, Summer/Fall, 43(2), p. 38.

2.5 Digital tools in formal and informal dance education environments

Rosemary (Rosa) E. Cisneros, Marie-Louise Crawley and Karen Wood

Dance, the digital and ethical practice: navigating new landscapes for teaching and learning

As dance education scholar Mila Parrish has suggested, the 'last 45 years have seen people [artists and educators] investigating methods for including digital technology into their practices' (Parrish 2007: 1381). Digital tools can reveal dance thinking and processes in a manner that presents information in compelling ways and, in recent years, clusters of new technological developments have been arising. Facilitating dance students' reflections using tools and technology, such as video cameras, is now commonplace in higher education (HE), community dance, private dance studios, and choreographic and dance company class settings. Digital practices, such as annotation and motion capture, are also entering the training space.[1] In such a context, these digital tools and technologies can harness the power of transmitting knowledge and provide multiple ways of seeing dancing bodies. These digital tools are not intended to replace the body-to-body experience of being in a dance studio or classroom but can support and prime the dancer to consider the dancing body in different ways. This chapter aims to look at formal and informal dance environments, such as HE and private studios, and to make the case that digital tools can have a place in both of these spaces. The rise of online and/or blended learning during the Covid-19 pandemic has served to highlight an increase in the use of digital tools and interfaces in dance education. More significantly, this sudden and ongoing shift from the body-to-body to a reliance on a digital environment to engage in a dance class, whether practical or theoretical, has opened up some important ethical questions about how dance is taught, learned and experienced, such as how accessible is the content, what support structures are in place and who has access to personal, sensitive data. With many teaching and dance practices moving online, ethics and acting ethically while delivering classes in a digital environment are of high importance. Throughout the chapter, we ask if and how dance technique might be influenced by the use of digital technologies and discuss what ethical considerations then need to be critically contemplated throughout the process.

DOI: 10.4324/9781003111146-13

At the Centre for Dance Research (C-DaRE), Coventry University, UK (where all three of this chapter's co-authors are based), ethics in a dance learning and teaching environment that includes digital technologies has been a core area of interest for several years.[2] C-DaRE has been developing an ethical strand of work considering the practical as well as the theoretical components of acting and carrying out research, uncovering the language that emerges within dance practices and/or the development of digital tools. The Centre has been advocating for ethical dance research and has defined areas to encompass morals, values and ethics, asking its researchers and partners to detail the value systems and beliefs that inform their teaching/research and how this might play out in the dance studio or in the development of a digital tool, such as motion capture kits. Examples include producing guidelines for the Centre that are used internally by other researchers and postgraduate researchers for working with industry partners and freelance dance artists. When forming part of project consortia, we have ensured that the ethical dimension is central to any development work with proof-of-concept prototypes. One such example is the H2020 WhoLoDancE project (2015–2018).[3] Such developments are grounded in questioning and ensuring that values of care, empathy, moral judgement and inclusivity are central to exploring the interconnectedness of the body and the digital tool. This chapter will argue how, through the potential of increased collaboration, participation and reflection that digital tools afford, they can help support dancers in training to develop these values. In particular, we will seek to underline the role that digital technologies can play in framing new dance education methods which can, in turn, forge specific ethical values for training twenty-first-century dancers.

A finding from the WhoLoDancE project was that for an educator, the ethical considerations of storage of data and clarity of use and/or dissemination of the data are important to promote good ethical practice. The chapter interrogates this finding and raises further questions alongside reflections from EU-funded research project, CultureMoves[4] (2018–2020), which investigated connections between dance, site, cultural heritage and digital storytelling, introducing a digital toolkit into dance training and education. In particular, this chapter will focus on a series of workshops which, in the context of the CultureMoves project, we call 'LabDays'. These revealed several possibilities for the CultureMoves digital toolkit (which comprises three digital tools – a digital scrapbook, MovesScrapbook; a plug-in, MovesCollect; and a dance annotator, MotionNotes) within the context of dance education – in terms of both practice-as-research and learning/teaching – and choreographic creation. These possibilities were situated across three main areas: in the teaching of dance material, in the remaking and transmitting of existing work and as a choreographic tool for creating new work.[5]

While we co-authors are dance artists and researchers with specialisms in practice-as-research, community co-creation, cultural heritage and screendance, ethical values and ensuring that an equitable dance workforce is possible has been a focus for all of us over several years. As researchers, we have positioned ourselves to work alongside artists and digital developers; in both projects mentioned here, we have used a methodology that is communicative in its foundation, leading to a dialogical and egalitarian way of working. Through sharing studio practice, as well as holding events and workshops, spaces were opened that allowed a diversity and plurality of voices to be included and celebrated, as well as for tensions to be safely expressed. The LabDay workshops, in particular, allowed the dance artists and learners involved to reflect on what ethics means to them and how ethical values might be embodied and expressed within the dance studio and in teaching environments when teaching and learning dance technique. Similarly, the workshops offered ways in which we, as researchers, could reflect deeply on the multifaceted and complex dialogue between dance, the digital and ethics. Within this chapter, we reflect critically on this dialogue, first outlining the ethical framework that informs our thinking, considering values of care, empathy and moral judgement, and then offering thinking on the ways in which the CultureMoves and WhoLoDancE projects have interrogated it. Furthermore, we ask how digital tools can help us develop new ways of teaching and learning to scaffold and support dancers through their journey of developing and refining their dance technique. The tools afford time for reflection and close observation of movement, which call for a process of care and attention.

Ethics of care and embodied ethics

There are theoretical and applied ways in which ethics exist in the world and ethical principles, such as truth, justice, right and wrong, care and responsibility, may be defined in a number of ways depending on the context, individual, culture and setting. In terms of our theoretical and philosophical scaffolding here, a focus on Ethics of Care (EoC) and Embodied Ethics underpins our analysis of the projects and the digital tools referenced. Ethicist Maurice Hamington (2004) developed an idea of embodied care that extends the work of Carol Gilligan, who first created the theory of EoC (see Gilligan 1982). EoC argues that attentiveness to a situation and context, which is inclusive of the material and immaterial, such as feelings, thoughts and bodies, can encourage empathy. EoC informs Embodied Ethics and is a term that choreographer and psychotherapist, Beatrice Allegranti (2011), and choreographer and teacher, Aneta Zwierzyńska (2015), have both carefully discussed, suggesting that the intrinsic and extrinsic can come together to develop an ethical relationship. Furthermore, Zwierzyńska posits that Embodied Ethics is not simply a cerebral and intellectual exercise but should include the 'unified body and mind and through empathy' (2015: 61). Choreographer and teacher Alice Chauchat (2017) argues that dance can become our teacher in matters of ethics: '[b]y scrutinizing the demands that each score places on the dancer, I want to propose that dancing might be a privileged terrain for practicing ethical relationships' (2017: 30). Bodily experiences must therefore be part of any ethical conversation that is happening within a dance/digital dance context. Dance scholar, Lenore Hervey, has explored ethics and embodiment within several contexts, arguing that ethical decision-making is not binary and that it is more than 'following rules or directives; it is a heuristic process that requires our full participation to be meaningful' (2007: 92). The *full* that Hervey is referring to is the embodied and lived experience of the individual. This lived experience corresponds to what dance scholar Sherry Shapiro (2016) would suggest is embodied knowledge. For Shapiro,

> Knowing through our bodies means too, understanding critically the way our deepest feelings and passions have been structured by the culture in which we live. No education aimed at human transformation of our beliefs and attitudes can ignore this deep substratum of embodied knowledge as it is this kind of knowing that can reveal to us the knowledge of life….
>
> (2016: 7)

This embodied way of knowing within an educational context is imperative as several ethical and moral questions begin to emerge. Sociologist Rhonda Shaw (2015) has looked at moral judgement and embodied ethics and in her research has suggested that one way of gaining insight into this subject is to present people with hypothetical scenarios, asking them to think through an ethical issue or to reflect on a past experience where ethical and moral principles were questioned. This method resonates with the research outlined in this chapter as we now focus on the CultureMoves project to reflect on ethical dilemmas and scenarios within dance and teaching/learning environments using digital technology.

CultureMoves

CultureMoves, which ran from October 2018 to February 2020, was a user-oriented project looking to explore the interconnections between dance, education, tourism and digital storytelling. As such, the partnering organisations encompassed an extensive variety of fields, from dance scholarship to digital innovation.[6] This wide-ranging interdisciplinarity framed the project's thinking about how the embodied knowledge inherent in various forms of intangible cultural heritage, such as dance, can be revealed differently through those same dance practices in relation to digital storytelling, documentation and annotation practices. Through qualitative research methods, such as interviews, questionnaires and practice-based studio practices, the project explored digital dance environments and produced tools that asked the researchers, dancers, educators, artists and choreographers involved to reimagine what a digital dance environment might look like.

The CultureMoves project developed a series of digital tools enabling new forms of touristic engagement and dance educational resources (primarily for HE and professional dance artists and practitioners, for example, a Massive Open Online Course (MOOC) exploring site dance within heritage settings)[7] by leveraging reuse of content from the European digital library of cultural heritage, Europeana.[8] The CultureMoves digital toolkit aimed to bring together the material body and the digital as a meeting place where dance artists, educators and students could consider the documented, the archival and the immaterial. As such, it presented an opportunity for artists, dancers and choreographers to reflect on different forms of collaboration and participation, as well as to encourage new horizons for their practices. Within the CultureMoves project, the digital toolkit was placed in a variety of choreographic and dance educational environments through a series of LabDays.[9] During these LabDays, it became clear that the multimodal learning possibilities offered by the toolkit were prompting dance artists and learners to think differently about their dance making, teaching and learning processes, as well as about the ethical ramifications of using such hybrid applications.[10]

While the WhoLoDancE project asked questions around the ownership of data that is produced within a motion capture session and the avatars that are retained within the virtual environment, CultureMoves demonstrated how the toolkit, and the annotator, in particular, can begin to exhibit 'hidden' aspects of the dancing body and the choreographic process. While both projects were not directly interested in a better understanding of ethics within dance training settings, the project team members slowly observed that ethics, annotation practices, motion capture and avatars were closely interlinked. For example, the WhoLoDancE project enabled a suite of prototype tools to be developed that saw the dancing body in the virtual space for the purpose of education and creation of dance for students and professionals. The live dancing body could be recorded, stored, annotated, used as a search tool, converted to a visual representation and combined with another body to create choreography. This resource for researchers and practitioners (although unavailable for use outside of the consortium at present) raised inquiry into the ethical considerations of storing information from the dancing body and ownership of the data, which in turn led to thinking about best practices for developing a choreographic educational environment that supports its participants to explore questions around data, ownership and embodiment. This sensitivity to such questions within a dance educational environment also emerged through the LabDay workshops that formed a key part of CultureMoves. We will now discuss and expand on the role that technology that encourages reflection can have on the training of a dancer.

Reflections on dance in the digital environment

While there are several beneficial aspects to the use of digital toolkits in expanding learners' understanding of how dance material might be created, transmitted, stored and archived, there also needs to be a recognition of the ethical ramifications of this material becoming digitised data. In using hybrid applications, this negotiation becomes a key part of dance educational experience. The space that digital technology occupies within an educational setting must question the infrastructure in which it exists, and tangible and intangible gains and losses must be explored. Such an iterative reflective process can maximise the benefits for the dance learner and ensure that the technology does not overpower the knowledge acquisition process but rather serves the people involved. For example, during the various CultureMoves LabDays, dancers discussed the usefulness of the annotator, in particular, for nuancing tiny detail and for finding a shared language to document the dance, pointing to the variety of different annotations as helping dancers to learn existing dance material through multimodal ways of learning. As dance scholar Rebecca Stancliffe has argued, the process of annotating dance – and developing what Stancliffe herself terms '*annotational thinking*' (2019: 274, emphasis in original) – creates complex, multilayered memories that can help support dance learners to train their 'analytical eye' (2019: 274) in ways that can further enrich and deepen their understanding of dance. In a dance educational context, the MotionNotes annotator revealed itself to be valuable in the teaching and transmission of specific vocabulary, due to the detail and precision that the tool potentially allows. Both the teacher and the student could use annotation practice to look at the same video clip, and this could be useful for assessments in modules. The accuracy fosters fluency with technique that in turn can build new areas of interest and also deepen engagement. This expanded and enhanced vocabulary set encourages the student to replicate and incorporate the exactness witnessed via the digital platform while also training the body to learn alongside a computer or similar device. This digital tool can be seen as another resource the dancer has in their training and creative 'toolbox' that facilitates fluency with dance training and choreographing.

The educational environment is not the only space that is transformed by the use of a digital tool. The performance space can also be positively influenced by the use of a digital tool where knowledge and relationship building can take place through the incorporation of such a resource. For example, dancer Sara Macqueen, who participated in the CultureMoves Dance and Architecture LabDay,[11] articulated how the digital tools allowed for a capturing of dance's momentary engagement with audience members, or of the very moment of performance, and enabled that experience to be shared differently, allowing for the combination of a variety of viewpoints and methodologies. Macqueen was drawn, in particular, to the *reflective* aspect of the digital tools and expressed an interest in how she could work with these tools as a dance educator, to articulate and detail the choreographic and creative process in the studio with learner dancers. The reflective component to which Macqueen refers links to the aforementioned idea of fluency, where the digital tool serves as an external space or mirror for the learner to deepen their understanding of, while becoming a witness to, their dancing. It also points to the importance of the potential for interdisciplinary collaboration that new technologies enable, allowing dance to work in the expanded field of arts education.

Dance learners interviewed during the CultureMoves LabDays also observed how the annotator could help them to better document and understand the movement of the body in space.[12] More significantly, while dancers nuanced the necessity of the three-dimensionality of bodily learning and the importance of body-to-body transmission for dance, they also noticed how the annotator tool could enhance this learning. Examples in a dance studio or classroom setting point to the potential for the annotator as a teaching tool, to create annotated video lectures, to be able to leave detailed notes and markers as comments on video recordings of practical work, and indeed to be used for the teaching of dance analysis. Importantly then, in negotiating dance as data, the key is to understand digital technologies as priming and supporting learners to consider their dancing bodies in multiple ways. Digital tools can reveal otherwise 'hidden' (Blades and Whatley 2019: 378) properties of the dance and articulate, document and highlight embodied knowledge *alongside* a 'traditional' body-to-body transmission. The revealing of hidden properties relates to the broader context where we see the use of social media in society – we can see into people's homes and lives where we otherwise might not be exposed to this information. Therefore, digital tools enhance embodied transmission and can reveal more about its properties; they are not intended to replace it. At the same time, when applying digital technologies to dance learning environments, at the heart of the process must be deep care about, and understanding of, the ethical implications of what happens when dancing bodies become bodies of data. This points to the entanglement between the physical and the digital, and the embodied care that is needed to negotiate it. The twenty-first century dancer is not removed from the presence of digital technology and due to this close and incidental concurrence, both projects asked dancers and dance teachers and developers to enter into an iterative process that bolstered how a dance education environment could ensure that care, empathy and moral judgement were part of any dance training experience.

Reflections on our digital selves

Again, drawing on Chauchat's thinking, it can be argued that the dance environment allows for the use of dance technique(s) to develop socially engaged individuals capable of interrogating ethical human relations that both respect the body – and body-to-body experience – and also keep up with the digital, online world. Through an engagement with the digital, the dance learning environment offers an opportunity to confront some of the more challenging questions around the values and rights of dancers. For example, dance education scholar, Tanya Berg, when discussing competitive dance in Canada, has suggested that new technologies are influencing the identity of young people to their imagined audiences. Berg also stresses how online competitions are 'marginalising groups of people who do not have the financial capital to participate' (2020: 148). An awareness of artistic and educational integrity is key here, alongside a recognition of the ethical implications of new technologies for young people and their effect on identity formation. On the other hand, filtering, navigating and using the digital environment can also encourage a reflective practice that can be radical and encourage social engagement. For instance, the speed of certain environments, such as mainstream educational spaces, dictates that time for reflection is not always a priority. Yet, a digital tool can quickly capture thoughts and processes and generate effective team building and collaborative workspaces. Through such engagement with the digital, new meaning-making is possible. Learning and reflective processes are not always discreet and the action of making that learning visible to a majority has a social component, as it displays habits, skills and mindsets. If a tool is able to capture and facilitate a synthesising of those ideas and display that *thinking in action*, then transformation becomes visible. It is important to note both that ideological tendencies are not removed from the tools that we use nor the ways in which we use them and to say that any use of digital technology within a dance environment always enters into socially charged questions is, in itself, contestable; however, what we are arguing for here is dance's potential to offer opportunities to critically explore those political, cultural and technological conditions directly impacting the sector.

A teaching environment within HE and/or private studios should encourage a teacher to consider their value systems and limits and reflect on their moral position. Teachers will have to make decisions based on requests from their students, moral obligations and financial constraints (Berg 2020). When a digital tool is placed within a dance space, there is a further layer of responsibility, as the entanglement of the body, the digital and the individual's teaching style and philosophy all consider the interconnectedness to the self and the external components. Furthermore, there are connections between the digital as tangible and the body as intangible elements and a digital tool can serve these. Within a teaching and learning context, a digital platform or tool need not encroach on a practice but rather should help deepen the work and support the uncovering of what may be 'hidden'. As dance scholars Hetty Blades and Sarah Whatley suggest, underpinning many enquiries involving the digitisation of dance is 'a desire to unearth more of the "hidden" aspects of the dance, such as the dynamic, relational and co-creative aspects of dance creation' (Blades and Whatley 2019: 378).

This is certainly true of both the WhoLoDancE and CultureMoves digital toolkits which reveal the potential of how intangible aspects of dance can surface through the use of either motion capture or annotation, and hence of how new knowledge emerges to be shared. At a CultureMoves LabDay with dance undergraduates on a specialist Dance and Technology module at the University of Worcester (UK), for example, learners discussed dance's ontology as ephemeral and immaterial and how the digital documentation offered by the toolkit might allow us to capture some of that ephemeral material, especially what might otherwise get 'lost' in the creative or archiving processes, revealing what is 'hidden'. The ability of the digital to uncover and trace those 'hidden' aspects of embodied knowledge of the dance is therefore an important one in enhancing dance education and can feed into digital dance learning environments (again, particularly important given the prevalence of digital and blended learning in the Covid-19 context). However, when dance becomes data, this generates new ontologies for dance, as well as raising important questions about ethics and corporeality.[13] Indeed, when 'dancing bodies are extended and constructed from data' (Blades and Whatley 2019: 379), how might we ethically approach such valuable dance data?

Dance data

Dance learners and educators interact with digital technology in a creative environment which allows them to access new knowledge of and about the body while evoking questions around the ethics of dance data. When dance becomes data, how might dance educators and learners respond to and negotiate these new ethical questions about dance's ontology, corporeality and ownership? Discussing the relationship between the performing body and (digital) technology, choreographer Isabelle Choinière writes of the fluid, interrelated and intercorporeal nature of the contemporary body (2019: 161). This problematises a desire to apply boundaries or differentiate between what is of ownership to the performer and what is not. However, once a collection of data from a dancing body is stored to reuse or repurpose, care is required in making involved parties aware of the future use of such data, whether for creative or educational purposes, and of its dissemination. This data is of a dancer that can be resurrected to represent the dancer in future scenarios. Therefore, carefully considering and making explicit what the dancer's data will be used for, as well as having clear guidelines before the recording itself happens, is good ethical practice when dealing with digital tools and the human dancing body. The dancer must be informed, consulted and be a part of the conversation discussing the ways in which the data will be handled. The dancer has the potential to be seen as a vulnerable component in the data-producing environment because once the dance is converted to data, such as an avatar, the assumption may be that this avatar no longer belongs to the dancer. However, we would argue that this data is indeed an extension of the live body and, without a nuanced conversation, there is a risk that an EoC might not be honoured. Furthermore, when using digital technologies in the teaching, learning and transmission of dance skills, such an awareness of the ethical implications of dance becoming data is something that dance educators should also try to support their dance students to reflect upon and better understand.

Considerations and care

Throughout this chapter, we have explored different ways of approaching the use of digital equipment and tools within dance education and learning settings, as well as how artists, educators and learners should consider ethics throughout such interactions. Through the project examples, the chapter has revealed processes that were designed to bring awareness to the responsibility for, and care and protection of, the data created by dancers' bodies when stored, reused, represented and repurposed for digital activity. We briefly discussed the WhoLoDancE project toolbox that developed prototype tools to assist the dancer learner/choreographer in finding new ways to see and create dance movement. Using both high-end and low-end motion capture equipment, like Notch sensors, conversations around the storage of body data become integral to how we value the dancer's contribution. Points of interest exploring the dancers' experience of wearing the sensors can spark conversations around the insights that an avatar representation can provoke, particularly concerns about movement perception and kinesthetic engagement. The CultureMoves project displayed a suite of tools where learners interacted with the tools to document and share content, highlighting the potential for aspects of teaching that involve looking at specific elements of technique and annotating video. Again, there is a necessity to not only consider the ethical implications of the storage of data but also how the data itself encompasses bodies in a 'liminal' space (Broadhurst 2006) – perhaps unfamiliar territory for some students and educators – and how this space is, to be treated with care. This needs to be a safe space, inviting the student and teacher to have a deep engagement with the process and material. It also needs to be a secure space in which the data generated can be stored (as this data is significant to the dancer to whom it belongs). This chapter aimed to share insights from working with digital tools in learning and creating environments and to highlight areas of consideration for good ethical practice. While students and educators may experience new ways of approaching and training dancing bodies when working digitally, it is important to see digital tools as not replacing the physical body-to-body relationship but, rather, as negotiating and complementing it. Finally, the use of digital tools in both formal and informal dance learning environments serves to remind us how, above all, we need to treat dancing bodies – and their data – with due care.

Notes

1 For some examples of these, please see Garland and Naugle (1997), Sun et al. (2017), Pereia dos Santos et al. (2018) and Lagrue et al. (2019).
2 Find list of projects here: https://www.coventry. ac. uk/research/research-directories/?var2=964
3 WhoLoDance: http://www.wholodance.eu/. The WhoLoDancE project brought together ten consortium partners based in the UK, Greece, Netherlands, Italy and Spain. The project, spanning three years from January 2015 to December 2018, was primarily focussed on developing proof-of-concept digital tools that assist with dance education and creation. Partners included dance researchers, professional dance companies, computer scientists, developers and motion capture experts. The partners thus spanned a range of experiences and expertise, providing a rich working environment wherein knowledge about dance practices and pedagogy could be shared, assumptions questioned and a common ground established. As an extension of the project, a pilot study was conducted at Coventry University using Notch sensors exploring the postural alignment of ballet and flamenco dancers. This collaboration allowed lecturers and students to share experiences of working with sensors to illuminate choreographic, pedagogic and phenomenological nuances of the dancing body.
4 CultureMoves: www.culturemoves.eu.
5 Cf. Cisneros and Crawley (2021).
6 The CultureMoves project consortium included C-DaRE (Centre for Dance Research), Coventry University (UK) alongside Universidade NOVA de Lisboa (UNL, Portugal), IN2 Digital Innovations (Germany) and the Fondazione Sistema Toscana (FST, Italy).
7 The 'Creating a Digital Heritage Community' MOOC (massive open online course) was co-created by the CultureMoves and Kaleidoscope (https://pro. europeana.eu/project/fifties-in-europe-kaleidoscope) project teams: https://www. edx.org/course/creating-a-digital-cultural-heritage-community.
    The CultureMoves team wrote a series of dance-specific modules for the MOOC exploring Cultural Heritage; Intangible Cultural Heritage and Annotation; Dance and Site; Im/material Cultural Heritage – Costumes, Masks and Museums; as well as a Historical Dance Module, developed in collaboration with the Early Dance Circle (UK) and Chalemie (UK), with guest tutors Barbara Segal and Sharon Butler. These modules offer a series of activities for learners ranging from undergraduates to PGR students, to showcase and encourage uptake of the CultureMoves tools. Learners are encouraged to critically engage with and discuss the intersections between culture, dance, tourism and digital technologies, with a particular focus on dance in unconventional spaces and in relation to touristic landmarks.
8 https://www.europeana.eu/en.
9 The CultureMoves LabDays held between 2018 and 2020 varied in size, approach and engagement. Of particular interest to this chapter are the Coventry Architecture and Dance LabDays (March 2019; September 2019), Manchester LabDays (November 2019), Birmingham Dance Network LabDay (December 2019) and the University of Worcester LabDay (January 2020). More information about the LabDays can be found on the project website and in the published White Papers that sit online. (https://culturemoves.eu/)
10 Here, we mean 'hybrid' in the sense of bringing digital storytelling tools and live dance/arts practice together in an educational environment.
11 This LabDay was held at C-DaRE, Coventry University, in September 2019 and was specifically designed for undergraduate and postgraduate architecture students to use the tools to engage with movement and choreographic practice, as

well as archival content. Dancer Sara Macqueen was also present in the space to respond in real time to the students' engagement with the digital tools through the creation of improvised choreography.

12 Here again, this corresponds to the potential of the tool for bringing dance and architecture students into a dialogue where drawing dance relates to spatial patterning and embodiment, as useful in the study of architecture in dance.

13 As in other LabDays, using the tools also prompted the University of Worcester dance undergraduates to think about the wider ethical questions and implications of the storage of dance data, and of the ownership of digital dance material and Intellectual Property Rights.

References

Allegranti, B. (2011) 'Ethics and body politics: interdisciplinary possibilities for embodied psychotherapeutic practice and research', *British Journal of Guidance & Counselling*, 39(5), pp. 487–500. http://doi.org/10.1080/03069885.2011.621712

Berg, T. (2020) 'Manifestations of surveillance in private sector dance education: the implicit challenges of integrating technology', *Research in Dance Education*, 21(2), pp. 135–152. http://doi.org/10.1080/14647893.2020.1798393

Blades, H. and Whatley, S. (2019) 'Digital dance', in Dodds, S. (ed.) *The Bloomsbury Companion to Dance Studies*. London: Bloomsbury, pp. 357–384.

Broadhurst, S. (2006). 'Digital practices: and aesthetic and neuroaesthetic approach to virtuality and embodiment', *Performance Research*, 11(4), pp. 137–147. https://doi.org/10.1057/978-1-349-95241-0

Chauchat, A. (2017) 'Generative fictions, or how dance may teach us ethics', in Edvardsen, M., Spångberg, M., and Andersson, D. (eds.) *PostDance*. Stockholm: MTD, pp. 29–43.

Choinière, I. (2019) 'Seismographies of mediated bodies: a logic of creation', in Choinière, I., Pitozzi, E., and Davidson, A. (eds.) *Through the Prism of the Senses: Mediation and New Realities of the Body in Contemporary Performance. Technology, Cognition and Emergent Research-Creation Methodologies*. Bristol: Intellect. ISBN 9781789380798.

Cisneros, R. and Crawley, M.-L. (2021) 'Moving, annotating, learning: Motion-Notes LabDays – a case study', *International Journal of Performing Arts and Digital Media*, 17(1), pp. 138–149. https://doi.org/10.1080/14794713.2021.1880141

Garland, I. and Naugle, L. (1997) 'A university dance course in cyberspace: the telelearning experience', *Journal of Distance Education*, 12, pp. 257–269. Available at: https://www.ijede.ca/index.php/jde/article/view/273

Gilligan, C. (1982) *In a Different Voice*. Cambridge, MA: Harvard University Press.

Hamington, M. (2004) *Embodied Care: Jane Addams, Maurice Merleau-Ponty and Feminist Ethics*. Champaign: University of Illinois Press.

Hervey, L. (2007) 'Embodied ethical decision making', *American Journal of Dance Therapy*, 29(2), pp. 91–108. https://doi.org/10.1007/s10465-020-09338-3

Lagrue, S., Chetcuti-Sperandio N., Delorme, F., Chau, M.T., Duyen, N. et al. (2019) 'An ontology web application-based annotation tool for intangible culture heritage dance videos', 1st Workshop on Structuring and Understanding of Multimedia heritAge Contents (SUMAC 2019), Oct 2019, Nice, France. pp. 75–81, https://doi.org/10.1145/3347317.3357245

Macqueen, S. (2019) Skype interview with the authors R. Cisneros and M.-L. Crawley, 8th October 2019.

Parrish, M. (2007) 'Technology in dance education', in Bresler, L. (ed.) *International Handbook of Research in Arts Education*. Springer International Handbook of Research in Arts Education, vol. 16. Dordrecht: Springer. https://doi.org/10.1007/978-1-4020-3052-9_94

Shapiro, S. (2016) 'Dance as activism: the power to envision, move and change', *Dance Research Aotearoa*, 4(1), p. 3. https://doi.org/10.15663/dra.v4i1.53

Shaw R.M. (2015) 'Moral judgement and embodied ethics', in *Ethics, Moral Life and the Body*. London: Palgrave Macmillan. https://doi.org/10.1057/9781137312594_3

Stancliffe, R. (2019) 'Training the analytical eye: video annotation for dance', *Theatre, Dance and Performance Training*, 10(2), pp. 273–288, https://doi.org/10.1080/19443927.2019.1610039

Sun, G., Chen, W., Li, H., Sun, Q., Kyan, M., Muneesawang, P., and Zhang, P. (2017) 'A virtual reality dance self-learning framework using Laban Movement Analysis', *Journal of Engineering Science and Technology Review*, 10(5), pp. 25–32. https://doi.org/10.25103/jestr.105.03

Zwierzyńska, A. (2015) *Ethics and Body Politics Building Social Relationships through Dance and Capoeira Classes*. MA Dissertation. Anton Bruckner University.

2.6 Staying alive

The dance technique class as a means for survival

Erica Stanton

This writing focuses on a period between 2015 and the present day. It tracks my diagnosis with breast cancer in August 2015 and the subsequent alliances *in dancing* which became – and still are – my survival strategies for being alive and present in my life and in my work. What has emerged from this time is a lived manifesto which combines the experiences of a dance class and the everyday awareness of still being alive. On this journey, the lodestones of Tim Ingold's propositions of storytelling and correspondence are important (Ingold, 2011: 164, 241); and my travelling companions in this (ad)venture are Sonia Rafferty and David Waring, both of whom are longstanding friends and exceptional artist-teachers. We have danced together, taught together and presented at conferences together. Our teaching of our dance technique classes has developed in complexity; into an entwined phenomenon, a process of 'togethering' (Ingold, 2011: 221) between people, dance and daily life. We have laughed, cried and drunk quantities of tea together, and in the spirit

Figure 2.6.1 Brighton Seafront February 2016. A place for breathing and recovery, and for waiting for blood results. Credit: Erica Stanton

DOI: 10.4324/9781003111146-14

of our embodied reminiscences and conversations, this writing becomes our work, our manifesto: our maxim – *Simply for the Doing*.

The notion of the dance technique class and the role of the dance teacher within it have become ambiguous. A dance technique class, a workshop experience of a particular artist's approach or the daily preparation of dancers for 'dance work' generate problems related to training (indoctrination), privilege (who decides that this is important) and heritage (inequality). The intangible myths and ghosts in the practices which define the traditions of 'dance theatre', or 'dance art', are too often revered and become preserved and, if we are not careful, entrenched in our daily work. However, the perceived borders among teacher, learner and the work are porous and offer routes for sharing and changing embodied wisdom and knowledge more explicitly and more generously.

As teachers devise classes and experience them with learners, the influence of prior learning and training is inevitable, but by using co-creation and an intertwining translation process among 'before, now and next', an exciting instability emerges as the identity of 'class' permanently evolves and changes and becomes ripe with possibilities. But there are still further and better questions – what is being preserved? What can be freshly (re)generated? Why do we do this? And a vexed question – what are we allowed to do? As the metrics of higher education become more and more pervasive, where data and surveillance are held up as evidence of expertise, where is the freedom to roam with the individual stories of the dance technique class? How are our classes staying alive?

Dancing 'you'

Working in the studio, at conferences and in collaboration with teachers in 'studio retreats', the *Simply for the Doing* project interrogates the narratives, currents and values which sustain our teaching of dance technique. Out of our desire to be *with* the work of a dance class and *with* others looking at the work, the workgroup first came together in July 2016 with its first 'studio retreat'. This summer marked the end of my cancer treatment and the beginning of remission. My desire to be immersed in the reality of dancing and teaching as soon as possible after the end of my treatment was vigorous. Just in case 'cancer-free' was not my eventual prognosis, this was a way of dealing with the uncertainty. It was a delight to be in the studio with colleagues, to be dancing and asking some frank questions about teaching dance technique. It was also a way of reassembling my body. What could I (re)discover about myself as an embodied subject after months of medical objectification?

The *Simply for the Doing* workgroup has a fluid constituency. It gathers current and former students, colleagues, friends of colleagues, and dancers and teachers who happen to be passing by. The work of the group has been documented so far as:

- videos; e.g. *The Practical Wisdom of Teaching*
- workshop presentation at the *Dance and Democracy* conference at Liverpool Hope University (November 2018) – *Democracy begins at home where home is the dance technique class*
- workshop presentation at *Dance Fields* April 2018, University of Roehampton
- workshop presentation at *Bridging dance training contexts: re-assessing techniques and skills for the social and cultural sphere*, University of Winchester

The workgroup has actively resisted sharing its practice through writing since its inception. Our facility to make sense of experiencing, thinking, feeling and 'doing dancing' in the studio emerges from the 'continuing, laboured, persistent attempts to resolve problematic situations through the transformation of the materials of experience' (Johnson, 2011: 151). The sticking point of our manifesto is our scepticism about how words can express this experience. This chapter is an opportunity to surrender to this work, to talk about our work and to satisfy a need to say something, a need 'that motivates search patterns in the work. Having a need to say, one looks more intently' (Eisner, 2002: 89).

As the recipient of the intense and invasive medical treatment for cancer, looking for patterns, looking for connections and finding 'togethering' (Ingold, 2011: 221) have required a new, closer attention. In me dancing me and you dancing you, how do we dance us? How do we do this in our culture of quantification where we demonstrate our effectiveness in competition with

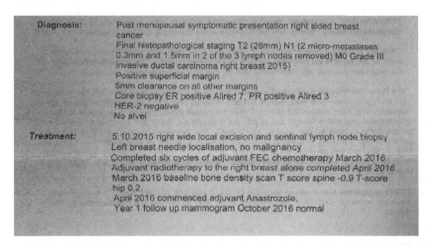

Figure 2.6.2 Extract from the sign-off letter from my oncologist following my treatment for breast cancer. Credit: Erica Stanton

our peers? Remember, 'not everything that matters can be measured. Not everything that is measured matters' (Eisner, 2002: 178), but from September 2015 to May 2016, I watched as my body become a place to gather data and, in so doing, demonstrate its incompetence.

September 2015

'It's not your fault', the consultant tells me. I'm curious about this statement. This tumour is me. I made it.

I hold very tightly onto the knowledge I have about my body. I'm the expert of this moving body. I become an expert at being very still, lying quietly as the recipient of high-tech beeps, surveys and scans.

Expert hands manipulate skin, tissue and limbs for a biopsy. This is complex choreography – this here, that there. I try to facilitate the micro-rotations of shoulder, elbows and thorax with the doctor. It's an invasion, but I'm maintaining a process of invitation. I'm reminded of Deborah Hay and her mantra, 'invite being seen'.

'You're very calm', says the doctor conducting the biopsy. Really? I'm still, but this is work. My attention is focused exclusively on the process of breathing slowly, of releasing muscular tension and quelling nervous twitches. Trying not to feel cold, trying not to feel pain. The biopsy needle feels and sounds like a staple gun. How many times? Be patient. Be a good patient. He's doing his job; let me make this easier for him.

He wishes me 'good luck' as I leave. What has he seen that I need luck on my side? This body which I believed to be invincible is vulnerable; is fallible. This experience will be life changing. This is about me.

'living in the midst of so much illness and death, I long to believe that dance, the practices of what [Deborah] Hay considers the altar of the body, might overcome the body's betrayals' (Satin, 1999: 183).

Dance adventures

André Bernard's invitation 'to enter an adventure into your own being' (Bernard, Steinmuller and Stricker, 2006: vii) is often quoted and is an important part of the *Simply for the Doing* manifesto. Many dancers have been inspired by the practice of ideokinesis and in the layers of possibilities which emerge from a meticulous, systematic, holistic approach to 'my body' and the invitation to be curious about 'my own being'. This being exists in and connects to a world. Gill Clarke used to remind us in class, 'we are grounded in the relationship with the environment which is changing constantly, what is coming into the present is us and the environment... in conversation' (Clarke, 2007). This is reiterated in Ingold's *Being Alive*, where he reminds us that movement, the flows of materials, place, action and the emergence of skilled activities are all intertwined – we are 'born and grow within the current of materials, and participate from within in their further transformation' (Ingold, 2011: 29). This interior adventure suggests solitude on the part of the dancer; the private dancer with an exhortation to dance as though nobody's looking. This has the connotation of singing in the shower, but discovering the private dancer amidst the public learning of dance is a complex adventure. I am doing this. How does it feel when I am dancing? How do I know when I am dancing? All of this needs to be resolved before we can countenance 'inviting being seen' (Hay, 1989: 72) or revealing our motional itinerary (Nikolais and Louis, 2005: 238) and here a paradox is revealed; by attending to our sensory processes, a viewer's curiosity is aroused. Not so much 'look at me' but 'let me tell you how this feels'. By 'inviting the onlooker to travel along vicariously. These movements can give both the dancer and the onlooker the sense of anything within the universe that is of a similar motional nature or that can be communicated by metaphor' (Nikolais and Louis, 2005: 28).

So much of our doing of dance, watching dance and thinking with, through and about dance gets bound up with the behaviour of first-person experience (the embodied subject), but as dance philosopher Anna Pakes reminds us, 'phenomenology's first-person perspective … is not a question of always speaking from the point of view of an individual "I," but of elucidating the "what it is like" of experience' (2011: 42). Choreographer and teacher Heike Salzer elucidates this further in writing about the experience of dancing and the importance of metaphor in her 'dance class manifesto' from the *Simply for Doing* retreat in July 2019:

> *Zefiro…* the soft wind that comes down from the Italian mountains in the beginning of summer and makes people fall in love. It gently dives along the steep hills taking humorous turns at the curves that it encounters on its downwards path. It mocks the branches of bushes and vibrates the leaves at the top of the crowns of the trees. It divides the golden stalks of the fields. *Zefiro* moves with care and an encompassing freedom. It connects all beings by bringing awareness to the surrounding air and its soft yet sparkly sounds invigorate all who become aware of its journey.
>
> (Salzer, 2018)

The sharing of dance adventures through 'what they are like' – through simile and metaphor – is an important seam of investigation in our dance practice. When we are not aspiring towards a compliant visual form, dance classes offer up multiple perspectives. They become adventures for all kinds of personal and collective artistic expression and places for profound and poetic expression and significant ways of being in the world. Conversely, we can also use this capacity for noticing 'what it is like' to find reverse metaphors: feeling movement from writing, as in this lovely example from Louise Erdrich's recent novel, *The Nightwatchman*: 'She stopped. The sense of something there, with her, all around her, swirling and seething with energy. How intimately the trees seized the earth. How exquisitely she was included' (Erdrich, 2020: 51).

Trialogues between the work, the learner and the teacher

When we are dancing, we bring our attention to aspects of the same thing and these may not mesh. Our curiosities are likely to diverge, and it is here that the possibilities of trialogue come to the fore. This triangulation stimulates conversations among teacher, learner and the work. If we imagine this as a triangle inside a circle which holds the context for the work; who are we, where are we and why are we doing this, then this positions the class itself as a 'metaphor for knowledge creation' (Paavola and Hakkarainen, 2005: 2) and simultaneously, as an interactive art. This does not focus on the aesthetic form of a work as it presents itself (a codified form inscribed on a proficient body), but on the response of the viewer (learner). 'The viewer then becomes a participant in the work, which behaves in response to the participant's actions. Interactive art needs behaviour on both sides of the classical dichotomy of object and viewer' (Massumi, 2008: 1).

Teaching a dance class necessitates simultaneous first-, second- and third-person behaviours. It offers opportunities to experience others' ways of knowing and is a way of knowing in itself. As a class is in progress, questions about what is unfolding come into view

- How is the 'thingness' of dance – its state of being, of being real to the dancers – emerging?
- How does it correlate with my experience in the role of the teacher?
- What use is my meta-awareness (I'm noticing, I'm feeling, I'm wondering) to the participants in the class?
- How am I participating in their first- and third-person views? (The trialogue of me, you and the work).

'The making of knowledge is the making of space, space is made in travelling, knowledge is travelling, and travelling like knowledge is a form of narrative' (Turnbull, 2002: 273), but in dance, knowing *is* travelling. Dancers are *in* motion. Travelling is not a metaphor for what we know, it is what we *do* – I am here on the way to there by means of this; where 'here', 'there' and 'this' may be any permutation of possibilities; new, half-remembered, familiar, strange, comfortable or daunting. Past and future are revealed in the present moment of dancing. This is a negotiation of our interior landscape (soma-mind-spirit) *and* a navigation of the shared space of class, corresponding with our peers who are engaged similarly. The story of the dance class emerges between us. We are doing this now.

In July 2019, the *Simply for the Doing* workgroup took the theme of kinship as its focus, in particular the notion presented by Paolo Freire, 'when … kinship develops we need to cultivate within ourselves the virtue of tolerance which "teaches" us to live with that which is different' (Freire, 1995: x). In being receptive to difference in teaching and learning and shifting the emphasis from dialogue to trialogue, the questions of why I teach/move/think this way come into view. I have been trained in the Limón technique which informs how I make choices about what we might do together in a class. I recognise that this is not only the work that we do, but it is also 'a process, a campaign, a dwelling, a conversation and it is ongoing work – a circulatory flow of regeneration' (Ingold, 2011: 29). Ideas from friends/kin near and far visit the work in these speculations. Karen Barbour's questions about, 'what movement we choose to teach and for what purposes in higher education, and how we might teach movement ethically and inclusively' (2016: 189), are salient reminders of our responsibilities as teachers. David offered this during our studio practice, 'the work is a proposal. The acceptance of the offer creates the work. The methodology is in us asking each other and ourselves about the work' (Waring, 2018).

A range of movement practices have been present in the Limón technique from its inception. Founder Limón dancer Betty Jones studied with Lulu Sweigard and not only incorporated imagery for alignment and attention to detail but also adopted principles of kindness in her teaching. Later on, Laura Glenn immersed Bartenieff principles in the technique, Jennifer Scanlon used Alexander technique, and in the present day, Geraldine Cardiel connects her Limón teaching with Feldenkrais Awareness through Movement (ATM). These ideas of care of the body and kindness sit at the heart of the principles of how to 'dance Limón'. Limón spoke of listening to the voices of the body in order to arrive at the heroic capacity of the human being to, 'with dignity and a towering majesty, dance. Not prance, cavort, do "fancy dancing," or show-off steps. … dance as Michelangelo's visions dance and as the music of Bach dances' (Cohen, 1965: 23). This lofty vision may raise a smile of recognition, or a sceptical eyebrow, but what can we do with the relics of the dancing past without being stuck 'worrying the carcase of an old song' (Thomas, 1952: 5)? My colleague and old friend Dale Thompson expands this notion,

> I can remember hearing these words in my Nikolais/Louis classes – or something similar. Somehow for me, the issues of presence/present allow us to avoid stale definitions of what was…It makes us involved in the 'now' process to which we 'responsibly' bring our socio-cultural, political selves.
>
> (Thompson, 2020)

The heritage of what we teach now has been passed down to us through and with embodied practice, but what else remains *as well as* the traces of these ways of moving/knowing? What stories did we miss? 'A way of seeing is also a way of not seeing' (Eisner, 2002: 25). The Limón technique insisted its way into the twenty-first century by deliberately avoiding didactic teaching and emphasising the joy of movement and of people moving together. This embodied heritage of a way of dancing that proposes 'we' rather than 'I' works from an assumption of kinship. Artist scholar James Moreno observes Limón's practice of the 'embodied gaze' (2017: 8) which:

> provided a dissident practice through which he could enact multiple stories of brownness, blackness, whiteness, queerness, and straightness. It allowed him to create a space in which he could assert a way of being in a world that his queer brown body would otherwise not fit.
>
> (Moreno, 2017: 8)

As teachers, how do we create possibilities within the forms that we teach? In the mixed ecology of our dance classes, can a 'both/and' approach generate openings for renewal, for surprise, delight and a sense of belonging. A student's incompatibility with the material, or 'failure', requires delicate observation. We learn publicly in a dance class – we're working it out empirically – so how is this private and shared experience manifested in a collective interest? How can we find ways to move together with desire, joy and confidence in our capacities *and* our frailties?

> If I have to learn in full view of everyone else, how do I work in a way that fulfils and satisfies my growth and development and keeps me curious and engaged whether I "like" what is being proposed or not?
>
> (Waring, 2018)

There is plenty of room for trialogue among the story (work), storyteller (teacher) and reader (learner) here. Only in class, is it possible to triangulate teaching, learning and the work. This triangulation is important to the *Simply for the Doing* manifesto as we explore how and why we are doing this together. In our July 2018 retreat, we identified some problematic tensions as we navigate the teaching of Dance in higher education. These tensions arose from conversations as we were working in the studio; institutions vs. embodied subjects and training vs. enquiry, for example. We also began to wonder what is in-between these perceived points of opposition and how we navigate this territory as teachers? We discussed strategies for students to engage actively with an assessment by helping to design it, to encourage them to value their process so that the 'product' can take care of itself; seeking antidotes for the 'how do I get a good mark?' culture.

Learning to dance by doing dance in the company of others is a unique phenomenon. The solo practice of the musician, painter or writer is not for us. Certainly, the conditioning and somatic work we engage with as part of our individual interests and maintenance are essential, but they are adjuvant to the vividly social encounter of class. The class is a gathering of people, dance and daily life. It is our lifeblood where we find both kinship with each other and a trialogue with our work. Paavola and Hakkarainen's concept of trialogue promotes an 'emphasis not only on individuals or on community, but on the way people collaboratively develop mediating artifacts' (2005: 5).

Making playful encounters with phrases and their problems

Phrases can be hierarchical so let's make them fun.

(Guttierrez, no date)

Learning phrases or combinations at the end of class is the culmination of all the warming up, practice and preparation. It is the fruit of the labour. Why is this part of the class also perceived as a problem? If 'the phrase' is seen as an apotheosis, how is it also perceived as problematic and how might it be dismantled? We can pursue phrases with irony, humour and scepticism, we can open up the 'empty sectors and dusty corners' (Rafferty, 2018) to our interest, rather than focus our efforts to get everything right. In order to be playful, we need to invite surprise and uncertainty into our practices – trial and error and the delight and mischief of making mistakes. In the delight of still being alive after treatment for breast cancer, I am aware that my desire for play and for social encounters, and my unruly disregard for rules have increased exponentially.

Writing this now in the midst of a global pandemic raises a number of old and new questions about dancing and its capacities and values. Avoiding risk, uncertainty and failure are a heightened aspect of everyday life and are also conditions which interfere with our learning, teaching and dancing. COVID data shift daily and unpredictably and determine whether we go out, or not. Our work as dancers places more importance on exploration and to what is distinctive (Eisner, 2002), so we should feel prepared. Uncertainty provides opportunities to be creative and improvise; to practise our survival skills. Uncertainty is cunning (Novotny, 2016) and the more that institutions desire their workforce to provide certainty and to be efficient and 'successful', the more artists and educators will shift and subvert. We make the space for trial and error, for failure, mistakes and uncertainty.

The cunning of uncertainty lets in the unexpected. It makes room for the new, even if the new is made from clever and unexpected recombinations of already existing elements. Poised on the threshold between the present and an unknowable future, it invites us to join the dance.

(Nowotny, 2016: 36)

Improvising with dance material and engaging in some point of interest within the scaffolding of the phrase, there is plenty to occupy our time purposefully. Self-directed interest (heutagogy) is the key player here; self-determined learning which challenges ideas about teaching and learning and identifies the need for 'knowledge sharing' rather than 'knowledge hoarding' (Hase and Kenyon, 2001: 4). Disrupting the need to know the steps or to embody the material quickly and efficiently (in auditions, for example) can help us avoid class situations which propel us towards 'oppressive unison' (Dryburgh, 2018), where what is produced steals our attention away from a playful encounter with 'I am doing this' and the 'what it is likeness' of our own dancing.

What we notice gives shape to our experience. Artist and writer Jenny Odell describes this as a process of 'rendering' (2019: 121). The playful encounter of the dance technique class can render an environment for and with dancing where we can fool around in the 'wild spaces of the body' (Ellis, 2020) with what choreographer Rosemary Lee describes as a 'creature mind' (2018). The joyful presence of peers presents a schema of 'listening rooms and side galleries' (Fisher, 2001: 12) and the potential for meaningful metaphors to rush into view.

Not knowing what we are doing

My diary takes on new importance. Counting down the days.
  Six treatments. Six months.
  I feel that this mapping gives some control back to my life, but before each round of chemo, there is a blood test. My blood must pass a test and it fails. Twice.
  Strangely I feel fine, but my blood says otherwise and so my treatment takes longer.
  I surrender – reluctantly – to the process I know nothing about.

Why is it so important for us to dance and how does going to class everyday address this and sustain its importance? Classes are unpredictable, we make detailed plans, but they are not a foregone conclusion – and nor should they be. During the first few months of COVID, the hiatus of not knowing what to do was turbulent. After 40 years of practising teaching, I was in a situation of not knowing; of being a novice. As teaching moved online, there seemed to be an obvious binary between those who embraced the possibilities of online engagement and those who mourned the contact of class, the space of the studio and the honest, sweaty, laborious joy of dancing. I had not encountered *Zoom* before and suddenly it was a necessity for teaching, but I felt that I needed to coax my students off their screens and into the 'outside studio'. Walking, running and improvising outdoors in our local environments allowed us to bring stories back to our online encounters; stories about how movement was helping us to navigate lockdown, how our sensorial awareness was more acute – no traffic, more birdsong, no aeroplanes, no contrails, cleaner air. It was a time to be quiet, to be grateful and to observe other species thriving at a time where humans were revealing their fragility. Alongside a walking practice (as a survival strategy), I encouraged our students to write their own dance manifestos. This manifesto by Azize Sousami was proposed during the final months of her BA studies during the COVID lockdown with all of its uncertainties and 'unknowing'.

Affirmation

Step by step, day by day, I transform.
Each version of myself feels different.
I dance for all of them.
For every reason I smile, cry, love deeply, try hard, give up
Warm up, run in the snow, try again harder, pay bills, swim in the sea, eat,
Sleep with music, face my demons, walk by lakes, talk to friends, dream of
Sunsets by the ocean.
I dance for each given breath.
I dance because I must, and I shall.

(Sousami, 2020)

This is now, I am here, we are doing this. I use this statement as part of the 'arrival' of all of my classes so that we can all become receptive to the potential of what we are doing and the capacity of class for renewal, for recovery, for starting from scratch and for finding new reasons for dancing. In our learning, failing and progressing in public, the trials and errors of each individual in the class (including the teacher) are readily available to everyone in the class. This yields a rich site for exploring our dancing, our capacities and our – usually self-imposed – boundaries inside the framework of the class. What we know as dancers is discreet; it is hidden – especially from those who choose not to dance. Embodied knowing, embodied enquiry and embodiment are sites for discovery, transformation, transgression and joy for dancers, but too often invisible to the non-dancer. Being a dancer means to be in the world in a particular way; a dancer is alive to the possibilities of being present in time and space with corporeal attention to themselves, to others and to their environment. Their engagement in class is haptic and the knowing is an implicit embodied experience which explores both the myths and realities that bind us together.

'Because I'm dreaming of you now as I plan it [the class], so it's already begun'.

(Gutierrez, no date).

What will happen today? How will this go? I'm not feeling up to the task this morning, how can I become the most enthusiastic person in the room? (Why is this necessary?)

'*You were very entertaining Erica, but what did they learn?*'

Words from the past resonate as I dream/plan a class. I recall this comment from dance lecturer Edith Stokes on observing my teaching practice as a second-year student. It has stayed with me for over 40 years... But back to this class I'm about to share: what will they learn? Remember: it's not about me. What did we try yesterday? What seemed to 'catch fire'? Where were the sticky bits, the delicious bits, the 'banana skins' and what Sonia calls 'the dusty corners and empty sectors'? Will we remember the phrase? Does it matter if we don't?

Walking to work, warming up. Pay attention. Cadence. Pattern. Pace. 1,2,3,4 ... Mix up the metre. 1,2,3. 1,2,3,4. 1,2,3,4,5... Breathe.

I've arrived. The studio is warm and there is time to warm up. Most of the students are here and are gathered in the usual 'camp' near the cubbyholes, catching up both live and virtually. A few of them have ventured into the space to warm up.

And we begin ... with our greetings, our welcomes, our checking-in, our stories of journeys, of events, of tired bodies, of eager bodies ... and all of the chatter in my head from the train journey and the walk to work evaporates.

The work of class begins. We are here: this is now.

'I am a teacher and I will do what I can'. (Gutierrez, no date)

Trusting our embodied knowledge and curbing the desire to demonstrate competence

The curiosity about embodied knowledge propels teachers of dance technique daily into the laboratory of class and into a practice of research, or a research of practice.

What we do every day is research. Our knowledge, our embodied bibliography – what we bring every day to our practice. One of our missions [of *Simply for Doing*] is to value and validate the everyday work that we do – creatively, intelligently, pedagogically – to have our students learn from us and with us.

(Rafferty, 2018)

This everyday thinking on our feet, problem-solving and looking *with* the material is a qualitative practice and in today's metrics-driven culture runs into some unhelpful paradigms. Simon Ellis addresses the ubiquity of data and surveillance in his blog. He reminds us that we unwittingly contribute to the growing market of surveillance capitalism through our smartphones. He urges us to turn them off:

> We can create a wild space. Like the body. A wild space: unpredictable and un-extractable. A place for our analogue selves and our radically analogue bodies. A place where something is not simply yes or no, this or that, 1 or 0, anything but boolean, untouched, untouchable. A body that, even just briefly, resists the facts and fictions of sampling, the logic and ideology of data, and the datafication of the world.
>
> (Ellis, 2020)

Universities gather information about students' attendance and achievements and their use of libraries and virtual learning platforms; they are data

---

June 2016

My chemotherapy has finished.

My radiotherapy has finished.

But what is this last part of the treatment? I was not expecting this – a daily oral dose of Anastrozole for the rest of my life which will inhibit oestrogen circulating in my body.

I'm uncomfortable with the idea of losing of bone density. I manage three weeks and stop.

During my cancer treatment journey, my companions were our incredible NHS nurses, technicians, doctors, consultants and surgeons. All armed with data about me (not surprising) and most with movement and dance practices that supported their work-ing lives (surprising). Their self-care in order to care for others. This felt life-affirming. Another entwined phenomenon. Another process of 'togethering' (Ingold) between people, dance and daily life.

Back to data and competence ... in my final sign-off meeting with my oncologist –

"How are you getting on with Anastrozole?"

"I've packed it in"

I ask about the data.

"Don't worry. Most drug trials are terribly inaccurate, they run at about 40% accuracy.

Think about it Erica – drugs are taken by human beings, they forget to take them, they don't

follow the protocols, and they don't fill out the data-capture forms correctly ... ".

subjects assembled from digital traces of educational activity. Demonstrating competence, it seems, is about producing good data.

Data colonialism exploits human beings through data; continuous tracking leads to stealthy opportunism in relation to discrimination or influences on our behaviour and interaction (Couldry and Meijas, 2019). This is in profound contrast to the embodied subjects we encounter every day in class. In response to this, dance teachers need to add vigilance to their toolkit; a state of careful watchfulness of our students' confidence, helping them to work with affirmation, helping to undo bad training, debunking the selfie and reminding them that *they* are doing this, it is not being done to them. On top of everything else, we are stewards of well-being and providers of antidotes as the data designed to make us 'competent' makes us unhealthy.

Dancers and dance teachers *celebrate* dance's diverse forms; we value its situated cognition and its creative embodied subjectivity. Its tools and skills change and shape the world around us. The dance class is where we learn to survive and thrive and encounter failure without failing. Dance does not continually need to be explained. Our core values are self-evident in the doing of our many dances and these cannot – and should not – be measured exclusively by criteria or outcomes. We celebrate dancing's capacity to resist the quantitative indices of performance and productivity. The tools for survival, resistance and kinship are all present in the dance technique class, but the story of the class has to be compelling, 'make the story itself so interesting that the teller just...disappears' (Pullman, 2017: 13).

Acknowledgements

My sincere thanks to Sonia Rafferty and David Waring for their extraordinary companionship and expertise and to these wonderful colleagues who have participated with us in the studio on our retreats:

Adesola Akinleye, Alice Sara, Anna Pakes, Arabella Stanger, Cristina Rosa, Debbie Lee Anthony, Elaine Thomas, Fiona Edwards, Gemma Donohue, Georgia Tegou, Hanna Gillgren, Heike Salzer, Helen Kindred, Jamieson Dryburgh, Jayne McKee, Kathy Crick, Lalitaraja, Nicoletta Bonanni, Nina Atkinson, Seema de Jorge Chopra, Simonetta Alessandri and Tamara Tomic-Vajagic.

References

Barbour, K. (2016) 'Embodied Values and Ethical Principles in Somatic Dance Classes: Considering Implicit Motor Learning', *Journal of Dance & Somatic Practices*, 8 (2), pp. 189–204. https://doi.org/10.1386/jdsp.8.2.189_1

Bernard, A., Steinmuller, W. and Stricker, U. (2006) *Ideokinesis. A Creative Approach to Movement and Alignment*. Berkeley, CA: North Atlantic Books.

Clarke, G. (2007) Mind Is as in Motion. *Animated* (Spring). Available at: https://www.communitydance.org.uk/DB/animated-library/mind-is-as-in-motion?ed=14048 (Accessed: 16 June 2021).

Cohen, S.J. (1965) *Modern Dance. Seven Statements of Belief.* Middletown, CT: Wesleyan University Press.

Couldry, N. and Meijas, U.A. (2019) 'Data Colonialism: Rethinking Big Data's Relation to the Contemporary Subject', *Television and New Media*, 20 (4), pp. 336–349. https://doi.org/10.1177%2F1527476418796632

Dryburgh, J. (2018) Teachers' Wisdom. *Simply for the Doing*, University of Roehampton/Trinity Laban Conservatoire for Music and Dance.

Eisner, E. (2002) *The Arts and the Creation of Mind.* New Haven, CT: Yale University Press.

Ellis, S. (2020) *Phones, Feelings and Radically Analogue Bodies.* Available at: https://www.skellis.net/

Erdrich, L. (2020) *The Night Watchman.* London: Corsair.

Fisher, H. (2001) *The Subjective Self. A Portrait Inside Logical Space.* Omaha: University of Nebraska Press.

Freire, P. (1995) 'Preface', in McLaren, P. (Ed.), *Critical Pedagogy and Predatory Culture: Oppositional Politics in a PostModern Era* (pp. ix–xi). New York: Routledge.

Guttierrez, M. (no date) *This Is Why I Teach Class.* Available at: https://www.miguelgutierrez.org/teaching

Hase, S. and Kenyon, C. (2001) 'Moving from Andragogy to Heutagogy: Implications for VET', *Proceedings of Research to Reality: Putting VET Research to Work: Australian Vocational Education and Training Research Association (AVETRA)*, Adelaide, 28–30 March: Crows Nest, NSW.

Hay, D. (1989) 'Playing Awake: Letters to My Daughter', *TDR*, 33 (4), pp. 70–76.

Ingold, T. (2011) *Being Alive.* Abingdon: Routledge. https://doi.org/10.4324/9780203818336

Johnson, M. (2011) 'Embodied Knowing Through Art', in Biggs, M. and Karlsson, H. (eds.) *The Routledge Companion to Research in the Arts.* Abingdon: Routledge, pp. 141–151.

Lee, R. (2018) Simply for the Doing Workshop at *Our Dance Democracy: Dance, Performance, Culture and Civic Democracy.* Liverpool Hope University. November 2018.

Massumi, B. (2008) 'The Thinking Feeling of What Happens', *Inflexions 1.1.* Montréal: Université de Montréal. Available at: http://www.senselab.ca/inflexions/pdf/Massumi.pdf

Moreno, J. (2017) 'Brown in Black and White: José Limón Dances', in Kowal, R.J., Siegmund, G, and Martin, R. (eds.) *The Oxford Handbook of Dance and Politics.* Oxford: Oxford University Press, pp. 33–49.

Nikolais, A. and Louis, M. (2005) *The Nikolais/Lewis Dance Technique: A Philosophy and Method of Modern Dance.* New York: Routledge, Taylor and Francis.

Nowotny, H. (2016) *The Cunning of Uncertainty.* Cambridge: Polity Press.

Odell, J. (2019) *How to do Nothing. Resisting the Attention Economy.* London/New York: Melville House Publishing.

Paavola, S. and Hakkarainen, K. (2005) 'The Knowledge Creation Metaphor. An Emergent Epistemological Approach to Learning', *Science & Education*, 14, pp. 535–557.

Pakes, A. (2011) 'Phenomenology and Dance: Husserlian Meditations', *Dance Research Journal*, 43 (2). Congress on Research in Dance, pp. 457–476.

Pullman, P. (2017) *Daemon Voices. On Stories and Storytelling*. Oxford: David Fickling Books.

Rafferty, S. (2018) Teachers' Wisdom. *Simply for the Doing*, University of Roehampton/Trinity Laban Conservatoire for Music and Dance.

Salzer, H. (2018) Movement Manifesto. *Simply for the Doing*, University of Roehampton/Trinity Laban Conservatoire for Music and Dance.

Satin, L. (1999) 'Autobiography in the Present Tense: Deborah Hay, Living and Dying at Once', *Women and Performance*, 10 (1–2), pp. 181–210.

Sousami, A. (2020) 'Affirmation', *Dance Manifesto*. University of Roehampton.

Thomas, R.S. (1952) 'A Welsh Landscape' from *Selected Poems* (2004). London: Penguin.

Thompson, D. (2020) Teachers' Wisdom *Simply for the Doing*, University of Roehampton/Trinity Laban Conservatoire for Music and Dance.

Turnbull, D. (2002) 'Travelling Knowledge: Narratives, Assemblage and Encounters', in Bourguet M-N et al. (eds.) *Instruments, Travel and Science. Itineraries of Precision from the Seventeenth to the Twentieth Century*. London: Routledge. https://doi.org/10.4324/9780203219010

Waring, D. (2018) Teachers' Wisdom *Simply for the Doing*, University of Roehampton/Trinity Laban Conservatoire for Music and Dance.

Part III

Conversations

Introduction

Part III comprises a series of ten artist conversations, exploring ideas of ethical agility, values and autobiographical explorations of training and experience of technique. Twenty artists or organisations were asked to take part in these conversational duets, split into pairs, bringing together multiple perspectives from across the dance sector with differing relationships to the people they were in conversation with. Some pairings were long established working relationships, others were meeting for the first time through this opportunity. Some conversations happened more than once, over a series of days, whilst others met only once. Different lived experiences, different training routes and different career trajectories (choreographer, teacher, lecturer, performer, producer) were brought together in dialogue. What is documented here are 'segments' of these longer conversations, edited not to strip away content but to sift for the concentrated meaning.

This method of engaging artists to be 'in conversation' with one another pulls from a number of methodological processes. By bringing together peers in dialogue with one another, a process of mutual exploration fuelled by interest and curiosity took place. While, as editors, we sat on the periphery during the discussion, prompts or starting questions were offered, including encouragement to consider values and the concept of ethical agility, although this was not predefined. This method pulls from relational interviewing, which brings people together in discussion to generate narratives or stories about themselves. Through these stories, as described by Lee Ann Fujii (2017), 'people locate themselves as agents in the various social worlds they identify with, aspire to, imagine, or inhabit' (3). Emphasis is on how these artists perceive the world and the phenomenon of 'technique' to expand understandings of what technique is, can, and should, be.

Examining the conversations together, patterns emerged between the discussions that connected people's stories, journeys and experiences. By interrogating their own training as a starting point, many of the artists reflect on their journey pre- and post-training, often recognising a process of unlearning or rethinking what training can be. Ideas of technique as both a personal

DOI: 10.4324/9781003111146-15

experience and a collective encounter were prevalent in many conversations, thinking about different bodies translating movement within a collaborative space. Attention was paid to the shifting social and political landscape in the UK, and how dancers embarking on careers in this context navigate their position and work in the world. In terms of the more practical aspects of teaching or facilitating technique, evaluation and assessment is a particular feature, either via the self or via others. Discussions consider language and listening as vital elements of creating inclusive and dialogic training spaces.

How technique is understood as both collective engagement and individual exploration is assessed through multiple conversations. Chris Crickmay and Miranda Tufnell discuss how participants come to movement exploration with their own sense of the world, bringing a personal perspective on their engagement. This personalisation (or need for) in technique was shared by Imogen Aujla and Laura Jones, who discuss the process of translation and adaption for disabled dancers. However, the individual experience of movement exploration is understood and practiced within a collective endeavour, as Ruth Pethybridge and Diane Amans explore, discussing inter-generational community projects and the relational dimension of moving together. Adam Benjamin and Olu Taiwo discuss this togetherness as a unifying action, exploring how dance technique can bring together groups of people with cohesive intentions. Aspects of authorship and negotiation in this collective approach to choreography and movement creation are recognised in Shobana Jeyasingh and Alexander Whitley's discussion.

Acknowledgement of the shifting socio-political landscape was a common feature of many discussions, both specific to the dance sector and considering the wider context of the UK and its relationship with the world. The volatile state of the UK dance ecology is recognised, with Theo Clinkard and Seke Chimutengwende discussing aspects of employability for current students, understanding that student training and career trajectories are directly affected by socio-political changes. Therefore, it is suggested that curiosity, multiplicity of experience and variety is needed within dance training to establish flexible and resilient responsiveness to the shifting landscape, as Scilla Dyke and Rosemary Lee also explore in their conversation. Related to this are discussions of political change, with decolonisation of the dance sector being discussed by Jonathan Burrows and Alesandra Seutin, within a broader discussion of anti-racist movements. Visibility within the dance sector and, more specifically, dance training is considered through multiple conversations, with the need to recognise who has access, what is valued in dance currently, and how this might be dismantled to open more possibility.

Practicalities of teaching or facilitating technique classes and movement exploration, such as evaluation or feedback offering, were common across the discussions. Magpie Dance, in conversation with Caroline Hotchkiss, propose and interrogate 'notions of success' and how traditional tropes and ideas of accomplishment can be challenged or dismantled to rethink virtuosity, expertise and talent. A reconsidering of language use and the importance of listening was significant in discussions, including inviting in different disciplines or multimedia to offer innovative ways of engaging with reflection and self-awareness.

The purpose and role of technique appeared across the discussions, with Ruth Pethybridge asking, 'what are we training for?'. Asking who is involved and why we are training was pressing, emphasising the importance of revaluating dance technique delivery. In thinking about their own experience of dance training, many artists recognise the 'training' they had before undertaking formal dance study, often through familial celebrations or engagement with popular music. Others spoke of a process of 'unlearning' or 'undoing' that can occur after completing undergraduate training, with Ivan Michael Blackstock and Henrietta Hale recognising the process of continual learning that occurs through the twists and turns of working in the UK dance sector.

The UK dance community is often viewed as being modest in size, with many commonalities and connections emerging from overlapping areas of activity. We not only move with one another but also converse in shared spaces, at various sector events and through social meetings. The conversations documented here in part III anchor the wider, emerging themes of the book in reality, through shared dialogue and future aspirations; viewing technique from within and outside of the studio for all to engage with.

Reference

Fujii, L.A. (2017) *Interviewing in Social Science Research: A Relational Approach.* Abingdon: Taylor & Francis Ltd.

3.1 Thinking together about the ethics of training

A conversation between Alesandra Seutin and Jonathan Burrows

Alesandra Seutin is an international performer, choreographer and teacher. She holds a Diploma in dance theatre from Laban and a degree in choreography and performance from Middlesex University in London, and is currently Co-Artistic Director of Écoles Des Sables in Senegal and member of the Artistic Faculty for the Rose Choreographic School, Sadler's Wells Theatre, London. Since founding her company Vocab Dance in 2007, Alesandra has progressively built an international reputation for creating thought-provoking and visually striking performances for small to large scale theatres as well as non-theatre settings.

Jonathan Burrows is a choreographer whose main focus is an ongoing body of pieces with the composer Matteo Fargion. He is the author of A Choreographer"s Handbook (Routledge, 2010) and Writing Dance (Varamo, 2022), and is currently Associate Professor at the Centre for Dance Research, Coventry University.

Alesandra: I think of my early days growing up as already being part of the training, but the word training came into my ear when I came to the UK. I've always been training because everything I've been doing is part of what I'm doing now. It started in the living room in Brussels with my mother playing records and my brothers dancing and my dad sitting on a couch with a pipe. It's very powerful – for me that's where the training began because my mum is moving and dancing and I'm following, my brothers are there too and we are sharing something that is movement, life, fun. When I look at what I'm doing now, it's really about this idea of exchanging something in the space, but not necessarily being taught skills because they are inside of us. In sharing we are finding joy, expression, subtleties and interaction. It's almost like I've done the whole journey to arrive to something that I always knew or always had, but with the additional knowledge and connections that are part of the journey of who we meet and what we keep or throw. I've gone through the traditional training of ballet, jazz and contemporary, but then my journey switched when I went to Africa and started training there. It was a different idea of learning, not always being told how it's done, but observing, learning by repetition and continuously

DOI: 10.4324/9781003111146-16

doing something in order to embody it. This is very different from most dance studios in the West where someone's telling you what to do and how to do it. I adopted this way and it's part of my practice when I teach. It's not about me being the master but being someone with knowledge that I will share. You have as much to give to me as I have to give to you, because your existence and your presence in the space is as important as mine, because it nurtures mine. I go by this idea of living in the movement. I work in a very performative way, where it's about our existence and continuously being aware of what we are saying rather than the shape we are creating. It's about us.

Jonathan: It's very interesting that you start with this image of training beginning before the training and continuing onwards after the training. I also had in my life this period that was called training, when I studied ballet for eight years, but for me, that time was less important than what followed, which was a kind of unlearning that expanded things and reconnected me to what I felt. The young person who turns up at a dance institution is full already, and what they come with will continue long after their official training ends. For me, the thing that's sometimes missing in dance education is being taught how to trust the physical knowledge you arrived with, and how to nurture it over a lifetime. The dominant image in dance institutions is that you will learn new skills, and after a certain number of years you'll be ready to dance. This is not what I experienced. I think at the heart of the ethics of dance pedagogy is that dance institutions could challenge this notion of a set period and endpoint of learning, and prepare people instead for how to go on moving through the world as a human being who was and is always in the process of embodying, and whose physical knowledge is useful in ways far beyond the act of dancing itself.

Alesandra: I agree with that. For institutions, it's a package to recruit people, but the idea that after three years you have arrived is not real. I'm still learning. I think that whole idea has to change. I was sharing this with past students a few weeks ago, telling them that you have to learn technique in order to let it go and to continue with something else. It's in you and it will be useful, but it's not something that you're holding onto so much that you can't let go and let anything else enter. With the form that I do, there's also a hierarchy of what is valid or not valid. I really notice it when I'm teaching. It's changing in Belgium, but in the UK, there is still an idea of what is the actual product, the technique or the style we need to have in order to be valued or valid.

Jonathan: It's that question of how we validate what we do. How would I know if what I was doing had value? We usually don't get any sense of that until long after we've moved on somewhere else and then look back. But the difficulty of this old model of three years of learning where you acquire the skills for professional life, is that the temptation is to come out from under all that technical training and then reject it.

Alesandra: Unlearning is better than rejecting.

Jonathan: I think people reject technique because after all that time in the classroom it comes to be seen as a colonising structure, rather than something which, if you approach it by a different route, might be recognised as a kind of embodied learning that's innate to human perception and being and being with each other. So, if you think of an ethics of training, what is it about training that it often fails to find a way to set up a situation where somebody can carry forward what is of them within that training, rather than rejecting the training as being something which came from the outside?

Alesandra: In order to unlearn it, you have to have learned it – to have embodied that training. That's why I value training and technique because it's given me a certain structure and awareness of my body that I didn't have in the living room. It's almost like I can step outside of my body and understand, feel and know structurally what's happening. I'm moving with consciousness. I find techniques very useful and it feeds my teaching, because with them I'm able to look at other bodies and support them to find their own path.

Jonathan: I'm thinking now again of what you just said a moment ago, that it's like you make a whole journey to arrive back at what you knew. I'm very aware that when I'm working with younger artists and in dance institutions, it feels like a lot of the work is to give that younger person permission to remember, not consciously, but rather the feeling of what they knew, which is what brought them there in the first place. Because it's that feeling which will sustain them after they've left the institution. What they learn at the institution won't keep them going. They have to come back to this core sense of something, which I guess is deeply personal and therefore sometimes also shameful. And the institution makes you feel ashamed of it.

Alesandra: I think for a long time you're doing this thing but you're not really sure if it's right. I kept going and now I'm more sure, more grounded with what I'm doing and more in control of what I want people to see. During the training in England in contemporary dance, I had to fulfil this idea or these visions, but it wasn't really about me, it was about needing to complete and to fulfil a certain idea. It really shifted afterwards when it became more about what I was actually doing.

Jonathan: One of the things I remember about my early life as a dancer, is that for a lot of the time when I was dancing in the way I liked to dance, I had the fear that I wasn't embodying things enough. I was surrounded by people who talked about embodiment, that told me about their embodiment and kept encouraging me to feel more embodied, but something set me up all the time to wonder if I was failing. I do now gravitate occasionally towards moments where I have a fleeting sense 'maybe this is embodiment?', but I'm aware that any real conscious perception of it is fleeting by its nature. It's a process rather than about arriving somewhere.

Alesandra: I don't think we ever arrive; I think it's a continuous process. It never stops for me. I always questioned what embodiment is, because you are dancing and you are feeling, and at the same time you're trying to feel this thing of 'I'm embodied'. You don't really know what it is, but there have been times when I thought, 'I'm really here. I'm here fully'. This may be the closest you get to the satisfaction of feeling embodiment – when you are fully in this space and there's something about how you feel inside the space, and the space inside of you makes you feel like maybe that is what embodiment could be. But there are times when you don't feel it at all.

Jonathan: For me when you're embodying something, it passes from a place where what you're doing seems separate and superficial, and then it slowly and consciously becomes you, until finally it reaches that place where you're no longer aware of it at all. At other times, you suddenly become aware of something you've embodied which was never you but belongs somehow to your past. It has moved forwards with you, and you have to question it. In reconsidering the ethics of dance, how do we cherish what matters that tails from the past and into the present and future, and at the same time do this work of questioning it? How do we review the past in dance history? This is important because that sets up how we might validate the future. I guess it's part of the work of decolonisation.

Alesandra: This word decolonising means many different things to different people depending on history or geography. In a way, it's about erasing something, but it's complicated because the impact of the history, while in some senses negative, is bringing you to what you are right now. For example, I don't do ballet anymore, but I value the training I got through doing ballet for a long time, even though the way I was being taught was not really positive. I can't throw it away completely because it's part of how I move today. It's still visible when I do certain things. I know it's there. But I don't know if it's really about decolonising, I think it's about choosing the things that we need, or the things that work for us. It's about leaving history where it is and just moving on with what is right for us, not trying to erase that part of myself.

Jonathan: The poet and philosopher Fred Moten said recently, 'Well, for me, decolonisation is about challenging individualistic possessiveness'[1]. I found myself wondering what that might mean in terms of dance training and what gets embodied. It brought me back to valuing the idea of dance knowledge as a process, rather than being about the acquisition of something which you could say has become yours or you own it. Because my experience as a dancer is that I've never really felt like I owned anything that was passing through me as embodiment. Occasionally, I've watched an old film of me dancing and thought it looked like I'd momentarily caught or understood something in my body, but I know that at the time I didn't feel like I'd really caught or understood anything. It's also the blessing of what we do, right? We let it go. It passes through.

Alesandra: Passing through. I like that concept, and the idea of the space and how we move through it with each other.

Jonathan: I've been talking recently with the anthropologist Stephanie Bunn, whose research has been focused on a particular form and practice of basket weaving in Scotland. She observes that there's an element of embodiment which exists and communicates in a more heightened state when you're in a situation of being and doing with other people. When I heard this, I recognised that the skilled practice I've experienced, of both technique and embodiment, is very connected to doing things with other people.

Alesandra: The value of technique is in a way more noticeable against others and with others and in relation to others and other bodies. An example is the first time I went to Senegal and I was invited into a baptism. During the baptism they have different circles, and you may have a circle where there are only the women (then only the men and then the children), and then towards the end, everyone comes together. I was invited into the circle of women and they were playing on pots and pans and dancing, but it was very, very subtle. And you had women who were 90-year-olds and 17-year-old young girls, all dancing the same dance. But it was amazing to notice the difference and see how the elders had embodied this thing that the young girl was doing, but in such a grounded, calm way. And I thought watching this 90-year-old woman dancing, that this is as valued as the young girl jumping higher. I want to aim, not at the really high excited energy, but to this grounded, calm and very assured physicality. It changed my perspective; I thought this is something really special. For me this is virtuosity, this is technique. There is something there that I don't have yet.

Jonathan: If we speak of an ethics of dance training, then this sense of collective learning is sometimes missing. The doing together is there, but it's still under the thumb of the idea that talent rises. There is still at the heart of dance training the image of individualistic self-improvement. What might the future of dance training look like if there were more balance between individual learning and the realisation that without the doing together it can't really function? It's something about how the process of learning with other people, by observation and repetition, is how we function as human beings. What you say raises the idea also that there is a possible ecology of dance training and practice which might be less binary between younger and older performers, which could recognise embodiment as a process that precedes training and continues until the end. Right through to a 90-year-old woman dancing – fully validated.

Alesandra: I agree, there is perhaps something missing in schools about the wider idea of collective culture and ideals, about tools and resources for life practice and values. I think this may also influence the culture of dance training.

Jonathan: There's been a proliferation of dance schools all over the world recently, and most of them still focus on old-fashioned linear models of career, rather than wider resources for life practice and values. And at the same time, there's a lessening of the amount of paid work that people have access to when they come out at the end of their training. As a teacher, it feels like we're making a wrong promise to young people, that there will be work available for them. I don't want people not to have access to the experience of dance, and on an ideal level, I think it does give people something they can take forwards into all aspects of their life. However, I would like to see the possibility that it be spoken about from the first day of their entry into the dance institution, that what they learn isn't limited to the idea of them becoming the next big dancer or choreographer. That the knowledge they gain can be useful towards other disciplines, other places and other ways of giving and receiving within the wider community.

Alesandra: Yes, because I've studied dance, there's so much more I can do. Dance is a great skill; it opens up many other possibilities.

Jonathan: Thinking about history, I'm old enough to have lived through a period of time when there was a strong sense of historic development within contemporary dance. There was still this notion of the next important artist, but it was a very particular bubble of dance culture, which excluded many people and many different approaches to what dance may be or might mean or offer. This is changing now and it's much harder to say that this or that particular artist or way of doing things is more important, but there is still in dance institutions the echo of this notion of a timeline, and who will be the next important person. What I like now when I look at the wider dance ecology – I mean not just contemporary dance – is that I see people finding ways to sustain a practice or a process of being as an artist that is much more horizontal, and so has more breath in it and life. I guess it's about how we orientate ourselves within that, as individuals going forwards.

Alesandra: I don't really think we have so much control of all of this. It keeps changing and at the moment it's all about black people. You take opportunities when you can because there's a period where the white male dancer is also at risk or being pushed away because he's been privileged for so long. Suddenly the privilege, or success, is given to someone else. Who is in the books? I really encourage all the writers to just write about the people who may not have a place in a book – to mark new histories. It is changing because there are more conversations happening and younger people writing with new ideas.

Jonathan: I find that idea – that we can't always have control of it – in some ways an enabling thought. It seems in contrast to the way education still moves towards the notion that you will have control. I think one thing that dance gifts people is the endurance of change. To learn how to live with change. I think if I get better at anything, I get better at that. I think that's what becoming older blesses us with. The best work happens when you understand the limits of your ability to control what's happening.

Alesandra: On the other hand, there is also a pressure for constant rein-vention in dance. Sometimes you just want to go into your own process and develop within it, but you need to find a new way of getting money, so you're obliged to add a new thing to your practice. Something is changing within the world with technology and social media. People don't stay with something for a long time, so the notion of slowing down has become important. It's really difficult with younger people. I value this idea of slowing down and repeating things, but it doesn't exist as much anymore in training. You must impose it as a teacher, and when I do it, I'm really conscious about it. When I'm travelling or teaching in Senegal, I'm finally slowing down and suddenly I value everything around me. Even the ants walking. I have time to observe them and hear the birds and nature, and suddenly everything slows down around me and I can take the time. The way of life and teaching or training in London doesn't have the time to value the slowing down or repetition.

Jonathan: I had an experience recently that made me think about the value of slowness, rather than being overloaded with too many possibilities. I was working with hip hop crews in London with Jonzi D, and the French hip hop artist Mohamed Belarbi, founder of Vagabond Crew, was passing through. Jonzi had invited him to come in and work, and it was a room full of hyper-skilled dancers. And Mohamed Belarbi led a two-hour session where he made them work only on toprock, the opening steps that precede the floorwork in Breaking. And he went into extraordinary slow detail. Jonzi and I stood watching and saw that everybody, even the most skilled and confident in the room, was super immersed in what was happening. And at the end of these two hours, Belarbi let them all come into the cypher, and he played music and there was a half hour of absolutely sublime dance and understanding and togetherness. Somehow the return to a slowness deepened and released something. It made me think that sometimes it's about going more deeply into less, rather than trying all the time to embody more. When you practice, you can pass through moments where you think nothing is happening, but these are often the most important moments. Again, it's about moving back towards what you already knew.

Note

1 From Fred Moten 'Blackness and Poetry', a talk given as part of the Mixed Blood Project, University of California Berkeley, 2015.

3.2 'Movement is not something you do, but something you are'

Balancing the development of technical skills with attentional practices in dance training

A conversation between Ivan Michael Blackstock and Henrietta Hale

Ivan Michael Blackstock, born and raised in London, is a dance innovator and cultural observer who first established himself in the UK underground dance scene then as a professional dancer and choreographer, working on music videos, advertising and television. After establishing a successful commercial career, Ivan went on to create his own work as an independent artist creating intense, thought-provoking and political theatre, leading up to his critically acclaimed production TRAPLORD. Ivan is founder of festival and talent incubator CRXSS PLATFXRM and media company ALTRUVIOLET.

Henrietta Hale is co-director of Independent Dance, an artist-led organisation supporting the development of dance through radical enquiry. Their international programme of classes, workshops, projects, and festivals invites artists to co-create learning and exchange ideas. She has worked extensively as a performer and choreographer, co-founding a performance/research collective, Dog Kennel Hill Project, in 2004. She is currently embarked on a PhD with Coventry University and Tavistock Institute of Human Relations.

Personal experience of dance training

Ivan: The way I came about dance was a little bit unbeknownst to me. I had family members that were musicians and work in the reggae dub music and sound systems, so that kind of vibration was already there for me, and obviously with my Caribbean culture we have all these parties all the time. We celebrate everything, even if it's a funeral, birthday or a wedding, there's going to be a celebration. It wasn't like I wanted to be a dancer. I wanted to be something. At that time, video was important and I was watching Michael Jackson on TV and it would make me go, 'Whoa, what is that?'. And I realised actually I wanted to also be a star. That means also using my voice. And then possibly be a rapper or a singer. But over time, through the education system, or as I grew as a person, I felt like I was starting to slowly

DOI: 10.4324/9781003111146-17

become mute, I felt that I started to lose my voice. Things happened in my life, it triggered something, and I held on to some ideas. I think that is where the movement came from for me. When you lose your sense, you pick up other things and I discovered I was good at moving. So, I realised when I do this thing, I become a star in this way and maybe I'm gonna keep doing this.

The way I saw my training then was through music videos and people being on stage and people going, 'Wow, you are amazing'. This is not something I heard a lot in the environment I grew up, so overtime I feel it became escapism. When you're young, you want to move your body. You want to run, play football, climb a tree. Some people push their energy into a certain frequency and vibrate that way and hold onto that.

So, for me, I realise when I do this thing, I feel good after. But it came to a point in my life, I started to understand creative processes and how it might work in different areas of my life. Hip-hop training already did that: from learning, doing something, making something from nothing but my training made me empower myself. It also made me learn how to empower others and pass on how one may transform oneself though training.

A lot of that work has been internal. When I've done that internal work and apply it as an external work, it is a lot easier for me. I know where I need to put my mind to do this external work. I know where I need to be shifting and understanding things and analysing things logically or intuitively.

This led me into doing formal training, studying at Lewisham College at first, then I moved onto Urdang Academy and then I went to London Contemporary Dance School. But my roots are street culture. I feel it's a lot more open. And I like open spaces so I can move. Not restricted spaces. What is good from my formal training, I've been able to kind of share it with other people who are not in that sort of mindset but can find new ways to move and manifest that sort of energy. Dance from the streets is forever manifesting. It's constant, it's a constant energy and you could say it is part of youth culture. I say street culture but I'm not necessarily saying hip-hop, I'm saying punk, all sorts of youth culture. It's forever manifesting, forever moving. But what is missing is the hip-hop philosophy. A lot of people don't know hip-hop has a philosophy underneath it and that's why it's not just a dance, it's bigger than that. It's a culture. There's certain understanding. It is government of self. Street culture allows people to make up their rules too. And we understand that it's their rules.

When I went into formal training, it felt that the Western ideas are the apex of the knowledge, but I thought differently. For me, it was important to be able to learn from each other and not be conformed to other people's way of moving. At the moment, I am going back to my independent training and still learning. I'm still moving my body. It is interesting to fuse two ideas together: a European idea of what dance is and this other space, which is actually very multicultural. I think there is a need for bringing things together in dance training.

Henrietta: It's great to hear because so much of what you said has so much resonance but there is also a huge amount of difference in contexts. As a child, all that was available at the time in terms of training was ballet, so I did ballet classes, which was typical for a little girl. I was really struck by what you said about this feeling that there were potentials or possibilities in a non-verbal space that couldn't be accessed so much in verbal spaces such as in school. I found myself quite shy but when I was dancing, I found this ability to work with dance and music and feeling this sort of power from it. I wonder if that's got very little to do with training. That's about people finding a space that's fulfilling for them. They're kind of in tune with movement spaces more than verbal spaces. You're obviously a really natural talent. So before even going to training, there was obviously just a lot there. That's a very different thing from someone who goes to train where maybe they haven't had those kinds of experiences, and I wonder if training can even offer those experiences where you really feel the sort of specialness of movement and you really understand it as a creative space, or a space of possibility and transformation. I notice that when I teach a lot in university. Some people arrive and they have that already and then some people seem to sadly lose it through training. But sometimes people can really use the training to forge something through that training. I'm curious about whether a dance training programme can offer the opportunities to experience dance as a creative space of possibility and transformation.

Paying attention: internal processes, repetition and multiplicity of movement outcomes

Ivan: It's not necessary for people to go through a lot or to go through trauma to have these experiences with movement but it's about how we look at who we are and bring dance and movement out of that. When I went to conservatoire schools, teachers would say, 'you move like this to feel dance'. It didn't work for me. In martial arts, or Eastern kind of dance practices, the same movement is practised over and over but the expectation is that an internal feeling emerges out of that repetition. I am interested in these two different ways of thinking. How can we bring both of these ways of thinking into conservatoires? More hip-hop improvisational techniques are what I think is missing. There have been a few leaders in the UK, such as Jonzi D and others, who are trying to shine a light on this need to bring these different approaches to dance because it is transformational.

Henrietta: My early background was classical but my whole life has been a sort of reversal of that classical training. It's been more and more about re-finding a kind of childlike quality. Training to really listen in to your own desire and to be committed to that desire. This might resonate with your idea of knowing your own mind and doing internal work first. This practice of listening to internal voices feels like a hugely important aspect of dance training.

In learning anything, there is a shift between not getting something and then getting it. That transition is so impossible to name or even to sort of locate. It's a combination of things that requires a kind of muddiness, or it's enveloped in muddiness. Improvisation classes for me were a key transition moment. Coming from my ballet background, I just remember standing at the edge of the studio and thinking, 'I don't know how anyone knows what to do. How do they know what to do in this space?'. But maybe a year later or six months later, I was doing it and realising that it was completely easy. Suddenly through practice, I got into a place where I could feel comfortable improvising. It is interesting when we think about education, because we're always asking students to articulate their learning as though it was some kind of really clear-cut thing that they went from A to B but most of the time it's more nebulous and kind of blurry. It's a constant process. It's not like you learn it and then you have it either. You are just constantly in process of adjusting or renegotiating what you think you know or the relationship between doing and not doing. The messiness of learning doesn't get acknowledged enough in academic settings. I love when you said, 'I am dance'. Movement is not something you do, but something you are. And I don't do learning, I just am learning. In that sense, everything is training. It's practising with a sense of non-attachment. It is important to not get fixed on the thing that we do. Embodied practices give us the potential to pay attention to what the learning could be in every moment.

Ivan: Yes. I have realised that there is different level of trainings: you can do the training internally or you can do the training outside of yourself. Not physically doing but thinking about the movement and processing it mentally. This is another approach to learning technique which is not talked about in dance training. How can we bring confidence in young people that they can create their own rules while training and learning dance technique?

Henrietta: I want to return to the notion of repetition that Ivan you brought up earlier. Training for me implies something that is kind of repeated in order to become more automatic in a way so that you might train your stomach muscles in order to get stronger so that you can lift people, for example. I like to use the word recursion rather than repetition. It's actually a term one of my students Alice Gale-Feeny spoke of with me and I loved how they used it. Recursion implies that it's the repetition of something that is the same but felt differently. Each time you repeat your practice it evolves slightly. You go through a series of exercises and each time it becomes something different, which feeds into the next time you do it. This notion of practice as recursion is about training your attention rather than training a body part. Although I admit that sometimes it's really useful to train a body part if it's weak. You might want to work on your ankle so it doesn't keep wobbling.

Ivan: Movement has helped me as a tool to learn and understand the world. I process things very differently. I struggled a lot with the way that was taught at school. It didn't make sense to me. I talk in riddles, or metaphorically, because that's how I see the world. I learn from other people that had a bit more of a free way of thinking. Improvisation helps me to build structure or system that can be described as map – but this is not the only way. Other people can try that map and see if it works for them. Conservatoire training can be seen as a map.

Henrietta: In relation to this question between improvisation and set materials, there are just different kinds of systems to tune things. Sometimes you could have really rigid improvisational systems and it's still improvisational. You are still making choices in a live manner. The question isn't always about whether I'm doing a set technique or whether I'm doing improvisation, because for me they are all basically on a spectrum of choice-making. However, it becomes problematic when there are set outcomes and set ideas of success. There is a need to recognise the multiplicity of systems you are talking about. There are many maps.

I can see this multiplicity could be a real problem for universities and conservatoires because if you sort of value everything, how are you upholding things? I could be seen as 'anything goes' and it could undervalue the whole point of getting an expensive institutional education. How are you deciding what rigour means? How do you decide whether someone is rigorously engaged with their practice when there are multiple understandings of what that might mean? But I think that's where the learning then becomes more about the students themselves, even defining what rigour is for them. We have to sort of underpin the notion of value because people have to still be paying their fees. There has to be some kind of value that people are going to get, but that needs to be less fixed. It needs to be not the sort of single identity of what value is, but it needs to be sort of the value in multiplicity, for instance, the value in process or the value in making change. It is about creating a space where you think you're one thing, but then something else happens that you weren't expecting. The student is going to work with systems and maybe they will try something that they hate, or something that they don't hate. It is useful to learn a new system to have it as resource, but creating the space for the unexpected feels really important. And it's important that we're not fixing out outcomes, we're not telling people what they should be or what they should look like.

Contemporary dance and cultures

Ivan: What I find interesting, in training and in the current state of dance, is the street culture. It is thriving. The conservatoires are struggling to hold up contemporary dance because they are not bringing in contemporary culture.

Henrietta: I work for Independent Dance, which is an experimental organisation, based on embodied somatic practices. It aims to be inclusive of all styles, but it's very rare that we have hip-hop. It's not because of a lack of intention, but it's just because these cultures of experimental movement research and hip-hop don't really meet. Also, we are so busy upholding the research into experimental practices that it feels like when cultures become quite commercially successful – like much of hip-hop is – they somehow sort of fly away from us. Why would you interrogate it? It's great, what everyone's doing is great. Does it need the interrogation? This points to a gap between the notion of learning and interrogation and then the notion of actual professional practices that become commercial.

Ivan: What I find interesting with hip-hop is its spectrum. Peace love, unity and having fun, do it yourself. Make something from nothing. And it empowers everyone. Maybe it's more of a spiritual, holistic way of training.

Beyond the dance move, you need to know the music and the role of the music so that you can understand the body rhythms etc. Conservatoires can learn a lot from hip-hop and street culture and the diverse people within these cultures.

Henrietta: It makes me think that Western contemporary dance is divorced from a culture. When we learn contemporary dance, we are learning moves and shapes and things, but we are really not learning it as a sort of cultural practice. Whereas, with hip-hop, you can't just do the moves. You have to learn the culture and it's got as much to do with the music and the clothes and the context. So maybe we need to think of dance training as part of cultural practices and really naming the cultural contexts of things more than we do. I recognise that in my field, we claim some kind of neutral identity, like anyone from any culture can come and just do improvisation, but actually it's more complicated than that.

Ivan: Yeah, and I do feel like there is a European way of dancing. It's like it feels very severed from spirit. But if I'm going to a punk club and everybody is thrashing, now that feels like there's a connection to spirit. I think you can learn your movement language through different ways of thinking, but I think that the real power is bringing thought and feeling together.

Henrietta: Many people in my field are now doing movement research that is dealing with a sort of spiritual shamanic notion. This points to a desperation to redefine the spiritual to refine ritual or cultural practices.

Working with young people

Ivan: One of the biggest things I've learned is not telling them what to do. I've been working on a project for about five years now and I have had many different young people within the project. Some were professional dancers and some were young people who were not in employment, education or training. I created many different kinds of spaces, depending on who is in the room. There are certain universal rules of how you have to move your body but you can try and break the rules. Sometimes I might use different forms. I might speak, I might put on film. I might do a physical exercise. For example, we go for a run to get a certain energetic vibration going or just play a certain type of music. For some of them, it was really transformational, in a sense of getting them to physically move and making their own choices, how they want to physically express. The best result when I work with young people is to let them mould themselves. To empower them to believe that they have the strength to make their own choices.

Henrietta: I'm more and more interested in the kind of 1:1 approach where, exactly as Ivan was saying, it is not about telling people what to do. Less and less as I get older do I feel like I'm any way responsible for telling someone what they should or shouldn't do. It feels like that's not my role, but my role is really about a kind of listening. And then through listening, trying to sort of pay attention to things where people are getting stuck or where they feel like there is a massive gap and it's about helping them to bridge a gap. It is like providing some kind of possible, maybe they're tools, or strategies, or maybe they're just ways that you can go, if you're stuck but it's really not didactic. It works best when I feel like I'm learning from students, and I feel like I'm kind of getting excited by what they are making. However, it is not about just total freedom. It is about finding strategies to notice what you are doing anyway. If students are in that place of not knowing what to do, then I helped them to pay attention to the fact that you are always doing, that doing is happening, like things are changing constantly. The idea of movement and change being a default and that everything is constantly in flux and impermanent. Paying attention to that is where we begin. Noticing that things are happening to start to have a creative journey. I can set up a task that is really strict and rigid like we're going to work with sitting and standing and everyone just does that. The task is there but what they're doing with it is up to them. So, I am not denying that I would give people possible structures or maps or scores but what I'm more interested in is for people to get to a place where they realise they're doing it anyway. People get so busy being neurotic about not knowing what to do. Tasks can help them to stop over thinking, then they're usually able to release which is again a bit of a spiritual practice. A bit like meditation.

Ivan: Thank you for that. It triggered a few things for me. Sometimes with hip-hop, the technique is made straight away. There it is! You spin like that or I'm going to contort my body like this and that's it. It is the technique, sometimes it is that simple. You don't need to do this move over and over and over again in a repetitional way. Sometimes I teach my body once and we keep it as a resource. That's the technique. That's the strategy. But it comes from a place that is attached to a feeling. That is also what I meant by spiritual practice. I think it's really important that we see how powerful it is. For instance, certain practices such as yoga or some sports which use the adrenaline of the push of energy to get to this place are really important. When you watch hip-hop dancers, the technique is very fresh. It's very new. However, there is also repetition to gain technique in hip-hop, especially when you see breakdancers and B-boys to get them to do a windmill or a head spin, it takes them months. Just as people who want to do a triplet, it might take them months.

Henrietta: We both have a resistance to telling people what to do, but actually it's so layered, it's much more layered because it is not like there aren't skills that can be taught. There's like particular skills, like a head spin or a triplet. Those skills are useful things to develop a pallet of tools. It is really useful to teach students the techniques, the strategies that might make those skills more possible. But somehow it's again about the end outcomes notion. Young people can't just end up with a package of skills – it doesn't add up to being a dancer. There is something more to being a dancer. I can't be the person to tell you what kind of dancer you should be or what kind of work you should make. Most of my training for young dancers has been more about attentional practices so that they can listen in to what's happening already and start from that as their starting place. This allows for a safer place where they can start making up their own ideals.

3.3 Being faithful to the complexity of the creative dancing body

A conversation between Shobana Jeyasingh and Alexander Whitley

Shobana Jeyasingh has created over 60 critically acclaimed works for stage, screen and unconventional public spaces. Her work has toured extensively to Europe, USA, India and the Far East and is now part of the national curriculum in the UK. Shobana is the recipient of numerous awards for choreography as well for her contributions to dance discourse. She holds an honorary MA from the University of Surrey and honorary doctorates from the universities of Chichester and De Montford.

Alexander Whitley is a choreographer working at the cutting edge of British contemporary dance. He has created work for Sadler's Wells, the Royal Opera House and several of the UK's leading dance companies. His collaborations across a range of media and technology platforms have gained him a reputation for a bold interdisciplinary approach to dance-making.

The politics of classical training

Alexander: I trained at the Royal Ballet School. I mean I'd obviously trained a bit before that. If we go right back to the beginning, I started dancing in a small village in the North of England, in Cumbria, and I think I was very fortunate to have a good teacher in that rural environment. If it wasn't for her, I probably wouldn't be doing what I'm doing now. She was able to accommodate the competing demands of a young boy's life, growing up in that kind of environment. She was also great at pointing me to other teachers and ultimately to the Royal Ballet School, to give me the training that she felt I needed, because I was, for most of the time that I trained with her, the only boy.

    Shobana: Yeah, I was going to ask you, whether that was difficult or not, being a boy and doing dance?

    Alexander: Yes, that was the challenge, as I was getting older, I played a lot of sports as well and was interested in other things that, I guess, a more conventional young boy would do in that kind of setting. I think that's where she was a great teacher, she understood that and was flexible enough to allow me to do those things and keep me dancing. While I was interested in dance,

DOI: 10.4324/9781003111146-18

it wasn't like I had a huge burning passion to do it. There were many other things that interested me as well and I think that was the case throughout all my training. So, there was a substantial question for me to whether it was the thing I really wanted to do. Sadly, a lot of the boys that I trained with and grew up with were defeated by the tough approach and gave up. Dancing was never the be all and end all for me. So, I think that somehow enabled me to be able to take a step away from it and not be too affected by that. You come out of those institutions with skills. Obviously, we had excellent training on the face of it, in terms of the technical rigour, exactitude and work ethic, because it's really drilled into you that if you don't work hard enough, then you won't succeed. But it certainly was and remains a very narrow approach in terms of what technique is and what skills are, ultimately.

Shobana: I understand that. I always liked dance when I was a kid, but it was an adjunct to school, to the main curriculum. I finished my A Levels; I went to university then I took my postgraduate degree in Shakespeare Studies. So, my dance training remained private and separate from main-stream education. A completely different route to yours! When I finished my studies, I began to concentrate on Indian classical dance in a more profes-sional way, and I spent every summer for about ten years seeking out a good teacher and learning that way.

When I first started learning Bharata Natyam as a girl of seven, all Indian middle-class parents wanted their children to learn Indian classical dance as a way of asserting their heritage. However, as an adult, I realised that Indian classical dance is extremely contemporary in many ways. It is a political and politicised activity. The British Empire meant that there was a devaluing of Indian dance, and by the end of the nineteenth century, Indian classical dance had literally ground to a halt. Its association with Hindu practices and its perceived promotion of female sensuality meant that it fell foul of Victorian social reformers. Female Indian dancers had caught the eye of European travellers long before the Victorians. I think it was Marco Polo who first commented on it. He noted that the dancing women wore something to support their breasts – a bra-like contraption. It must have caught his eye because such garments were not used in Europe. So, Indian dance and female dancers have always attracted the European gaze and often, a very male gaze. So, the struggle for independence from colonial rule also involved a move to reclaim and respect all aspects of Indian heritage, including dance. Children like myself learnt Indian classical dance, not to become professional dancers but to nail our colours to the patriotic mast. So my dance learning was part of a general political movement.

Alexander: It's similar to ballet, I guess, in that most of the ballet institu-tions, for example, the Royal Ballet, were only founded in the 1930s. It's a very modern classical tradition.

Shobana: Dances like ballet and Bharata Natyam have not been captured on videos until recently, so it only goes as far as one's memories, which is just two generations if you're lucky. Bharata Natyam, for example, historically started with very religious roots and was performed in the temples and then it moved to courts under the patronage of kings. Specific rules may have changed but it was very rule bound. Interestingly, Bharata Natyam shares one primary rule with ballet, that of a turnout. However, the turnout is done in plié in Bharata Natyam as opposed to straight legs. It's a very particular type of shaping of the body. The minute you think about turning out you immediately make the body into a very particular physiological entity; it's a very open, iconic shape. Something as exact and rigorous as a body in turn out is often taught in a way that can cancel out the people who aren't robust enough to take on the psychological and physical battering. 'If you can't take it then I'm afraid you can't be in the club.' However, for me, the training in Bharata Natyam was more than learning the technique. It was also an education in understanding the politics of what impacted on my life, it made me understand the effects of empire and the fact that I was a post-colonial person. When I see ballet, I am also aware of its politics – its imperial history and courtly etiquette.

Alexander: That's largely what was behind my feeling uncomfortable. There's a point you raised earlier about the tendency of these kinds of classical techniques to eradicate the individual and that's something that I really experienced, especially moving from that very rigorous classical training where I became very skilled in a very particular way, gaining the ability to be very exacting about certain aspects of how I moved my body and learning within a set repertoire of movement very quickly. As soon as I was asked to improvise, or do anything that involved contribution from me, I was at a complete loss and that was the quite painful transition I had to make in going to Rambert; unlearning a lot of the features of ballet training that were deeply engrained in my body and in my mind. The letting go of habits and the ways of thinking about myself as I was dancing. That's what made that process so enjoyable in that it opened a new way of understanding myself and thinking about or through movement.

Negotiating choreographic language and authorship

Shobana: For a while, I was choreographing people who were Indian classical dancers because that seemed to be the logical thing. We had a language in common; a shared terminology as classical dancers that made it easy to communicate ideas and movement in the studio. I did that for a few years and then I came to the end of that road. Mainly because the language is set and did not take kindly to being shifted out of its context. One can do wonderful things if the narratives match the history and aims of the style, but when one takes it out of context, it can become very strained and then communication breaks down. So, I found myself very gradually working with contemporary dancers and, for me, that helped find the language that I wanted, that I was interested in. Now, of course, there are many other languages one can co-opt to help one communicate, for example projections or post-production footage. So, we can enrich the communicative power of the body moving on stage or site.

Very often I don't share the same movement language as the dancers I work with. At the beginning that really used to worry me, and I did go and do some ballet classes and contemporary classes, as I'm interested in all different ways of moving. Now I see the studio being a bit like a lab, with different groups of people working in different corners, trying to realise and test the concept that I bring in. Older dancers who have gone through that phase of exploring their own physicality but who are now interested in exploring ideas with that physicality are great to work with. It also promotes a more equitable relationship in the studio. It gives agency to both parties, and over the years, I've had to find ways of leading as well as following. You have to lead but you don't have to lead from the front, you can lead from the middle or the back. I love working with imaginative dancers, who are inventing and putting so much of themselves in, so that at the end, I hope, they feel ownership and authenticity, which is very different from the way that I was choreographed on.

Alexander: You were saying something about authorship and the relationship between choreographer and dancers. I think I was fortunate in a way, to have an experience in my performing career of working with lots of different choreographers in a lot of different ways. Over time, I was able to appreciate the benefits to both the process and the outcome of a production when space is created for the dancers to contribute ideas creatively, generate material and ultimately be more invested in its underlying concepts. Then they take that investment and ownership onto the stage and are given tools to keep searching and finding more in the material, in the ideas and to work with that in the performance. Working with Wayne [McGregor] towards the end of my career was a very open space, which, at that stage of my career, was incredible to witness and be a part of. I was really interested in the different ways of generating material but also the conditions you can create for a process to unfold and that does require a certain level of maturity and creative willingness from the dancers you are working with. Often, it's hard to expect that of dancers that are coming straight out school, because you need to know yourself enough to have the confidence to explore.

Shobana: Yeah.

Alexander: There are exceptions. I've come across dancers that do somehow come out of school and have that self-confidence, technically. Personally, I think it took me a long time to get to the creatively interesting place to be able to contribute in a way that I would hope and expect from the dancers I work with. My work is still, to some extent, informed by that technical rigour from my ballet training, although there are many other approaches and strategies that I like to employ in the dance-making process. It's rare to find dancers who possess an equal balance of technical exactitude and creative freedom. The training in the UK, partly because of the dominance of the ballet tradition, is skewed in one or other direction, whereas I experienced in other countries that it tends to be more balanced. For example, in the Western Australian Academy of Performing Arts (WAAPA), they somehow seem to be able to strike a balance between training their dancers with that strong technical grounding and the creativity and ability to let go, improvise and explore. I guess there are other places in continental Europe, perhaps because of the different dance traditions and the likelihood of going into employment.

Balancing rules and creativity

Shobana: It's true. It's very difficult to have both those things because it's like being faithful to two totally different ideas of the dancing body. You do need to teach that very rule-bound technique in a very hierarchical, slightly oppressive way otherwise you can't inhabit the rule. The idea of being strict comes from having rules, whereas the other quality that we treasure, imagination, seems to lead in a different direction. On the one hand, you have poets like Wordsworth and Shelley with the idea of the artist as someone slightly mad, as someone who can be irrational, who is not going to follow the normal rules. That's a popular and accepted way of hallmarking an artist. Someone who is going to break all the rules. In dance, we are seeking to inhabit two different traditions of art making: the ultra-disciplined, craft-led and the ultra-free and rebellious! I notice that I get on very well with dissatisfied classical dancers, because you want someone with rigour, but you don't want someone who's going to think that's the be all and end all. They know rigour is for a creative purpose.

Alexander: Rebellious ballet dancers. There's something in the relationship between rules and creativity that I think is significant because, in the classical sense of training, rules are applied in a very particular way to the idea of technique and to the relationship between teacher and student. The understanding of creativity as being free imagination, that creativity is complete freedom, I would argue, is totally wrong. The rules are essential for creativity and defining clear terms and having the skill and the ability to stay within defined parameters is an important thing. The task isn't to make something 'a bit like this,' it's saying make something within this very specific set of rules and terms so that we can define material that has a particular character and quality. The ability of dancers to grasp and work within those rules is a key difference in what I see as a different technical ability.

Shobana: That is so difficult to find because often one very quickly gets to the end of somebody's creative output. It's sometimes because of the specificity of attending to a task. Crafting the task and communicating it is a very creative activity! To craft the task so it has the best possible chance of producing something that you want to see as well as stimulating the dancer. Creating the limits of a concept is the hardest thing sometimes; it's the opposite of the romantic idea of what an artist is. To be a successful artist without rules is not possible because first you've got to set the limits yourself before you can make something. That's probably the hardest thing, setting the limits rather than embracing the freedom.

Alexander: I think it's the use of tasks that provide useful frameworks for a dancer to think within but aren't so constrained as to eradicate their ability to act freely through. This process enables the best kind of creativity, especially when working with a group of dancers. Setting a task in the hope that you'll get five or six different versions of something quite similar. Variations on a theme rather than five completely unrelated things. I'm constantly in negotiation with those, often contradictory, forces of wanting to be clear enough with the dancers, of finding a way of explaining a task so they can get it quickly but not spending hours talking about the meaning of words for them to understand. You can get bound up in these definitions so there is this common understanding that can end up ironing the joy and creativity out of the situation but then also not wanting to be so pedantic that I end up feeling like the teacher I had when I was younger. What keeps me fascinated and curious about the process is constantly negotiating these features and aspects of how you can design and facilitate a process and understand the relationships between the actors in that space.

Understanding context to deepen experience

Shobana: I think dance institutions are still very much into just educating the body, rather than educating the imagination and the psyche. I don't know why dance more than anything else is so devoid of history or historicity, you know? Dance seems slow in understanding its own context in a way that literature or theatre or even music is not. Dance seems to be in an eternal bubble of its own making! When young people are learning a technique, that's really when one needs to understand a little bit of historical context and where your history sits within the history of others. There is nothing like learning a second language to make you realise that primacy is a very subjective thing!

Alexander: I can speak from experience of being in Rambert, for example, and training and performing in a lot of Cunningham work. I learnt next to nothing about why Cunningham devised the technique he did and the approach to choreographing the way he did and his relationship to John Cage and the whole art movement he was a part of at that time. It was only afterwards, because I had a particular interest in choreography that I sought that out myself. It seemed like such a missed opportunity because had I been provided with that knowledge, I probably would have performed the work quite differently.

Shobana: Yeah, it's only people who are intellectually curious, like yourself, who might understand how much Western contemporary dance was influenced by Sri Lankan, Indian and Javanese dancing and the whole impetus for contemporary dance really came from people looking outside to other

European cultures. I'm sure if someone was studying the visual arts and they learnt about Picasso they would know his cubism came from looking at African sculptures. It is good to understand the context of what you're doing, so you realise and understand how and why it looks the way it does. But also, I remember my classical dance teacher in India, who used to say 'stop analysing if you want to be a good dancer'. He felt that the moment you start over-thinking, you lost instinctive things like grace. I can't dismiss his warning completely!

Alexander: From my experience of training in ballet, there was an anti-thinking or a reluctance to encourage inquisitiveness or questioning because that would tend to undermine the authority of the teacher. If you don't allow for questions, then you don't get students asking you difficult ones or challenging your authority. Maybe having different visions of success or different ideas of what success can be as motivators would help, to somehow support them to find meaning for themselves in that context rather than to imprint a very particular idea of success. You're asking dancers to commit, not just their mind but their feelings, their emotions, to the process and you change the way you feel, you change your body, you change yourself as you train. It's a huge commitment to make.

Shobana: It's a very holistic thing. Whereas in other subjects, your body isn't that involved. Obviously if you're a musician, maybe, but it's not the same.

Anti-flow and choreographic unpatterning

Shobana: I don't think I'm anti-technique, perhaps anti-flow because what I realised was that while contemporary dance may not be as rule bound as ballet or Bharata Natyam it is bound by its own passionately held values. Release and flow are very desirable in Western contemporary dance, and they have wonderfully good things to offer making the body move seemingly 'organically' creating a seamless and holistic dynamic. For many reasons, I'm interested in 'anti-flow' of the body pushing back against the space around. It probably comes from my Indian dance training.

For example, in Indian classical dance, you really hold back the tension from flowing out of your arms, by using these very strong shapes which act like the walls of a building keeping the energy in. You are pushing the energy back and making your body as self-sufficient as a statue. You incise yourself into the space as opposed to flowing through the space. So often, I ask dancers to consider space as an opponent rather than a colleague. So that every movement must be negotiated. Beware of countermove from the space around you! It's probably because I'm Asian and I live in Britain and to define my place in Britain was never easy. It's a place that I had to fight and negotiate very, very hard for. To achieve anything, you always feel like you must expend a lot of energy and you just cannot take anything for granted;

so that's why I'm always attracted to bodies which move with tension, as opposed to releasing tension.

Alexander: I can relate to that in a way, thinking about the tendency of technique and training to unify and cohere. To instil a stable technique, you need to work really hard to pull coordination in the body together or pull a consistent process of thought or quality in the body, together. But choreographically, I am far more interested in breaking that apart and finding ways to de-cohere and unpattern because it falls too predictably into a pattern. I've been really inspired by William Forsythe's work and using the Laban cube to distribute, to have multiple centres of balance across the body which conflict with each other. To problematise the body rather than just to say, it's easy. As a choreographer, to assume a position of knowing that some of the things you are going to be asking might not always be met with pleasure, and you're not going to please everyone in the room equally. It's often quite a lonely position to be in.

Shobana: It is. Very lonely. There's something in the indirectness of the use of language in dance. More so in contemporary dance than in traditional techniques, where language and terminology are very specifically associated with corresponding movements. In contemporary dance, choreographers increasingly have hybridised forms where you can't define a particular movement or call it out objectively. We are drawing on many different techniques and methodologies to describe the kinds of movements that we're doing. So often we have to use indirect terms and sounds.

Alexander: I'm really interested in that. In the different strategies that can start to point people in a direction where they can then discover things for themselves, supporting young people to make those discoveries.

3.4 'Choosing a lens of values'

Dance training as relational practice

A conversation between Seke B. Chimutengwende and Theo Clinkard

Seke B. Chimutengwende is a choreographer, performer, movement director and teacher. His work *It Begins in Darkness* is a group choreography looking at ghosts and colonial legacies. Seke has also recently choreographed a new group work for Candoco Dance Company, *In Worlds Unknown*. Seke is currently exploring long solo improvisation performances of 50–60 minutes and working as a performer with Forced Entertainment. He is a visiting lecturer at London Contemporary Dance School.

Theo Clinkard's practice spans choreography, design, performing, movement direction, mentoring and teaching. Following eighteen years working as a dancer, he launched his company in 2012. Choreographic commissions include Tanztheater Wuppertal Pina Bausch, Danza Contemporanea de Cuba and Candoco. He leads workshops internationally, including engagements in Chile, Australia, New Zealand, United States, Slovenia, France, Cuba, Finland and Sweden. Theo is an Associate Artist at Brighton Dome, The Hall for Cornwall and an Honorary Fellow at Plymouth University.

Early training influences: pre, post and around

Theo: When I was young, I remember dancing around at home to Kate Bush, wearing Mum's clothes, wafting fabric and tuning into something which felt innate and very central to me. When I eventually went to a ballet class once a week, and despite having a very creative and generous teacher, I was introduced to, 'Here's an image of how you should look'. Dancing was no longer just about how I felt and expressed myself, it was about looking a certain way. I went away to Ballet School at eleven. It was fairly commercial training: musical theatre, acting, singing, jazz and tap – ballet was just one part of it. I then did three years at Rambert School which seemed much more creative, yet my overwhelming memory is of a physical training, with no improvisation, for example. So, when I was studying, it felt like I was preparing to be a kind of 'neutral body' – ready to be adaptable and to receive choreography. It makes me think about how much has changed since, in terms of intellectual or creative demands of dancers as collaborators.

DOI: 10.4324/9781003111146-19

Seke: There are some similarities and some big differences with our pathways. For a long time, I had this idea that I started dancing really late. I started going to contemporary classes regularly when I was 18 and I didn't start full-time training until I was 20. I graduated when I was 25, so that was all very late. But from as long as I remember, I was performing for my family, for friends, in front of the whole school at primary school and I was getting up and doing stuff, so I've been doing this all my life. This was all improvised. I'd put on a Michael Jackson song or *Cats* or *The Jungle Book* or whatever it was at the time, and I would just go for it. And people would watch that, whether that was in a talent contest or school disco or in my parents' living room. I didn't think of it as practice at the time, but actually, I do think of that as part of my training, in a way.

Theo: It's great to frame that early stuff as practice and note how that freedom can so easily be trained out of us while something else could be trained in such as a value system or an idea of what good dance looks like. When you're surrounded by lots of influence it becomes harder to sense, 'What do I love' or 'How do I actually move'. I always want to get closer to the kid that danced around at home.

Seke: Yes, there's something about practice and doing something over and over again. Often, I feel like we don't notice the things that we're practising. Making people laugh all the time is a kind of practice for example. You don't think, 'I'm practising comedy', it's just what you do. In terms of formal training, I left school and I think I had half an A level. I dropped out of the sixth form twice. And I was like, 'I'm gonna try dance'. I was thinking about going to drama school, but at the time, being mixed race, I was like, 'What jobs will I get as an actor?'. I couldn't really see it. I was really interested in dance and in dance I thought, 'It doesn't matter what race you are because it's abstract'. That was my logic at the time anyway. I had a love-hate relationship with training, like a lot of people do, I think. The whole way through I was very much doubting whether it was a sensible thing to be doing. I felt like a lot of the training was about what I couldn't do. That's how I experienced it and that filled me with doubt.

Fixed forms vs agency, creativity and enquiry

Theo: I often think about how dance study pre-internet was very different. As students, we engaged with people that came to the school and the work that we saw in person. My training encouraged a strong relationship to aesthetics and valued how quickly we could pick up the style of something. It got me a lot of work early on, this ability to recognise the physical codes in the room, take them on and change myself. We didn't have any improvisation at school, so I had none of that practice of physically tuning into your own movement. There wasn't really much discussion, theory or even a choreography class, so we created choreographic work based upon the influences that had bashed up against us, usually from shows that came to the school. I remember there was a gang of us who would go to The Place to do Sean Feldman's class on Sundays because we recognised this emerging Release technique, or it seemed emerging to us as we were new to it. It makes me think about the learning that happens after our training stops – this was massively significant for me. Upon graduating I had to ask, 'Who are my guides now? Who are the people I orient towards?' It's almost like that moment is when the real training started. I wonder what happened to you after school? Did you find new teachers?

Seke: After I graduated, I started working straight away with one of my teachers and, through that, I went to lots of improvisation classes and workshops, with different practitioners that were really influential to me. I did a lot of that post-training. It felt like a training after training.

Theo: If I look at training now, I still witness an almost determinist, 'existing mould' training, where there's a toolkit – 'You need this toolkit to make a career' – but also, in contrast, an approach that stimulates the student to ask questions and expand their thinking to be more aware of more things. I feel like I missed out on contextual studies, so that's what I did after training. What else is out there? I tried to see lots of shows and meet people and take part in workshops. I tried to get networked and understand not only what I had, but also what I might need and what I didn't know.

The idea of developing your own practice as a dancer, like moving for yourself, whether between, before or beyond choreographies was foreign to me. I wasn't around that thinking and I didn't know how to access my own dance. When I started to create work, I had a slow process of trying to discover my voice amidst all these varied external influences in my body.

Seke: Yeah, I definitely had that. There are these ideas with dance: the rep dancer, the company dancer, doing class every day and learning from different choreographers and touring. That's all I knew about, – big companies. That was my frame of reference. I feel it was a real dissonance for me between what I was already pretty good at and what I thought I was supposed to be working towards.

Theo: What kind of work has visibility? What kind of work has a big platform? I suppose with online platforms it feels a little bit more egalitarian in terms of what we can access. But, having not grown up in London for example, in terms of what I was exposed to, it was whatever show came to my local city and that was often these big companies. So my formative understanding of what a career in dance might look like was in relation to these big dance ships that sailed in.

Seke: Exactly. I feel that things are concealed from students. I think this exclusive thing is quite appealing to people. It's like this is an elite thing and if I make it in this, then I've gotta be worth something. Instead, we could have a different framing – 'I'm already worth something so what do I want to do with that worth', rather than thinking that worth is something to be gained by joining a special elite club.

Theo: Absolutely, I think it's perpetuated by not only a lot of teachers, but also younger dancers who either want it or they think they want it at that time. When I consider my own teaching, I started out trying to hone this very refined and virtuosic skill base dance and then tried to teach that. Then, after a few years, I realised I needed to break that down a bit and understand it as one way. To contextualise what I'm doing with the body I've been given – a certain ease or fluidity – and recognise that other people were coming into that space with different bodies. I started challenging the politics around that a bit and shifting my teaching, opening it up to other ways of working, less demonstration for example. I sought to remove myself from the centre of the room to talk through ideas of orientation or senses or perception, or egalitarian things that don't draw on my specific background in recognition that we all have different possibilities. I still think that there is value in leading and sharing from another body, it's just how it is framed and what else goes along with it, where the emphasis is put. It might not be about approximating what the teacher is doing, but what we notice while our bodies are in action, for example, so that it might not be a means to an end, but a tool for something else to take place, something more open-ended.

Relationships, hierarchies and responsiveness

Seke: Yeah, I have never really taught technique in the sense of teaching steps or even in the sense of, like how to use your body. I've had this similar dialogue around sharing experience and perspectives and knowledge. I tend to give people a space in my classes to explore their own ideas. For a long time, I felt like my classes had to be fun and people had to be having a good time. But it's alright if people struggle sometimes, are confused or bored. It felt helpful for me to acknowledge that this isn't necessarily about customers who need to be pleased with this. It's about learning, and learning isn't always easy.

Theo: I like challenging the thinking around expertise in the studio and the assumed hierarchy. For me, it doesn't feel natural or interesting to be like, 'I come from this history and I'm up here and this is how we get you here'. I realised it could be more like a conversation in the room if I understood myself differently within it. How can we all be there together with the ideas and notice how the developing conversation changes our moving. So, I guess I'm thinking about how removing a particular aesthetic – one that came from my body, from my bones and the mechanics I was born with – enables me to open up to what is actually happening in the space and shifts that idea of a one-way learning. And something that keeps coming up in my classes is about strategising ways of letting go of a particular aesthetic in order to really engage in an actual experiment.

Seke: In terms of values, I feel like I'm concerned with the idea of the experiment, in terms of teaching improvisation. It's a form that embraces the idea of a genuine experiment and it's interested in what's happening in the moment, in the now, which is always unfolding. In terms of values, that's important in my teaching and being awake to it. I try to create a space that feels safe for people to experiment in.

Theo: As a maker or teacher, I notice that working with companies that have more of a classical history and developing spaces with permission for creativity, dancer agency and inviting conversation in the room is generally met with enthusiasm and an appetite from dancers. However, occasionally dancers find that almost unsafe because of the conditioning that comes with more formal training. I've witnessed people who are used to, 'Here's the bar. You need to do it over again until you meet it', freak out in the most generous creative spaces. It just makes me think about this formal training and how it can collapse that creative, inquiring mind.

Seke: Yeah, that's true. With that idea of safety, you never know what's going to trigger something for someone. If you're engaging with performance, you're engaging with liveness, and it's risky. It's emotional and physically demanding. It's not about removing all danger. Openness can feel like a restriction or even feel traumatic.

Expanded technique: attributes and skills

Seke: I'm often teaching myself when I'm teaching, reminding myself of things that I should be doing and reminding everyone with that, deploying the relevant skills or mindset or state for a particular situation. What if you're improvising with a group of people. What do you need in that moment? What can you let go of in that moment? Doing a group improvisation with people is very different from doing solo improvisation, or improvising in an audition, or performing a repertory piece of ballet. There are some tools that you can use in all of those settings and some tools that are really specific to specific contexts, and it's about becoming alert to what is needed. This relates to the idea of the emergent and what is happening right now. I really like your expanded idea of technique and I was talking to some students this year about the importance of being able to talk about what is emerging for them as we are working in the studio. Being able to talk on the spot in front of other people about something you've just seen or done. That's an important thing to be able to do. You'll be asked to do that all the time. You can learn on the job, or you can start thinking about that during your training. It seems now there's an infinite pool of tools that anyone might need and it's ridiculous to imagine that somebody might be good at all those things or even have time to learn all those things.

Theo: When you talk about improvisation, I'm considering this massive spectrum, from moving within a very particular score or tone or certain conditions, to walking into the room and opening up to anything and everything being available. Often there's a binary of codified technique and improvisation but there's a massive spread within that. We will only see part of the picture, and there are other influences in other countries that we're not even aware of.

Seke: Yeah, like these words do fall apart quite quickly. Improvisation, it's not a very good word really because it encompasses too much. It means different things to different people.

Theo: It makes me think a little bit about La Manufacture in Lausanne, which is run by Thomas Hauert. They decentred classical ballet so it is one module among many others, challenging the long-held idea of it being foundational. We're slowly seeing a genuine decentralising of a certain abstract, contemporary dancer aesthetic too, which only certain people feel tuned into, can access, feel represented by or are interested to watch. I've personally been trying to expand beyond a way of moving that felt very studied and almost precious. I'm very much led by the younger people around me and I perceive a shifting mood. Part of that is urgently asking who doesn't feel welcomed, who is not in the room or what is not in the room; and I'm interested to see how I could make space for more in my work.

Seke: I'm thinking about the idea that performance and dancing are dialogues and teaching should be in dialogue form, rather than imposing or coercing, technique should be responsive. Teaching technique or dance teaching in general should be responsive to and in dialogue with what's happening. I'm questioning the idea of training and employability. The idea of employability is exclusionary. It feels to me like it's an idea that has a winner/loser framing. There's a sense that you might get this, you might not but, in terms of ideas around decolonising, and inclusivity, that framing is going to privilege certain types of people. Certain bodies, certain people with certain economic backgrounds. It doesn't feel fair, unless there were jobs for everyone, in which case that would be very different.

Theo: I was training at a time when there were enough projects around to be a jobbing project dancer. The Covid-19 lockdown made me more deeply appreciate that studying dance might be about developing your own practice, which you do for pleasure and it's not about the professionalisation of the form. That thinking is much more in my foreground now.

I wrote something a little while back for *Dance4* magazine about this term 'transferable skills' because it has been used a lot in terms of dance, and in the past, it has mostly been understood to reference a dancer's resilience. As a dancer, you understand what failure is and you know how to push back, try again, and therefore, it really suits the capitalist neoliberal system. Now, when I think about the expanded use of the term technique or things like community mindedness, good humour, keeping perspective, care or calling out bullshit – all these things I personally think about as technique – then dance becomes a practice for how we can exist in the world, as an engaged human finding fulfilment on a really core basis. There's a huge amount which is transferable in that sense, which is not this old-school dance thinking.

Seke: I really agree. The idea of training, I don't know what's going to be out there in a few years. We don't know what the possibilities will be. It's about empowering people to feel like they can explore what they want to and offering whatever perspective I might have. Although in some sense, we're all in the same boat, in that we don't know, but that's not truer now than it was ten years ago. The possibilities that there were ten years ago weren't there ten years before that.

Developmental shifts: politics, awareness and aesthetics

Theo: I want to share a quote which relates to what you're saying. This is from Juliet Fisher, who was teaching at The Place in the early 1990s: 'It is difficult for teacher to know if she was doing her job well, since the teachers' job is to prepare students for choreography that hasn't been made yet and that we couldn't yet imagine'. That made me think about not only participating in a choreographer's vision but also considering how the whole landscape shifts, the political climate shifts and the technology shifts. Teaching doesn't have to be about looking backwards and bringing your own history to this moment and can instead be an act of being with the students to imagine forwards. To have this expansive idea of where you might take your dance. That whole system seems to be evaporating before my eyes anyway: the company dancer job is almost mythical now. Some students start their studies with a set idea of dance based upon company 'X' which they saw five or ten years ago when they were forming their idea of what contemporary dance was. You can find that you're having to not just teach them, but unteach an existing idea of what they thought a dancer's life would be.

Seke: Yeah. I do feel like students are more and more interested, the ones that I teach, in doing their own thing straight away, compared to when I was training where I feel like almost all of us wanted to be in a company, whatever that meant. But now there are a lot of students who are already making their own work outside of training, and so that's changed.

Theo: And also, in forms of collectives, which is so encouraging. It's not a model that I'd seen much until recently.

Seke: That's really inspiring. I think there's a little bit of a twin problem of there's a very understandable bleakness. The general reality isn't your specific reality necessarily; that is something that I'm trying to cut through sometimes, and then the flipside of that is a little bit like what you were talking about before about this neoliberal – almost a little bit American dream – attitude. It's the flipside of the bleak. How can I use this moment? But I feel like it's fuelled with something that's too optimistic and idealistic and a little bit self-centred. So there are the two things that I notice that were not so present when I was training: this entrepreneurial vibe and this like, 'Oh, it's all fucked' attitude.

Theo: Yeah, I was thinking about the fact that I trained during New Labour and an economic ease and what that climate meant for the industry, in high contrast to people like Lloyd Newson, Michael Clark and Liz Aggis, making work in the early 80s, fighting against the system. There are parallels with this moment and for what I understand to be very politicised generation of young dancers. They are calling out staff, asking their institutions to do better, to follow through with Black Lives Matter promises, and they're holding them to account. Not to romanticise this time because it's shit, but just to know that there are some very vocal, smart young people around, and I for one, think of them as my guides, as well. I don't work with this top-down older/younger thing.

Seke: It's a very, very different vibe.

Theo: I'm just thinking about the manifesto that I wrote about technique and where that came from. A student before my class asked, 'Is it creative/improvisation or is it technique?' It was as if the latter was where the real work took place. It made me reflect on the hierarchy within training and where technique sits in that. What if we expanded the term to include curiosity, humility, care, listening, critical thinking or to include activism, for example? There is more and more performance work or work situations where, what is needed of dancers is for them to understand themselves as engaged humans in the world and bring that to the work. All these faculties and values we hold as humans can be integrated within our dancing rather than being this peripheral thing that is left at the door. I think there is a need for values to be more central in the work that is made. I, for one, choose to look through a lens of values more than I did in the past.

3.5 Improvisation

Inclusivity and race

A conversation between Adam Benjamin and Olu Taiwo

Adam Benjamin was joint Founder/Director of Candoco Dance Company, a founder member of 5 Men Dancing, an award-winning choreographer, author and National Teaching Fellow. He has been a Wingate Scholar, Rayne Choreographic Fellow and Associate Artist at The Place. He is currently developing the Dancers' Forest to raise awareness of sustainability within the dance industry.

Olu Taiwo is Senior Lecturer in Performing Arts at University of Winchester and teaches in acting, immersive and digital performance as well as physical theatre. He has worked on identity and performance and is a well-established performer using digital technologies. He is engaged with critical debates around the interaction of body, technology and the environment. Olu is a member of the University's Centre for the Arts as Wellbeing.

What is dance in society?

Olu: I remember when I was at the Laban Centre and I first saw the work of Candoco, the influential dance company of disabled and non-disabled dancers; my level of ignorance genuinely shocked me. The sheer beauty of movements that was being generated by the dancers forced me to re-evaluate what dance means. You know I'm a street boy, I grew up breakdancing and body popping, but those performers could not spin on their head and do crazy legs steps but they did something else which was as fantastic.

Adam: It's interesting that you mentioned the Laban Centre, which is now very much a centre of technical excellence but if we go back in time, as you suggest, and look at dance as a shared space; people danced to share different temporal experiences to connect with each other and to the spaces they danced in. It was very much a community practice that Laban originally envisaged and hoped to build on.

Olu: If we are going to discuss improvisation, we need to go back to the fundamental ideas of how we construct what dance is in society. The premise of all improvisation affects people's experience of race, which is a social construct to validate whiteness. The concepts behind improvisation invite more questions about how we conceive and perceive of dance as a cultural

DOI: 10.4324/9781003111146-20

phenomenon in Britain. If you're trying to tackle racism in football, it seems to be a tall order because football exists in society, racism is a social issue and it goes back to very fundamental ideas of how a particular aspect of society engages with difference in culture. Dance is not immune from the effects of cultural assumptions.

Adam: When you look at the way so much of dance is taught now, particularly technique, what we see is a cultural imposition. The way conservatoires compete to attract students is due to a culture that is increasingly profit-driven. The notions of space and time within these educational models are very regimented and if we unpick that a little bit further, we find that whilst the department might foreground its 'artistry and education', the institution itself is primarily concerned with financial income. As a result of this, we are seeing a lowering of entry-grade requirements and an artificial inflation of grades – all of which of course impact on the quality of teaching.

The conservatoire is turning out bodies for the 'industry', a term that I actually hate, but most of us work within the industry. So, you've got this notion of a culture defined by profit that is imposed on dance training in order to ensure utility; a uniform kind of embodiment. It really weighs against everything that Candoco has questioned with regard to identity and dance. I think that inclusive experience within dance training is still rare. And particularly so over the last maybe three or four years, when more institutional programmes are suffering cuts and courses are closing. I suppose the questions are where can these destabilising experiences now take place if the conservatoires are gearing more and more to training for industry, and where does the individual person and their story fit within that system.

One of the problems is that the more industrialised dance training becomes the less improvisation provision will be allowed to do what it is actually capable of doing, you might even say 'designed to do', which is to challenge the status quo and create space for disruption and disturbance. Improvisation is going to be subverted into just another way of feeding the choreographer, feeding the dance machinery. It is going to be less and less interested in personal story and matters of equality. I think we are heading into murky waters. It's not enough to offer improvisation. It really depends on how improvisation is offered and how it is understood by those who teach it.

Construction of the self in dance

Olu: You see growing up in South London in a Yoruba community, we have this notion of dancing; which is attached to the very essence of language. In the Yoruba language, it's 'mo n jo' or 'o n jo'. 'O n jo' means you're dancing, 'mo n jo' means I'm dancing. It is a kind of onomatopoeic word because it is a way of describing the visceral experience when you start to dance. For example, if you say good morning, 'e kaaro', if you say hello, 'o kaabo'. Ka means to 'read' or to 'count' well, in other words, to 'measure' and to 'project'. It is a term to facilitate well-being. It's like saying, 'how's your soul', or 'happy soul day'. It's difficult to translate into English because English has specific ways of categorising thoughts, which can negate the concept of spirit and soul.

'Good morning' within the West is very much a kind of pleasantry, polite statement. You're not saying, 'I hope your soul is good this morning as it arises from the spirit of existence'. It doesn't come across in the kind of good mornings scenario you know where as…

Adam: I wish it did.

Olu: When you say 'o kaabo', it's a way of elevating that person and helping them to come into the morning. It's seen as a prayer. Not just a pleasantry you say to be polite, and so the same with 'mo n jo'. If you see a dog and its very pleased to see you. It's dancing, it's dancing because it's pleased to see you. Its soul is dancing; so 'jo' is that kind of resonance of the soul. So, everything else that happens after that are forms, techniques, prayers, structures and entertainment. Or a language of the soul coming out: A 'mo n jo'. If we start with 'Jo' as a concept, then we foreground the spirituality of movement. Laban understood this. He was looking at the mystery of movement: the reasons for moving, the philosophy of the movement, the love of movement.

The Western perspective on improvisation is that it is a kind of cognitive exercise imposed on the body to generate, as you said earlier, frames and forms for a chorographic event, which at best might disturb or find ways to create happy coincidences. Whereas improvisation from an African point of view, traditionally, it is the voice of the soul. If we're gonna talk about improvisation for differently abled bodies, and for people who are of different cultures, you have to start interrogating the ways in which self is manifested and constructed in dance and what are the existing assumptions about this manifestation and construction.

Adam: One of the delightful things that happens when you have an inclusive group is that immediately and evidently injustice is visible. You are in a place where if, as a teacher, you don't address the whole group's participation, your avoidance is noted. Young dancers are super aware of these things, so they'll be seeing these injustices, and they'll be going, 'Ah, we are in a place where we don't talk about that'. In good inclusive work, the injustices, the inequalities are immediately acknowledged: this person can't walk or this person can't see. So we have to build bridges. We have to build understandings and what I've always found super interesting within those environments is that when you're working in a group where injustice is recognised, sooner or later, the injustice of race emerges.

It's always been there, it's just no one has ever mentioned it, so it's been invisible. If improvisation is not taught by experienced practitioners, then race can be ignored. It can even be denied, like, 'we're not here to deal with that, we are here for disabled people!'. We've got to find ways of acknowledging that improvisation really is not only about actually the joy, the spirit of dancing, but it is also about the way we use space, who that space belongs to and who is free within that space. Issues of freedom of movement are essential to improvisation and these go beyond disability.

Considering barriers to equality and freedom

Adam: Dance training can and often takes away the dancer's voice. There have been lots of people who have challenged that – people like Wendy Houston – who have kind of said, 'No actually, I'm a dancer and I *have* a voice'. But there is relatively little time or space for this exploration of who we are as people and how we question the structures that we find ourselves in within our trainings. When you introduce inclusive practice, it opens all of that up.

I'm not specifically interested in disability. It's not actually the thing that fascinates me or drives me. What fascinates me and drives me is equality and freedom. Finding the place and the value for that subject within our training programmes, that to me seems essential; particularly within the university experience which ought to be about education in the widest sense. When I first arrived in academia, I was doing a lot of that kind of teaching across dance and theatre – with art students coming in and photography students and theatre students and dance students and disabled students. It was very rich, but my experience over eight years was a gradual eroding of this artistic freedom. So, by the time, I left HE I was down to one hour of that kind of teaching and the department had redefined itself as a conservatoire. The inclusive degree programme at Coventry University had gone and the programme at Plymouth where I taught has since been replaced with Musical Theatre. Dance education has been redefined according to financial profit to the institution and this really doesn't bode well for improvisation because meaningful improvisational groups need to be small and need to practice in safe spaces, and if you've 30 plus students in a class, then it is a hell of a task to create a meaningful experience for all of them, and the institution actually doesn't want students to be trained to ask difficult questions, it wants the opposite – obedient bodies that do as they're told…and conveniently ignore the political and cultural implications of this stance.

Olu: It's about the visibility and invisibility, and if one is made invisible, then it doesn't belong to that space. It is kind of the enlightenment project for me. The enlightenment project is all about freedom and fraternity and individual for human beings, but that only really represented the white middle-class and upper class man. Working-class men weren't involved in freedom. Women weren't included in that freedom, and if you were an enslaved person, then you were basically property, so you certainly didn't have any rights to freedom. That kind of perception or assumption is found in movement and aesthetic education. If we think about contemporary dance, then the word contemporary should mean something that's happening now, in the moment, so colleagues around the world that are producing work would be considered contemporary. However, that's not what it means in aesthetic practice. Contemporary means contemporary Western so if you do contemporary African dance, if it's not involved in some way of addressing Western contemporary dance, then it's not seen as contemporary. So you can have contemporary Bata or contemporary Zulu dance that is maybe a new way of perceiving Zulu dance today, but that wouldn't necessarily be seen as contemporary dance, because contemporary is being kind of shoehorned into a limited and limiting Western concept of aesthetics. I would also include in the injustices that we perceive in dance, the idea of untold stories – untold stories from the invisible bodies. And untold stories from invisible bodies are based on a different paradigm of being. This shift of values creates the space for us to look at Aboriginal dances, the dance of creation, or the communal line dances of the bear dance, by the Southern Ute Bear Dancers, or the syncopated rhythms of the Yoruba's Bata dance, or the Fulani Men Dance at the Gerewol Celebration in Niger, or the particular dances of the Mongol horse dancers. That is not to negate or to take away any kind of developments of the Western contemporary dance. I don't have a problem with that. I do have a problem with it thinking it's the only arbiter of the contemporary.

Improvisation is a bit like our conversation, we improvise as we talk, and when we talk, we are exchanging ideas, seeing similarities and expressing ourselves. This is a dance of the soul, 'mo n jo'. Growing up in Deptford, London I remember going to a party where they would play Jùjú music (Nigerian rhythms). For example, someone like the musician Ebenezer Obey, who represented the post-colonial era. Everybody would come to the dance floor and the dancing would be an improvisation. The music was a context for improvisation. The community would come together to share their dance through improvisation. Big movements and usually smaller movements were performed by the adults and then the real stars were when the elders would come onto the space, and they had that very small movement that articulated all the rhythms and all the patterns, just with a flick of the hand and a nod of the head, and we all turned round, not to say, 'Oh look they're still moving, how gorgeous. It's nice. Look she's 80 and she's still moving. Oh isn't it lovely'. There's not that kind of stuff here. Our reaction was more like, okay stop, let's have a look at this person. This person is at the bookend of their life, and they're giving us a masterclass in improvisation.

Adam: When you are talking, I was thinking about improvisation and the practice as the product, rather than *towards* the product. And I think there's an ironic kind of situation at the moment whereby the professionalisation of disabled dancers points towards adaptive technique as an essential for those who want to train and want to become professionals, rightfully so, but it shifts the attention away from improvisation towards adapting so improvisation becomes a tool to adapt technique towards an inclusive practice. On the one hand, it's enabling people to train, and on the other hand, it diverts everybody away from the value of a practice that can actually break things open and that provides space and time to make new artistic discoveries. I understand that desire to be part of the industry. And of course I have been instrumental in facilitating that progression, but it certainly isn't where my passion lies, nor is it where I feel collective change can happen during training. You were saying before we can't just change the racism that exists within football, that we have to create a much deeper shift in society. And it's the same in dance. Any student who has gone through their training in the presence of a disabled peer is going to be changed, hopefully, for the better. But if you've got a group of students, a cohort of students, and you've got one disabled student and two black students and everybody comes out with a better understanding of disability, then there's absolutely no guarantee that everyone is going to come out with a better understanding of race. There is no guarantee.

Olu: Yeah. That's a very good point.

Adam: I had a lovely moment, I think it was in my final-year teaching at the university where I was working with some theatre students and there was one black student in the group. They decided to create this piece which was about exclusion, and they somehow decided that they would work with one of them as the outsider and the rest working as a group. And the person who got chosen, I don't know how they got to that, I don't know how they made that choice, but it was the black student. And I said to them, 'Well, um, that's quite a statement you are making there? How do you think an audience will read this'. And it was as if for them, the question wasn't visible like it wasn't there. I just thought 'Why in you training and in your education has this not been addressed? If you don't see this, then you just haven't been educated'.

Olu: Adam, that's a fabulous story, thank you for sharing it. I think it comes down to exactly what you're saying previously is that people who don't see the relevance, think, 'We haven't got a racist problem because we've got no black people here'. So non-visibility or non-appearance equates to not having an issue. And if I link that back to the issue about adaptation, then I have realised that the thing to do when you're working with people who are differently abled is to ask and address the differences – to engage with what is possible rather than trying to adapt as near as possible as the original form as possible. If there are two different peoples with differently abled bodies and different issues, then those issues can be the context by which a dance can occur. And I think the same is when I go into a room and someone says, 'We don't see colour'. And I'm thinking, 'What is wrong with your head? Can't you see that I am black. I'm not invisible. You're all white. I am black. What's your problem? Let's talk about that'.

Spaces for improvisation

Olu: I think that dancers communicate what the inner life of an individual has. For example, Pina Bausch's choreographic work resonates a lot with African dancers in the way that she used people's emotions and experiences and rendered them into the movement. Physical theatre, that tanztheater explosion, is closer to the African expression of the voice, the inner soul. Where improvisation comes in, I think for me is to develop this process of different ways of perceiving personal voice, what does it mean to have a voice? You know, dance as a technique is one thing, but dancing is as natural as breathing. So, to commodify that in some ways, and to reject bits of it, is a bit... You know, you didn't breathe like that, you breathe like this. No, no, if you don't breathe, then you don't live. From an African perspective, if you're not dancing, if you're not improvising, expressing yourself, then part of your inner life dies. So how we create a space for that is crucial. Things like Butoh, like Jazz dance, not jazz dance as in jazz hands. I'm talking about listening to music and finding your own ways around the rhythm, those kinds of things. There are certain African dance pieces where you learn a technique and that technique launches improvisation and the improvisation is your voice. The relationship between that and the drum, for example. When you are working in a drum ensemble, you first learn the basic rhythm and the cross rhythm, then the bell pattern and the bass drum pattern. This creates the rhythmic architecture that is continuous and flowing, revolving around the return beat. The Master drummer would then drum within the rhythmic architecture as a solo; this would be the voice the drum speaking to the dancer. The dancer will respond, and there would be a dialogue.

I think that some of the movement techniques, for example, Jacques Lecoq's work is heavily technical, but the process by which one learns a language of improvisation allows the inner voice to speak. So, you're looking at how do you express or move like the colour blue. Now that is something which doesn't make sense in the first instance because 'blue' doesn't move, but of course it links into our poetic intelligence. And then with that comes a kind of freedom of movement to explore. I can point to techniques which will start to break away from the limitation of aesthetics. Another example is Butoh and the work of Kazuo Ohno whose movement practice can be best described as watching a flower, that's it, the expression of a flower. Its scent, its movement, its tracking the sun. I think that these approaches to technique move away from trying to recreate the goal of some kind of aesthetic beauty, based around classical assumptions of beauty and form, and instead engage in disharmony, asymmetry, difficulty, failure and their manifestations and expressions. Understanding how we engage in the process of life is the goal of improvisation in these practices. Most people still think of improvisation as a way to generate material. In that sense, the material is policed by an internal aesthetic. You could never really do pure improvisation because you're always trying to generate material. Whereas if the process is the goal engaging with the person you're with, their difficulties, their pain, their pleasure, where they're at in that moment and that's the goal to be in that moment, then actually you are free from generating material. Your only interest is in the engagement with flux and change in that moment. What's your thoughts on that so?

Adam: We are talking about a wide-ranging palette of approaches and understandings: Bausch and Jazz and Butoh and Lecoq and music and colour. They are extraordinary artists but not necessarily people whose actual practice we would necessarily want to embody. In the case of Bausch for instance, a lot of people were savaged by working with her. A lot of the dancers that worked with some of the Butoh training have been brutalised. Same for Lecoq. So, whilst I'm absolutely with you with regard to seeking different approaches, I think what's missing in these trainings is the time and space to develop pedagogic practices and understandings. If you tackle self-expression and self-revelation in a space that's not safe, then all the things that are flourishing won't be contained or held in a way that they can grow and instead students can feel exposed and resentful of the experience. For me, it is about the positioning of the dance leader, that if you're in dance, you're going to be dealing with human beings and whether that's in training, in a professional company or in a community setting, you have a responsibility that goes along with the care of those you're working with. And you need to make sure that they are safe and well and that they are valued and that their voices and concerns are heard. Improv, when taught well, provides a space where the hidden or unacknowledged voice can be encouraged, where young

Figure 3.5.1 Tom St. Louis, one of the first black disabled dancers, Kate Marsh and Lucy Moelwyn-Hughes in rehearsals for *Wallpaper Dancing* – choreographed by Janet Smith. Credit: Adam Benjamin.

dancers can begin to interrogate who they are and respond to the world as they experience it – and this how we grow as artists and people.

It seems to me that this is what is being brushed out of contemporary dance training. Particularly if, as it seems, we are increasingly involved in the commodification of the 'industry ready' dancer, then also what we're involved in is the notion of the 'dispensable' dancer, and 'if training or performing breaks one, then it doesn't matter as we've got plenty more similar ones to replace them'.

Olu: That's so true and I have to thank you for highlighting something which is really useful for me, in my current practice not only as a researcher but also as a teacher. In my teaching, I am working with undergraduates who are rarely people predisposed to some of the rigours that I wanted to go through as a student. So, I found a way to expose people to the essences of Pina Bausch and the essences of Butoh and Lecoq, in a way that is comfortable. I start from where they are at – to create a safe space for people to be challenged. I do think that it's important for people to be challenged and that difficulty is an important part of the process of growth and training. However, safety is even more important.

3.6 'There is no line'

Valuing individual potential through inclusive and collaborative dance technique

A conversation between Alison Ferrao, Laura Graham (Magpie Dance) and Caroline Hotchkiss

Alison Ferrao joined Magpie Dance as a volunteer in 1997 and has never left! In 2019, she became Artistic Director, seeing the organisation grow from two classes per week to currently delivering 22 different programmes catering for all ages and abilities. She has been instrumental in securing partnerships and collaborations with Royal Opera House (UK), Martha Graham Dance Company (US), Propellor Dance (Canada) and Arts with the Disabled Association (Hong Kong).

Laura Graham trained in dance, working as a professional dancer before moving into Arts Marketing working in venues such as New Wimbledon Theatre, Churchill Theatre Bromley and Laban London as the Arts Marketing and Press Manager. Deciding upon a new challenge, Laura joined Magpie Dance in 2009 as the General Manager. Stepping up as Executive Director in 2019, she finds Magpie Dance rewarding to work for and is proud and excited by the way it's evolving.

Caroline Hotchkiss has been a performer, choreographer, director and education practitioner for almost 20 years. She graduated from the Northern School of Contemporary Dance in 2000 and London Contemporary Dance School in 2001, after which she performed with many leading dance companies and choreographers. Caroline was formerly a co-artistic director for Blue Apple Theatre with responsibility for choreography and she now leads the Blue Apple Core dance collaborations with students from the University of Winchester.

Personal training

Alison: I was accepted into dance college, but at the time, I just couldn't afford to go, so I took my ISTD teaching qualifications. My dance school was very much of that kind of ballet, tap, musical. You had to have a certain look, aesthetic. It was all about the performance of being on stage. But as part of this training, I did a work experience with Union Dance company and that

DOI: 10.4324/9781003111146-21

was it! A big turning point really. Because up until then, anyone I'd work with – either in a class or teaching – was in pink leotards, hair in a bun, it had to be like this and then suddenly people were wearing what they wanted, they were doing what they wanted in class, and that was such a breath of fresh air. When I came to Magpie as a volunteer 26 years ago, it was also about the individual and what they could gain from the experience of dancing and how it could be shared. I thought it would be a terrible thing to not go to college, but it's allowed me to just stand in the corner and watch what's going on and that's really helped and affected how I work with dancers.

Laura: I started as an employee with Magpie Dance 14 years ago and before that I was a volunteer trustee for three years. So, we both have been at Magpie for a long time. I trained in dance and did arts marketing and PR at Trinity Laban and then worked at the Wimbledon Theatre before becoming General Manager at Magpie where I merged my interests together.

Caroline: I trained at the Northern School of Contemporary Dance in Leeds, and I did a year at The Place as well and after that I was lucky enough to perform in various settings. I started with Richard Alston Dance Company and then worked in Europe and the UK with smaller and larger-scale dance companies. I stopped performing quite early because I worked quite a lot in education. I work in schools to develop holistic performing arts professions based on the curriculum. My role at Blue Apple Dance Theatre Company (BA) has been changing from being a choreographer to be the artistic director for a while and now I work freelance, and I mainly coordinate the collaboration between the University of Winchester Dance students and the core performers at BA.

The value of assessing progression

Alison: Magpie's values are people, access, challenge and excellence, that's what we strive towards. Over the last three years, our whole programme at Magpie has changed and developed. We now offer technique classes which we didn't before. So previously it was focusing on creative ideas and tasks and people would have an input in that choice, but now we have two youth technique classes, a drop-in class that is open for people with and without learning disabilities and that's ballet, contemporary and body conditioning. The ethos is always about ability rather than disability. We always focus on what people can do. In classes, we go from age three to adults and upper age adults as well. We now have a choreographers group who focus on creating their own work and then our latest addition is our dancer development course. We are looking at individual potential and how our dancers can progress and how we monitor, assess and evidence that.

Laura: There is now the opportunity for someone who has a learning disability to join an inclusive dance company. Creating progression routes is the reason we have so many sessions in a week. We started with adults, and we saw how they developed their skills and how we felt it would have been beneficial for some to have developed those at an earlier age.

Caroline: There is also progression in terms of technique or skills for the university students and for Blue Apple performers. My focus with the university/BA collaborative project is to show that we all have strengths and qualities in different places. I made a document to demonstrate where everyone is in terms of skills. I document spatial awareness, body awareness, timbre awareness, pitch awareness, character awareness, movement quality, awareness of the quality of movement. If you look at one student from the dance degree and one Blue Apple performer and evaluate their spatial awareness, the Blue Apple performer might be extremely high on that skill level and perhaps the dance degree student is different. But if you focus on different skills, pulse awareness or pitch, the student might have developed stronger skills. It's quite interesting because the document shows everyone is scattered around. My intention was to demonstrate how we are all the same and different! I wanted to show that there are no lines!

Alison: I think one of the main values that I took from my kind of background has been about expectation. I've always had extremely high expectations and I expect everyone to achieve and if they don't, then it's my job to change what I'm doing to facilitate that journey for them. I think I would say that underpins what we do at Magpie. It's about everyone's individual journey. The ultimate expectation is that everyone will reach their potential, but that does not mean that the outcome of what they do is going to be the same. It is going to be completely different for each person in the room. Our job really is to support that. Each dancer has a voice and can input to the session so everybody is valued equally. I think that's an ethical approach. It's an individual's journey. An equal opportunity is not the same opportunity for everybody. It is what you offer them to get to where they need to be.

Laura: We have expectations, but we don't have expectations of the group as a whole. We have expectations of each individual. That each individual will achieve and flourish and they will improve but they won't all improve at the same speed or at the same level.

Alison: So, instead of thinking of going from here to there, from A to B, we like to say that you are going from A to B but you might go out here a little bit first and have a look at C and D and then you get back to B. So, it might take a bit longer and it might be a different way and it will be a different route but you'll still get where you want to. And that's not adapting down, that's exploring what works for that individual. I think the thing that jumps out at me is the importance of empathy in facilitating dance. You're not doing something to or for someone but you're doing it with them, and once it becomes a shared experience that really changes things. You have learnt skills and techniques but when you are in a session, that individual may respond that way, but may not, and it's being attuned to that and being able to then support that person.

Technical motivation and adaptation

Caroline: The way that I approach physical skills in the collaboration with Blue Apple is very much focused on the motivation behind the movement, its origin, where is the movement coming from. We start with actions, and I have no theme. It is about understanding how to create movement qualities which match the different bodies and experiences of dance training in the project. They have an idea of what technique is … I guess sometimes I really like to say we are going to work with this technique, but I don't want to do that because it is about physical skills and how you apply your body to what is asked of you… that is your physical skill.

Alison: There is this idea with technique work that we have at Magpie. We all learn a way of doing it, but everyone can have an adaptation that suits their body or their level of challenge. So there is more speaking in the class. People can raise their hands if they have questions. We'll stop and go through it for everyone, rather than just go along. We'll explain what we're doing, how and why each time. And that has to be repeated. It needs to be done for several weeks in a row to consolidate the knowledge.

Laura: I think having our dancers as role models is a really important step forward in terms of inclusive dance. It is about being visible. Some of our adult dancers were going to our junior, our youth, our younger classes and would be there to help assist. We also encourage them to lead classes themselves. We tend to do everything in a circle, but in some cases, we will prompt the dancers to take charge and demonstrate to others.

Alison: From feedback, we understood that our dancers were enjoying technique and that they wanted to be pushed more. But one dancer who appears very able and copes very well with everything said, 'I know we always do roll down and I think I'm doing right but I've never actually had someone explain how you do a roll down'. And so one of the things that we're aiming to do is to make YouTube tutorials, where our dancers go through all that simple technique, but they are the leaders. It is about a lack of representation. If you never see yourself on stage, what is there to aim for? So often performance opportunities are at disability festivals or it's an arts or a dance festival and we can be the disability act. So we pushed the idea of not only being included in disability festivals.

Laura: It's a tick-box exercise quite often and our dancers know that and that needs to change. There is no normal.

Alison: So, if there's a dance festival, why aren't we just included in that? Rather than the tick box? We're hoping to continue developing these tutorials so that our dancers are the ones on screen demonstrating and explaining what to do. Because I think that's part of it, you need to see yourself and having those role models will start to change things.

The role of music in inclusive dance technique

Alison: Our methodology is very much participant-centred. One of the important aspects of our quality framework is the role of live music. It's really integral to the way we work; in everything we do, right from our warm-up with the name and shape exercise at the beginning of a class. A musician can build a score more flexibly, we don't have to ask our dancers to change. It's about facilitating that individual person's involvement.

Caroline: Working with music and rhythms is really resonating with my approach. On stage, the challenge in performances is the need to respond. I like to work on that with the students and the Blue Apple performers. The performers I work with are quite experienced performers. They've been performing, touring for ten years, and they're very confident and high-quality theatre performers. I try to nurture an environment where it is about responding to what's coming to you, but responding in a way that you are allowing the person you are working with to achieve their highest possible on the day. So you respond in moving forwards in a positive way, so it's just whatever is presenting to you... we all face different challenges, whatever they may be, so it might be our life experiences, it might be our physical way of being ... whatever it is, but we all share some experiences, and we will all meet from our different place of challenge. We train to respond to these challenges on a personal and collective level.

Alison: Music allows us to be really participant-led. If you've maybe got someone in a group that isn't so confident in contributing their ideas, then that one person might come up with a move and I might go back to that other person and say, 'How many shall we do? Shall we do two or four?' and then when they come up with 7/4, you can do that because the musician can play 7/4 time, which you just couldn't do if they weren't there. We work with facilitators rather than teachers and it is very much a team-taught session.

Caroline: It is about approaching music as a skill. And if we use sound or music, it tends not to have a pulse. So then they just know, if someone decides to start in a different section, then we can go with that but there's a universal understanding of the section and what rhythm or pulse that section is in, but we're not tied to the music, so they can work together to begin, pick up, move on and that's led to some really interesting moments in performance.

Laura: With our adult choreographers, if they are leading a section, then they will count our musicians in, and they will tell our musicians when to start and stop, so I think it's also, like you said, a learning process of being a professional as well. For our facilitators, it's so nice that they don't have to go forwards and backwards to the cassette. They can be like 'Right, stop!', 'Okay, start!'. We often have funders looking at the figures and say, 'Well cut the musician out and use pre-recorded, this will save you loads'. But it is actually part of our ethos, it is part of what we do. Our musicians will follow how our dancers will move. So again, it goes back to our ethos of our participants taking ownership and we follow. It's allowing people to blossom themselves, without us moving people around.

Collaboration

Alison: We now have a partnership with the Royal Opera House, and in 2019, our dancers got a special permission to perform a piece for World Ballet Day. Ballet is not the main aim of the company but this opportunity presented itself. That kind of initiative starts to break down the industry by asking what is dance and what is acceptable and how things should be. This project really felt like a partnership. It wasn't just that they were doing something for us. They wanted to learn from us as much as our dancers had these amazing opportunities. There were really simple things that we just take for granted because we do them all the time at Magpie. And they said that when they did their tour and they went to Japan, they managed to use some of that in sessions to engage people in ways that they hadn't before. So, sometimes it's the simplest things, but it was the fact that they were wanting us to lead the way in that respect. They really did invest in not just giving our dancers those opportunities but also to have dancers there and learn from them firsthand, rather than just have a training session with me. We were allowed to be visible.

    Laura: It was very much an exchange. They learnt from us and we learnt from them.

    Caroline: For us, there are different layers of exchanges in the university collaboration. One of the layers is that the Blue Apple performers are quite experienced in performance because they have been fortunate enough to have had this opportunity to perform and train as a performer for many years. They have been out there, and this is obvious when they come in to work in the room. I think the dance students respond to Blue Apple as artists and as performers. For example, when we went on tours, the Blue Apple performers would go into a new space at each different venue, and they would be leading the rehearsals professionally, not being intimidated by the new space. They could be in the performance, and if something went wrong, then they would respond, 'it is fine we are just going to keep going', and they would take the students with them. So, you had the students with the technical dance movement training ... you had the Blue Apple performers who did not get the opportunity to have a physical training, but they are performers, and they are very clear about that.

Individual potential: language and presence

Alison: One of the things we do in technique sessions is that we might teach the actual name for a move, but we then create our own Magpie name for it. So that we can see what people understand in terms of the quality of the movement or the action. For example, when we do 'echappe saute', that's what we call 'McDonalds jump' – we know that we need to jump up and out and up and in. We use visual images to rename things and make them make sense. And then when we did our residency with the Royal Opera House, we started with a ballet class led by their creative associate and it was interesting that when he got halfway through the pliés, one of the dancers stopped him and said, 'Actually David, what I think we should do there is take our arm over and do this…'. It was not the way he would normally teach but he loved it because what we then found is week-on-week we would think back to what our bodies had done the week before and start to put those movements in to our warm-up. What we were doing in the technique session was building up muscle memory, so that when we got to perform, we'd learn the technique of it and our bodies were used to it. And that was a new way of working for them. It was a new way of working for us as well because we would let the dancers lead everything.

Caroline: Adults with learning difficulties don't always have so many inhibitions, so it creates a very open way of communicating. It also enhances a sense of being present in the moment – now – and I think that the being present in the now is something that actually seems to almost shock the dance students to begin with. They don't know what it is at first, and they come around to realising that they are challenged by a very immediate presence created by the Blue Apple dancers. You have permission to be in the moment. You have to be more relaxed in a way. Students gradually become aware of this 'in the moment' way of working and being. Just right now. Don't worry about what's going to happen in a minute or be anxious whether you are going to remember that piece of material, or is it working, or anything like that. It is just slowly training themselves to go, 'Okay, it's just right now and that's it'.

Alison: It is interesting to bring inclusivity and rigour together. The way that Magpie's approach merged into the Royal Opera House's ballet class was fascinating because traditionally in ballet, there is the barre, then the centre, then you do the dance, and suddenly one of the dancers might suggest something else, like running around and changing places. I think that's how the creativity has merged with the technique to make it inclusive, because the whole idea of copy me and do what I'm doing (a) doesn't fit people's bodies and (b) is, kind of, lip service because you don't understand fully what you're doing. And I know our dancers are very keen to have that detail so that they can get it right, even if it's a completely different version of what everyone else is doing. It's still that they're reaching as much as they can, or they're bending as much as they can.

Laura: And actually, where we have different abilities, we might use a different name based on an image like Alison's example of the 'McDonalds' jump but the actual professional technique name for that step would still be given and there would be a percentage of dancers who would call it by the technical name, and those who have the Magpie name, slowly, will understand what that technical name is. Magpie methodology is about blending the two approaches. We don't want to patronise people either and we want people to learn ballet language so the approach is to question how you can still use professional technique lingo, as well as adapt it to your own lingo, such as the Magpie names. And let there be dancers who call it one name and other dancers who call it another name, but ultimately they are doing the same movement.

Caroline: In the collaboration between the students and the Blue Apple performers, I work very hard on stripping away any preconceived ideas about movement or technique. I don't specifically say that to them, but I do speak explicitly about stripping away dance language. So if you are talking about going to the floor, then it is important to use imagery if you want to be inclusive. For example, I will use expression such as, 'diving to the floor' rather than 'reach down to touch the floor' because not everyone can. We do use images in my traditional dance training, but here it is really focusing on that language and imagery and quality that emerges from that approach.

Alison: I guess our perspective on technique is that instead of having this aesthetic ideal, it is individuals reaching their goals in their own way. They get to do a balance, or a turn, through their own route. And that is what I was saying before that it's not a direct route for everybody, and you take a wavy pathway to get there, and not everyone will get to the end place but it's about them getting as close to it as possible. Their approach to technique is valued even if the end outcome doesn't look the same as the person next to them.

Caroline: Yes, it's the integrity of that approach. I agree with that.

Laura: Most families, parents and carers of people that work with Magpie often say that where they have been given the opportunity for choice and to make decisions themselves, that confidence has enabled them to go on to do things or even get jobs. We are a dance company, and we deliver dance but there are these spinoffs such as enabling people to develop their skills to feel confident to go and work.

3.7 Developing bespoke inclusive technique for mainstream dance training

A conversation between Imogen Aujla and Laura Jones

Imogen Aujla is a freelance dance psychology researcher, lecturer, and life and well-being coach at Dance in Mind (www.danceinmind.org). Her research centres on psychological well-being, inclusive dance, and the working lives of freelancers. Imogen is passionate about the application of psychology to enhance participation, performance and well-being in dance.

Laura Jones, Co-Artistic Director of Stopgap Dance Company, joined in 2001 and has been integral to the company's growth and direction. She is a fierce advocate for dance inclusion and equality, advancing the sector through training and consultancy work. She has extensive teaching experience, with a passion for empowering future generations of diverse dancers, and developing accessible training opportunities. Her broad creative and performance experience includes working with numerous choreographers and performing nationally and internationally.

Training

Laura: I trained over 20 years ago now. Although, no, I take that back. I'm still training, you never stop learning! But in terms of a formal training, I started dancing at about four or five years old, doing Royal Academy of Dance (RAD) and Imperial Society of Teachers of Dancing (ISTD) ballet and modern. As I grew up, I realised dance was something I was passionate about and wanted to do as a career, so I enrolled at college to take A Level dance. However, in the first week of the course, I had my spinal injury, which left me paralysed and needing a wheelchair. At that point, I had no concept that there was much in the dance world outside of a fairly limited career path and training. Because I wasn't aware of other options, I thought, 'Well that's it! End of that career dream!'. So, I count myself very lucky that having started the course, my tutors stayed in contact with me and encouraged me to come back the following year, after a year in hospital for recovery and rehabilitation. In the meantime, I found some other dance experiences, including a week's residency course with Candoco. Then I went back to college the following year and completed my A Level in dance, becoming the first person

DOI: 10.4324/9781003111146-22

in a wheelchair to do so. My tutors were new to teaching dance to someone in a wheelchair and I was new to being in a wheelchair, let alone dancing in one. I definitely learnt a lot about how to adapt and make things work for my new body, but it was relatively limited because we were all new to this way of working. There was a good conversation happening but it was also frustrating feeling like I was the only one who was different. I did initially consider going on to further training after my A Levels, but at the time, nothing I found was right for me. I had done a couple of workshops with Stopgap Dance Company and, at that time, they happened to have funding to employ two new dancers. I was invited to audition for them and got the job, which, being just out of A Levels with very limited experience, was incredibly lucky. Having been a dancer in the company for many years, my role developed to Head of Talent Development, and now Co-Artistic Director, so I am able to support others in the way I was supported when I joined the company and create opportunities that weren't around when I was younger.

Imogen: My beginning is similar to you. I started Cecchetti ballet when I was about four. I liked how you talked about what your ideas of success were back then because certainly for me I wanted to be a ballerina, although I think I always probably knew that I didn't have either the talent or commitment to actually make it! But my ideas about success were very limited to ballet, which is largely white, very lean, non-disabled dancers on stage. It was quite a rarefied world. I probably came across contemporary dance when I was about 16 and I also did GCSE and A Level Dance at my dance school, and not at my school because they weren't offering it. I don't think I thought about values or ethics. When I was 18, I went to university to do a Dance degree and we did a couple of Community Dance modules and I remember we had introductory sessions on inclusive dance, dance for children and dance for the elderly. I don't remember ever having the conversation about 'why would we do this, why is this work important, what's the value of this practice'. I think it was implied that we would understand and we were all very keen 19-year olds, it was brilliantly taught, I really enjoyed it, but there was no conversation about what place it had within the industry, where might that lead – for instance, if you teach a young disabled dancer who wants to do more than recreational dance is there anything for them and back then, there was probably not a huge amount.

Questions around the ethics of technique in particular really did not start to occur to me until after I did my PhD. Technique was just technique. It was a given that it was done by a certain type of body to achieve a certain end. At the start of my PhD at Laban, one of the teachers did a footwork exercise and she said, here are eight counts – improvise! And I kind of went, huh? Because improvisation belonged in the choreography class, that was my mindset. I never had that sense that it was something that technique could be. So, I suppose from my training and background, technique was a very limited thing and it was your tools that you then used to create work. But that creating work took place in another studio or another session.

My PhD was about talent development at the Centres for Advanced Training (CAT) in dance. I was looking at all sorts of different things around talent development and around people's physical and psychological development. My post-doc research explored how talent identification and development processes could be made more inclusive. I was asking questions such as 'What would we look for in an audition, for instance, if we were looking for young disabled people to join a CAT? How would we train them? What would be the model of training? Would we do specialist classes for disabled students? Or would technique include both disabled and non-disabled dancers?', and that's really the first time I thought of technique training in that way and that's when it really became clear to me that technique could be a whole lot more flexible than I had understood it to be.

Broadening technique through flexible approaches to teaching

Laura: I think that's interesting, that idea of ethics or values, because I'm not sure when I really started considering these ideas. If I hadn't had my injury, I don't know that I would've been aware of or have got into inclusive dance practice so now I'm keen to make opportunities accessible, not just for those who need them because of their access needs but also to bring that awareness to other students or aspiring dancers that there is this much wider dance world. Like you say, technique is so much broader than often it is initially introduced to be. It's now with hindsight I want people to have those opportunities that I might not have had.

Imogen: I did a project with the Imperial Society of Teachers of Dancing (ISTD) who were interested in making both their syllabi and examinations more inclusive, because private dance studios or independent dance studios are often a young person's introduction to dance, so if their doors aren't open, so to speak, then if you want technical progression as a young disabled dancer, you may not know exactly where to go. There's always been that perception that contemporary technique can be as broad as you like, it can kind of be whatever you want it to be, therefore that's the most suitable dance genre for disabled people. That's been the sort of implicit belief in the dance industry. Ballet, on the other hand, is not accessible. The ISTD is quite keen to challenge that perception. If we want dance to be truly inclusive, which is hopefully what we all want, then all genres have to be accessible. So how do we do that and how much can you change a syllabus while remaining ballet. So, for instance, if you teach a plié exercise to a young dancer with Down's Syndrome, then they may find it difficult to use first position if that's their initial introduction to a plié. It is more inclusive to start in second position, then try in parallel, and then we work up to first position. So, it is trying to find ways of reaching that end point but the journey to get there is different for each dancer in the group. Of course, Laura, you can talk more about this with the Stopgap training scheme IRIS (Include, Respond, Integrate and

Specialise). The project being a specifically inclusive contemporary dance syllabus, how much flexibility is available in IRIS, would you say?

Laura: It's been a challenge because as we designed and developed IRIS we really wanted to make sure that there is flexibility and that it is inclusive to anyone, any degree or type of disability, but also, relevant to any young person who is interested in developing dance skills. There's something about making sure that it is created to be recognisable as technique, as skills development, as something that has rigour built into it. I'm aware that there can be fear around technique for a disabled dancer, but I suppose for me, my definition of technique is about learning and developing skills for dance, and therefore, that can be anything, whatever those skills are. What is going to help progress you as a dancer? That's technique! Sure, there are set techniques with particular names, but it can be as broad as developing skills. So, you can develop your technique within improvisation, you can develop it with set movements. With IRIS, we've tried to break down what skills are important for dance. Whether it is spatial awareness, use of breath, control, coordination and then start to filter down. How can we develop them into something that's more set and formal? We talk about wraparound work. So, it might be a game or an exploration to introduce and help to develop a specific skill, and then actually the exercise just becomes something to show that they have the skill, rather than learning the skill solely through that exercise.

Imogen: It's sort of almost the opposite approach to the traditional approach. Where the exercise is the end goal, rather than the exercise is the way that you display or demonstrate what you've been working on.

Laura: Ultimately, as long as we're seeing the skills, then that's success. Technique is more of a vehicle to show the skills rather than 'it needs to be this'. You don't go on stage and do your exercises and your technique. It's a vehicle for then developing dance in a broader sense.

Imogen: It's about rethinking how we describe or define technique as a vehicle for developing skills, rather than a set of exercises. It shouldn't be that contemporary dance is better suited for disabled bodies though. In the recent project, the ISTD was looking at translating three of their codified syllabi; part of the process was that teachers were given permission to make changes. For example, one of the expert practitioners who helped the teachers to translate the syllabi suggested: 'You don't have to have a barre. That's not where you have to start. If you feel like the students are getting tired, let's do some improvisation. Stick on some loud music and just do what you want'. And it was a bit like, 'Oh, can I do that?'. The modern teacher had a few standing dancers with cerebral palsy in the class who found it really difficult to do turns, so the expert inclusive dance practitioner suggested that they put ballet shoes on or jazz shoes so that they can turn more easily. It was about giving permission to make those changes: You are allowed to do this because this is your class. So you can think, 'Okay, I'm going to make this change, actually, because this suits my students rather than being chained so much to the syllabus'.

Laura: As a teacher, when you get the revelation of that freedom, you are more able to understand what your students need and how you can draw things out from them, and what skills and talent they do have and can help that development, rather than feeling like you're a slave to the syllabi. Training should be focused on the students rather than trying to shoehorn them into a format.

Bringing inclusive translation processes to the mainstream

Imogen: As a non-disabled dancer, what I've observed in my research is that there will always be a sense of conversation or dialogue around how this work happens, because it's not the case that if you have ten dancers with sensory difficulties, then they will all have the exact same presentation. For example, with people who have cerebral palsy, you might have one person in a wheelchair and one person who's a standing dancer. Each person will have their own particular presentation as well as lived and bodily experiences. Many people believe that technique should be like this for everyone; we're all translating to our own unique bodies. This idea was such an alien concept compared to how I was trained where we all had to try to look the same in every possible way. There's so much more value to everybody being part of that process of translating. So if you're in an inclusive class, then you aren't singled out as the one or two disabled dancers who have to do the translation. This is work for all of us and it also makes technique more interesting, perhaps, to do? And more complex to teach, but I mean that in a good way, because as a teacher you have got to think, 'What am I trying to get out of this exercise? It's not just a swing exercise. What are we trying to get out of it? And how can everybody achieve this aim in ways that might be very different?'.

Laura: When I teach in an inclusive setting, it improves my 'mainstream' teaching skills as well, not just my concept of what is important in teaching but also the skills used to deliver that approach to young people. Rather than learning a technique that they try and fit on themselves, they learn their own technique. Inclusive work and integrated work bring that translation process to mainstream. The concept of bespoke technique should be for everyone! It would create better dancers that have a better understanding of their own body, are probably less likely to get injured, maybe a bit more thinking for themselves, which maybe some teachers and choreographers might find a challenge.

Imogen: Hopefully more confident, as well.

Laura: I think healthier, certainly in terms of mental health as well. You are not constantly trying to be something that you're not. You're still trying to develop and be the best that you can be, but it's less about comparing yourself to someone else, for example, they can get their leg that high and I can't. This way of working needs more self-discipline because you are having to work for yourself and push yourself for what you can do. I think that makes for a better, more rounded, healthier, happier (hopefully) dancer. This approach takes longer and maybe that's an issue for some people, because maybe people aren't getting through the exams as quick, but it takes longer because it's going deeper and it's getting a better quality outcome.

Imogen: If you're working to your own goals and you're trying to better yourself rather than compete with other people, then you're likely to perform better, you'll be happier, you'll be more confident and less anxious. So, actually, that's a win-win situation and yet it is such a radical departure from your typical technique class where you're a passive body in the space, desperately trying to copy what your teacher's doing and looking in the mirror to see if you've got it right.

Talent and virtuosity in inclusive dance practice

Imogen: We talk about talent in dance all the time, without really defining what we mean by that. There's no one factor that indicates talent, there's no one factor that predicts talent either – talent is multifaceted. We know that it probably falls into some sort of broader categories such as physical and psychological factors and artistic skills. Looking at inclusive settings, there is also the degree of support the young person has in terms of parents, carers and logistics like what transport needs they might have, and just also things that might need to be in place before they start some kind of programme of training. But the talent development process is arguably more important than the talent identification process. So what happens between finding a dancer that we think is talented and developing their potential and getting them to where they have the potential to be. In inclusive settings, young people will probably have had less exposure to dance training. In that context, we are looking more for potential than already developed skills. So rather than looking at flexibility and strength, for instance, we are looking at a certain type of interesting movement quality and bodily awareness, embodied movement.

Laura: An aspiring disabled dancer will most likely have faced challenges in terms of access to dance. They might not have had the same options, or access or opportunities as their non-disabled peers, but quite often I think someone with a lived experience of disability or an impairment is likely to have developed good body knowledge because of life, because of having to deal with situations where there are barriers and there are challenges, they already have a deepened understanding of their body. For me, you know, when I come across a situation that's not accessible, I know my body well, so I know how I can manage this. I have developed that ability to be flexible and adaptable and problem-solve because I've had to problem-solve as a disabled person living in a world that's not yet fully accessible. Those are skills that are relevant in dance and it is about finding processes in the training to draw them out and make use of them within a dance setting.

Imogen: And some of our non-disabled students have very little understanding of their own bodies. They sometimes come with these bad habits that you have to undo. And sometimes, they're not that adaptable. To develop flexibility in learning would again benefit everyone.

Laura: Looking at this idea of talent and virtuosity, which is a term that I know this book is reassessing, and that is something that we talk about in Stopgap, but it's about finding your own virtuosity and that might be very different to other people's. So our role is about helping dancers to identify what their own version of virtuosity is. For example, when we lead teacher training, we often ask the teachers what they think makes a great dancer and it's interesting because it is often similar things that come up like dedication, motivation, adaptability, body awareness, creativity, all these sorts of things, and never actually anything about physical attributes. Considering that dance is such a physical art form, it is interesting that when we ask teachers what they think is important, it rarely comes down to, 'Oh that you can kick your leg high or do the splits'. We also discussed the idea of what success is. Both of our career journeys were unexpected from what we initially set out. So, when you are looking for talent, you need to be aware of the possibilities and journeys that people might take on. Sometimes the skills or the benefits of dance and dance training might not necessarily take someone to be a performer. There's such a wide range of dance careers and also careers that might not even be dance-related, but you can benefit from the skills developed through dancing.

Imogen: When I'm talking about these sort of talent identification criteria, this is all based on the idea that we're talking about somebody that becomes a professional performer but you're absolutely right, that it is a narrow idea of what we might want to look for. Dedication and the love of dance as an art form are so fundamental to a range of those career trajectories.

Laura: With the IRIS syllabus, we have been focusing on different phases of development in relation to skills. So, for example, the 'Include' level of the programme looks at dance skills, contact skills, exploration, performance and textures as the way of breaking that down into the skills we think are important. And then with the 'Respond' phase, we look more at the dancers individually. We examine their skills on a personal level and help them to develop their own bespoke technique. We have this awareness that obviously the dance world is incredibly broad and there are lots of different potential options, but a lot of that potential is not designed yet to be completely inclusive. So, for 'Integrate', we support people to go to what you might call a mainstream dance group to find an area that they might be interested in. The final phase is 'Specialise'. We look at particular areas such as performer, teacher or choreographer.

Moving away from competition: individual achievements and collective observations

Imogen: We have got to be careful, I think, of not reinforcing those traditional hierarchies: choreographer at the top and then the dancer and then the teacher. It came up in a separate research project into freelance dance practitioners. It still felt like being a choreographer or a performer is the pinnacle and, actually, that's so relevant for training young people, that we're not inadvertently reinforcing that hierarchy.

Laura: If you don't 'make it' as a dancer, then that's not a failure. Actually, it's about finding what's right and where your talent lies and what interests you. It's perfectly fine to be doing something different.

Imogen: There is also a perception that to be a 'real dancer', you have to have gone through some kind of hardship in relation to the training and rigour of the discipline. The assumption is that it is all very well to be nice to students when they're in training but that we should start being a bit harder on them, being a bit mean to them as they get older, so they're ready for the profession. I don't think that's a true reflection of 'the profession', and I don't think it's a good way to train people!

Laura: It is more important that, as an individual, you are challenging yourself and working to your full potential. There is this fear that if we're too relaxed, in order to accommodate for people's differences or disabilities, it waters down or dilutes the quality of dance. I don't think that's necessarily the case. If you're challenging yourself, then as long as you are doing that within what your capabilities are then that's the important thing. With this more inclusive approach to dance and technique (or dance skills), it's down to each individual to push themselves and actually that's what you want in dance. You need people who want to push themselves and better themselves and that don't just rely on whoever is in charge of the space. When I'm teaching, I try to give options to make people aware that they can challenge themselves. So I can say, 'This is the class, this is what I'm leading, but please feel free to add your own challenges, whatever you need to challenge yourself for today', whether it's to do with memory of movement, or adding an additional layer or focusing on a particular skill or body part. If we're developing dancers who are more thinking dancers and more self-aware, then they should have more of those skills to be able to challenge themselves and know where they need to be challenged. For example, the teacher might not necessarily give all the movement for the lower body so that the dancers can add an extra balance or can add an extra transference of weight here, because that's a challenge that is important to them at that time.

Imogen: This approach to learning is underpinned by really well-established psychological theory. Achievement goal theory refers to being more task-orientated. It means that you are focused on mastering a particular task, your motivation is about learning, it's about enjoyment, it's about what is inherently satisfying about what you're doing and it's about doing better than you did before. So you're in competition with yourself. Essentially, it means that you are able to set and monitor your own goals, and then to challenge yourself accordingly. And those are the kind of dancers that we want across the board. That kind of approach to learning and motivation is much better for us in terms of both our well-being and our overall performance and what we want is to get away from this other form of goal, the ego orientation which is more about being in competition with others.

Laura: However, creating a space for observation of others is important. Observing others dancing is an important skill. If you're working with another dancer, to be able to observe them and see how they move and how they use their body, can help inform you, to be aware of both differences and similarities.

Imogen: I think it's really hard to teach students in a lecture space about different bodies or psychological approaches, because the extent to which they then apply that in the studio is questionable.

Laura: Yes, in training settings, there is still such limited diversity, so it's difficult to show the importance of how difference and learning from and valuing those differences can enrich everybody's practice.

Imogen: It's hard though because it takes a certain amount of maturity to have that mindset and when students come to us at 18, they're still children really. They'd hate me to describe them like that, but they still have so much development and growth ahead: physically, cognitively and emotionally.

Laura: If there are more opportunities and inclusion for disabled people or a more diverse range of dancers from a much earlier age, then maybe that will help with the understanding and the appreciation of different needs and bespoke approaches. This will help to develop a more mature approach to diversity and inclusion and a healthier approach to training as a whole, which can be taken on into their professional lives and even beyond the dance world into the broader society.

3.8 Participating in worlds of our own making

Inclusive training in community dance practice

A conversation between Diane Amans and Ruth Pethybridge

Diane Amans is a freelance dance artist, lecturer and consultant offering professional development, arts and health projects, evaluation and mentoring. Diane is one of the leading practitioners in community dance and her textbooks – An Introduction to Community Dance Practice and Age and Dancing- are set books on undergraduate programmes in the UK and abroad. Diane is a 2014 Winston Churchill Fellow and has worked with community dance practitioners in Australia, New Zealand, Korea and Japan.

Ruth Pethybridge is a choreographer, facilitator and researcher. She has delivered dance in diverse settings with all ages. Her socially engaged practice emphasises creativity in choreographic processes and blurring the lines between social gathering and performance. She joined Falmouth University as a lecturer in 2013 and completed her practice-based PhD on concepts of community in cross-generational dance in 2017. Ruth regularly presents her work nationally and internationally and most recently has been working on an interdisciplinary research project with Oxford and Kent University that looks at the role participatory arts interventions can have in adolescent mental health outcomes.

Introduction

Agility is associated with the capacity to adapt to changing circumstances and events as they happen, to be able to move quickly when needed, and to respond to a situation as it evolves, something that the Covid-19 pandemic asked of everyone in the performing arts sector. Community dance artists have often developed all of these skills too as a result of many practitioners 'learning on the job', or 'learning through doing'. It is notoriously difficult to train in some of the relational skills and tacit understandings that underpin what a dance artist needs – in addition to physical techniques – in the variety of contexts and situations that working in community dance requires.

It has been widely acknowledged by dance scholars and in practice-based research more broadly that there is knowledge inherent in the practice of dancing and making dances with others. It is a form of cultural knowledge as well as a social practice and a performing art with artistic works available

DOI: 10.4324/9781003111146-23

for analysis and dissemination. It is vital that these ways of knowing continue to be valued in and of themselves, but if this knowledge is to be shared, then write and discuss it we must! This conversation between two experienced practitioners and writers in the field is an exchange of ideas and an opportunity to find language to communicate shared and distinct experiences of the potential for community dance. We reflect in particular on what training means in an inclusive context and how active participation and collaboration creates dancing worlds that we might all want to inhabit.

– Ruth Pethybridge

Purposeful training

Diane: When I started out, there wasn't any training in dance. The most I got was a Laban module as part of my teacher training course. After that, I did a special needs diploma and a course in counselling and one of the things that has been most important in my development has been the fact that I worked in the department of Applied Social Sciences at a college, where I was working with social workers, people who were doing counselling. I realised when I came to do my MA that I really absorbed quite a lot of the elements of person-centred practice, and that influences my approach to dance in the community. In thinking about the ethical principles and values that are most important to me I realised that in all aspects of my work, whoever I'm working with – but it definitely applies to intergenerational work, I'm interested in creating the right conditions for the participant to be actively involved in decisions, rather than being a passive recipient of what I've got to offer. I'm committed to establishing collaborative relationships with participants. So, I'm actually trying to set things up where nobody has priority, that we're all in this together. I'm interested in a leadership style that promotes autonomy, where people feel they've got ownership of what they're doing. And I feel as a leader, I've got to create an atmosphere in which people feel secure and able to take risks, and I recognise that has been informed by my contact with the counselling people and social workers.

Ruth: I was thinking about my own, somewhat antagonistic, somewhat ambivalent relationship towards technique, which comes partly from a constant feeling of not living up to a standard. A more positive spin on that is that it's an unfinished process, you never arrive anywhere, and that's the wonderful thing about movement, right? It's always shifting, so there's always that potential for growth and change and those moments of discovery where something shifts and clicks. I'm always asking students, what are you training for? Because if you're just training, what even is that? It's just self-reflexive back into the body. So, this idea of what are you training for then implicates values and a context beyond that. I think Diane's point about the social aspect coming into your education is part of what, maybe, a university education can offer, bringing in these different perspectives.

Diane: I think that's a really good question, Ruth, what are you training for? And it's really valuable that we have that in mind with our students. If their ultimate aim is to do some participatory dance, then that is very clear, what they are training for. If they are aiming to be performers or they don't know, at the end of the day, the reality is, unless they're actually going to do that as a leisure pastime, they're going to have to find some way to earn a living out of it. So, that is a really valuable question.

Ruth: Yeah, I think for me it also has to do with choreography and the form of dance and how dance communicates, so the training depends on what it is you're wanting to communicate. So, certain techniques are useful to you, and some aren't and it's partly about forming some kind of sense of identity, which again is where that overlaps with values and ethics around what it is you want to do with your dancing. Which, like you say Diane, might be about a career path, or it might be about what I need to communicate, what form I need in order to be part of a particular conversation.

Diane: Listening to you, I'm just reminded of the process-product continuum as a model. I find that quite interesting too, where are we on that and why? Why are we choosing the process-product continuum and also the leadership style, you know? The collaborative leadership style or the more authoritarian leadership style? And there are places for both.

Ruth: Technique forms are difficult because they have this history. These tropes immediately start to arise in our bodies as soon as we're in a line in a classroom or in front of a mirror. So some of the inspiring uses of technique that I've seen have been about simply the way that the space is used, for example, so you're teaching technique but you're doing it in different configurations, which is something that community dance has long recognised and long engaged with. Teaching tendus in a circle will have a very different relationship to each other and to the body than standing at the bar. I've also seen dance practitioners coming into a university context who've really worked with leading and following in a very particular way. It's not about demonstrating and copying, but it's through this constant exchange of copying and then refining, so it's still really technical in the sense that you're trying to refine and work towards something that is really clearly executed. But it's less of this demonstrating and copying model, which just brings with it all that history which is really hard to escape from.

Diane: We can move away from the demonstrating and copying model. I remember once someone said, good choreography should surprise and delight and, I feel, be a little less predictable, where something unusual happens. It can be a much more inclusive approach because there are going to be some participants who can't perform some of the technique which has been handed down. When you're working with somebody who is in a wheelchair and can only move one side of the body, you get the most fascinating opportunities for choreography and it's about shifting, getting the fit right for what we offer as leaders, as choreographers and what is most likely to result in something which is interesting, engaging and also interesting to observe.

Ruth: Moving away from that one-size-fits-all is really important in how we think about training now I think, which is where we get that more passive engagement from learners, and it's political too how power manifests itself in those kind of didactic teaching environments. Making the links between theory and practice is an ongoing challenge for dance and it all seems to disappear sometimes when students start their technique class. But I am not anti-technique, I just think it is necessary to interrogate it, particularly in the current climate considering decolonisation too, we need to be asking ourselves which techniques are considered more rigorous and relevant, etc., not just doing what we have always done. Judith Butler wrote that it is possible to critique something that we can't live without, so there's this sense that just because we critique it doesn't mean that we're dismissing it.

Language

Ruth: I think there's something interesting about the relationship between technique and language too and the way that different practices and teachers will use language as something which also is integral, and what it can bring out is very different to just thinking about the muscle tone or the ability to hit certain points. It's about a qualitative presence, rather than what you can do, it becomes about how you're doing it.

Diane: What you're saying about language is lovely. Sometimes I choose not to use very much language at all because I work with people who either don't understand, don't speak that language or can't hear. Sometimes we could do with looking at less verbal ways of facilitating what we're doing.

Ruth: Yes, for sure. I have been to some classes that work with a much less verbal way of leading. I think what I was talking about though was very considered use of specific language and language tools to bring out certain qualities or extend certain possibilities within a technique class. And it comes back to that, to my original, very simplistic question of 'what is it for?' Because if technique is considered a training system, then we were never meant to do that on the stage. We're not transmuting directly from the classroom onto the stage. The performance itself is always going to be an amalgamation of all these different things, including technique. So, Diane, you used the term performance skills, I used the term presence, and we're talking about technique, so is technique a set of skills? Perhaps. For me, presence – which is a performance skill – is something that has a bit more ambiguity to it, in a good way. I like a bit of ambiguity, it opens up for these non-verbal experiences.

And I think the thing around language, in inclusive sectors we've really had to be thinking about how we use language for a long time. I should credit Kate Marsh, who's a former Candoco dancer and is at Coventry University and who has run some brilliant workshops on this, using words, such as 'shift' rather than 'walk', for example, and then allowing the multiple responses to that to come to the fore which don't rely on a person's specific physicality. It shows the difference between offering language and images rather than complex sentences that describe the movement very precisely.

Shared values

Diane: I think it was Yoko Ono once who said about being an artist with people skills. And I thought that's how I see myself; an artist with people skills and cultivating person-centred practice where the participants, the people in my groups, are actively involved in decisions rather than being passive recipients. I've got a commitment to establishing a collaborative relationship within my groups. Creating an atmosphere where maybe half the group perform and the other half observe, even if it's pair work, but that they're not going to be exposed and observing the whole time. Getting the fit right between what I offer and what is likely to create enjoyment and engagement. Creating an atmosphere in which people feel secure and able to take risks.

Ruth: Yeah, I think it's lovely to hear all of those thoughts, Diane, because it's often really confirming of these shared values, I guess, which have long been articulated by the community dance sector. I think People Dancing, the Foundation for Community Dance, has also done a lot about articulating what those values are, and that sense of democracy and co-ownership in a choreographic or creative process is central to that. When I think of my personal values and how that crosses over with those values, I definitely feel like there's a range of contexts and projects. You might go in there with a set of values, but those can also be broken open almost by the situation and what it requires of you. So some things need to be more artist-driven I would say, whereas others can be more coming from the community, a grassroots, bottom-up approach. I think it's important to acknowledge that it's not always easy to even do that co-ownership stuff, because sometimes people genuinely want to be led. We can try to create a safe space, and we might value their ideas, but they might not value their ideas because of years of various forms of oppression. Ethics sometimes involves shifting and evolving because you are being responsive to what's being brought to you.

Unlocking movement

Ruth: I was thinking about an example of a much older participant holding hands with a child and skipping around the room and how that feeling of skipping, for her, was like 'Oh my, I don't move like this anymore. This is not a movement that is part of my vocabulary anymore.' But it's not actually to do with ability, because she can skip, that's something that her body is capable of doing, but it's outside of the lexicon of what's deemed appropriate or necessary for her age category. And she described this sense of freedom that came from the skipping. So that was a really interesting way in which the movement itself brings up these associations or memories or reactions and how that crosses over with where you are in your life span, and that there's something around that, in terms of, if you were thinking about what kinds of things come out of intergenerational dance that for training, it's maybe addressing some assumptions around literally how we move our bodies.

Diane: I think that's a lovely example. You just described the person with the small child skipping and one of my notes on ethical perspectives of what to train for in relation to career paths is about people skills. You, as the facilitator, observe people and when we're actually moving towards choreography, when we're making a piece, it's about clocking where people are at, so observation skills. The volume needs to be turned right up so we can see who seems to be comfortable with what. So, the dancers have got some freedom between how they actually get to that point in moving and so on.

Ruth: I think it's interesting to think when you're clocking where people are at and so you're then adjusting your expectations and making sure that they're comfortable. Then how that goes on to affect the choreography, down to decisions about where people are in the space, even. When I think of the idea of training, there's this feeling of pushing or wanting to advance something, so then I suppose it depends if we're talking about training for facilitatory skills or something else. Through understanding where boundaries come in, then you can unlock something or from a place of discomfort learn something still.

Diane: What you said about unlocking stuff, implicit in what you just described is reflecting, and having opportunities to listen to people's reflections about what's going on for them. The 'How do I know what I think I know?' is about this experience for these participants. And it's about checking in in an objective way. If we're wanting some objective feedback, we need to ask those objective questions. And again, it's part of the people skills repertoire, isn't it?

Ruth: There's always this sense, in community practice, that people are needing to advocate for themselves and their practice and so the potential for critique in the sense that it's moving things forward and shaping ideas gets a bit lost. The practice often relies on reports and evaluations from projects, so the emphasis is on positively framing outcomes and the metanarrative around critique is not as developed. The capacity to evaluate and say, 'Well, actually, these aspects didn't work for me', is vital to the form and the sector evolving.

Diane: Yeah, and you're right about the emphasis, I found this when I ran my own company for those years, the emphasis on written reports and that kind of documentation, it really made me take a step back and think we need to get the right fit between how we check in with participants and measure what's going on. We need to satisfy people who want something concrete and so on, but we're creative people for goodness' sake, we need to have a creative approach to checking in with what's going on for our participants.

Ruth: I guess the thing is for intergenerational practice, which we have both worked in quite a lot is that those differences, the particular differences, are often heightened by age, or because of the different ages – so how do you speak to that multiplicity in different ways? Because everybody might be in a peer group, they are still having very different experiences and that's what you're always dealing with that counterpoint between equality and the specific lived experience of each person. There's always a counterpoint there between wanting to present something that has a sense of equality of opportunity but also recognising there will be different entry points, different experiences and different outcomes.

Diane: It comes back to the question you asked earlier, Ruth, 'What is the training? What are you training for?' And actually that's linked to progression. If we work backwards from what we're training for, the notions of progression and what we're looking for are going to be determined by that. So what are we training for? Are people doing this work so that they can perform high-quality dance for an audience in a number of different contexts? Or are we training people to facilitate other people's dance experiences, and choreograph work with them so that they can perform work? And both of those, they not only have some overlap in skills sets, but they also have some different skills sets, and the second one I mentioned is going to include people skills like active listening, observation skills and so on.

Ruth: Thinking more broadly about the aims of inclusive practice too, there are these artist-led projects where it might be, for example, about an aesthetic that involves different ages, because that represents or embodies somehow the sense of the scale of humanity, rather than having trained dancers all of the same age, I am thinking about not only Rosemary Lee's work in particular here but also others. In these cases, there's a qualitative presence that is required by the artist as much as it being a participatory experience for the dancers. Then there's the more socially engaged kind of project, which is much more about the experience the participants have, the person-centred stuff that Diane talks about in relation to recognising people's needs within that and what they might get out of a project. And it's not that the former 'artist-led' model wouldn't recognise people's needs but I do think there are these differences in why and how work and projects are produced that change what you're measuring, what success is, those kinds of things.

Performing micro-topias

Diane: There are some people in one of the groups I have worked with who definitely didn't want to perform, but over the years, I've both developed myself and seen other people develop different ways of performing. A film that I worked on was with a group of Korean farmers, and originally, they asked me to work towards a performance as part of this showcase. I just looked at the timescale, looked at the fact that they were total beginners, and I thought it would be more valuable if the audience watched the sixth session. I structured it in such a way that there was very little of me in there. We did what we had been working on and they could do it in a way which was confident, which had presence, and which showed their enjoyment, as opposed to showing frightened rabbits in the headlights, trying to remember what they're supposed to do. So, I wouldn't rule out doing a performance in a more traditional way, but I also think there are other ways of doing it, which are actually interesting to take part in and interesting to watch.

Ruth: I've been able to engage in a way of performance-making whereby the performance would come, and I would realise what a small part of it it was. The performance was important, it was a culmination, and it was a moment of sharing, but it was one small part of an ongoing process. There's dialogue and reverberations and things that get taken forward after the performance. That open-endedness allows for failure. When there isn't this performance pressure, it can allow for a kind of failure, or repetition. But performance also makes sense of things and gives momentum – it feels purposeful and I've found it can be hard for some groups to find motivation without it.

Diane: You can have a little, mini performance within the session. I find that's really valuable.

Ruth: I think that's really good as well to think that you can also be teaching and learning and practicing performance skills without necessarily the fanfare of a huge performance ta-da moment. These kinds of moments also allow more vulnerable participants to begin to feel safe and build trust with their peers in the group.

Diane: Yes, as a dance leader, I have a responsibility to facilitate the relationship building between the group because that is going to actually come through in their performance work. So, it might only be three or four minutes at the beginning of the session but there will be something on relationships, whether it's a very brief thing with the person next to you, or something about relationship building within that group. It's part of my session plan.

Ruth: Also, we haven't talked about the shared movement vocabulary and how, with technique, there's a recognised codified system that everyone knows, the community builds up around a technique and through the shared vocabulary and the shared understanding of what that technique is. It does also generate a sense of co-ownership in a very different way through moving together, at a biophysical level, generating a feeling of togetherness and of shared experience. And I've seen, certainly in Rosemary Lee's work, attempts at almost creating that feeling through other things, such as flocking or a rhythmic thing that is being built up.

Diane: Yeah, and I think that's a really important part of warm up to me even if you're doing a traditional dance, whether it's a folk dance or something where we're all doing the same thing. It doesn't actually matter if you start with your right leg or your left leg, as long as you're doing the rhythm together, but there's no right or wrong way of doing it.

Ruth: For me, a big part of participatory practice and intergenerational practice is trying to plug a hole that exists because of the way that society has evolved to become more fractured, especially now. – I think because of the political and social climate we have started to develop new strategies and ways of moving together that are really progressive and exciting and needed to happen. It's really significant who is dancing together and how we're doing it in terms of how we're modelling life and being with each other – writer Claire Bishop called them 'micro-topias' – these ways that artistic practice can create temporary communities – and the way that life overlaps with art and dance, maybe we don't have to separate them so much. A lot of community practice is saying, if we bring dance more into the everyday, look what happens! Actually, we really relate differently to one another, we are closer to one another, and we are able to share in this experience and be more in touch with our own bodies and responses and therefore present in the world, so for me that's how dancing is a vital part of political and social life.

3.9 Technique as a way of building an ecology of practice

A conversation between Scilla Dyke and Rosemary Lee

Scilla Dyke MBE FRSA is an independent artist creating bespoke interventions between classical and contemporary dancers (having nurtured career transitions with more than 2600 artists internationally). Her career has included roles with the Royal Ballet, English National Ballet, Royal Academy of Dance and One Dance UK. As Founder Director of DanceEast, Scilla was instrumental in creating a dance ecology nurturing artistic talent and access to dance. She is an Honorary Fellow of Liverpool John Moores University and in 2022 was appointed as Patron People Dancing and nominated for an AWA DANCE Woman in Dance Leadership Award.

Rosemary Lee, choreographer and filmmaker, makes work in a variety of contexts and media, ranging from video installations to large-scale site-specific performances, often involving cross-generational casts. Her work is characterised by a special quality of care and attentiveness to the art, cast, audience and surroundings. Rosemary is an Associate Professor at C-DaRE-Coventry University, she holds an honorary doctorate from Roehampton University, is an honorary fellow at Trinity Laban and was awarded an OBE in 2022.

Virtuosity, knowing and imagination

Rosemary: Some of the reviewers of my early work implied that it was not physically rigorous enough, they seemed to assume that the work required no technique or even skill to perform because it was simple. Yet I see the work I make as being very virtuosic, in fact a close colleague once said it was the hardest work she had ever performed and she had had a long professional performing career. To be attentive and so finely tuned in your attentiveness and in your listening to others is a real and learnable skill. But it seems to go unnoticed, it doesn't look like a skill, because it's not a leg up by an ear. Certainly, through my career, the term virtuosity has plagued me a bit. I wondered what you felt about that, since you had a ballet training didn't you, originally?

    Scilla: I inhabited classical ballet throughout my formative training and artistic life… my teachers and choreographers were pioneers, experimenters,

DOI: 10.4324/9781003111146-24

with restless minds, intent on stretching us to exploit understanding and deep knowing. I've always been a chameleon and crossed boundaries of elite virtuosity and different genres – the strength of the Graham technique; the fall and recovery of Limón; the precision and uniqueness of Cunningham; and the synergy of Laban's movement analysis. Additionally, I have found the dance in science, music, art, philosophy... harnessing the movement/mind response to deepen my knowledge of the moving body, and the development of technical skill and virtuosity. I would describe an impromptu performance by my former dancers with Down's Syndrome as having incredible presence, joy, sentiment and virtuosity. Each dancer spontaneously rose to their feet and recreated our last dance together from ten years previously, their voices their own, the power, nuance and potential of dance resonating.

Rosemary: I can just picture that. It used to be a worry for me early on in my career because virtuosity was seen as a yardstick of success particularly for reviewers. I'm all for virtuosity, I love seeing people that are skilful, I love rigour, I love people who have trained for years and are brilliant, like a Tai Chi practitioner that has practiced for 50 years. That kind of virtuosity I adore, where it's in every cell of their body. I'm not against virtuosity, but I'm against it being equated with athleticism alone in dance. I'm in great favour of the word technique meaning something very broad, without losing the rigour and expertise.

Scilla: I couldn't agree more. I am fascinated in the process and passion underpinning any skilled performance. During the extraordinary lockdown intervals, dancers had to find ways to sustain their physical and mind-body skills, what was really challenging was sustaining what is missing when virtual or not in a live class with other dancers, the deep intuitive connectivity, the joy of the interactive explosions of exuberance, the knowledge that resides in touch, the imaginative response to anything that happens as life unfolds.

Rosemary: I'm thinking back to my own training and the experience of technique classes in the 1980s. We knew that Cunningham and Graham techniques, for example, came from the authorship of individual choreographers, from their desires as artists. Is that happening now so much? Is contemporary technique class now perhaps less prescriptive? Maybe that's good because it prepares people for many different kinds of styles and forms of expression.

Scilla: It undoubtedly is although I think lineage and legacy are important to the way of moving forward, in terms of people's identity and stories. We were 'au fait' with our roots and understood how we connected. Intellectually appreciating something is not the same as deep knowing so that it's in the fabric of our being. We evolved it and built an ecology, but these things were born out of the experience and experimentation of the original thinking. Conversely, now you have a multiplicity of different strands, dance and community, dance for health and well-being. This less prescriptive approach to technique disrupts brings about radical change and creates new methods, narratives and ethos.

Rosemary: You are reminding me of how I once researched the roots of the word 'knowledge' in different languages and so often there are two words for the two different ways of knowing – to know cognitively and to know through the body. How do we know when our third fingertip and toe are inline? We know it not only through the mirror feeding back but also through how it feels. We have to recognise that sensation in order to know we have that line. That's technique isn't it – a recognition of awareness and sensation. For me, it feels like the best way to promote deep knowing with young people is to promote constant exploration, curiosity and sensory awareness. I think it's important to really fire the imagination, because metaphor is what makes my body change the quickest. For an example, Bonnie Bird who was one of Graham's first dancers didn't teach us technique when I was training at Trinity Laban (then the Laban Centre), but before our last graduate performance, she warmed us up. She said 'imagine your ears are like fox's ears', and when she said it, my whole back came into line and I felt a new and vibrant sense of alertness. I found something for the first time in the three years of doing Graham five times a week. In that moment I realised, this is the way I want to teach and this is what dancing is for me. The imagination is giving me the sensation, it's changing my embodied experience. I suddenly found this upward-ness, because my ears came up from the back like the tufts of Red Squirrel ears and no one else had said anything like that to me. They'd always said, put your ribcage on top of your hips and it was very biomechanical. I wonder if feeding the imagination through imagery and metaphor is recognised enough as an important part of dance education. We need to keep fighting for imagination, exploration and training attentiveness as part of education – not just of the dancer for that matter. If you can teach and nurture awareness and attentiveness, then I think you'll facilitate a deeper knowing through touch and proprioception.

Scilla: I also worked with Bonnie Bird and relate implicitly to the power and potential of metaphor unleashing imagination. The power and legacies of approaches to metaphor can reach across decades, genres and space. An anecdote: Robert Cohan, Celeste Danker-Arnold, Beryl Grey, Gillian Lynne and myself all climbed into a lift, a neutral site-specific space. The door closed, the lift went up, and down, and up, and down. Lynne was in control of the button choreographing an improvisation with us through the common language we all shared. The metaphor was to dance 'as if caught in a lift'. There was a poignancy, tenderness and laughter that was arresting. Dancers from different decades and genres were all held together through a shared metaphor. The joy in our collective body, the performative presence and the experience of a shared experience grew amongst us from deep knowing, embodied knowledge and lives well lived.

Rosemary: Performative presence. This is reminding me that presence and what it is to perform doesn't seem to be addressed so much in training. I love discussing with students why a performer might be memorable to them or draw their eye. We try experiments to explore the different performative presences we can embody and witness each other's changing presences. It is fascinating but I suspect not often explored.

Meaningful relationships and ethos

Rosemary: Over the last 15 years or more, I have facilitated workshops centring on the relationship to our environment – the flora and fauna, landscape and the elements. For example, on the North Norfolk coast, we walked with naturalists, visited an astronomer and brought to the fore the sense of ourselves as creatures, as nature, equal and related to all other living things. I'm really interested in those kinds of multidisciplinary ways of looking at what dance is as a human behaviour.

Scilla: Me too, my work throughout my artistic life has continually involved collective and collaborative process. This emerges from curiosity, listening, nurturing, growing people, working together to bring about change. We can evolve dynamic conversations that ponder, free and reveal in a completely different way. Understanding other approaches into genres and techniques is part of technique.

Rosemary: Do we talk enough in training or as artists about who the work is for? Personally, if I'm only making work for my colleagues, then I'm not an artist. I want to make work for the general public, that somehow speaks to a passer-by or to someone that has no knowledge of contemporary dance. That's why I put my work outdoors. I'm trying to push myself to quite difficult places where the work actually might not work. Maybe a part of training is constant gentle questioning about the relationship to audience? Who might those people be? What do you want to give them? I see my work as an offering. Is the transactional relationship between the maker and the audience explored enough?

Scilla: Ooh, this is interesting – the process you are talking about resembles the idea of an eye which is reflecting images endlessly. There is nothing heavy or imposing about this process but there is something quite improbable. You can't prescribe how it evolves, that is part of its mystery and dignity. I always work with the notion of there never being a one-off but a practice that is evolving. Where is the legacy? Where is the understanding? Where is the connection? How can we generate work for people to be able to grow audiences, to grow their and your understanding? I like to think that we can open up the dialogue through training and through the way we create by going back to the essence of how we work with people. As Founding Director of DanceEast/Suffolk Dance, I created and built a bespoke dance ecology – project to project, initiative to initiative, artist by artist, dancer by dancer, person by person, community by community ... we lived it forwards, learning it backwards and then... evolving and moving it forwards again – with reflective eye.

Rosemary: You just poetically described how this ecology spreading through and influencing our humanity is about treating each other with respect, with open-mindedness and no judgement. We're talking about long-term, incremental change – that one generation will affect another, for real lasting change. We have to believe in that and help our young people in training believe in that kind of behaviour – full of generosity for each other.

Scilla: It comes back to the way that we engage with dialogue, the experiences that we furnish, how we disturb the air and engage in collective listening. For real understanding, engaging and having resonance with our communities, we have to live in the moment and work inclusively, intuitively and flexibly, adapting and being open to chance, challenges and solutions, ponder our creative instinct and honour individual voices. One of the critical things always is about forging meaningful lasting relationships.

Rosemary: Kindness, trust and respect are at the heart of building relationships and communities and nurturing change, learning and growth. I remember consciously considering when I made Common Dance (Dance Umbrella 2009) with 50 people of all ages, what I would need to do to immediately create the most nurturing environment for fast and profound transformation and learning to occur for each cast member as I had so little time. It is like gardening, I've got to give them the right soil, the right conditions, to help a sense of belonging to be fostered from day one. You have to model good practice through how you are with them. This is a methodology and what I'm looking for in the dancers' approach too – it's what I value. If I'm selecting someone to be in my work, then I look for that generosity and humility in someone's presence. If I am looking for a young, trained dancer, then it's finding people – who are curious, open, who watch other people – will watch a child or watch an older person and see the dance in them. There will not be any kind of judgement and they will be invested in seeing it. They are looking for the potential or looking for the embodied light. It's about the human condition. Perhaps it is a technique – a skill to be brave enough to have an open mind and not feel they will be lost, to put egos aside and to know when to come forward and when to hang back. We have to value each other with no judging or competition. The only way I can make work is if there is no question of whether one person is better than another. They need to sense from the moment they come through the door that they are valued equally.

Scilla: Expertly put. That is the ethos that guides me too. You absolutely create an environment of, I guess, inclusiveness of people being able to contribute and to feedback. It's wonderful, Rosemary, when you reflect and talk about this process... and so fundamental.

Rosemary: But I guess that is quite hard when you are in a conservatoire training. It is quite hard to keep that because of judgement inherent in the system.

Scilla: Maybe this is the challenge of engaging and enabling people to look at this differently? The people that we engage, inspire and work with now will be taking dance into the next century.

Rosemary: I think there's not only some wonderful ethical practice going on in dance, but there is also still learning and rehearsing through fear. The praise-giving method of encouraging and expanding people is seen as quite female and is sometimes seen as 'wishy-washy', and yet, for me, it is efficient, ethical and professional practice.

Scilla: I agree, to direct ethically with praise-giving is an effective approach. It strikes me when working with a person you both see and hear that person. Whoever you work with, choreographers, performers, audiences, curators, treat them as an artist who has a voice, knows how to talk about their work, and share feedback. This process is vital to building a company, cast, ensemble, team, and to ethical collaborative-working. Through ethical working practice, individuals in roles as dancers, choreographers, members of a group, establish meaningful relationships. From this will emerge new voices, new relationships, new opportunities, impacting performance, curation, audience development into the future in discrete and overt ways.

Inclusivity

Scilla: In terms of risk taking and ethics, the notion of transition is fundamental within how we look at training and technique. Retiring and injury cause sadness, loss, disrupt and unemployment yet if we are constantly evolving in our dance lives, then how might we be able to reignite in different ways all through our lives?

Rosemary: It's an approach of expansion and curiosity. If you view dancing as a display of physical prowess, then you will lose some of those things when you get older. But if you look at dancing as a kind of state of being, as an approach to life, then you can have it the whole time. How do you instil in young people this broader approach to what dancing is or can be and still give them a rigorous training?

Scilla: You're talking about challenging the whole way that we engage with our practice and our training. Reinventing the notion of transition in our dance lives, of valuing, yet challenging pre-conceptions will precipitate new intentions, ideas, approaches, creative practice, training and language to unleash fresh collaboration, choreographic commissioning and ecology vital to anyone that dances or with the desire to dance. The future of dance as an art form is vital to society. Just imagine, the richness, the intensity and potential of our dance lives and those who love and desire to dance alive with possibilities.

Rosemary: How are we going to engage with and support people wanting to bring their artforms, their ways of moving from their different cultural backgrounds and experiences to the fore?

Scilla: We need to be enabling, finding opportunities and seeking ways of galvanising a view of emerging forms. In reality, training across dance and movement-related genres fosters inherent multiple intelligences and complex mind/body connections that influence the way we understand, approach, engage and communicate with people, communities, an ever-changing world. This somehow equips us to reflect, question, reinvent, create, provoke, sensitively challenge, socially engage and find solutions that can ricochet, and impact far beyond any studio or stage.

Rosemary: We need to keep finding more opportunities for more people to enter. If only!

Scilla: How exciting and essential, to be looking at enhanced opportunities and ways of engaging in dance.

Rosemary: It's such a balancing act, isn't it? On the one hand, you want to develop more excellence, that's how the CAT schemes came into being. I was a timid little girl that couldn't dance that well, except in my heart. My technique was lousy but, in my mind and imagination, I was desperate to be a performing artist. How would that ever have been seen? You might not see potential if you are sifting for the visibly very technically able. For a lifelong career in dance, it's as much about a creative energy and a breadth.

Scilla: Unequivocally. At DanceEast/Suffolk Dance, we had companies where people just loved to dance and move – conservatoire training for young people in classical ballet and contemporary working in synergy with a network of dancers who danced, inspired by social agendas. You could see the person, the individual, the potential. Now, as an independent artist in transition, I continue to collaborate, listen, nurture individuals discovering their path and shape their narrative towards a life filled with dance. Perhaps their dance becomes a catalyst for change, opening up new worlds. Individual agency, equity and authenticity inform the crux of this coaching, supportive, mentoring relationship.

Rosemary: I am thinking of the Black Mountain model of educating. I would love to see some liberal arts colleges that are really delving into that creative practice in different ways – with clay, with cooking, with your body. Or even just as a foundation year for artists interested in a variety of media.

Scilla: There should be years of experimentation. How can we find those opportunities and things that we love to do that can then give us an opening to continue to work in and engage with dance or pursue other interests or yet undiscovered pathways.

Rosemary: The valuing of dance solely through its instrumentalisation has worried me for decades – of course, we all have amazing examples of where dance has had life-changing effects. But I want to advocate the view that dance is a human behaviour, and an ancient and extraordinary art form. It's essential to human existence.

Scilla: It's about understanding the resilience, isn't it? If we want to keep dance in our lives, how do we do that? There are so many things that dance reveals. We need to understand how people who are suddenly faced with forced transition or injury gently discover how dance can be a really strong factor in recovery, reinvention and moving on. Dance in the Community broke the mould. Women are engaging in ever-evolving leadership roles creating challenging, and championing, real change. Daring to dream.

Rosemary: This makes me think about flow – about movement and change and finding pathways through when things become too fixed, or when people become entrenched. My job as a facilitator is to find what is going to loosen a pathway. Is it a state of mind? Is it just a way of feeling relaxed or having a laugh, or is it a particular metaphor or musical input? What is going to unlock something that's become a bit solidified whether that's in the physical body or mental state.

Scilla: Yes, it's about how we enable people to know what their ethos is. Nothing we share stands alone or is complete in the present. Nothing living is still.

3.10 In the fullness of ourselves

Some skills and intentions of improvisation

A conversation between Chris Crickmay and Miranda Tufnell

Chris Crickmay trained in architecture and subsequently taught fine art with a social and community emphasis in various colleges and universities, including Dartington College of Arts and UWE Bristol. His own creative practice involves collaborative work with dancers, exploring movement and interactive performance environments. This has included an ongoing collaboration with Miranda Tufnell in research, teaching, performance and writing. Together they have written two illustrated books on improvisation exploring approaches to creative practice. http://candjcrickmay.co.uk/

Miranda Tufnell, having read English at UCL, trained in dance and from the mid-1970s was one of the pioneers of New Dance. She became well known for her mixed-media dance pieces combining light, sound and movement to form mysterious performance landscapes. Her intense interest in the body led her into a parallel practice as an Alexander Teacher and Craniosacral therapist. Her innovative work in the field of arts and health has included a recent book. www.mirandatufnell.co.uk

Introduction

In the conversation that follows, we look at four linked improvisation exercises – ones that might occupy the first morning of a two, or three, day workshop. We've chosen to discuss these beginning exercises because they say something about the skills and intentions behind this work. We are talking about improvised movement sourced in the experiencing body, rather than in any given dance style or technique. What we mean here by 'body' needs to be understood in all its complexity and mystery. We draw upon a dance practice that has grown up over the last half-century or so amongst an ever-widening circle of practitioners. Our own work extends beyond dance into other arts, especially writing and work with materials, objects, places and spaces, which we explore in combination with movement. That range of activity is reflected here in our choice of exercises. Once or twice in the conversation, we make a diversion to discuss a broader issue that has arisen. One thing we stress throughout is the value of working with others – often just one other person as a partner. Improvisation, at its best, calls upon all

DOI: 10.4324/9781003111146-25

the parts of ourselves coming together – hence our title. In particular, we are drawing attention to three things that practitioners need to cultivate. These may seem more like states of mind and body rather than techniques as we usually understand the term, but they do also require specific kinds of skill. They include

- an open and embodied presence in relation to wherever we are and whatever is occurring;
- a breadth and flexibility of attention that can move between the detail and particulars of our surroundings and the wider imaginal worlds we inhabit;
- a capacity to be curious and playful towards the things we come across and the creative possibilities they offer.

The type of work we discuss here may be used in many different circumstances: as a form of training; as a regular studio practice; as a way of sourcing material for performance; or as a means of connecting more deeply into one's world, both inside and out. The chances are it will be some combination of these, where one's life and work become intertwined and inform each other. In addition to the original recorded conversation between the two of us, we have added comments and clarifications which appear in italics, or as footnotes at various points in the text.

Exercise 1: the mysteries of an object

Chris: Often, at the very beginning of a workshop, we ask everyone to pick an object from a collection we have previously arranged around the edge of the work space. We ask participants, first, to wander about in the space, then, to pick something that appeals to them. Once they have made their choice, we ask them to pair up and take turns to explore their chosen object, while speaking to their partner about what they notice. They begin by saying what drew them to the object in the first place. Then they close their eyes and begin to explore it through touch and other non-visual means, savouring its various qualities and allowing associations to freely arise from whatever they are sensing or feeling. As they continue to explore, they share with their partner whatever is going through their minds. As we dwell on an object in this way, it begins to open out beyond what we thought we knew about it. All it requires is attentiveness. Then, something of the richness of the object itself and of that person's world of connections and associations begins to reveal itself.

Miranda: This way of people getting introduced to each other begins to open the door to a more poetic, particular and personal sense of who they are and how they perceive the world. It's different in kind to the familiar stories we tell about ourselves.
***

From the start, we are encouraging both a physical/sensory and an imaginative relationship to a chosen object, letting go of our everyday, generalised, idea of what an object is, or does. In its particularities, the object begins to lose its common identity and to seem more mysterious. In doing this exercise, we engage with the material and the more-than-materiality of things. It sets the tone for all that follows.

Exercise 2: going for a walk

Miranda: I always like to begin with an activity that's ordinary and familiar. Simply getting on the move immediately brightens our awareness. Walking gives us time to breathe, to loosen up and to let go whatever 'shape' we may be stuck in. We walk forwards/backwards/sideways, alone or with another. Gradually, we wake up to what is around us: the feel of air on our skin; sense of light, shadow; feel of our feet on the floor; others in the group; the qualities and details of the room itself. As we play with rhythm and tread – skip, tiptoe, stomp, slide – we may discover a cast of characters.[1] We explore simple spatial patterns of walking: towards, away from, joining; adding a stillness; then back into walking, or running; solo, or with others. We pass through spaces that suddenly appear between people, or join up, hand to hand, elbow to elbow, maybe become like a pantomime horse, where front and back end may not agree. As everyone's attention deepens, the sense of a group mind begins to emerge, each person tuning in to the spatial interplay of the whole. In leading such a group, we are not directing the movement, as in a traditional technique class, but offering frameworks that encourage a co-creative process, where each person's initiative contributes to the whole.

Chris: 'Pedestrian Movement', including walking and other everyday actions, is what made this work accessible to me as a non-dancer, when I first came across it in the mid-1970s. I love the playfulness that invariably emerges in this process of walking in a group, and the way it tunes us in to what is going on, both inside and out. As attentiveness in the group builds and people begin to see the possibilities of interaction, it is marvellous to experience the build-up of energy and the changing patterns that result in this most ordinary of all activities.

I often find a comparison between walking and drawing helpful. If you just scribble on a bit of paper for a while, then that can free you up. In this case, the space of the paper in drawing is equivalent to the space of the room in walking. As with the walking, your attention gradually expands from the individual marks you are making to take in the whole. Sometimes I like to do this kind of drawing with a partner on a single piece of paper – each alternately adding a mark, line, shape, etc., responding to the other, as in a conversation.

Miranda: Yes, our various approaches to this work always seek to dissolve habits and generalities – in our posture, our gestures, our movement and our thinking. Scribbling and walking are both very good ways of just lightly shaking things up.

Chris: You often introduce walking by talking about the anatomy of the feet.

Miranda: Yes, in all our work, I like to introduce anatomy wherever it's relevant. Drawing attention to the detail of the foot, or any part of the body, refines our awareness so that we sense and see and create with more clarity around what we are doing.

For me, developing an understanding of the body is key to everything else. It strengthens a person's self-awareness and therefore their sense of choice and possibility. It also awakens one's sense of curiosity and wonder at how amazing the body in fact is. Becoming more conscious of the body in all its variety and subtlety vastly extends one's movement palette. The structure of the foot itself is amazing. All our weight meets the ground through 26 small bones in each foot. The articulateness and sensitivity of the feet and their capacity to read and receive from the ground can be understood as a metaphor for the whole body – for how we meet and engage with everything around us.

On skill and training

Miranda: Improvisation was once seen as sloppy, a lazy form of dancing, in contrast to what was regarded as the rigours of traditional technique. While there is no set pedagogy for improvised movement, it does involve particular skills. These are primarily skills of attention – learning to listen to the body and its surroundings. For most people, this is an acquired skill, not a given. In offering a training, we are seeking to awaken and stimulate a person's innate bodily intelligence and imagination, as distinct from any set style, or method. Movement, from this perspective, is deeply personal – it reflects our individual lives.[2] For me, training the mind in the body is the basis of all our work.

Chris: The question of technique can often be a thorny one in relation to improvised movement. An acquired technique, or skill, in any field, is generally understood as the ability to match action to intention, whether this is learning to perform a sequence of dance steps, or learning to hit a tennis ball over the net and land it on a given spot. But what if the sequence is reversed and intention emerges out of action, as is the case with improvising? This complicates and challenges our common idea of what technique and skill are about.[3]

Miranda: In refining awareness, we free ourselves from habit, both postural and perceptual, thereby strengthening our capacity to open a door into a wider landscape of self and world. Training in this respect often includes a process of unlearning. For me, I had to undo much of my traditional training in ballet and Graham technique in order to become sensitive to the numinous, metamorphic world of my own body. A key part of improvising is cultivating an openness to the unexpected, the element of surprise. We thought we were exploring one thing, then we find ourselves in an opposite, having let go of the first intention. Surprises and accidents are vital disruptors of habit; they rebalance us when we get too heavy and serious. I love the anarchic nature of what can happen. We are always seeking a more varied, richer palette of energies and qualities.

Exercise 3a: breathing with a partner's touch

Learning to listen to and move from the breath is a key to all this work. How we breathe, or fail to breathe, along with developing an awareness of gravity, is fundamental to our sense of being present. Tuning to the breath brings mind and body more fully into alignment and deepens our sense of pace and rhythm.

* * *

Chris: This exercise, like much of our other work, is done with a partner. To start, one person lies face down on the floor, bringing their attention to their own breathing.[4] Their partner helps to focus this attention to the breath, first by simply resting a 'listening' hand on the back of the person lying down. This hand is like an ear, tuning in to the fluctuating tides of the breath. After a little while, the attention of both partners begins to deepen. The one offering hands-on begins to add pressure to the exhalation, as if expelling the breath – washing it through and out of the body, much as a wave might rise up a beach and then empty away back into the sea.

In your book about dance and health, you say, 'how effectively we meet and connect creatively with another is determined in large part by how we are in ourselves and the relational field we create through our presence' (Tufnell, 2017: 106). The quality and spaciousness of one's own presence and attention profoundly affect what can happen to one's partner. The person who is offering hands-on in this exercise needs to hold dual attention, aware of their own body while listening to the other. Without that, our hands can pressure or crowd another person's awareness.

Miranda: A capacity to listen, not just with the ears but also with the whole body, to be in relationship, co-creative and receptive towards another person, to be open and available in how we meet and respond, with all our wits, our intuition and imagination. That's one of the things I feel this work can offer to the world at large.

* * *

Given present anxieties about touch in institutional settings and the risks of abuse, the use of touch as part of any movement practice requires particular consideration. Our own belief is that we need to educate our sense of touch rather than apply taboos or prohibitions to it. An activity such as the above, which depends so much on reciprocity, seems an ideal circumstance in which to explore this. Certainly, the power and value of touch is huge in focusing and freeing the body. The work would be much diminished without it.

Exercise 3b: moving from the breath

Chris: In the second part of this exercise, the person who has been lying on the floor gradually finds their way into movement, sourcing this in the rhythms and energies of the breath. As this person begins to move, their partner continues to offer touch in support of the moving, sensing what is needed from moment to moment. As in a conversation, they lightly offer suggestion, support or resistance, bringing attention through touch to neglected parts of the body.[5] After a while, when they feel ready, the mover asks their partner to withdraw while they continue to move on their own, still following the breath. The whole process happens bit-by-bit, starting from the mover on the floor as described in Exercise 3a. The mover may at any point choose to work with eyes open, or closed.

Miranda: The initial moment of transition into movement is a delicate one. The shift from passive to active should not be forced. Above all, the supporting partner is listening, inviting and responding. It's a mutual relationship, just nudging things forwards until the mover is really 'singing the breath' with their movement.

Beyond this particular exercise, we often use touch to support one another in movement, especially as a way of getting going. The quiet hand of another person swiftly focuses and refines our awareness, reflecting us back to ourselves and making visible the subtle, ever-present currents of movement and response in the body. The sensitivity of the hand, and through it our capacity to read the nuances of another's body, is always extraordinary.

I love the Zulu term, 'Ubuntu', which means 'I am, because we are'. In our own work, I see each person's creative process strengthened through the partnering presence of another. This is a partner who travels with us as we create. It's a companion, who listens and also responds creatively, amplifying whatever we do. In moving, a partner's undivided attention offers a containing space that adds concentration to what is happening and enables the mover to explore more widely and deeply.

Chris: For me, moving, or watching somebody move with breath and touch, is invariably absorbing. It's something about the depth of focus that it brings about in the body and the unselfconscious movement that results, which makes it so personal and particular. Attending to the breath gives something to occupy the mind, which then frees the body to move with its own intelligence. The variety and particularity of the movement that results and the unpredictable timing of it is very satisfying to witness. As movers, we don't need to 'perform' flow, or expressiveness, or whatever stereotypes of freedom we may carry in our heads. We just need to attend quietly to what's happening in the body and around and follow the thread wherever that may lead.

* * *

Movement is a silent language. In waking up the body through movement, we wake up to previously unrecognised landscapes within us – landscapes that reflect all the parts of our lives. Images, memories and stories surface that, if we give them form, can refresh our everyday perceptions – our sense of ourselves and our lives.

On improvising and getting lost

Chris: To improvise is to be an explorer, always curious to know what you may find. In improvising, you are deliberately choosing not to know what's coming next. You follow a certain thread, allowing yourself to be drawn along without knowing where it's going to lead. In Rebecca Solnit's book, *A Field Guide to Getting Lost*, she says: 'Leave the door open for the unknown, the door into the dark, that's where the most important things come from, where you yourself come from and where you will go' (Solnit, 2005: 4). In this work, getting lost is not for its own sake. It's a way of drawing upon the hidden world in all of us that lies just beneath the surface. As we loosen the grip of the controlling purposive mind, we discover what is waiting to be expressed through us. This is why we invite an element of surprise into our working, deliberately subverting our own habits and expectations. All the time, we seek to enliven and refresh our working and open ourselves to unforeseen possibilities.

Of course, there are different forms and degrees of getting lost and not all are productive. Sometimes our everyday preoccupations, the ongoing flood of thought or feeling, drown out our ability to attend to the present moment. In consequence, we feel lost and unable to begin. This is where simply returning to breath, or weight, or receiving the touch of a partner, may help us to focus and to find our way in to the work. At other times, even in the middle of working, our attention glazes over and becomes too generalised. The whole working process may begin to feel empty and pointless. In such moments, slowing down and letting our attention be drawn to particular details of body, or surroundings, is invariably a way of finding a new thread and restoring a sense of engagement.

Exercise 4: finding words

Chris: After moving, we often write.[6] When working with a partner, one person has just moved and the other has been watching. Now both write in response. Writing lends words and imagery to the silence of our movement. Here, as in so much of what we do, the role of a partner as witness supports, extends and amplifies whatever we create.

Miranda: In writing, we stay on the edge of the unknown, letting the words and images appear in the same way as we have been moving. Writing in this way captures the feel of our moving without deliberately trying to do so. These are words that we discover – feeling words, embodied words and images that rise up of their own volition in the wake of moving and surprise even ourselves with what they have to tell, since they arrive spontaneously and speak in stories or metaphors, rather than in literal language. As in any improvisation, we don't know what we want to say, or express. The very act of writing tells us this. It speaks to us indirectly and in depth, giving form to our silent inner worlds and feelings.

Chris: The purpose of this writing is not to record, or describe what we have just seen, or done. What we are looking for here is a more open response. That's why, in leading a group, I often say, write a loose kind of story, or some story fragments – let characters, places, events emerge and trust that they will turn out to be relevant. But you have to take the risk of diving in, then seeing what comes. This kind of writing has been called 'discovery writing'. It's writing as a way of finding things out. It's rather different to the convention of using words to express something already in one's mind. In this exercise, we write with attention to the words themselves, letting images arise in the writing of their own accord. This is not what is sometimes referred to as 'automatic writing' – a random outpouring of words. It is not incoherent, any more than improvised movement is incoherent. We need to trust that some kind of sense will emerge, even if it's oblique and metaphoric. But maybe we have to take the risk of losing meaning and coherence in order to find another kind of sense.

When we read the pieces of writing back to a partner and ponder each one in turn, we almost invariably find that we've taken in a lot more from the moving than we realised. If we attend to the images and associations, the feel of the writing, rather than its literal sense, it often seems that, in some indirect way, we've noticed not just the dance itself but also what was shaping the dance from within the person moving.

* * *

Finding words for where we have been is another step in learning to see and in being more fully present. In these times when we are often deluged by words and images, finding our own words, as with finding our own movement, can be life affirming.

Why do this work?

Chris: Over the years, we have sought to find ways of working that bring a sense of personal meaning to this work. But the concept of self (or person) that is dominant in our culture somewhat undermines this personal approach. In Western culture, we sometimes assume a rather narrow and static idea of 'self' that exists in isolation from other selves and other things. In contrast, the self which emerges in this work is always found in relationship – to others; to surroundings; to the course of events; to what we are physically making or creating; to all that we know and feel. It's a self that is best understood obliquely, through metaphor and image, embodied yet fluid in its boundaries, always in touch with the world beyond our edges, beyond what we choose to call ourselves.

* * *

In our second book, we named and shaped an area of exploration we called 'body and imagination' (Tufnell and Crickmay, 2004). It is based in improvisation and in a grounded sense of the body. It involves curiosity and sensitivity, not just towards the body itself but also through the body to the objects, places and materials of our surrounding worlds.

Chris: Generally, in our practice, we are interested in states of awareness and strategies for working that carry us beyond the everyday and the prosaic. We are looking to sense and explore hidden worlds that exist in the body and in our surroundings. Above all, the work is about unearthing that part in ourselves that feels personal, particular and alive.

Miranda: I've always felt that improvisation in movement has a far wider relevance than simply within the field of dance itself. An experiential knowledge of the body, so much part of this approach, contributes to our sense of autonomy, strengthening our ability to manage our lives. Conversely, a lack of body awareness disempowers us, blinding us to a vital aspect of who we are and how we live. In my professional work as a movement teacher and health practitioner, I have always been deeply touched to witness how awakening imagination through movement, writing and making brings out a person's wit and humour and strengthens their ability to connect more fully to others and to their environment. It helps a person to find and follow what really matters to them in their lives. Art making of any kind offers a space where we can step aside from the inarticulate jumble of thoughts and feelings, the nebulous flux of moods that bedevil us all. Movement and related work in the arts, sourced from the body, quietens the chattering mind and brings us into a fuller more connected state of being.

Notes

1 Charlie Chaplin found his character of the tramp through a large pair of shoes and a particular walk.
2 Speaking in Lisbon in 2019, Steve Paxton noted that dance, as he and others viewed it from the 1960s onwards, became personal. From that period on, there would not only be technique, but it would also be to do with people developing their own way of dancing (Paxton, 2020).
3 In our first book, *Body Space Image* (Tufnell and Crickmay, 1990), we outlined what we saw as some of the fundamentals of improvisation and what it requires in terms of skill and approach.
4 In bringing our attention to the breath, it can happen that we inadvertently begin trying to control our breathing. To counter this tendency, it is often helpful to pay particular attention to the way the length and depth of each breath naturally varies. The ability to notice and allow rather than control is one of the basic precepts of improvising.
5 Also, when in a group situation, they make sure the mover is safe from collision and not endangering other movers in the room, especially if some are moving with eyes closed.
6 Or, instead of writing at this point, we may choose to draw, paint or make things with materials in response to the moving.

References

Paxton, S. (2020) 'So here you are, against all obstacles...', a recorded talk at Culturgest, Lisbon, 2019. *CQ Unbound.*

Solnit, R. (2005) *A Field Guide to Getting Lost.* Edinburgh: Canongate.

Tufnell, M. (2017) *When I Open My Eyes: Dance Health and Imagination.* London: Dance Books. Re-published 2023 Axminster UK: Triarchy Press.

Tufnell, M. and Crickmay, C. (1990) *Body Space Image: Notes on Improvisation and Performance.* London: Dance Books. Re-published 2023 Axminster UK: Triarchy Press.

Tufnell, M. and Crickmay, C. (2004) *A Widening Field: Journeys in Body and Imagination.* London: Dance Books. Re-published 2023 Axminster UK: Triarchy Press.

Part IV

Manifestos

Introduction

The final part of this book is a collection of manifestos written by dance artists, researchers and teachers. Manifestos have long been recognised as a mode of expression involving statements of intention, belief or motive from an individual or collective. Traditionally politically, socially or artistically driven, manifestos enable people to communicate their views in a way that has not always easily fit within academic or mainstream publication channels, often being linked to activism or a call for change. The manifestos in this part vary from short collections of artistic statements to longer prose exploring reasons for enacting change in the delivery of dance technique. These contributions work to further the chapters and conversations that have gone before. Whether read singularly or as a collective with the rest of the book, the aim is for these manifestos to encourage ideas, collaboration and action in the development of dance technique in Britain (and beyond). As Sonia Rafferty, Erica Stanton and David Waring express in their contribution, 'Manifestos are mission statements; they are not empty words' (286).

In his manifesto 'As technique', Theo Clinkard explores the notion of 'value' through a collection of statements considering what does (or could) constitute technique. First written in response to approaches to technique delivery that placed value elsewhere, Clinkard reconsiders what might be central to our thinking of what technique could be and encourages us to embed these ideas in the 'doing' of moving.

Next, Eline Kieft explores connection among the body, heart, mind and spirit in her manifesto 'The Way of the Wild Soul: A Map for Embodied and Nature-Based Spirituality'. Outlining her '13 ingredients to explore embodied and nature-based spirituality', Kieft offers a series of questions and guiding techniques to help readers engage with the self as an act of reconnection.

Reflecting many of the ideas explored in her earlier chapter, Erica Stanton collaborated with Sonia Rafferty and David Waring to create 'Simply for the Doing: a manifesto for the work of a dance class'. In this manifesto, the trio present their shared values for teaching dance technique, reflecting on the

DOI: 10.4324/9781003111146-26

ideas that motivate and sustain them, emphasising the studio as a 'place of growth' through dance technique and movement exploration.

The next manifesto, 'Breaking the mould: a manifesto for a future-facing and accessible dance course', explores curriculum design that locates access and social justice, student well-being, and professional outcomes as central tenants. Authors Baptiste Bourgougnon and Lise Uytterhoeven share recent changes that have been made at London Contemporary Dance School as a way of reflecting on the changing landscape of dance higher education, and how this might be responded to.

Kate Marsh's 'Manifesto for Inclusion' draws on lived experience as a disabled artist and career working with disabled dancers to present a series of statements offering questions, actions and prompts to encourage more inclusive dance technique teaching. The opening contextualisation of the manifesto grapples with language for, history of and representation in inclusive dance as a useful framing for the manifesto itself.

In 'The value of 'South Asian' dance technique to 'contemporary' dance training', Magdalen Tamsin Gorringe opens with a series of exercises for the reader to engage with before exploring what South Asian dance styles can offer to Euro-American contemporary dance settings. From the understanding that South Asian styles are also contemporary, Gorringe, with Shivaangee Agrawal and Jane Chan, encourages the creative potential of 'unsettledness' as expansion of our own vantage points.

Exploring similar ideas around the concept of 'contemporary' in dance, 'Funmi Adewole examines artistic praxis and citizenship in 'Towards Decoloniality and Artistic Citizenship: a manifesto'. Emphasising the importance of context to embodied understanding of Dance of the African Diaspora (DAD), Adewole considers authenticity and integrity in the training, performance and practice of DAD for students.

In 'The world needs more dancers', Jorge Crecis advocates for a formalised, structured approach to training consciousness within the technique class. After exploring the meaning of consciousness, Crecis sets out a series of reasons why consciousness should be trained and reflects on the role of the teacher in facilitating this to support dancers of the future.

The final manifesto is 'A chorus of dancing voices', curated by Katye Coe in collaboration with Temitope Ajose-Cutting, Ay De La Fe, Elena Rose Light, Catherine Long, Patricia Okenwa, Amy Voris and Natifah White. Punctuated by questions to or tasks for the reader, this collection of poem-like responses explores personal experiences of dancing, reflecting ideas such as intention, ownership, survival, ambiguity and transcendence.

4.1 'As technique'

Theo Clinkard

Theo Clinkard's practice spans choreography, design, performing, movement direction, mentoring and teaching. Following 18 years working as a dancer, he launched his company in 2012. Choreographic commissions include Tanztheater Wuppertal Pina Bausch, Danza Contemporanea de Cuba and Candoco. He leads workshops internationally, including engagements in Chile, Australia, New Zealand, United States, Slovenia, France, Cuba, Finland and Sweden. Theo is an Associate Artist at Brighton Dome, The Hall for Cornwall and an Honorary Fellow at Plymouth University.

DOI: 10.4324/9781003111146-27

'As technique'

listening as technique,
curiosity as technique,
offering ideas as technique,
elastic mindedness as technique,
rest as technique,
initiating conversation as technique,
getting comfortable with the mess as technique,
speaking your truth as technique,
waiting as technique,
waiting a little longer as technique,
diving in courageously as technique,
establishing boundaries as technique,
interdependence as technique,
volunteering as technique,
care as technique,
self-care as technique,
good humour as technique,
keeping perspective as technique,
offering perspective as technique,
critical thinking as technique,
generous thinking as technique,
activism as technique,
calling out bullshit as technique,
humility as technique,
taking responsibility as technique,
sharing responsibility as technique,
stimulating your imagination as technique,
trusting your intuition as technique,
kindness as technique,
appreciation as technique,
voicing appreciation as technique,
rethinking technique as technique,
knowing when to stop as technique.

List regularly updated

Current iteration 2.3.2021
First iteration 27.11.2016

4.2 The way of the wild soul

A map for embodied and nature-based spirituality

Eline Kieft

Eline Kieft (Ph.D.) is an independent scholar, consultant, and coach, who combines her background as anthropologist, dancer, shamanic practitioner, and change facilitator. Combining these different modalities, she invites movement as a different way of knowing that reconnects us with ourselves and with the world around us. Her experiential pedagogy sprouts from a deeply lived connection with nature and her passion for personal growth and embodied spirituality. https://www.elinekieft.com and info@elinekieft.com

A trail of fluid enquiry

Dance and dance technique have many facets. This brief manifesto is a warm invitation to consider the role of spirituality in dance experience. It includes different levels of awareness in dance education and training to support an all-round, inclusive, and holistic approach to movement and expression. It aims

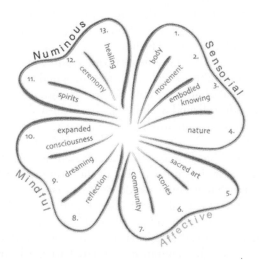

Figure 4.2.1 Thirteen Wild Soul practices. Credit: Eline Kieft

DOI: 10.4324/9781003111146-28

to contribute to the physical, emotional, and mental health and well-being of the dance student and dancer.

In this manifesto, I offer a combination of techniques that draw on the healing power of expressive movement, archetypal wisdom, and nature-based spirituality. These include conscious dance, qi gong, and shamanic practice. My approach provides a safe, authentic, and creative invitation to return to self and soul, always in relation to the tangible and intangible aspects of our surroundings. It includes various activities, practices, and techniques that help us to thrive in life.

Reconnecting with what is meaningful and inspiring helps us face life's challenges in an empowered way and take action that we believe in and dare to stand for. 'The Way of the Wild Soul' offers an experiential pedagogy that fuels positive motivation and creates room for the soul.

The image of the four-leaf clover serves as a map of the landscape. Its curving lines reflect a meandering among body, heart, mind, and spirit, each represented by one of the leaves. The individual soul at the centre is the guide of the journey, always in direct relationship with the world around us. The notion of a trail invites an inward journey, in which we hone skills of multi-layered literacy through all aspects of our being and with an awareness of personal growth and healing as an ongoing process. Simultaneously, exploring the various dimensions also invites an outward journey, through being in community with others, with nature and with the numinous. The exploration draws on deep knowing within our physical structure, fluidity of emotions, and cognitive and intuitive functions to re-embody all of who we are.

Leaf 1 represents the sensorial domain and includes Body, Movement, Nature, and Embodied Knowing as specific further ingredients. Leaf 2 engages affect and the heart, offering a space for Sacred Art, Stories, and Community. Leaf 3 reflects the area of mind, combining Reflection, Dreaming, and Expanded Consciousness. Leaf 4 symbolises spirit and the numinous and is home to Ceremony, Spirits, and Healing.

These four Leaves and 13 Ingredients propose gateways to deepen existing practice and enter the unknown when we feel intrigued to try something new. This supports a sense of strength and fluency in different perspectives that contributes to our health and well-being, decision-making strategies, self-confidence, inner peace, contentment and happiness, and general empowerment and inspiration.

The principles of Ethical Agility (EA) are present in The Way of the Wild Soul's philosophy. Relationship is visible in the Community Ingredient, and the general premise that nothing we do exists in isolation. Other EA principles are woven into the Trail's groundwork and underlying assumptions. Responsibility compares with diligently walking (or dancing!) our talk, putting our thoughts, words, and intentions in action so that these become aligned and strengthened. Reputation is related to the heart, feelings and emotions, and the skill to navigate them, while Results refers to intuitive faculties, which would be part of the fourth clover leaf.

13 Ingredients

Below are practical reflections and invitations related to each ingredient, grouped together under the four Leaves of Body, Heart, Mind, and Spirit. Each of these ingredients offers strong medicine and can provide a rich life-time practice. The diversity, however, provides a responsiveness to different needs as well as energy levels that we experience at various times in our day, year, and lives.

Inquiries Leaf 1: body and the sensorial

1 **Body:** How well do you know and nurture your body so that you can have optimal understanding, harmony, and health in your dance practice? What does your body need in terms of nourishment, activity, and relaxation? Also, how do you take care of your body when you are tired, injured or otherwise unwell? Put your body in 'the driver's seat'.

2 **Movement:** Tune into the movement that is already there, emerging from your breathing, heartbeat, and blood circulation. Listening deep within and connect to what is present and alive for you in this moment. Let that inform your movements. Let go of any performance anxiety or preconceived ideas of what movement is supposed to look like. If your heart is heavy with grief, how does grief move (through) your body? If you are full of zest and sparkles, let this flow into your limbs and out into the space. If you have very little energy, what is the most nurturing movement you can find, perhaps lying down on a soft blanket and simply caressing your body? Move in a way that feels authentic to you in this very moment.

3 **Embodied Knowing:** How can dance help you move fluidly between different places in consciousness and sensitise your body to access 'other' knowledge? Let your dancing body become an instrument to receive information and insights on any topic you would like to focus on. What do you learn from truly inhabiting your body?

4 **Nature:** Can dancing in nature add to your practice? What happens when you mirror, or even *become,* the movements of nature? How does it feel to move *like*, *with*, or *as* a river or a tree? Do different landscapes influence your movement? Can you reciprocate what you receive from your surroundings, giving the quality of your presence back through movement?

Inquiries Leaf 2: heart and the affective

1 **Sacred Art:** When you engage with an art project, a painting, a poem, can you approach the activity as a dance? Can your movements (however minute) be a dance? Making art can also help reflect on an experience you may have had while dancing. Distil it in a painting or a collage as this can help to further integrate the learning.

2 **Stories:** Can you consciously apply story-telling techniques while you are dancing? For example, what is the theme of your dance? What are you trying to express? Does it have a beginning, a middle, and an end? Can you dance a timeline of a specific experience or explore the archetypes of a story through movement? How does it feel to dance in the shoes of the Adversary? The Ally? The Stranger? The Lover? The Wise One? The Hunter or the Prey? What does this add to your understanding?

3 **Community:** Dance with awareness of the circles and communities you are connected to. Which of them inform, support, or perhaps hinder your dance? This can also include the non-human communities of animals, eco-systems, as well as the community of cells and organs within your own body. What would you like to express to your communities, through your dance?

Inquiries Leaf 3: mind and mindful

1 **Reflection:** Can you dance with a specific event or experience, to view it from different sides, dance around it, move away from and come closer to it? Can you perhaps even step into it and see how it informs your movements and affects you? Can you let your dance be like light, reflecting from your experience, to see what you see?

2 **Dreaming:** Can you dance your dreams, both your literal night-dreams and your life-dreams? Can you bridge dreaming and waking reality on the dance floor? Can you bring a powerful healing dream onto the dance floor, to dance it even deeper into your awareness? Can you reach out to the dream world on your left, and to the world of manifestation on your right, and let your dance be the place where you embody both? Does this help you to 'live' your dream?

3 **Expanded Consciousness:** In your dance, can you let your awareness expand and contract? This is like a muscle you can train, to zoom into specific fields of attention. Play with awareness close by and far off. Notice the sensations inside your body, and just around your body (like your skin meeting the air). Notice what or who is in the space with you, and what is beyond that space, outside the building, the park, the city. From your body as anchor, tune into the 'essence' of the phenomena you notice.

Inquiries Leaf 4: spirit and the numinous

1 **Spirits:** With that sense of expanded consciousness, you can greet the essence, or spirit of anything around you. If you have a cat, dog, plant, (bonsai) tree, favourite natural place, then can you greet and dance with its essence? Begin by introducing yourself through movement and explore if they are willing to be your dance partner. Pay attention to subtle clues in your body, and always respect the answer. When the answer is positive,

you can ask this being to teach you their dance, move around, play with different postures, heights, density of movement, etc. Respectfully withdraw if you feel a negative response to your question – this simply might not be the right time.

2 **Ceremony:** Can you make your dance a ceremonial experience in which you consciously connect to the sacred, the source, or the mystery (use whatever name you connect with most)? Do something such as lighting a candle to acknowledge this as a special activity. Can you touch the air, the earth, and your body with reverence? How does that change your experience? Then dance your questions, concerns, longings, gratitude, or prayer for connection, help, and guidance and surrender to what arises. Another enquiry might be to make ordinary tasks like washing the dishes into a ceremonial dance, honouring the water, the soap, the fact that you had food on your plate, so that you have dishes to wash.

3 **Healing:** Knowing that you are always already on a path of integration, healing, and transformation, can you let your dance be an enquiry of balance in your system? How are your left and right sides balanced? Your front and your back? Your lower and upper body? But also, do you observe places where energy is lost, stagnant, or disrupted? Is the three-dimensional energy field around your body intact and vibrant? You can address anything you find through your dance, by soothing, calming, releasing, balancing, calling back, and mending whatever you find through your movements.

Further reading and exploration

Kieft, E. (2018) 'Clearing the Way towards Soulful Scholarship', in Ellis, S., Blades, H. and Waelde, C. (eds.) *A World of Muscle, Bone & Organs: Research and Scholarship in Dance.* Coventry: C-DaRE Coventry University, pp. 456–479.

Kieft, E. (2020) 'East Wind: Dancing the Story of My Ectopic Pregnancy', Online Performance, Available at: https://www.youtube.com/watch?v=10ZOsDjYFJ0

Kieft, E. (2021) 'Calibrating the Body: Embodied Research Strategies for Attuning to Subtle Information', in Wright, J. (ed.) *Subtle Agroecologies: Farming with the Hidden Half of Nature.* Boca Raton, FL: Routledge, CRC Press, Taylor & Francis Group, pp. 191–202.

Kieft, E. (2022) *Dancing in the Muddy Temple: A Moving Spirituality of Land and Body.* Body and Religion. Lanham, MD: Lexington Books.

Kieft, E., Spatz, B. and Weig, D. (2019) *A Somatics Toolkit for Ethnographers.* Coventry: Coventry University, Available at: http://somaticstoolkit.coventry.ac.uk

4.3 Simply for the doing

A manifesto for the work of a dance class

Sonia Rafferty, Erica Stanton and David Waring

Sonia Rafferty is senior lecturer and programme leader for BSc Dance Science at Trinity Laban and a freelance teacher, performer, choreographer, director, researcher and author. She has delivered professional/master classes for over 35 years, with a technical teaching philosophy strongly influenced by Limón principles and incorporating applied dance science knowledge. Sonia is a consultant in healthy dance practice, co-founder of Safe in Dance International (SiDI) and co-author of 'Safe Dance Practice: An Applied Dance Science Perspective'.

Erica Stanton is a dance teacher and choreographer. She co-founded the collaborative dance company *Mothers of Invention* with Marion Gough and, following Marion's legacy, has supported the professional development of dance teachers for over three decades. Erica specialises in Limón technique which she has taught in the UK, the USA and New Zealand. Her work in curriculum development includes the first MFA Choreography programme in the UK which is based at the University of Roehampton.

David Waring is an independent dance artist and formerly artistic director of Transitions Dance Company and co-programme leader of MA/MFA Dance Performance programme at Trinity Laban (2002–2021). He has taught professional technique classes nationally and internationally since 1997 and performed his hustler series throughout the UK since 2006. David is author of Heroes of the Stage: Connecting with the Joy of Performing (Mindful Heroes – Stories of Journeys that Changed Lives, 2019, Aberdeen, Scotland: Inspired By Learning).

DOI: 10.4324/9781003111146-29

Sonia Rafferty, David Waring and Erica Stanton have been bringing their work together in the studio, at conferences and in collaboration with other teachers in 'studio retreats' for the past five years as the *Simply for the Doing* collective. Our project interrogates the narratives, currents, underscores and values which sustain our intangible heritage of teaching dance technique and ponders on questions, such as what is a dance technique class for? What does movement do and how does it support complex and nuanced embodied meaning? Who does practice belong to?

We work on these and other questions through active participation in dancing; positioning the dance technique class as a place for growth where the teacher participates in and amongst a world of active materials (Ingold 2013) and looks with the work of a dance class rather than at it. This third-person perspective is not in the interest of an objective view but instead locates the work as a shared interest: *we* are doing *this*. Our attention moves to allow the work to 'have an opinion' and so disrupt the obvious binaries between teacher and student, dancer and pedestrian, or expert and novice. We foster a community of engagement with 'the work' – the labour of dance in relation to the dancer who is doing the dancing.

Following our workshop presentation at *Our Dance Democracy: Dance, Performance, Culture and Civic Democracy* at Liverpool Hope University in November 2018, our manifesto emerged as follows:

This is a place for you to dance you.

This class is an adventure into our own being.

We will understand dance as a site of embodied knowing and curb our desire to demonstrate competence.

We will appreciate the value of not always knowing what we are doing.

We will encourage trialogue among teacher, learner and the work.

We will make playful encounters with phrases and their problems.

Once you see these six motives in writing, very quickly you grasp that there is nothing new here; these intentions consort with the dead, sit on the shoulders of giants, and borrow and steal from peers. This manifesto is indeed a palimpsest and underneath we find –

This is a place for you to dance you.

Who are you? If you're you, don't try to dance like him or her. Dance like yourself.

(Lester Horton 1953)

This class is an adventure into our own being.

> You are about to enter an adventure into your own being.
>
> (Andre Bernard 2006)

We will understand dance as a site of embodied knowing and curb our desire to demonstrate competence.

> Approach your dancing with a creature mind.
>
> (Rosemary Lee 2018)

We will appreciate the value of not always knowing what we are doing.

> The unknown becomes a friend, absurdity is worn well and the tyranny of trying to be interesting is overcome
>
> (Andrew de Lotbinière Harwood 2014)

We will encourage trialogue among teacher, learner and the work.

> Learning as a process of knowledge creation which concentrates on mediated processes Where common objects of activity are developed collaboratively.
>
> (Sami Paavola and Kai Hakkarainen 2006)

We will make playful encounters with phrases and their problems.

> Phrases can be patriarchal so let's make them fun.
>
> (Miguel Gutierrez 2014)

Manifestos are mission statements; they are not empty words. We not only use them as signals and signposts for future development, but we also trace the runes of past examples with all their inherent problems of canonicity. In the interest of developing as better people, better teachers and better dancers, 'what do the dead people want from us?' (Otake 2009) and how do we stay alert to the participatory dialogue (Ingold 2011) of doing, taking and sharing dance classes?

References

Bernard, A., Steinmuller, W. and Stricker, U. (2006) *Ideokinesis. A Creative Approach to Movement and Alignment.* Berkeley, CA: North Atlantic Books.

De Lotbinière Harwood, A. (2014) *Awkwardness, Failure and Redemption: Adventures in Contact Improvisation.* Available at: https://www.impulstanz.com/en/archive/2014/workshops/id2548/

Gutierrez, M. (2014) *What Is This Class. Old School Technique Class with New School Questions.* Available at: https://www.impulstanz.com/en/archive/2014/workshops/id2539/

Horton, L. (1953) *Technique. Expression. Life.* Available at: http://lesterhorton website.wordpress.com

Ingold, T. (2011) *Being Alive. Essays on Movement, Knowledge and Description.* London: Routledge.

Ingold, T. (2013) *Making. Anthropology, Archaeology, Art and Architecture.* London: Routledge.

Lee, R. (2018) Simply for the Doing Workshop at *Our Dance Democracy: Dance, Performance, Culture and Civic Democracy.* Liverpool Hope University. November 2018.

Otake, E. (2009) Like a River. Time Is Naked. Available at: http://ww.eikoandkoma.org/index.php?p=ek&id=1989

Paavola, S. and Hakkarainen, K. (2006) An Emergent Epistemological Approach to Learning, *Science & Education 14*: pp. 535–557.

4.4 Breaking the mould

A manifesto for a future-facing, accessible dance course

Baptiste Bourgougnon and Lise Uytterhoeven

Baptiste Bourgougnon graduated from the National Conservatoire in Paris. During the first 15 years of his career, Baptiste focused on performing and worked as a dancer with numerous choreographers internationally. Since 2012, Baptiste has developed his pedagogic work and has been teaching floor-work, release technique and improvisation to dance companies and schools around the world. In 2019, Baptiste became the Director of Undergraduate Courses and International Development at the London Contemporary Dance School (LCDS) at The Place.

Lise Uytterhoeven is Director of Dance Studies at The Place. She is the author of Sidi Larbi Cherkaoui: Dramaturgy and Engaged Spectatorship (2019) and co-author of What Moves You? Shaping your dissertation in dance (2017). She has published in Contemporary Theatre Review, Research in Dance Education, The Bloomsbury Companion to Dance Studies and The Ethics of Art. Lise is co-chair of the Society for Dance Research and part of the Associate Board of Dance Research.

Problematising conservatoire training

Over the last 40 years, dance education and training in the UK have increasingly been situated within higher education. LCDS began to offer the first university-validated professional dance course in Europe in 1982. Since then, course design has benefitted from wider evidence-based pedagogic frameworks,[1] especially in the last 20 years. The professionalisation of dance educators as higher education teaching professionals, through formal learning and teaching qualifications and through engagement with the UK Professional Standards Framework for higher education, has increased understanding of how students learn. Furthermore, universities' scrutiny and approval processes are also helpful in generating critical dialogue with peers within and outside the subject, rationalising and justifying course design decisions.

However, general perceptions of what constitutes conservatoire dance training seem to have stagnated within students', applicants', teachers' and other stakeholders' perceptions. Conservatoire dance training traditionally

DOI: 10.4324/9781003111146-30

means high contact hours (around 30 taught hours or more per week) and a focus on developing technique primarily through daily practice in traditional codified dance forms, –predominantly ballet. Conservatoire training becomes an unchallenged shorthand for accessing coveted, prestigious performing jobs after graduation, including in famous dance companies or on the West End stage. New 'conservatoires' continuously emerge, promising excellence achieved through hard work and a smooth transition into industry.

Despite the pedagogical advancements made over the past decades, a tension is still felt within dance institutions between the need for genuine constructive alignment of learning outcomes, learning activities and assessments on the one hand, and dogmatic approaches to conservatoire training on the other (Biggs, 2003). At LCDS, the faculty decided to confront these issues head-on during our latest course redesign that was led by Lise Uytterhoeven, the Director of Dance Studies, and Baptiste Bourgougnon, the Director of Undergraduate Courses and International Development. Integrated in this exercise were Lise's background in dance learning and teaching leadership and her engagement with decolonial thought through research, combined with Baptiste's extensive industry knowledge stemming from his international, professional dance career.

LCDS is a key part of The Place, the creative powerhouse for dance involved in the entire lifecycle of dance – from education and training to the creative process that leads to new ideas and conception of new work, through to its creation, production and performance. Our vision is a world with more dance. For over 50 years, The Place and LCDS have paved the way within the dance industry, with innovation, internationalism and experimentation woven at the heart of the institution.[2] Mining our past as a pioneering arts school, the organisation is looking to challenge the notion of what 'contemporary' means.

In 2020, LCDS started a new validation partnership with University of the Arts London (UAL), sharing a strong focus on facilitating students' independent exploration of creativity. In preparation for this, the team spent two years listening to students, artists, audiences and industry leaders, to understand the conditions needed for change and to take on board what they felt was necessary to succeed within the industry and within society. Galvanised by the recent calls for decolonising the curriculum and anti-racism, the school embedded a seismic shift in the pedagogical model, beyond that of the conservatoire and towards that of the art school, working with UAL's pedagogic frameworks.

In this manifesto, we will share the key drivers that have emerged from and guided us through our recent undergraduate BA (Hons) Contemporary Dance course redesign. The key drivers are access and social justice, student well-being, and professional outcomes. These drivers have manifested themselves across significant paradigm shifts for learning and teaching, assessment and admissions.

Paradigm shift 1: learning and teaching

Key driver 1: access and social justice

As part of our endeavour to decolonise the curriculum, we decentred our focus away from ballet and Euro-American contemporary technique classes as the pinnacles of a hierarchical structure. LCDS has now introduced into the curriculum practices from various cultural backgrounds as they intersect and influence each other in London as an urban centre, including South Asian dance practices such as Kathak, and practices from the African diaspora such as house, vogueing, locking and traditional African dance practices. The students develop an embodied understanding of dance and movement practices and ownership of how they engage with these practices. They also undertake to understand the lineages and historical contexts that contribute to the development of dance practices.

In the process of introducing new-to-us dance practices from the Global South, we realigned the unit content and structure to provide students with an experience of multiple dance cultures and how they intersect with each other in a globalised society. Rather than simply adding these practices to the Euro-American dance forms already studied and hence adding the new subjects into the margin, it was necessary to decentre the hierarchies between these dance forms.

What one studies for the most hours and for the longest duration inevitably is understood by the students as being the most valuable. Therefore, we must make space in the curriculum for practices from the Global South by doing less of something else. In turn, this leads to questions about values and priorities of specific practices or asking what should be at the centre of a contemporary dance training. Our students no longer study ballet every day; rather, ballet is placed on a par with other dance practices. They still encounter ballet, but for limited time periods. Alongside, students develop a wider range of understandings of their body and how it moves through popping, Kathak, hip hop-based floorwork and Flying Low.

The shift in conceiving of the purpose of what is traditionally referred to as 'technique training' is significant. What the students are working towards is no longer the emulation of an aesthetic ideal that is permeated by fixed cultural values of what constitutes excellence in dance, namely the ability to precisely reproduce complex movement patterns. Instead, the focus of the learning activities is themselves as dance artists, as they encounter a range of dance practices and let these influence their understanding of how their body moves, what it can do, and how they can develop their own practice in dialogue with other techniques, traditions and ways of working.

Key driver 2: student well-being

We have implemented findings from our ongoing internal dance science and pedagogical research on periodisation, which aims to optimise students' physical and mental health. Periodisation works with the principle of workload management, with load being defined as intensity multiplied by duration. It is not effective or desirable for a dancer to work at high intensity all the time. Instead, the ebbs and flows of dance training need to be accounted for and designed to prepare dancers for moments of 'peak' performance. This helps create the necessary time to invest in independent study (reflection, research, writing, exploring).

Furthermore, we have embedded learning activities to increase students' knowledge of dance psychology as part of safe dance practice, with the aim of developing students' psychological tools and skills. Students engage indepth with models for reflective practice, as well as insights into motivation and tools for goal setting.

Key driver 3: professional outcomes

Our focus on professional outcomes means preparing students for their survival as independent dance artists, performers and makers within the reality of the cultural landscape they will be a part of and shape. Our undergraduate course outcomes are designed to prepare students for the realities of working as an independent dance artist in a portfolio career, combining different short- or medium-term contracts flexibly across performing, creating, teaching. Stable jobs as dancers in a company are very rare, and so we have stopped promising the students jobs that do not exist. Even in established companies, dancers need a variety of skills to facilitate workshops. The demands on dance artists are varied and increasingly value creativity and playfulness when approaching creative processes, along with a readiness to engage with new approaches and concepts. Providing the required tools to develop an independent artistic vision and creative practice is central to the professional outcomes of our training.

Paradigm shift 2: assessment

As a general note, we have embedded assessment modes that may have previously been atypical for institutions such as ours, so that the assessments were genuinely aligned to the learning outcomes. This meant letting go of traditional ways of assessing. We are using a portfolio-type assessment mode, in which practice is always accompanied by the student's reflective voice. For example, we are using blogs/vlogs, e-portfolios, auto-ethnographic films and self-evaluations.

Key driver 1: access and social justice

In the portfolios and reflective assignments, the student creates the lens through which the assessor is invited to engage with their practice. Further decentring the hierarchies of value that might be seen to exist between dance and cultural practices, the students develop their personal artistic voice within the broader context in which their work emerges. This means that the assessor's cultural values and aesthetic preferences are not simply superimposed onto the student's work and give way to an individual cultural and aesthetic framing through the student's reflective voice.

Key driver 2: student well-being

The shifts in assessment modes ensure that the students are proactively engaged with the assessment process, rather than assessment being something that they undergo passively. The new modes prioritise the students to develop their own individual voice as artists in relation to the learning activities they participate in. We anticipate that this will help to reduce both students' anxiety around assessment and the incidence of injuries, which in the past tended to peak around assessment time.

Key driver 3: professional outcomes

Shifting the focus from aesthetic values to reflective processes, our summative assessment modes are no longer concerned with merely observing students in class or on stage in order to judge how well they can dance. Instead, students submit creative portfolios, combining reflection and research, or blogs/vlogs. The reflective voice is much more important and allows the student to frame their artistic practice without the assessing staff imposing a certain aesthetic lens. The students position themselves as artists in relation to the dance practices and creative processes they encounter within a broader artistic, intellectual and socio-cultural context.

Paradigm shift 3: admissions

Key driver 1: access and social justice

We believe that excellence without access is exclusion. LCDS works proactively to achieve clear targets for the recruitment of students from groups that are underrepresented within our school, namely people of the global majority, those from low participation areas in higher education or first-generation students, and those from socio-economically disadvantaged backgrounds. We have made changes to the admissions process not only designed to be more genuinely aligned to the new course outcomes but also deliberately designed to increase access through contextualised admissions.

The admissions activities attempt to cut through essentialised notions of 'talent', which may be more accurately conceived of as prior access to training, cultural capital and taste. By conceiving of the admissions activity as a 'workshop' rather than an 'audition', we endeavour to make the process less daunting. This led us to take the decision to remove ballet from the selection process in 2020.

Key driver 2: student well-being

Our aim is to make all applicants feel welcome, regardless of how much access to technical training they may have previously had. We aim to create an inclusive and welcoming environment with an increased sense of belonging for applicants from groups that have previously been underrepresented in the school. Details about the process, including the list of questions for the

Table 4.4.1 LCDS's mapping of key drivers across pedagogic paradigm shifts

	Paradigm Shift 1: Learning and Teaching	*Paradigm Shift 2: Assessment*	*Paradigm Shift 3: Admissions*
Key driver 1: access and social justice	• Encounters with dance practices from Global South • Decentring hierarchies of value • Student-/artist-centred • Technique shifted beyond reproducing aesthetic ideal	• Student creates aesthetic lens through which assessor is invited to engage with their practice • School's lens is not superimposed	• Excellence without access is exclusion • Cut through essentialised notions of 'talent' • 'Workshop' over 'audition' • Contextualised admissions
Key driver 2: student well-being	• Principles of periodisation and dance science • Increased knowledge about safe dance practice • Development of psychological tools and skills	• Increased student ownership and agency, less 'violent' • Reduced assessment anxiety and injuries around time of assessment	• More inclusive culture with increased sense of belonging • Reasonable adjustments • Details of the process and conversation questions shared in advance
Key driver 3: professional outcomes	• Constructive alignment starting with course outcomes • Preparation for portfolio career as independent dance artist • Rebalanced credit weighting, emphasis on creativity and transferable skills	• Portfolio – student choice in selecting elements of practice put forward for assessment • Integrating practice/ reflection/ research • Student-/artist-centred • Assessment for learning	• Increased emphasis on assessing creative potential and communication skills • Digital admissions channel

conversation with the panel, are provided in advance to enable all candidates an equal opportunity to prepare.

Key driver 3: professional outcomes

We have radically reconfigured our admissions processes, away from a traditional audition that started with a ballet class, followed by a contemporary technique class. The attempt to decentre hierarchies of value between dance practices starts here, as students are invited to make choices in how to present their strengths to the school in the admissions process. Students attend a workshop, in-person or online, which has a stronger emphasis on improvisation, creative tasks and group discussion. Then, there is a conversation, in which applicants respond to questions made available in advance and are encouraged to ask staff questions. These new admissions activities are much more aligned to the new course outcomes and allow the school to assess applicants' skills, potential and motivation to study more effectively/reliably (Table 4.4.1).

Final thoughts

We have committed to a radical overhaul of our BA (Hons) Contemporary Dance course, influenced by our three key drivers (access and social justice, student well-being and professional outcomes); and through the course design principle of constructive alignment, we have significantly shifted the three paradigms of learning and teaching, assessment and admissions. We believe that this radical change was long overdue and right for us a unique organisation that leads the way in innovation.

Notes

1 Selected examples of evidence-based pedagogical frameworks: Biggs, J.B. (2003). *Teaching for Quality Learning at University.* Buckingham: Open University Press/Society for Research into Higher Education (second edition); Advance HE (2011). UK Professional Standards Framework. https://www.advance-he.ac.uk/guidance/teaching-and-learning/ukpsf; Advance HE (2019). Advance HE Essential Frameworks for Enhancing Student Success. https://www.advance-he.ac.uk/advance-he-essential-frameworks-enhancing-student-success; University of the Arts London. Creative Attributes Framework. https://www.arts.ac.uk/about-ual/teaching-and-learning-exchange/careers-and-employability/creative-attributes-framework; University of the Arts London. Assessment Criteria. https://www.arts.ac.uk/about-ual/teaching-and-learning-exchange/careers-and-employability/creative-attributes-framework.
2 Bannerman, H. and Bannerman, R. (2020). *Changing the Face of British Dance: Fifty Years of London Contemporary Dance School.* Binsted, Hampshire: Dance Books Ltd.

4.5 Manifesto for inclusion

Kate Marsh

Kate Marsh is a self-identified Crip Artist-Researcher with over 20 years of experience in performing, teaching and making. She is an Assistant Professor at C-DaRE, Centre for Dance Research at Coventry University. Her interests are centred around perceptions of the body in dance and notions of corporeal aesthetics. Specifically, she is interested in each of our lived experiences of our bodies, and how this does (or doesn't) inform our artistic practice. Her PhD explored leadership in the context of dance and disability and draws strongly on the voices of artists to interrogate questions around notions of leadership, perceptions and the body.

The writing offered here is a response to a request to produce a manifesto for inclusion. Specifically, a manifesto for the inclusion of disabled dance artists into dance, and more specifically still into technical training in contemporary dance.

I am interested in highlighting the vast knowledge that exists in disabled dance artists, not just about access or participation but also a rich and diverse ontology of dance and bodies that has the potential to enrich and improve dance training and dance practice (Figure 4.5.1).

I use the term 'we' in this chapter in relation to disabled artists, and I do this to locate myself in a community of artists and to make myself visible as a disabled author-researcher.

I write from a place of lived experience. I am a disabled artist who has worked for over two decades in the contemporary dance sector. Anecdotal experience is a key element of what moves the dance training sector forward and disabled voices and experience must be part of this. The thinking in this writing is informed by my own experience, and by the many conversations, I have had and continue to have with other disabled artists.

The question of 'including' people with disabilities into training frameworks for contemporary dance has been present in academic thinking and practice in different iterations for many years. As a benchmark, we might focus on the emergence of disabled artists into the professional landscape of contemporary dance practice around 20 years ago, with the increased visibility of notable companies such as Candoco and StopGap.

DOI: 10.4324/9781003111146-31

Figure 4.5.1 Artists: Sindri Runudde, Jo Bannon, Noa Winter. Credit: Kate Marsh

The presence of the disabled dancer in existing training models is problematic for the dance sector – we do not easily fit.

Disabled artists were historically 'found' primarily through workshops led by those interested in increasing access and participation into dance. Often these individuals had not undertaken 'formal' training on their entry into the professional contemporary dance sector. For example, the performance skills of the late David Toole, who worked for the Post Office at the time of his introduction to Candoco, were unarguably 'natural', and much of Candoco's early success was centred upon iconic examples of Toole's performance. There are numerous similar examples of individual artists.[1] There is a term that exists in relation to disabled dance artists in the professional contemporary dance field and that is 'bespoke training'. In this context, this means that these artists stitched together a training in dance through experience, taking classes and workshops, and they were generally 'working' their way into a knowledge of dance. Whilst 'bespoke training' enabled artists to develop skills and knowledge of the art form, it highlighted a key problem. As we were in the process of autonomous training, the wider dance pedagogy field was somewhat 'let off' the work of considering how to 'include' disabled artists in existing training. Without the rite of passage of 'traditional' training, we remain transient, moving through our dance careers, without feeling a link to those that have preceded us or those for whom we might be making a path. Much dance training is based on the passing on of knowledge and skills from generation to generation, and it is additionally based on an initiation into a cultural framework of what contemporary dance has been and can potentially be. There are still very few disabled teachers and trainers working in UK education systems for dance – a disabled student will rarely, if ever, see themselves and their experience represented in the people leading their training or in the history of dance that they are taught.

This causes a problem. The dance sector highly values training in dance, and there is a perceived currency of how and where dancers receive their training. This currency is directly linked to opportunities for work and professional development. Within a system of 'bespoke' training, disabled artists are faced with two options: to limit their practice to the so-called inclusive dance field, mainly as performers, rather than makers or teachers, or to 'bend' themselves into a 'normalistic' model of training in which their bodies and experiences do not fit.

It is not my intention in this writing to make recommendations to the mainstream about how best to include disabled artists into existing training. This has been tried and tested and the work of this lands almost exclusively on the shoulders of disabled individuals. It seems important to note a fundamental tension that exists between contemporary dance and the disabled dance artist. Dance is a form dominated by notions of the 'ideal' body. We operate in an etymological framework of highly codified language to share knowledge and learn about the art form. What does a plie mean if you are a dancer who does not use their legs? How relevant are Martha Graham or Merce Cunningham to disabled students of dance when disabled artists that have gone before them are absent from existing historical understandings of dance (Figure 4.5.2).

I want disabled dance artists at various stages of their career to claim their space in the dance training sector, not politely or quietly, not by attempting to

Figure 4.5.2 Welly O'Brien, Robbie Synge, Jo Bannon, Catherine Hoffman, Julie Cleeves. Credit: Kate Marsh

'try on' the training that is aimed at normative ideas of the dancer's body, but loudly, proudly, impolitely stating what we already know, not just through our experience of dance but also of living itself. I want disabled artists to emerge from borrowed corners of dance training such as a module in 'inclusive' dance, or a dissertation case study produced by a non-disabled dance student. I want disabled dancers to take up the studios and corridors of dance conservatoires, not as advisors or experts on how to fit a disabled body into a ballet class, but as leaders, adding their voices and experience to the future of contemporary dance.

A Manifesto in progress (this should be added to by more disabled people, it should be fluid and changeable).

- Let your first question be 'who is in this room' and often more importantly 'who is not'. (This means dance studios, staff rooms and conferences.)
- Consider your language, how much of what is offered in your training is based on an assumed shared knowledge and experience? (Accessible language is better for everyone.)
- Consider how you teach dance history, acknowledge that we are invisible in dominant understandings of cultural heritage in dance.
- Be prepared to do the work of understanding access and inclusion, and don't expect disabled dancers and dance students to do this for you.
- Be ready to let go of modes of training that are outmoded and inaccessible. If they do not serve or account for a wider community of dance artists, then should they still inform our training?
- Be an ally, do you really need a disabled student present in your class in order for you to highlight a lack of proper access?
- Be ready to reconsider the relationship between the mainstream and the periphery, good things happen in the margins.
- You will make mistakes, we will all make mistakes. Creating spaces for disabled dancers to experiment and fail is an essential part of the training process.
- Acknowledge that disabled dancers might do some things 'better' – we are not always catching up with our non-disabled peers. The experience of disability brings about a deep understanding of our bodies and bodies in general.
- Engage with discourse around critical disability studies.
- Be ready to reconsider time, time taken to achieve something, time allotted to learn, break time, rehearsal time. We do not all operate within the same time and pace. Needing longer or different timings is not a weakness.
- Look at your learning spaces, not everyone learns best sitting in a row of chairs, or in a 'traditional' formation for learning technique.
- Understand that best practice serves everyone, there is no one size fits all, we are all different and our needs can change from day to day.

Consider 'checking in' with what is needed to improve learning at any given time. (This does not mean giving students everything they want, it is about attempting to create an environment of discussion and readiness to listen.)

Note

1 Any list might include, for example, Welly O'Brien, Kimberley Harvey and David Lock.

4.6 The value of 'South Asian' dance technique to 'contemporary' dance training

Magdalen Gorringe with Shivaangee Agrawal and Jane Chan

Magdalen Tamsin Gorringe started learning bharatanatyam during her childhood in Madurai, South India. She freelanced as a bharatanatyam dancer, workshop leader and administrator for a number of years before starting a funded PhD at the University of Roehampton. She gained her doctorate for her thesis – 'Towards a British Natyam: The Professionalisation of Classical Indian Dance Forms in Britain' in 2021.

Jane Chan is an independent dance artist who works at the intersection of making, performing, teaching, project managing, mentoring and change instigation. Empathy, care and a people-centred approach are at the heart of Jane's artistic practice. Jane performs regularly with Amina Khayyam Dance Company, lectures and mentors, and works in an artist-advisory capacity at Sadler's Wells and Akademi.

Shivaangee Agrawal is a dance artist with a practice that concerns choreography, writing and advocacy. She draws upon her regular training in bharatanatyam, as well as folk and experimental practices of movement. She performs and presents work. She is also a trained audio describer and offers an embodied AD practice. You can find out more at shivaangee.com.

Exercise 1

Repeat to yourself:

> *Ta jam tari taka ta*
> *Taka jam tari taka tai*
> *Ta jam tari taka jam tari*
> *Ta, di, kitatakatarikitatom*
> *Ta jam tari taka jam tari*
> *Ta, di, kitatakatarikitatom*
> *Ta jam tari taka jam tari*
> *Ta langu tom kitatakatarikitatom*

DOI: 10.4324/9781003111146-32

Exercise 2

Repeat to yourself again, this time keeping time by clapping a beat of three.

Exercise 3

Take this position: Stand, feet apart but heels together, legs bent out into *aramandi*. This approximates to what in Euro-American contemporary dance/ballet is a *demi-plié*. Except that it is deeper and more elastic. The best dancers can sustain a position that is somewhere on the way from a demi to a full plié. Now put your arms out in *natyarambe*. This is a position with your arms stretched out to the side, but with the crease of the elbow facing forwards, so that the triceps are engaged and the arms end up very slightly curved. Where your hands continue the line of your arm, bend your ring finger on each hand, so that the top two phalanges extend perpendicularly from the rest of your hand. This is *tripataka*, one of the 28 single hand gestures (or *hasta mudras*) found in bharatanatyam.

You are now in *aramandi*, with *natyarambe*, holding *tripataka*. In this position, imagine that the ceiling is so low that it touches the top of your head. Now jump on to the balls of your feet. As you jump, make sure that your head stays at the same level – if it rises, it will hit the ceiling. As jump, make sure you do not lose the depth of your *aramandi*. Now lower the heels again so that they hit the ground with sufficient impact to make a slapping sound. Repeat. Jump on to the balls of your feet, slap the heels down. Jump on to the balls of your feet, slap the heels down. And repeat. And repeat. And repeat.

Exercise 4

Consider how the three previous exercises made you feel. Clumsy? Confused? Curious? Constrained?

Hold on to the physical experiences of these exercises and the emotions they engendered as you reflect on the following.

The question of what 'South Asian dance forms' (or to be more specific, what bharatanatyam, kathak or odissi, these being the three most commonly practised classical Indian dance forms in Britain today) might bring to, or of why their techniques are important to 'contemporary dance' is tautologous. These techniques are contemporary. They do not *bring* anything to contemporary dance because they *are* contemporary dance. In one way, this is the most important lesson of their practice. The identification of the label 'contemporary dance' with a genre of Euro-American expressive dance forms that developed in the mid-twentieth century implicitly positions all dance forms that lie outside this designation outside of the presumption of 'nowness'. Other dance forms are left with the burden of proving their contemporaneity. This is not merely a question of semantics. Labels matter.

It is important to disrupt the grip that Euro-North-American[1] contemporary dance forms currently hold on 'the present' (Kwan, 2017).

When we think about the way that education, particularly education and training in dance, can help create socially engaged individuals, capable of forging ethical human relationships, one of our most urgent tasks must be that of decolonisation. It is urgent because until we decolonise, we continue to posit one particular value system (Anglo-European) as the measure for all others. And as long as we do this, we greet others with non-recognition or misrecognition. This is unethical because, in the words of moral philosopher Charles Taylor, 'non recognition or misrecognition can inflict harm, can be a form of oppression, imprisoning someone in a false, distorted and reduced mode of being' (Taylor, 1994: 25).

By decolonisation I mean the recognition that there are multiple value systems, multiple aesthetic codes, multiple forms of cultural capital, multiple means of contemporaneity – and that no one set is worthier than another. This is not to return to some sort of multiculturalism, whereby Otherness is comfortably encountered from the safety of one's own space. To recognise, or even to glimpse the multiplicity of codes and conventions requires an unsettling. A discomfort. What philosopher of race George Yancy terms an 'un-suturing' (2017: 256). A not being sure where you are, how you fit, how you are supposed to be. To create something of the feeling that may have been elicited by the exercises above. It involves breaking open the blinkers on your vision to see, 'This is where I am, but there is more'.

Such unsettledness is the everyday reality of many. An enforced reality, not a choice. It is the reality for everyone who learns English as well as their 'mother-tongue' because English is the language of international discourse and of power. For everyone who modifies the way they walk and talk so as to be taken more seriously. For everyone who has to work out how their dance forms will fit into a landscape formed by a very different set of values.

In classical Indian dance forms, the legs are rarely held straight and lifted into the air. The focus is more on the performance by the legs and feet of precise, rhythmic and physically demanding patterns, without unsettling the centre of gravity, while the upper torso conjures fluidity and ease. Creativity lies not so much in the making new, but in the making again. And yet classical Indian dancers continue to be urged to train in 'choreography'; to break away from tradition (as if tradition is necessarily excluded from the contemporary; as if the past is not contained within the future).[2]

So, what can bharatanatyam or kathak or odissi bring to (Euro-American) contemporary dance? An embodied discomfort. A frustration. An unsettledness. The creative itch of 'not being able to'.

Why is this important? Because unsettledness helps us to widen our worldview. Because unsettledness can help us towards the ethical position of understanding others on their own terms.

Experience of bharatanatyam or kathak or odissi is critical within the teaching of (Euro-American) contemporary dance, in other words, because these dance forms bring to (Euro-American) contemporary dance an awareness of limitation. Which is at the same time, an awareness of possibility.

Of course, there are dancers who are able to flit between channels of embodiment and perform multiple physicalities. This can only occur, however, where there is parity in the level of commitment, of application and of hours of training put into embodying the different dance styles and understanding their narratives (or their histories and artistic conventions). This is because, as dance scholar Susan Leigh Foster identifies,

> ...imitating movements and shapes is just the first step. It must be accompanied by studying and internalizing elaborate anatomical, functional and expressive metaphorical systems that give colour and meaning to movement.
>
> (Foster, 1997: 64)

For Agrawal,

> Without such knowledge the industry of dance is myopic in its invitations to choreographers and artists of South Asian background. It is myopic even when it encourages work by practitioners of South Asian forms. It is myopic in its description and translation of artists' work into written text, reviews, analysis, legacy. It is myopic in its invitations to audiences, in what they may be able to experience by engaging with dance. Without such knowledge, the colonised world of dance risks creating huge inequity in what visions contemporary dancers are allowed to imagine of their dancing bodies, and what visions South Asian dancers are allowed to imagine of their dancing bodies.
>
> (Shivaangee Agrawal, personal communication, June 2021)

In sum, an experience of training in bharatanatyam, or kathak, or odissi is important (even essential) to Euro-American contemporary dance training because it provides 'a tool to a have a different perspective into the body'; it permits a glimpse of 'a different channel into dance as a craft' (Jane Chan, Interview, 2021); and it offers 'a different perspective and portal into accessing the body, movement vocabularies, rhythm, musicality, culture which are all of value to movers and dance artists' (Jane Chan, personal communication, June 2021).

Or in choreographer and dance artist Jane Chan's words:

> I would like to propose, invite and welcome a more horizontal dynamics where ballet, 'contemporary' dance (however we wish to define this...as for me it is about the present, the now), Odissi, Kathak, Bharatanatyam, indigenous, folk dance from all corners of the world, Butoh, Hip Hop,

Break, Lock, Salsa, Lindy Hop, Jive (the list goes on) are of the same importance as each other and are valued equally.[3]

(Jane Chan, personal communication, June 2021)

We owe such an equal valuing in the teaching of dance (as in other subjects) because of the 'educational debt' (Ladson-Billings, 2006) or the 'historical accumulation of educational inequality' (Banks, 2010: 29) that has, within dance curricula, so long upheld ballet as the 'apogee of the performing arts' (Kealiinohomoku, 2001: 35). We owe it to 'all young people who need cross-cultural epistemological resources for constructing knowledge' (Banks, 2010: 30). We owe it to ourselves, if we hope to envision a future with any degree of ethical integrity.

Notes

1 I thank Jane Chan for highlighting to me the importance of using this term rather than cementing the colonial binaries of 'East' and 'West'.
2 See dance and theatre scholar Royona Mitra's interview with Akram Khan in which he emphasises his 'relationship to time as cyclical "perceiving" the interconnectedness between pasts, presents and futures' (Mitra, 2017: 41).
3 Note from Jane Chan: I am aware of the power dynamics within my knowledge which continue to be at play even when I wish to resist it, however, I will continue to learn and aspire to stay as open as possible in the spaces that I take up, pass through and hold. As an artist I offer my perspective and experiences only from my context and that is by no means exhaustive.

References

Banks, O. (2010) Critical postcolonial dance pedagogy: the relevance of West African dance education in the United States. *Anthropology & Education Quarterly, 41*(1), 18–34.

Foster, S.L. (1997) Dancing bodies. In: Desmond, J. (ed.) *Meaning in Motion: New Cultural Studies in Dance.* Durham, NC and London: Duke University Press. pp. 235–258.

Kealiinohomoku, J. (2001) An anthropologist looks at ballet as a form of ethnic dance. In: Dils, A. & Albright, A.C. (eds.) *Moving History/Dancing Cultures.* Middleton, CT: Wesleyan University Press. pp. 33–43.

Kwan, S. (2017) When is contemporary dance? *Dance Research Journal, 49*(3), 38–52. DOI: 10.1017/S0149767717000341

Ladson-Billings, G. (2006) From the achievement gap to the education debt: understanding achievement in U.S. schools. *Educational Researcher, 35*(7), 3–12.

Mitra, R. (2017) Beyond fixity: Akram Khan on the politics of dancing heritages. In: Nicholas, L. & Morris, G. (eds.) *Rethinking Dance History: Issues and Methodologies.* London: Taylor & Francis Group. pp. 32–43.

Taylor, C. (1994) The politics of recognition. In: Gutmann, A. (ed.) *Multiculturalism: Examining the Politics of Recognition.* Princeton, NJ: Princeton University Press. pp. 25–74.

Yancy, G. & Alcoff, L.M. (2017) *Black Bodies, White Gazes: The Continuing Significance of Race in America* (2nd ed.). Blue Ridge Summit: Rowman & Littlefield Publishers.

4.7 Towards decoloniality and artistic citizenship

A manifesto

'Funmi Adewole

'Funmi Adewole has a background in media, education, arts development and performance. She started out as a media practitioner in Nigeria and moved into performance on relocating to England in 1994. For several years, she toured with Physical/Visual theatre and African dance drama companies. She continues to practice professionally, performing as a storyteller and working as a dramaturge with makers who are interdisciplinary or cross-sectorial in focus. In 2019, she was awarded a life-time achievement award by One Dance UK for her contribution to changing perceptions of the Dance of the Diaspora in the UK. She has a PhD in Dance Studies from De Montfort University Leicester, where she now works as a lecturer in the Dance department.

DOI: 10.4324/9781003111146-33

Dance of the African Diaspora (DAD) is a term used mainly outside of Africa. It represents a category of dance forms, practices and techniques which originate or draw from the cultural repertoire of Africa and the Diaspora. DAD includes dance practices which draw attention to the historical, socio-cultural, artistic, philosophical, political or spiritual lineages of dance practices as well as the communities and social groups that the dance artists might engage with. The term does not describe how dance practitioners who identify with these forms of dance classify their work in terms of genre. Such practitioners might also consider their work to be contemporary dance, physical theatre, dance theatre or a somatic practice, or they might align their practice with one dance form or group of forms, for example, dancehall, Hip-Hop or Afro beats.

Several universities in Britain have now included the DAD in their training provision. The opening of the UK HE curriculum to dance forms, practices and techniques based on non-western repertoire has moved forward the on-going process of decolonialising the curriculum, the decentring of the epistemologies of the Global North from dominating knowledge production. However, this development, which has increased since the 1990s, begs important questions as to what theory should support dance teaching.

> In a curriculum that provides less space for theory, how is the process of developing the foundations of dance study (one of theorising and reflexivity) supporting students who wish to base their practice mainly on Africanist dance forms or principles?
>
> How does dance training support students to work from their aesthetic, embodied vantage points – working in and between spaces which are formed by communities, working places and artistic genres?

Theory should contextualise dance training and engage with the artistic citizenship and praxis of dance artists teaching DAD

Students are best served if the university training in DAD they are given is contextualised in relation to how it has developed within the professional context in the UK, rather than a-contextual definitions of what African and Diaspora dance is. This would provide them with an intellectual and research context for what they are learning, and an understanding of how studio-based training relates to DAD in other settings. DAD artists train their students through dance practices or pedagogies which they have devised from their social dance experience, academic dance training or from dance company repertoire, whether their practice draws from Hip-Hop, or other social and traditional forms of dance from the Caribbean, Africa or African American cultures, or dance techniques derived from these. Nevertheless, their teaching is informed by pedagogic theories. Students should also be made aware that pedagogic theories inform how DAD is transmitted for example one pedagogic theory that informs how traditional or rather neotraditional dance is taught is called 'authentic learning'. Designing authentic learning experiences is a pedagogic skill through which the teacher teaches a dance in relation to the knowledge and parameters of the original cultural context. Teachers select dance movements and materials and set them in an order which facilitates transmission. Some add the prefix 'neo' to signal this shift in context. It is worth mentioning that many dance and teach in various contexts and their practice could be described as intercontextual.

Contextualising dance practices or pedagogies devised by practitioners brings their praxis to the fore and clarifies our understanding of DAD as a category. To not do this provides an inaccurate depiction of social and traditional dances as performed in their original contexts. Contextualising DAD in HE will clarify the relationship of how dance is taught for artistic and professional purposes to how and why it is transmitted in other contexts. A-contextual definitions of authenticity and integrity in the practice of DAD overlook the fact that how meaning is generated through dance may shift from one context to another even though there might be overlaps. Performance in social, ritual, popular dance contexts require the student to learn technique, physical skills of execution as well as philosophical or spiritual perspectives to be able to deliver an appropriate performance of the dance or participate in dancing in the given context. Moreover, social dances change completely or add new steps as lifestyles of people in a community change and new ways of living and social practices appear. They are not static.

Artistic citizenship can be used as a framework to engage with the histories of artistic activities and contribute to enhancing the cultural aspect of dance pedagogies in the UK. The centrality of praxis to artistic citizenship is significant in that it reveals the common, though unequal, terrain that DAD artists navigate with others. No doubt the concept of artistic citizenship has uses beyond those discussed here. The concept however can be used as a space for DAD artists to communicate the politics, aesthetics, ethics, choreography and socio-cultural context of their work in terms of their subjectivity or lived experience which will reveal that the appropriation of western codified forms or compositional technique is only an aspect of their work. It can support cross-cultural conversations. Black artists like their white counterparts are professional practitioners whose context of work involves the public sphere and civic arrangements. Euro-American dance practice pedagogy is generally offered as if it is devoid of a cultural perspective even though 'euro-american' cultural values inform how this pedagogy has evolved.

The dance curriculum in higher education in Britain evolves in tandem with the evolution of dance as a profession and the various practices that dance artists devise to interrogate what it is to live in the world. Artistic praxis can, when put in dialogue with postcolonial theories, provide a means of generating discourses for artistic work which allows a critical discourse to be generated that opens up academic study across borders.

An appropriate discourse, one which does not 'other' DAD but engages with its complexity, offers lecturers and students an opportunity to gain an understanding of the relationship of aesthetics and artmaking to race and race relations, cultural politics, identity politics and a sensitivity to power dynamics in various contexts. Such academic discourse expands the knowledge of aesthetics and artmaking and enables dance students of all racial and cultural backgrounds to develop as culturally literate practitioners who are able contribute to problem-solving in the various contexts they will work after graduation.

Further reading on examples of how a focus on artistic citizenship or how praxis is implicit or has been used to design curriculum and shape the dance sector:

Adair, C. and Burt, R. (2017) *British Dance, Black Routes*. New York: Routledge.

Adewole, F. and Palmer, J. (2017) *'Dissecting Principles'* Collaborative Research Project. Dance Exchange. Available at https://www.africanheritageuk.com/dissecting-principles-dance-exchange

African Heritage UK: Authentic Music and Dance. (2017) Available at: https://www.africanheritageuk.com/

Akinleye, A. (Ed.) (2018) *Narratives in Black British Dance: Embodied Practices*. London: Springer: Palgrave Macmillan.

Amin, T. N. (2016) Beyond hierarchy: Re-imagining diaspora dance in higher education curricula, *The Black Scholar*, 46:1, 15–26. DOI: 10.1080/00064246.2015.1119634

Casteleyn, S. (2018) 'Why I Am Not a Fan of the Lion King: Ethically-Informed Approaches to the Teaching and Learning of South African Dance Forms in Higher Education in the United Kingdom', in A. Akinleye (Ed.), *Narratives in Black British Dance: Embodied Practices*. London: Palgrave Macmillan, pp. 115–129.

Elliott, D., Silverman, M. and Bowman, W. (2016) *Artistic Citizenship: Artistry, Social Responsibility and Ethical Praxis*. New York: Oxford University Press.

Hakeem Onibudo. (n.d.) Available at: https://www.hakeemonibudo.com/

Igbokwe, V. (2020) 'Black Dance: Decolonisation of Dance Curriculum', in Léna Blou, et al. (Ed.), *My Voice, My Practice: Black Dance*. Leicester: Serendipity Artists Movement, pp. 100–109.

Impact Dance Foundation Ltd. (2022) Available at: https://impactdance.co.uk/

Quinn, L. (2019) *Re-Imagining Curriculum: Spaces for Disruption*. Cape Town: African Sun Media, 2019. ProQuest Ebook Central. http://ebookcentral.proquest.com/lib/dmu/detail.action?docID=6321180 (Accessed 23 05 2022).

Pedro, R., Stevens, K., & Scheu, C. (2018) Creating a cultural dance community of practice: building authentic Latin American dance experiences, *Research in Dance Education*, 19:3, 199–215. DOI: 10.1080/14647893.2018.1476479. Downloaded 22 04 2022.

4.8 The world needs more dancers. Consciousness can and should be trained through the practice of dance

Jorge Crecis

Jorge Crecis has a degree in Sport Sciences, studied at the Royal Conservatory of Madrid, and holds a PhD by Goldsmiths. He worked as a professional dancer and lectured in universities worldwide. Award-winning choreographer who has been commissioned by companies, including Scottish Dance Theatre and Acosta Danza among others. He also coaches professional dance companies and athletes. Author of the book: Designing Presence: Entering Towards Vivencia. Featured in the book: Fifty Contemporary Choreographers.

Context

When I lead a new training session, I usually start with the following provocation:

'List the skills you have acquired through the practice of dance'.

The answers are varied but rarely are they referring to purely mechanical abilities such as jumping, flexibility, coordination and balance.[1]

Although virtually all dancers develop these and similar abilities..., the answers are always far more profound:

- I am more capable of listening to what I need
- I have more empathy
- I have developed more awareness
- I am able to respond to difficult situations more effectively
- I have a stronger willpower
- I work better with others

...

As I have experienced personally, and what has been corroborated time and time again by other dance artists, the skills and values developed through **the practice of dance** are, in fact, a perfect vehicle to facilitate awareness of the self, or what is arguably the same: the development of consciousness.

There is no single, universally agreed upon definition of what consciousness is. But, for the purpose of this manifesto, we can define it as, 'what it's

DOI: 10.4324/9781003111146-34

like to be'. Consciousness is both an impossible subject of study and likely the most important subject of study.

Impossible because we cannot be separated from the subject of study itself and because we cannot fathom how anyone (or anything) else experiences consciousness.

And, the most important one, because it is the beginning and the end of what it means and what is to experience life.

Definitions aside:

- Consciousness is at the heart and is the motor behind everything concerning humanity's manifestation: ethics, politics, sciences, race, religion, love, reason.
- It is the mechanism that makes sense of physical sensations and labels emotions.
- It is what allows us to know that we are; the tool that provides us with a sense of the universe and its rules.
- There are even some schools of thought that assert that the known universe is only a model created by our consciousness in order to comprehend and interact with the quantum chaos that is our environment.
- And... although discussing whether there is a spiritual realm or not is beyond the subject matter, if there is one, we will only be able to experience it as an altered state of consciousness... altered yes, but consciousness after all.

By dancing, we increase our knowledge of 'what it's like to be me', and 'what it's like to experience something'. Therefore, generally speaking, dance can be a vehicle for the development of **human consciousness**. Meaning that specific dance practices have the potential to target specific aspects of consciousness.

Traditionally, dance training focuses on shaping the mechanical/ musculoskeletal system of the performer. The mechanical/musculoskeletal system is easily observable. In principle, cause-and-effects are measurable, replicable and, to the contrary of qualia, they are independent from the observer. Even if we approach dance training solely from the mechanical/ musculoskeletal perspective, it is not a stretch to imply that we are unavoidably also impacting the most inner self. When we focus the work on achieving perfect turnout, or executing beautiful triple pirouettes, we are also holding what makes those performers who they are and ultimately how they experience who they are: we are shaping their consciousness. However, this focus on purely mechanical/musculoskeletal aspects leading to an unintentional impact on the self does not always translate into a structured, healthy, productive, decisive, effective, positive, expansive, clear, thorough and poignant consciousness training. Unfortunately, the repercussions that dance training and its environment has on the identity of the performers' consciousness and on 'what it's like to be me' is sometimes damaging and harmful.

Therefore, dance training should, and needs to, include specific practices that specifically, positively and intentionally address the performers experience of 'what it's like to be me' through a balanced and holistic approach.

Current dance training programmes need to incorporate methods that help students to:

- Understand the mechanisms of the autonomic nervous system to maximise rest and repair periods as well as minimise the harmful effects of stressful situations.
- Increase their neuroplasticity to adapt better and faster to an ever-changing world:
    - Maximise their ability to learn how to learn
    - Increase motivation and expand their experience of joy
    - Create long-lasting impacts on how they approach all aspects of their lives.
- Increase empathy and compassion for oneself and others. Resulting in more mature and ethical individuals with integrity and strong values.

In short, dance training programmes need to direct a substantial part of their efforts to train the performers' consciousness.

Luckily, it can be done. It is time to describe the basis that can be incorporated in any dance training for future performers to be able to create their own systems to train consciousness, for themselves and/or for others.

So...

Manifesto

Consciousness can and should be trained.

Dance training

Dancers already indirectly impact their consciousness inherently through their daily practices. Therefore, there needs to be a shift towards incorporating specific practices that directly impact and bolster the positive and healthy development of consciousness:

- The study and the exercise of empathy, compassion, self-empathy and self-compassion.
- Basic knowledge of the functioning of the nervous system.
- Playfulness. Commitment. Discipline. Curiosity.
- Aesthetics. The study of the nature of beauty.
- Practices that incite non-ordinary states of consciousness: Whirling Dervish Dance, meditation, apnoea training, etc.

- Reflex exercises, endurance, resilience and problem-solving in real time.
- Tools for reflection, reflexion, self-reflection, to offer feedback and critical analysis.
- Physical, mental and spiritual self-care.
- Ethics.
- Tools to build, lead and/or be part of multi/trans and interdisciplinary teams.
- Celebration.
- Nothingness.

Some readers might be thinking that they already include most of the previous items in their teachings. However, consciousness training should not be casually, accidentally or superficially implemented. Instead, a structured system for training consciousness should be included separately and not collaterally as a fundamental component of any performer training programme. The training of the performer will never be complete till this aspect is not only formally addressed but, what is more, it is constantly, methodologically and relentlessly worked on.

Dance training should prepare future dance artists to be able to dissect how dance develops human consciousness in order to craft their own praxis facilitating consciousness development in themselves and others.

Dance training should be of the highest quality possible, accessible to anyone who chooses to delve into its study and extend its reach beyond vocational training into fundamental education systems, not as a means to train professionals, but to train consciousness point blank.

Performing is an integral part of the education of dance artists. Therefore, all future dance artists should experience what it is to perform, not as an act of sheer self-fulfilment, but from a place of service to moving humanity forward. They should be well practiced in the delicate balance of permanence and impermanence, not only infusing the piece with their unique signature as performers but also dissolving the self to allow the performance to exist through them, as a channel.

Teachers and dance training institutions

The teachers, lecturers and professionals in charge of educating future dance artists should hold the highest possible standards, possess the most exquisite integrity and promote the values that benefit the community by benefiting the individual.

Teachers should practise an unconditional passion for the art of teaching.

They should teach everything they know and only what they know.

They should teach everyone equally with loving discipline, seeking nothing from their students but their most complete well-being, not allowing them to leave any unfulfilled potential through setting excessively high, unrealistic and generic expectations.

Teachers should keep studying, researching and understanding the newest and most relevant advances in social, cognitive and neurosciences, pedagogy, philosophy, biomechanics, economics psychology and anthropology.

Being qualified as a teacher is a lifelong endeavour.

Teachers should be supported, encouraged and valued to be able to do their job in the best possible way.

Institutions in charge of curating the teachers who would be designing and imparting dance training do not have any excuses to not get the best professionals in the sector. Through online education, elite knowledge has never been so accessible, so affordable, so profitable and so environmentally friendly.

The core of a systematised/professional/vocational dance training should be far away from trends, box-ticking and tokenism.

What do the dance artists of the future look like?

Dance artists should be driven by three principles:

First: Do no harm
Second: Aim to serve
Third: Do everything possible to facilitate the evolution of human consciousness

The dance artists of the future are the fierce makers and the masters of themselves. They are their primary and ultimate piece of art; an unfinished work in constant progress that they will envision, shape, polish and only complete in the last instances of their lives, during their very last breath when the lights switch off forever.

Dancers of the future will be the agents of the mind, the deputy of the self and the advocate for a life force that can be felt but cannot be tamed.

The dancers in the future will have scarcity erased from their mindset and they will live, serve and exist in abundance, acting from a place of a more evolved consciousness.

The dancers of the future will contribute to society beyond its use for entertainment, artistic inspiration or alternative physical education.

The dancers of the future will be a key piece, among others, that will lead us all towards consciousness in an ever-evolving journey.

Last words

Dance is already a vehicle that contributes to the development of human consciousness.

Dancers with a specific consciousness training will be able to lead and guide others for a more developed and ethical global society.

The world needs more dancers, and we need to train those dancers to support the world's needs.

Note

1 These examples come from a survey conducted with students of the TWV Academy, a hub for online classes offered during the COVID-19 pandemic between March 2020 and December 2021.

4.9 A chorus of dancing voices curated by Katye Coe

Katye Coe

Katye Coe is a dancer and activist based in the UK. Her work as a performer spans over 20 years of international performance practice. Katye teaches independently across the UK and internationally and her teaching practice is an extension of her performance practice. Katye is a certified Skinner Releasing Technique teacher and has worked extensively with Helen Poynor through the Walk of Life Training. She guest teaches regularly at London Contemporary Dance School and at Independent Dance.

> … I extended an invitation to a handful of dancer performer folk that I have been inspired by/ disarmed by/ learned from in recent months. Each of their responses came in the form of a 'prayer, spell, incantation, or wish'. I have curated them here as a chorus of dancing voices.

Contributing voices

Temitope Ajose
Ay De La Fe
Elena Rose Light
Catherine Long
Patricia Okenwa
Amy Voris
Natifah White

DOI: 10.4324/9781003111146-35

This is a calling in and a breath out
This is why and this is what I have
This is ordinary and this is loving
   This is thinking and resisting and listening and multiple doings and
getting on with something useful
   This is not steps or fitness or flexibility or special intelligence or youth
or class or philosophy or on stages or being good or better ... this is body
attention training and taking care and giving attention and being ready
and it is about preparation and practice and
This is about showing up and getting out of the way
This is to-get-her ... these dancings

KC *(she they)*

Let's get lost.
   Let's move until our bodies disentangle themselves from language, until
we don't know who or what or where or when we are anymore, until there
is no more until.
   Let's disorient our directions, lose our center, grasp at the air, fall into
the sky.
Let's root so deep into the Earth that we come out the other side.
Let's unbecome ourselves.
That will be dancing, I think.

ERL (they them)

Before considering what 'dance' and 'technique' mean to you, please pause
and take a moment to breathe. Staying present with your breath, allow yourself to notice what happens internally when you hear the word 'technique'...
and what happens when you hear the word 'dance'?
   There may be as many different dance styles as there are people in the
world, but techniques are often prescriptive and exclusionary. What might
happen if we rethink technique as methodology and begin from the notion
that the impulse and desire to move is 'enough' and 'right' exactly as it is.
   When dancing is imbued with intention, disciplined practice and supported
knowledge, and you inhabit that movement, that technique becomes yours.
   It does not require the fulfilment of any normative ideals.
   It makes a priority of exploring, expressing, communicating, surviving in
one's body as an emotional experience.
   Is there a way you can take ownership of your body and the way our
bodies are positioned in a society? Can technique be a path to belonging or
not belonging?
   Is it about truth, and 'pride'...?

CL (she her)

Softening towards

what is present

following
desires and curiosities
for moving

receiving
the details of experience

and the uniqueness
of each moment

   allowing things to
   surface and
   pass through

   welcoming
   shifts in intensity
   and duration

   welcoming the presence of
   imagination and emotion
   as companions

   witnessing
   your movement
   and your movement
   witnessing you
   your movement
   as a witness
   to this space and time
   this space and time
   as a witness
   to your movement

   movement growing out of
   and grounding in
   the particularities
   of circumstance

   working with what is
   present
   and what is
   potentially present

AV (she her)

Contemporary dance is a seed seen, seeping, seeking, receiving and sealing – say this three times

NW *(she her)*

Ode to spider

Take note, take heart: From her legs, she shoots out fine silk. She allows the wind to carry her fine threads and she continues to fire her silk threads along its path. Up to 25 metres, until a suitable anchor is found. She secures and strengthens her threads and builds diligently a pattern intrinsic to her DNA. The silk web is stronger than steel. Her silk will feed and sustain her. Take note, take heart.

T A (she her)

A symbol as full answer. Lazy? No, not lazy. Ambiguous, surely. Ambiguous yet to the point. Dot, dot, dot. Three dots forming a recognisable and semantically multilayered punctuation. Known by many names; Open to interpretation. Or rather, sentencing-awarding you with the embracing of the paradox.

A mutis. From mutating, changing, and use with a meaning of changing location and ultimately of leaving the scene. Getting off stage. Making an exit. Or is it from mute? The impossibility, inability, indifference or refusal to speak/ing. A silence.

Either way, mutis as an imperative would have the same effect regardless of its etymology. Yet, it will probably leave us wondering:

Ellipsis or censorship? Termination or adjournment? Break or Broken? Void or Hope? Absentmindedness? Exhaustion? Resignation? Wait? Pause? Or end?

ADLF (they them)

Only If dance was an entity, what would Dance want from us, with us, for us? Would we listen, follow, use, distribute with upmost care and sufficient irreverence, so Dance would be free? Self perpetuating, omnipresent, evo- and revolutionary and consistently abundant Dance?

Would Dance help with the answers or become a distraction? Dancing on the precipice, dancing into the abyss, dancing while the world goes up in flames and could we find the movement and the hunger to travel through, around, beyond to find the ways and be fed while we do so?

Could Dance be for all, everywhere, like open sourcing a technology, or just remembering that it has been there all along, is always there, potentially transcending categorisation, but embrace variation and nuances, as a way off being together and apart, stringing, flowing, navigating, standing or holding close, aligning, making space, magnifying, surrendering, remembering and being present, staying present, taking space...

Figuring it out as we dance it through?

PO *(she her)*

Index

Note: **Bold** page numbers refer to tables; *italic* page numbers refer to figures and page numbers followed by "n" denote endnotes.

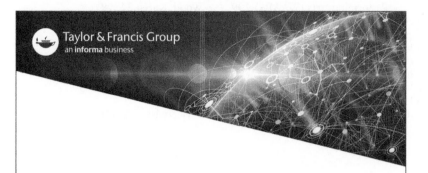